Epic Undertakings

PAPERS OF THE 12TH WORLD SANSKRIT CONFERENCE
Vol. 2

Epic Undertakings

Edited by
ROBERT P. GOLDMAN
MUNEO TOKUNAGA

MOTILAL BANARSIDASS PUBLISHERS
PRIVATE LIMITED • DELHI

PAPERS OF THE 12TH WORLD SANSKRIT CONFERENCE HELD IN HELSINKI, FINLAND, 13-18 JULY 2003
VOL. 2

General Editors:
PETTERI KOSKIKALLIO & ASKO PARPOLA

First Edition : Delhi, 2009

ISBN: 978-81-208-3382-1

MOTILAL BANARSIDASS
41 U.A. Bungalow Road, Jawahar Nagar, Delhi 110 007
8 Mahalaxmi Chamber, 22 Bhulabhai Desai Road, Mumbai 400 026
203 Royapettah High Road, Mylapore, Chennai 600 004
236, 9th Main III Block, Jayanagar, Bangalore 560 011
Sanas Plaza, 1302 Baji Rao Road, Pune 411 002
8 Camac Street, Kolkata 700 017
Ashok Rajpath, Patna 800 004
Chowk, Varanasi 221 001

PRINTED IN INDIA
By Jainendra Prakash Jain At Shri Jainendra Press,
A-45 Naraina, Phase-i, New Delhi 110 028
And Published By Narendra Prakash Jain For
Motilal Banarsidass Publishers Private Limited,
Bungalow Road, Delhi 110 007

PREFACE

Recent years have witnessed continued and growing interest in the massive, ancient, fascinating, mysterious and culturally rich poems we know as the Sanskrit epics. This interest has manifested itself in the continuing translations of the critical editions of both texts, a steady stream of monographs and edited volumes, and numerous scholarly meetings involving members of the international community of Sanskrit epic scholars.

A number of these scholars assembled in Helsinki to constitute the Epic Section of the 12th World Sanskrit Conference convened in that beautiful city in the summer of 2003 under the auspices of the International Association of Sanskrit Studies and the University of Helsinki. The present volume places before the Indological community the sixteen learned papers presented at the conference by the distinguished group of scholars who were in attendance.

The topics and methodologies of the authors are as varied and diverse as the contents of the monumental poems themselves but each, we believe, sheds new light on some aspect of the genetic and/or receptive history of these popular and massively influential works, their relationship to each other and to other Indic texts, or the representation and analysis of specific characters and episodes in the poems.

Putting together a volume of this kind naturally takes a great deal of time, energy and support from a number of individuals and institutions. We, the editors, would like to express our thanks to those who have made this publication possible. First, we would like to thank the authors for their scholarship and their gracious cooperation during the long editing process. Special thanks are also due to Dr. Petteri Koskikallio for his long and tireless efforts to organize the edition and to see it through to its conclusion. In addition, the editors are deeply indebted to Dr. Kensuke Okamoto for his hard and fruitful labours on the volume's unusually detailed and excellent index. Finally we would like to express our gratitude to the Finnish Cultural Foundation for their generous support without which the volume would never have seen the light of day.

ROBERT P. GOLDMAN
MUNEO TOKUNAGA

CONTENTS

CONTRIBUTORS

HORST BRINKHAUS
Seminar für Orientalistik
Abteilung Indologie
Leibnizstrasse 10
D-24118 Kiel
GERMANY
e-mail: hbrinkhaus@indo.uni-kiel.de

JOHN BROCKINGTON
3 Eskvale Court
Penicuik
Midlothian EH26 8HT
U.K.
e-mail: john.brockington@btinternet.com

MARY BROCKINGTON
3 Eskvale Court
Penicuik
Midlothian EH26 8HT
U.K.
e-mail: mary.brockington@btinternet.com

SIMON BRODBECK
Dept. of the Study of Religions
School of Oriental and African Studies
University of London
Thornhaugh Street, Russell Square
London WC1H 0XG
U.K.
e-mail: sb4@soas.ac.uk

NICOLAS DEJENNE
13, Boulevard du Val-de-Chézine
44800 Saint-Herblain
FRANCE
e-mail: nicolas.dejenne@gmail.com

DANIELLE FELLER
Section de langues et civilisations orientales
Anthropole
Université de Lausanne
CH-1015 Lausanne
SWITZERLAND
e-mail: danielle.feller@unil.ch

JAMES L. FITZGERALD
Department of Classics
Brown University
Macfarlane House
48 College Street,
Providence, RI 02912
U.S.A.
e-mail: james_fitzgerald@brown.edu

ROBERT P. GOLDMAN
Department of South and Southeast Asian Studies
7303 Dwinelle Hall MC #2540
University of California at Berkeley
Berkeley, CA 94720-2540
U.S.A.
e-mail: rpg@berkeley.edu

SALLY J. SUTHERLAND GOLDMAN
Department of South and Southeast Asian Studies
7303 Dwinelle Hall MC #2540
University of California at Berkeley
Berkeley, CA 94720-2540
U.S.A.
e-mail: sjsg@berkeley.edu

ALF HILTEBEITEL
Department of Religion
The George Washington University
2106 G Street, NW
Washington DC 20052
U.S.A.
e-mail: beitel@gwu.edu

MISLAV JEŽIĆ
Department of Indology and
Far Eastern Studies
Faculty of Philosophy
Ivana Lučića 3
HR-10000 Zagreb
CROATIA
e-mail: mjezic@ffzg.hr

PAOLO MAGNONE
Università Cattolica di Milano
Istituto di Glottologia
Lingua e letteratura sanscrita
Largo A. Gemelli 1
I-20123 Milano
ITALY
e-mail: paolo.magnone@unicatt.it

RAM KARAN SHARMA
International Association of Sanskrit Studies
63 Vigyan Vihar
Delhi – 110 092
INDIA
e-mail: ramkaransharma@yahoo.com

GEORG VON SIMSON
Düstere-Eichen-Weg 56
D-37073 Göttingen
GERMANY
e-mail: gsimson@gwdg.de

RENATE SÖHNEN-THIEME
Department of South Asia
School of Oriental & African Studies
Thornhaugh Street, Russell Square
London WC1H 0XG
U.K.
e-mail: rs2@soas.ac.uk

MUNEO TOKUNAGA
Graduate School of Letters
Kyoto University
Kyoto 606-8501
JAPAN
e-mail: mtokunag@bun.kyoto-u.ac.jp

ABBREVIATIONS

(More specific lists of abbreviations are given in the bibliographies)

ABORI	*Annals of the Bhandarkar Oriental Research Institute*, Poona
AS/ÉA	*Asiatische Studien / Études Asiatiques*
BhG	*Bhagavadgītā*
BORI	Bhandarkar Oriental Research Institute
DICSEP	Dubrovnik International Conference on the Sanskrit Epics and Purāṇas
IIJ	*Indo-Iranian Journal*
JAOS	*Journal of the American Oriental Society*
JIPh	*Journal of Indian Philosophy*
JOIB	*Journal of the Oriental Institute*, Baroda
Mbh	*Mahābhārata*
MLBD	Motilal Banarsidass
ms(s)	manuscript(s)
OUP	Oxford University Press
PPL	Purāṇapañcalakṣaṇa
Ram	*Rāmāyaṇa*
RO	*Rocznik Orientalistyczny*
v.l.	*varia lectio*, variant reading
WZKSA	*Wiener Zeitschrift für die Kunde Süd (und Ost-) asiens*
ZDMG	*Zeitschrift der Deutschen Morgenländischen Gesellschaft*

Manu Vaivasvata as *śrāddhadeva*: On the Insertion of the *Pitṛkalpa* into the *Harivaṃśa*

HORST BRINKHAUS

The *Harivaṃśa* has traditionally been regarded in India as a supplement (*khila*) to the *Mahābhārata*. In my view,[1] this especially refers to the core of the HV, which was devoted basically to embedding the events and main heroes of the epic into a history of the world mainly along genealogical lines from creation to the narrative present shortly after the Bhārata war. As the core of the HV I regard those parts of it which have been included in Willibald Kirfel's compilation of the Purāṇapañcalakṣaṇa,[2] though I take this core of the HV to be late epic and pre-Purāṇic.

The concluding part of the Purāṇapañcalakṣaṇa bears the heading *vaṃśānucarita*; and in essence it deals with the two most important dynastic genealogies, those of the Sūryavaṃśa and Somavaṃśa. In the HV, the presentation of these genealogies is interrupted between the Sūrya- and Somavaṃśa by a relatively extensive excursus, the *Pitṛkalpa*, which comprises nine *adhyāya*s (CE-HV 11-19) and deals with the death ritual (*śrāddha*) and the origin and significance of the *pitṛ*s. One may wonder what the

---

[1] Cf. Brinkhaus 1990 and 2002.

[2] Kirfel 1927; included are the passages of the Vulgate HV which correspond in the Critical Edition of the HV (Poona 1969-71) to the *adhyāya*s 1-10 and 20-30.

motive was for this interruption of the genealogical text. According to the text itself, it is the term *śrāddhadeva*, previously mentioned in the work, that has occasioned the excursus. In the preceding Sūryavaṃśa, Manu is named as the first son of the sun god Vivasvat, and this Manu Vaivasvata is there called *śrāddhadeva* without any further comment.[3] In a *Śravaṇaphala* at the end of the account of the Sūryavaṃśa, the sun god Vivasvat and – at least as far as I understand the text – his first son, who bears the epithet *śrāddhadeva*, are mentioned once again;[4] and here the fact that a mere human being is being called a *deva* obviously was felt to require some explanation, and thus the additional remark *devasya prajānāṃ puṣṭidasya* ('a god [in the sense of] a giver of prosperity to [his] subjects') was appended.

This double mention of *śrāddhadeva* and the need that was felt to explain this term were evidently what triggered the excursus that directly follows the *Sūryavaṃśa* in the form of the *Pitṛkalpa*. It comprises two parts: the first of them (CE *adhyāya*s 11-13) is a didactic discourse mainly upon the *pitṛ*s, and the second part (CE *adhyāya*s 14-19) consists of an illustrative episode about the relevance and effectiveness of the *śrāddha* ritual. The didactic portion ends with a passage in which for the third time Manu is

---

[3] HV 8.6-7:

trīṇy apatyāni kauravya saṃjñāyāṃ tapatāṃ varaḥ |
ādityo janayām āsa kanyāṃ dvau ca prajāpatī || 6 ||
manur vaivasvataḥ pūrvaṃ śrāddhadevaḥ prajāpatiḥ |
yamaś ca yamunā caiva yamajau saṃbabhūvatuḥ || 7 ||

("O descendant of Kuru, that best of luminous beings, the son of Aditi, begat on Saṃjñā three children, one daughter and two [sons as] lords of creatures. First [was born] Manu Vaivasvata, the deity of *śrāddha* and lord of creatures; Yama and Yamunā were born as twins.")

[4] HV 10.80:

paṭhan samyag imāṃ sṛṣṭim ādityasya vivasvataḥ |
śrāddhadevasya devasya prajānāṃ puṣṭidasya ca |
prajānām eti sāyujyam ādityasya vivasvataḥ || 80 ||

("By reading well this [account of] creation of Vivasvat, the son of Aditi, and of the deity of *śrāddha* (i. e. Manu) who is a god [in the sense of] a giver of prosperity to [his] subjects, a man attains to the same status as the progeny of Vivasvat, the son of Aditi.")

called *śrāddhadeva*,[5] and the explanation is added that he is known as such because he is the one to initiate the practice of the *śrāddha* ritual and is responsible for the primeval creation of the *pitṛ*s as well.

Manu as the founder of the *śrāddha* ritual is already known from the *Āpastambadharmasūtra*.[6] Another work of the Dharmaśāstra literature, however, can be identified beyond all doubt as the main source of the elucidative excursus of the HV, namely the *Manusmṛti*. In this Dharmaśāstra, even the Brahmins who participate in death rituals were generally called "gods at the *śrāddha*",[7] because they were devoted to the prosperity of men. The expression *lokasyāpyāyana* is again used in HV 13.70,[8] and it may perhaps have been resorted to precisely as a paraphrase of *prajānāṃ puṣṭi-* in 10,80. But this is not all: almost the whole conclusion of the didactic part of the *Pitṛkalpa* (13.64-70) displays a clear connection with the *Manusmṛti* passage 3.202-213; and the

---

[5] HV 13.64-65:

teṣām athābhyupagamān manus tāta yuge yuge I
pravartayati śrāddhāni naṣṭe dharme prajāpatiḥ II 65 II
pitṝṇām ādisargeṇa sarveṣāṃ dvijasattama I
tasmād enaṃ svadharmeṇa śrāddhadevaṃ vadanti vai II 66 II

("On behalf of them (i.e. of the *pitṛs*), my dear, Manu, the lord of creatures, from time to time, whenever right conduct is neglected, introduces the performance of *śrāddha*. Owing to the primeval creation of all the manes, o foremost of the twice-born, they designate him as the deity of *śrāddha* since this is his specific observance.")

[6] ĀpDhS 2.7.16.1: *athaitan manuḥ śrāddhaśabdaṃ karma provāca.*
("Now, Manu proclaimed this rite bearing the name *śrāddha*.") Manu Vaivasvata is also mentioned as *śrāddhadeva* in Mbh 12.122.39.

[7] Manusmṛti 3.213:

akrodhanān suprasādān vadanty etān purātanāḥ I
lokasyāpyāyane yuktān śrāddhe devān dvijottamān II 213 II

(Bühler 1886: "They (also) call those first of twice-born men the ancient deities of the funeral sacrifice, free from anger, easily pleased, employed in making men prosper.") On the problem of the term *śrāddhadeva* cf. Bühler 1886: lx.

[8] HV 13.70ab: *śīghraprasādā hy akrodhā lokasyāpyāyanaṃ param* I
("They are easily pleased, freed from anger, and confer supreme prosperity on men.")

preceding passage of HV 13, in which the seven *pitṛ* classes are delineated, is for its part again dependent upon the preceding passage in the *Manusmṛti* (3.194-199), even though the *pitṛ*s were derived there from the seven sons of Manu Svāyaṃbhuva instead of Manu Vaivasvata.

According to my exposition up to now, the text of the HV may seem to be altogether conclusive as regards the term *śrāddhadeva*. But there is a serious textual problem that needs to be mentioned: In my view, the *Śravaṇaphala* in HV 10.80 (cf. fn. 4) is talking about both the sun god, Vivasvat, and his son, called *śrāddhadeva*, i.e. Manu Vaivasvata. In so reading the text, I am aware of contradicting all the modern translations and interpretations known to me of the HV verse – and, by the way, of the equivalent *Brahmapurāṇa* parallel, too.[9] All of them take *śrāddhadeva* here as referring to Vivasvat. Up to now that *ca* in *pāda* d has commonly been suppressed, and indeed, according to the critical apparatus of the Critical Edition, this *ca* has been replaced in 7 North Indian manuscripts with *ha*. The reason for this common interpretation of HV 10.80 is clear. The *Pitṛkalpa*, which follows it directly, begins with a line in which *śrāddhadevatva* refers unambiguously to Vivasvat;[10] and this line is to be found in all the manuscripts which were used for the Critical Edition. However, the question it poses is nowhere answered nor even referred to within the following *Pitṛkalpa*.

On the basis of the considerations which I have presented up to now I am very much tempted to regard the first line of the *Pitṛkalpa* as an interpolation and, at the same time, as a corruption of the text. However, I am glad to be able to say that I am not totally

---

[9] As for the HV I know the translations and/or interpretations of Langlois 1834-35: 72-73; Dutt 1897: 61; Bose [1940?]: 47; Saindon 1995-96: 378; Saindon 1998: 177; as for the *Brahmapurāṇa* parallel in 8.95 (ed. Schreiner & Söhnen 1987) I refer to the *Brahmapurāṇa* translation 1985-86: 53, and Söhnen & Schreiner 1989: 23.

[10] HV 11.1ab: *kathaṃ vai śrāddhadevatvam ādityasya vivasvataḥ* |
("How did Vivasvat, the son of Aditi, become the deity of *śrāddha*?")

alone in my specific interpretation of HV 10.80 and at the same time in my disregard for the opening line of the *Pitṛkalpa*.

The HV version being characterized here is found to be confirmed in Kṣemendra's *Bhāratamañjarī*, which contains a detailed summary of the contents of the HV. In the first place, HV 10.80 is there interpreted wholly in the way I have done, namely with *śrāddhadeva* being explicitly made to refer to Manu, who was mentioned in connection with this epithet earlier in the *Sūryavaṃśa*'s description of him;[11] secondly, there is no reference at all to the first line of the *Pitṛkalpa* (HV 11.1ab): according to Kṣemendra, at the beginning of the *Pitṛkalpa*, the question is raised, à propos the mention of *śrāddha*, about the *pitṛ*s, not about *śrāddhadeva*.[12] There are two possibilities: either Kṣemendra knew a HV text in which the first *Pitṛkalpa* line was still absent, or he felt disturbed by this line and therefore passed over it in silence.

Kṣemendra's *Bhāratamañjarī* is known to have been written in the 11th century. There is, however, older evidence we can consult, namely the parallel versions of the Purāṇapañcalakṣaṇa mentioned at the beginning. In Kirfel's renowned compilation of these texts, though, the *Pitṛkalpa* was left out. But a similar treatment of the latter was later supplied by Kirfel's student de Vries[13]. Since our problem refers to the exact point of transition from the *Sūryavaṃśa*

---

[11] Kṣemendra's *Bhāratamañjarī*, HV 57 (referring to HV 8.6-7):

tasyām ajījanat putraṃ śrāddhadevaṃ manuṃ raviḥ |
yamaṃ kanyāṃ ca yamunāṃ yamalatvāt kṛtābhidhau || 57 ||

("The Sun begat on her his son Manu, the deity of *śrāddha*, and Yama as well as his daughter Yamunā, [the latter two] called thus because they were twins.") *Bhāratamañjarī*, HV 105cd (referring to HV 10.80):

ity ete śrāddhadevasya bhuvi vaṃśadharā manoḥ || 80 ||

("These were the perpetuators on earth of the race of Manu, the deity of *śrāddha*.")

[12] Kṣemendra's *Bhāratamañjarī*, HV 106 (= beginning of the *Pitṛkalpa*):

pṛṣṭaḥ śrāddhaprasaṅgena pitṛkalpaṃ mahībhujā |
muniḥ prāha ...

("When questioned apropos of [the mentioning of] *śrāddha* by the king about the precepts relating to [rites in honour of] the *pitṛs*, the Muni said ...")

[13] de Vries 1928.

to the *Pitṛkalpa*, we need to bring both back together again. On closer examination, it is two versions of the text that prove to be of particular interest as parallels to the version in the HV, namely the versions of the common cores of the *Brahmāṇḍa-* and *Vāyupurāṇa* (Bḍ-Vā), on the one hand, and of the *Matsya-* and *Padmapurāṇa*, on the other.

Among them the conception of the Bḍ-Vā parallel corresponds exactly to that of Kṣemendra: Here, as in the HV, Manu is called *śrāddhadeva* within the Sūryavaṃśa,[14] and at the end of this section there is a *śravaṇaphala*[15] that reads almost the same as HV 10.80; but a slight change in the text of the Bḍ-Vā core makes it clear that now *śrāddhadeva* unmistakably refers to Manu Vaivasvata. The didactic part of the *Pitṛkalpa*, which in the HV directly follows, again has a largely word-for-word parallel passage of text in the Bḍ-Vā core; but this passage has been shifted to before the *Sūrya-vaṃśa* section – a move which presumably must be judged as a conscious streamlining of the text on the part of the "diaskeuast" of the Bḍ-Vā version.

Remarkably enough, the parallels to the HV here again begin exactly with the second line of the *Pitṛkalpa*;[16] and the introductory passage of the *Pitṛkalpa* of the *Brahmāṇḍapurāṇa* concludes with the statement that it is the task of the *śrāddhadeva* Manu to establish the *śrāddha* ritual.[17] This obviously has been taken from HV

---

[14] PPL 285.6b-7.

[15] VāP 88.213-214 / BḍP 2.3.63.214c-216 (Cf. PPL 338.97-98a):
paṭhan samyag imāṃ sṛṣṭim ādityasya vivasvataḥ I
prajāvān eti sāyujyam manor vaivasvatasya saḥ II
śrāddhadevasya devasya prajānāṃ puṣṭidasya ca I
vipāpmā virajāś caiva āyuṣmān bhavate 'cyutaḥ II

("One who reads well this [account of] creation of Vivasvat, the son of Aditi, becomes endowed with progeny and attains a status similar to that of Manu Vaivasvata, the deity of *śrāddha* who is a god [in the sense of] a giver of prosperity to [his] subjects. He becomes free from evil and from *rajas* qualities; he becomes long-lived and does not swerve from the righteous path.")

[16] The word-for-word parallels with HV 11.1cd ff. start in VāP 71.6cd and in BḍP 2.3.9.5 respectively.

[17] BḍP 2.3.9.15cd:

13.65 (cf. fn. 5), and it supplies the finishing polish, as it were, to the textual model. In fact, the assumption that the "diaskeuast" of the Bḍ-Vā core may have known the HV-*Pitṛkalpa* without its first line appears to me to be rather unlikely for the following reason: The *Pitṛkalpa* of the Bḍ-Vā core, it is clear, is particularly closely akin to the South Indian recension of the HV, represented in the critical apparatus of the Critical Edition particularly by the Malayalam manuscripts M1-3.[18] Since, however, the first line of the *Pitṛkalpa*, after all, occurs in all the manuscripts that have been made the basis of the critical version of the HV, we are forced to assume that it had been already in place before the textual development of the HV divided into a northern and a southern recension. This would mean for our line of argumentation that the first line of the *Pitṛkalpa* was deliberately left out in the Bḍ-Vā parallel in order to avoid the awkward inconsistency of its model. This assumption is indirectly supported by the fact that in the parallel verse of HV 10.80 the term *śrāddhadeva* appears to be virtually highlighted with reference to Manu Vaivasvata.

Now I come to the second pertinent Purāṇic parallel, the common text of the *Matsya-* and *Padmapurāṇa* (Mt-Pd). In the first place, the Mt-Pd version is closer to the similar version in the HV, inasmuch as in it the *Pitṛkalpa* appears again between the *Sūrya-* and *Somavaṃśa*. It may be further noted that the Mt-Pd parallel throughout follows the version of the Critical Edition of the HV since it displays no asterisked passages. Thus it gives the impression of being close to a relatively old version of the HV.

śrāddhakriyāṃ manuś caiṣāṃ śrāddhadevaḥ pravartayet || 15 ||
("It is Manu, the deity of *śrāddha*, who will initiate the *śrāddha* ritual unto them.") The parallel line of the VāP (71.17ab: *śrāddhaṃ caiṣāṃ manuṣyāṇāṃ śrāddham eva pravartate* |) seems to be corrupt here.

[18] A concordance of the word-for-word correspondences between the HV-*Pitṛkalpa* and the parallel passages in the VāP and BḍP shows that the purāṇic version almost regularly follows the S-version of the CE-HV; just to mention the clearest cases, it includes parallels to the exclusively South Indian HV passages 246*, 247*, 248*, 249*, 251*, 260*, 263*, 264*, 266*, 279* and App. I, No. 3.

On the other hand, though, content has systematically been altered: First of all, in the *Sūryavaṃśa* section, *śrāddhadeva* is missing in both parallel passages: the term is not mentioned in the verse where Manu is introduced as the son of Vivasvat,[19] and at the end of this chapter there is no similar *Śravaṇaphala* at all. Nevertheless, the *Pitṛkalpa* section is emphatically introduced with the question of the *śrāddhadevatva* of the sun as well as of the moon![20] This, however, is no longer motivated by any allusions to it in the preceding text. Thus, here we do have a parallel to the first line of the HV-*Pitṛkalpa*. And where reference is subsequently made once more in the HV to Manu Śrāddhadeva, in the Mt-Pd parallel the sun now indeed explicitly appears under this epithet.[21] Neither here nor in the following is there any explicit mention of the moon as *śrāddhadeva*, but at the beginning of the following *Somavaṃśa* section, at least in the *Matsyapurāṇa* text the moon is expressly introduced as the lord of the *pitṛ*s,[22] presumably in order to be consistent with the preceding declaration.

Altogether, the Mt-Pd version made a systematic change in the form of a different notion of *śrāddhadeva*: on the one hand, this term was consistently avoided for Manu Vaivasvata, perhaps in

---

[19] MtP 11.3c-4b / PdP 1.8.38c-39b:
... suṣuve tvāṣṭrī saṃjñā tathā manum ||
yamaś ca yamunā caiva yamalau tu babhūvatuḥ |
("... and Saṃjñā, the daughter of Tvaṣṭṛ, gave birth to Manu. The twins Yama and Yamunā were also born [to her].")

[20] MtP 13.1 / PdP 1.9.1:
bhagavan śrotum icchāmi pitṝṇāṃ vaṃśam uttamam |
raveś ca śrāddhadevatvaṃ somasya ca viśeṣataḥ || 1 ||
("O adorable one, I wish to learn about the best family of the *pitṛs* and particularly about the status of a *śrāddha* deity of the Sun and the Moon.")

[21] MtP 15.42ab / PdP 1.9.70cd:
haviṣmatām ādhipatye śrāddhadevaḥ smṛto raviḥ |
("The Sun, the deity of *śrāddha*, is said to be the chief of those who receive oblations.")

[22] MtP 23.1a: *somaḥ pitṝṇām adhipaḥ* ... ("How did the moon ... become the sovereign of the *pitṛs*?") The *Padmapurāṇa* parallel passage has a different reading there: *somavaṃśaḥ kathaṃ jātaḥ* ...; cf. PPL 398.1.

order to emphasize his human nature as opposed to his divine origin. At the same time, however, the use of the term was expanded by the inclusion of the moon. With a view to the composition of the "*vaṃśānucarita*" chapter as a whole, this may have been meant as an attempted improvement: As was said before, the *Pitṛkalpa* in the HV version gives the impression of an excursus between the *Sūrya-* and *Somavaṃśa* chapters, whereas in the Mt-Pd parallel the term *śrāddhadeva* seems to be used to form a bond among the sun, the moon and the *pitṛ*s, and thereby to better integrate the former *Pitṛkalpa* excursus into its context.

Now, the question that forces itself upon us is: How do the versions of the Mt-Pd and of the HV relate to one another? Generally, there are two possibilities:

- Either the redactor of the Mt-Pd text was familiar with the HV version together with its disruptive opening line in the *Pitṛkalpa*, and given this lack of accord, he looked around for an alternative. In that case we would have to explain the insertion of the said line entirely on the basis of the HV text itself. Is it probable that the misunderstanding of HV 10.80 provided the occasion for its insertion? And even if we can imagine a single redactor or scribe tampering with the context as a whole, the question remains why this alteration was adopted into the entire text tradition of the HV. For, as we have seen, the contradictory nature of the text was fully taken note of by the Paurāṇikas, by Kṣemendra and, be it added, by the HV commentator Nīlakaṇṭha;[23] and it was eliminated in one way or another by all of them.
- The other possibility is that the Mt-Pd redactor knew the HV in a form without the said line. In that case he may have looked askance upon the fact that the human being Manu is there termed a *deva*, and so have introduced the change. Contrari-

[23] Nīlakaṇṭha even preferred to understand here Yama as being called *śrāddhadeva*; cf. Saindon 1995-96: 377-378.

> wise, a HV redactor who knew this alternative version may have reacted later by adopting the striking word *śrāddha-devatva* from it into his own corresponding insertion, making it refer – in the linguistically clear phrase *ādityasya vivasvatah* – to the ambiguous verse 10.80.

I tend to give the preference to the latter explanation, though I am far from being sure of it; and it is not the first time that I have been confronted with such a situation. During these past years I have been dealing closely with various portions of the core of the HV, and on more than one occasion have come up against the same situation: whereas the HV exhibited internal contradictions, the Purāṇic parallels displayed consistent versions, in some cases ones that can be proven to have been cleaned up from the HV version.[24] Thus more seems to have occurred in the textual transmission of the HV than in that of the corresponding Purāṇas. This is demonstrated clearly by the Critical Edition for the later transmissional phase of the HV: the Vulgate HV version was reduced in the Critical Edition to almost a third of the text. As to the older phase, that lies between the original conception of the World History at the core of the HV and the archetype of it reconstructed in the Critical Edition, the same appears to have been true, too.

REFERENCES

BOSE, Dhirendra Nath [1940?]. *Harivamsha.* Translated into English prose from the original Sanskrit Text. Ed. by D. N. Bose. P. O. Dum Dum (Bengal): Datta Bose & co.

Brahma Purāṇa (1985-86). 4 vols. Translated and annotated by a board of scholars. (Ancient Indian Tradition & Mythology, 33-36.) Delhi: MLBD.

BRINKHAUS, Horst 1990. Zur Entstehung und textgeschichtlichen Entwicklung des HV. In: *24. DOT, Köln, Ausgewählte Vorträge:* 415-425. Stuttgart: Franz Steiner Verlag.

---

[24] I am referring here, for example, to duplicate passages in the *Somavaṃśa* account of the HV; cf. Brinkhaus 2005.

BRINKHAUS, Horst 2002. The division into parvans and the Bhaviṣyaparvan of the HV. In: Mary Brockington (ed.), *Stages and Transitions: Temporal and Historical Frameworks in Epic and Purāṇic Literature. Proceedings of the Second DICSEP*: 157-176. Zagreb: Croatian Academy of Sciences and Arts.

—— 2005. Duplicates in the Somavaṃśa account of the *Harivaṃśa*: early text-historical developments in the Harivaṃśaparvan. In: P. Koskikallio (ed.), *Epics, Khilas and Purāṇas: Continuities and Ruptures. Proceedings of the Third DICSEP September 2002*: 363-387. Zagreb: Croatian Academy of Sciences and Arts.

BÜHLER, Georg 1886. *The Laws of Manu.* (Sacred Books of the East, 25.) Oxford: OUP.

DUTT, Manmatha Nath (trans.) 1897. *A Prose English Translation of Harivamsha.* Calcutta: Elysium Press.

KIRFEL, Willibald 1927. *Das Purāṇapañcalakṣaṇa: Versuch einer Textgeschichte.* Bonn: Kurt Schröder Verlag.

LANGLOIS, M. A. (trans.) 1834-35. *Harivansa ou histoire de la famille de Hari, ouvrage formant un appendice du Mahabharata.* Paris: Oriental Translation Fund of Great Britain and Ireland.

SAINDON, Marcelle 1995-96. Les deux divinites du śrāddha selon le Pitṛkalpa du HV. *Bulletin d'Etudes Indiennes* 13-14: 369-386.

—— 1998. *Le Pitṛkalpa du* HV*: traduction, analyse et interpretation.* Sainte-Foy: Presses de l'Universite Laval.

SÖHNEN, Renate & Peter SCHREINER 1989. *Brahmapurāṇa.* Summary of Contents, with Index of Names and Motifs. (Purāṇa Research Publications, Tübingen, 2.) Wiesbaden: Otto Harrassowitz.

VRIES, J. D. L. de 1928. *Der Śrāddhakalpa im* HV *und in fünf anderen Purāṇen*: Gekürzte Einleitung. Bonn: Kurt Schroeder.

Vālmīki's Portrayal of Hanumān

JOHN BROCKINGTON

Learned yet at times foolish, wise yet also impulsive, Hanumān is clearly a major figure in the *Vālmīki Rāmāyaṇa* but, in contrast to later tellings of the Rāma story where his devotion to Rāma is the outstanding feature of his character, in the original story his primary loyalty is to Sugrīva and it is Sugrīva's obligations towards Rāma which lead him to serve Rāma's cause.[1] In this article I focus on the different facets of Hanumān's portrayal in the earliest levels of the *Rāmāyaṇa*, those that for convenience I would designate as composed by Vālmīki,[2] and the ways in which – and the reasons why – these develop over time to the point where his birth and childhood had to be treated at such length in 7.35-36. If we disregard the very brief mentions in the two tables of contents at the start of the *Bālakāṇḍa*,[3] Hanumān is introduced surprisingly abruptly at the start of the *Kiṣkindhākāṇḍa* without any real back-

[1] I acknowledge with thanks a grant from the British Academy which funded my travel to the 12th World Sanskrit Conference.

[2] I am here basing myself on the sequence of stages of growth first proposed in Brockington 1985.

[3] These are, however, extremely brief and are not elaborated subsequently – there are no expansions of the basic mentions in * passages (indeed several manuscripts lack the reference at 1.3.14b), although several manuscripts do add towards the end of the first *sarga* a reference to Rāma's dismissal of Hanumān on his return journey to Ayodhyā (1.110*). Also, several manuscripts name Hanumān, along with Nala and Nīla, as monkey leaders serving Sugrīva and Vālin when the gods take birth as Vānaras (1.503*).

ground and, although he is involved in almost all the action of the rest of the book, he is rarely in the foreground there, whereas he plays a key role in the *Sundarakāṇḍa*, before reverting on the whole to a lesser role in the *Yuddhakāṇḍa* (the main exceptions being his fetching of the mountain of herbs and his being sent by Rāma to bring the news to Bharata, both of which occur in passages expanded during the second stage of growth).

Hanumān is the name by which he is designated in the great majority of instances (just over 450 times) and slightly more than half occur in passages which I have identified as belonging to the first stage; this is true overall, even though his name is rather more frequent in the second stage in the *Sundarakāṇḍa*, no doubt because much of the expansion in this book is intended to enhance his importance. The forms with short and long *u* seem equally frequent in these two stages but, whereas Hanumān is more frequent in the *Bāla* and *Kiṣkindhā kāṇḍa*s, Hanūmān is more frequent in the *Sundara*, *Yuddha* and *Uttara kāṇḍas.* The main difference in their distribution consists in the *pāda* where they are found, with Hanumān being more frequent in the first or third *pāda*s (except in the *Kiṣkindhakāṇḍa*, where it occurs as commonly in the second or fourth) and Hanūmān more frequent in the second or fourth; some of this variation is for metrical reasons but much is not (and the figures are undoubtedly influenced by editorial decisions). His next most frequent designation is as Mārutātmaja, occurring 68 times in the text; however, not only is this regularly linked with his name in the formula *hanŭmān mārutātmajaḥ* (found 42 times) but it is also substantially more frequent in passages belonging to the second stage (40 times against 28 in the first stage). This greater frequency in the second stage is even more marked with the substantially less frequent patronymic Māruti (8 times in the first stage, 21 in the second, also 3 in the third) and is also found, though less markedly, with the remaining infrequent names or epithets: Pavanātmaja (the next most frequent with 18 occurrences in total in the text), Vāyuputra, Vāyusuta, and Vāyusūnu (13, 12 and 7 occurrences respect-tively), Anilātmaja (7 occurrences), Vātātmaja (5 occurrences), Pavanasuta (4 occurrences, all in verses in longer metres), Anilasuta (3 occurrences) and Anilaputra once, Gandhavahātmaja (3 occurrences, all in 6.61), and Pavanasaṃbhava (5.13. only).[4] By contrast, his metronymic Āñjaneya, does not occur anywhere in the constituted text but is found, for example, in the invocatory stanzas prefixed to the *Bālakāṇḍa* in many manuscripts (see 1.19*-22*, 33* and 42*) and becomes very common in later tradition. This distribution pattern is clearly relevant to a proper assessment of the birth story of Hanumān.

It does seem to be the case that his birth features mainly in later stages, when Hanumān himself has become more important. It is too drastic to attempt to remove it entirely from the original Ram, as Bulcke attempted to do with a rather rigid analysis, and Sally Goldman has rightly challenged some of his evidence (Bulcke 1959; S. Goldman 1999). Nevertheless, it would be entirely natural for greater attention to be paid to his birth and parentage as his importance increased. Certainly the two most explicit references to the rape of Añjanā by Māruta (the name most often used) – within Jāmbavān's reminder to Hanumān of who he really is (4.65.8-18) and Hanumān's own briefer narration of it to Sītā (5.33.73-74) – occur in passages identified on other grounds as expanded, as does a briefer, less explicit allusion at 6.61.18, while much the fullest narrative is that in the *Uttarakāṇḍa* (7.35-36).[5] Elsewhere Hanumān simply describes himself as Māruta's natural son (*mārutasyaurasaḥ putraḥ* 4.66.7c and 5.56.113c / *mārutasyaurasaḥ sutaḥ* 5.49.14b) in the same phrase as Jāmbavān had used (4.65.28a), which occurs also at 4.66.3c and 5.35.41d (four out of five of these further occurrences coming from the second stage). On the other hand, in a first-stage passage, Kesarin, as he joins the muster of the

[4] There are also of course occasional instances of uncompounded forms, for example *anilasya ca putro 'tra hanumān iti viśrutaḥ* (6.21.24cd).

[5] Incidentally, there are similarities between Māruta's rape of Añjanā and the third-stage account of Vāyu asking the hundred daughters of Kuśanābha to become his wives and his distorting their limbs when they refuse (1.31-32).

Vānaras, is named as Hanumān's father without further qualification (4.38.17cd), while in another such passage Hanumān is called both Kesarin's oldest son and offspring of the wind (*jyeṣṭhaḥ kesariṇaḥ putro vātātmaja iti śrutaḥ* 6.19.11ab), a linking found also at 4.66.27ab, which adds *vegavat* to his description as *mārutātmaja*, lending support to the idea that this term is meant symbolically and so does not contradict his description as Kesarin's son.[6] Epithets incorporating *vega-* are quite commonly used of Hanumān elsewhere too, for example *hanūmantaṃ mahāvegam* (5.59.4c) and his striking an opponent *vegena vegavān vāyuvikramaḥ* (6.64.16cd, cf. from the fourth stage *eṣa vāyor bale tulyas tadvega iva śighragaḥ* 4.1346*6).

As to the significance of these epithets, if we do not take them literally, the idea first put forward by Heinrich Lüders (1939: 95-98) that *vāyuputra* (a form which is not in fact at all common in the Ram, as noted above) is equivalent to *vidyādhara* in the general sense of a magician is plausible for the Buddhist context in which he was suggesting it but rather less so for the Ram, which he adduced as a parallel.[7] While Hanumān can change shape at will (sometimes adduced as the magician aspect), he shares this ability with all the other Vānaras, as well of course as the Rākṣasas. If we take account of the MBh evidence,[8] where Bhīma is also a *vāyuputra*, the more likely interpretation of the term involves the aspect, particularly prominent in Vedic literature (but also found in the epics, cf. Vāyu's epithet of *prabhañjana* at 4.65.23d), of the wind as a destructive force, or perhaps better as a powerful force capable of being realised destructively, along with its speed, the aspect

[6] Kesarin is also mentioned independently of his relationship to Hanumān (his name occurs a dozen times in all in the text, at 4.38.17d, 65.8d, 27c, 66.27a; 5.33.73d; 6.4.30b, 18.34d, 19.11a, 39.26c, 60.38c; 7.35.19d and 36.31a), whereas Añjanā is mentioned only in the context of Māruta fathering Hanumān on her (4.65.8c, 17a; 6.61.18a; 7.35.20b, 21b, 36.26c and 31b).

[7] Some such popular element is very probably present in the portrayal of Hanumān but regrettably Narendranath B. Patil (1979-80) gives no assessment of the folk element, despite his subtitle.

[8] On this see Brockington 2004 and the references cited there.

which is perhaps most often exploited in epic similes. While brute force is clearly more appropriate in relation to Bhīma, speed and strength are particularly relevant for Hanumān, but all are contained within the impetuosity of the wind. Certainly, such patronymics are not infrequently combined with a comparison with Māruta (e.g. ... *mārutiḥ* ... *mārutapratimaḥ* 6.61.23ab; this persists down to quite a late stage, e.g. *mārutir māruto yathā* 6.1384* 2 post.). Incidentally, Hanumān's regular weapon in later mythology and art, the *gadā*, may possibly be borrowed from his half-brother Bhīma, since in the Ram he fights like the other Vānaras with fists, feet and mouth or with trees, rocks and similar objects (some of which are broadly club-like);[9] but perhaps a more likely explanation is to be found in his repeatedly using the great iron bolt which secured one of the gates of Laṅkā as a weapon against the Rākṣasas (first at 5.40.26-33 and 42.14-15 in his initial conflict with them and then again at 5.51.37-38 when he escapes after having his tail set alight, all repeated in his narration of his exploits to his fellow Vānaras at 56.97-103 and 134), for the term *parigha* used to designate this is more commonly used of some kind of (probably iron) club or mace, similar if not identical to the *gadā*.

There is in fact relatively little information given about Hanumān in the earlier parts of the text; his role is primarily functional, as Sugrīva's loyal and shrewd counsellor in the first instance and thereafter as perhaps the chief forwarder of the action. The main mode of characterisation is through the various epithets given to him at various points in the narrative. There are limited exceptions to this but on the whole these seem to belong to the stage of secondary expansion, as I have just argued is largely the case with his birth story. Similarly, the story of the origin of his name also occurs in the last two *sarga*s of the *Kiṣkindhākāṇḍa* (at 4.65.19-22), which appear to have been developed in order to enhance the

[9] This is a point also made by Goldman and Sutherland (1994: 44-45); I am grateful to Robert Goldman for reminding me at Helsinki (where I put forward only the possible link with Bhīma) of the better explanation for Hanumān's association with the *gadā* propounded in the rest of this sentence.

significance of his leap to Laṅkā, narrated in the first *sarga* of the *Sundarakāṇḍa.* Certainly, the possibly earlier narrative of it in Śuka's report to Rāvaṇa (at 6.19.13-16) presents it rather as a mark of his rashness and has no mention of Indra's involvement, whereas again the fullest account is in the *Uttarakāṇḍa* (7.35-36). Indeed, it seems fairly clear that Jāmbavān's reminder to Hanumān at 4.65-66 of his exceptional powers was developed, if not inserted, in order to provide a build-up to Hanumān's feat of leaping over the ocean to Laṅkā, for which his leaping towards the sun supplies a suitably hyperbolic precedent;[10] it also provides one of the correctives to Hanumān's culturally appropriate reticence before Rāma and Sugrīva about his exploits.[11] The next step in the narrative, his search of Rāvaṇa's harem for Sītā, has been variously interpreted, including Masson's oedipal interpretation (Masson 1981). More relevant is the point to which Goldman and Sutherland (1994: 41) have drawn attention that the passage represents the *śṛṅgārarasa* and so enables the poem to conform to the theoreticians' requirements for the contents of a *mahākāvya.* In my view this is precisely the reason for its development by later redactors.

In addition that episode, as Goldman and Sutherland also argue, is very probably the starting point for the later general Indian tradition of Hanumān as the ideal celibate *brahmacārin* (although in many Southeast Asian traditions he becomes a philanderer). There is in fact as little evidence for Hanumān's sexuality or marital status in most of the text as there is for Lakṣmaṇa's (and that of many others), for the same reason that it is irrelevant to the narrative. The only other hint in fact points in the opposite direction; this is when Bharata presents him with 16 *kanyā*s as *bhāryā*s at 6.113.41, also from the second stage, when Hanumān is becoming increasingly prominent.

---

[10] Keul (2002: 57) has noted how many of the main episodes connected with Hanumān occur in passages that I have identified as belonging to the second stage of growth.

[11] On the subject of Hanumān's reticence see R. Goldman 1998-99.

In the basic narrative, as Sugrīva's counsellor and spokesman, Hanumān is quite often given epithets which indicate his wisdom and his rhetorical abilities (for example, *medhāvin* at 5.3.1c, *vākyavidāṃ śreṣṭhaḥ* at 6.3.6c, *hanumān sacivottamaḥ* at 6.11.41b) and described as pondering on his words or course of action (for example, *cakāra matimān matim* at 5.28.40cd and *hanūmāṃś cintayām āsa matimān mārutātmajaḥ* at 6.55.55ab). Being central to his function in the narrative, these are found widely in both first and second stages. Occasionally, these qualities are highlighted, as when Sugrīva, addressing Hanumān, declares that he possesses strength, wisdom, valour, responsiveness to place and time, and statesmanship (4.43.6, cf. Sugrīva's similar words at 5.62.31). There is also the well-known episode when he finds Sītā and, in order not to frighten her, decides to speak in ordinary Sanskrit (5.28.17-19); this has given rise in later tradition to notions of Hanumān as the great grammarian but in the original narrative is merely incidental to his desire to reassure Sītā, who before long is chiding him for his stupidity in asking her for a recognition-token after she has already given him her *cūḍāmaṇi* (see 5.38, especially 5.38.17-18). An intermediate stage in this aggrandisement of his learning is found in a Southern addition where Rāma, after listening to Hanumān's speech about Sugrīva, begins his encomium of Hanumān by declaring that no one who was not learned in the Vedas or had not studied grammar in its entirety could have spoken so (4 App. 3.1-4). Here we see both Rāma and Hanumān being shown in a more brahmanical mould.

Besides incidental epithets, another good clue to the way characters are viewed lies in the use of similes or the like. Quite apart from that version of the story of how he acquired his name in which Indra plays a major part, shattering his left jaw with his *vajra* (4.65.21-22, cf. 7.35-36), there are several other passages where Hanumān is linked in some way with Indra, most often in comparisons, but also for instance when he boasts that he could take on Indra and seize the *amṛta* (4.66.25) or when, at the start of his great leap, he invokes Sūrya, Mahendra, Pavana, Svayaṃbhu and the *bhūtas* (5.1.7). Perhaps the most striking simile is that of Hanumān fighting Akampana likened to Puraṃdara fighting Namuci (6.44.7) but there are several general comparisons with Śakra (e.g. 6.6.1d or 6.58.42b [*triṣṭubh*] – and notably in a fourth-stage passage the other Vānaras honour Hanumān as the Maruts do Śakra, 4.1404* 2) or links with Indra's accoutrements; for example, Hanumān is equated with Airāvata at 6.4.15cd and strikes an enemy *vajravegeṇa muṣṭinā* at 6.58.23d.

Such association with Indra does not exclude comparisons with other deities any more than his supposed fathering by Māruta rules out these comparisons with Indra, but they are rather less frequent. Indeed, interestingly, the next most frequent is that his striding out or leaping is compared to Viṣṇu taking his three strides (e.g. 4.65.35cd and 66.22cd, persisting even into the fourth stage, e.g. 4.1374* and 5.4* 6), while Rāma at one point declares that the ocean could not have been crossed by anyone except Garuḍa, Vāyu and Hanumān (6.1.3). Within the *Yuddhakāṇḍa* we find, not surprisingly, comparisons also with Antaka (6.44.24), Kālāgni (6.73.18b) and Agni (6.44.14d and 69.7cd). We even find comparison of Hanumān with Sūrya (e.g. 5.62.31), which sits somewhat oddly with the story of his youthful attempt to seize the sun, as do the comparisons with Indra. However, taken together, these comparisons do underline Hanumān's power and martial ability.

Let me emphasise, as I finish, the point with which I started: that in the basic narrative Hanumān functions as Sugrīva's counsellor and it is Sugrīva's obligations towards Rāma which lead him to serve Rāma's cause, even to the extent of reminding Sugrīva of his duty. There is no real sign yet of the devotion to Rāma which becomes so prominent later on. Nor therefore is there any trace in the ...*dhyā* to *Yuddha kāṇḍas* of the famous boon that he will live as ... Rāma story is told. The nearest to anything of the sort is ... reminding Hanumān of his origin, declares that ...anted him invulnerability from weapons and thousand-eyed Indra the boon of dying only when he wished (4.65.25-26), a boon elaborated in the *Uttarakāṇḍa* version into invulnerability from their particular weapons granted by all the gods (7.39.15-21). Even when Sītā at Rāma's prompting bestows a necklace on Hanumān at the end of the *Yuddhakāṇḍa* this is just a sign of gratitude and there is no other implication (6.116.71-72). Clearly, although Hanuman's status is being enhanced by both these episodes, we are still a long way from the concept of his being a *cirajīvin.* It is only at the end of the *Uttarakāṇḍa* that Rāma grants Hanumān the boon that he shall live as long as stories about Rāma circulate in the world (7.98.24-25). Thus, the rise in status of Hanumān appears to go in tandem with the increasing recognition of Rāma's divinity, both prompting and being prompted by the shift from allegiance to Sugrīva to devotion to Rāma.

REFERENCES

BROCKINGTON, J. L. 1985. *Righteous Rāma: The Evolution of an Epic.* New Delhi: OUP.

—— 2004. Hanumān in the *Mahābhārata. Journal of Vaishnava Studies* 12.2: 129-135.

BULCKE, C. 1959. The characterization of Hanumān (a bird's-eye view of its evolution). *JOIB* 9: 393-402.

GOLDMAN, R. 1998-99. *sundare kiṃ na sundaram:* the genetic and receptive histories of the Sundarakāṇḍa of the Vālmīki Rāmāyaṇa. *JOIB* 48: 83-106.

GOLDMAN, R. & S. SUTHERLAND 1994. Vālmīki's Hanumān: Characterization and occluded divinity in the *Rāmāyaṇa. Journal of Vaiṣṇava Studies* 2.4: 31-54.

GOLDMAN, Sally J. Sutherland 1999. A tale of two tales: the episode of Hanumān's childhood in the Critical Edition. *Purāṇa* 41: 132-153.

KEUL, István 2002. *Hanumān, der Gott in Affengestalt: Entwicklung und Erscheinungsformen seiner Vererhrung.* (Religionsgeschichtliche Versuche und Vorarbeiten, 47.) Berlin: Walter de Gruyter.

LÜDERS, Heinrich 1939. Die Vidyādharas in der buddhistischen Literatur und Kunst. *ZDMG* 93: 89-104.

MASSON, J. Moussaieff 1981. Hanumān as an imaginary companion. *JAOS* 101: 355-360.

PATIL, Narendranath B. 1979-80. The legend of Hanumān: a study of a folklore motif in the Rāmāyaṇa. *Journal of the Asiatic Society of Bombay* 54-55: 118-127.

Husband or Slave?
Interpreting the Hero of the *Mahābhārata*

MARY BROCKINGTON

Who is the hero of the *Mahābhārata*?[1] Certainly not any of the Dhārtarāṣṭras, who are openly villainous, nor Draupadī, who is disqualified by her sex;[2] yet the Pāṇḍavas in general and their leader Yudhiṣṭhira in particular often appear in a far from heroic light. Yudhiṣṭhira is the obvious hero of the epic, so why should he and his allies be presented in a way that makes them appear to the modern Western reader weak, devious, and amoral? B. K. Matilal's comment on the question posed by Draupadī in the *sabhā* was,

> I believe the dilemma of Draupadī is not only unresolved but also unresolvable as most moral dilemmas are (Matilal 1989: x-xi).

If such a perceptive philosopher as Matilal could not solve the problem by the application of logic, perhaps a different approach may help. Maybe the problem posed by the question is not primarily philosophical, but narrative.[3] In my paper at the last World

---

[1] I acknowledge with thanks a grant from the British Academy which contributed towards my expenses in attending the conference.

[2] Thackeray's *Vanity Fair* is sub-titled *a novel without a hero* and dominated by the female Becky Sharp, but this expedient was not open to the composers of the Sanskrit epics.

[3] Matilal's remark that in the Mbh "no dilemmas were left dangling or unresolved except perhaps the unique case of Draupadī's question" (Matilal 1989: 2) is a further hint that the problem to which it points is of a different nature.

Sanskrit Conference in Turin I examined Yudhiṣṭhira's refusal to intervene to save Draupadī from being molested after the dicing, seeing his restraint as saving the Pāṇḍavas from pollution from their wife's menstruation: a sign not of weakness, but of strength (M. Brockington 2001). I now turn to the dicing itself. Is it not shameful of the Dharmarāja to gamble away all that he and his brothers possess, not even excluding their wife? Shameful it certainly is, and it prefigures a number of other indisputably shameful deeds perpetrated by the Pāṇḍavas in the final battle to avenge their disgrace and win back what they have lost, but by looking in turn at the narrative constraints operating on the author, and then at the often undervalued factor of performance, I hope to demonstrate that Yudhiṣṭhira should not be seen as entirely culpable in wagering Draupadī; that in the face of almost overwhelming provocation and personal loss, Yudhiṣṭhira can be shown to retain honour, dignity and integrity.

In terms of structure and motivation of the Mbh as a whole, the authors chose to adopt a plot outline fundamental to a vast number of narratives in all genres and cultures: that of the hero who gains some great objective, loses it catastrophically, and regains it. The catastrophe may be some external disaster unrelated to the hero's actions, but in the more interesting plots the loss results from his own folly, ignorance or wrong-doing, and he must undergo some educative or redemptive process to make him more worthy of the eventual prize; the Mbh authors extend and develop this general outline with their exploration of Yudhiṣṭhira's shocked reaction to the Pāṇḍavas' victory at Kurukṣetra.[4] Such an outline can pose severe problems to a narrator who wishes to focus only on the positive side of his hero's character: it is difficult to see how he can preserve the image of the Pāṇḍavas as all-powerful and morally supreme while stripping them of their wealth and dignity and sending them into exile, yet without some initial fault or weakness on

[4] Yudhiṣṭhira's education throughout the Mbh is examined by Alf Hiltebeitel (2001).

the part of Yudhiṣṭhira the plot cannot even begin.[5] I believe that a careful appraisal of the author's attempts to resolve these problems may contribute to a better understanding of several of the puzzles posed by this episode. The fact that a narrative presents a number of puzzles and inconsistencies is not necessarily proof of a corrupt or carelessly expanded text (although there are valid reasons to suppose that not all of the present Dyūtaparvan is original).[6] Such oddities commonly betray an author's difficulty in constructing his plot: solving one problem creates another, which he either overlooks or ignores, especially in works presented orally where the audience cannot stop the performance and turn back a few pages to check the text.

One puzzle that has aroused much discussion and speculation is the exact nature of the compulsion that drives Yudhiṣṭhira to agree to the dicing, and to persist in it to the bitter end when he is convinced he is being cheated.[7] I have nothing to add to that discussion: it is sufficient that Yudhiṣṭhira is shown to be acting under compulsion of some kind (whether internal or external) to engage in a contest that goes wrong with an awesome inevitability which gives ample testimony to the power and skill of its narrator.

It is more pertinent to consider why the two distinct dicing sessions should have different outcomes. If what the author wants is to engineer the exile of the brothers, why have them first enslaved and

---

[5] The role of Dhṛtarāṣṭra presents a similar problem. He is presented as far-sighted, sympathetic to the Pāṇḍava cause, and aware of the disastrous consequences the dicing will have for his own sons, yet he fails to act decisively to stop it. This failure (in fact a narrative necessity) is explained away by his frequent insistence that the dicing is driven by fate. His role is discussed by Peter Hill (1993: 5-10).

[6] For a careful analysis of the construction of this scene according to the metres employed, see Söhnen-Thieme 1999.

[7] For differing explanations see e.g. van Buitenen 1975: 5-6, 27-30; Hill 1993: 14-20; Hiltebeitel 2001: 220; Lipner 1994: 201-203; Söhnen-Thieme 1999: 141-142, 152. Renate Syed explores the nature of the dicing in detail (Syed 1997: 235-247); for her suggestion that the rules of the game do not allow Yudhiṣṭhira to withdraw from the contest during a persistent run of bad luck, see Syed 1996: 274; 1997: 243-244.

then released? If two sessions are wanted at all,[8] it would be artistically more effective to have the second one repeat the outcome of the first. My answer is that he wants to take the Pāṇḍavas to Kurukṣetra not only fuelled by resentment at being cheated out of their rights of property and sovereignty, but burning with fury to avenge the shameful outrage to Draupadī – an outrage they have been unable to prevent.[9] But how can Draupadī be put in that position in the first place? How can the Dharmarāja be made to stake her, knowing that he will inevitably lose the throw?[10] Up to and including the point of wagering his two half-brothers, Yudhiṣṭhira has himself offered all his stakes, whether with increasingly reckless bravado or with desperation. Śakuni had originally envisaged winning for Duryodhana only the Pāṇḍava's kingdom and fortune (44.20, cf. 45.40 and 51.1), but now he sees his chance to humiliate Yudhiṣṭhira beyond his expectations and slily mentions Bhīma and Arjuna; Yudhiṣṭhira stakes them under protest, and only two throws are left. Śakuni taunts Yudhiṣṭhira by asking what he has left to stake, no doubt expecting the answer "Draupadī", but Yudhiṣṭhira gallantly and desperately evades the issue by staking and losing his own freedom – but with it, the freedom to make any further decisions. Yudhiṣṭhira's prime concern, according to Bhīṣma, is to preserve his integrity (2.60.41); he has entered honourably into the dicing-bargain, and now that he has lost, the only way he can remain true to himself is to accept his position as a slave. His obedience is immediately tested: it is now Śakuni's turn to protest that Yudhiṣṭhira has broken the rules by trying to keep back some of his

[8] Renate Söhnen-Thieme considers the possibility that originally there may only have been one game (Söhnen-Thieme 1999: 148). Mehendale (1995) also examines the discrepancies in this episode.

[9] The suffering involved in the Pāṇḍavas' inability to act in this and similar episodes has been explored by Greg Bailey (1983: 111-119).

[10] Even the gambling-crazed Nala is shamed out of his addiction by his opponent's outrageous suggestion that he should wager Damayantī; rather than do this he voluntarily gives up his kingdom and goes off into the forest with his wife, and only at the end, when he is sure of victory, does he hazard her (3.58.3-7, 77.4-5).

property, and (as Vikarṇa points out, 2.61.24) it is in obedience to Śakuni's command that Draupadī is staked for the final throw.

Draupadī is told the news by the attendant sent by Duryodhana to fetch her into slavery, and her shocked response is to send back a question to Yudhiṣṭhira, "Bhārata, did you lose yourself first, or me?" agreeing that she will go with the attendant when she knows the answer, with the clear implication that she will go *whatever* the answer. She does not challenge the order: she just wants to know exactly what has happened. The attendant first glosses the question as "Were you master of anything when you lost us?" then repeats her own words more emphatically, not to Yudhiṣṭhira, now a mere slave, but to the court as a whole, where the various Kaurava notables talk around the matter at length, without coming to any conclusion, and without ever formally either releasing Draupadī from her enslavement or alternatively declaring her never to have been lawfully enslaved:[11] only the men are released when Dhṛtarāṣṭra grants her the two boons. Nor in fact does the discussion address the precise terms of the question. It is interpreted in dry, legalistic terms to mean: "Were you legally entitled to stake me?" but another interpretation is at least as plausible: "Did you, or did you not, stake me, your beloved wife, of your own free will, or were you helpless because you were already enslaved yourself?" This interpretation becomes the anguished cry of a woman anxious for reassurance that she has not been willingly betrayed by her husband and protector. Once Yudhiṣṭhira had lost his freedom, and with it the freedom to make any further decisions, the answer can only be: "He was not free *not* to stake her."

As a slave, Yudhiṣṭhira behaves with perfect propriety, setting his excitable brothers an example of the self-restraint that is to characterise and sustain him throughout their appointed stay in the wilderness; in obedience to Duryodhana's wishes, he sends for

---

[11] Mehendale's interesting contention that "Arjuna resolves the deadlock [by declaring Draupadī not to have been lawfully staked, ... and] the Kauravas accept Arjuna's verdict" (Mehendale 1985: 189), rests on an interpretation of 2.63.21d that differs from those of van Buitenen, Edgerton, P. C. Roy and others.

Draupadī to come to the *sabhā*, but makes no further comment and takes no further part in the action until after he has been released from servitude. His silence and restraint are key elements in the scene.[12] As the Dharmarāja, he might have been expected to pronounce on the issues raised in the Dyūtaparvan in a way that would have obviated the slaughter at Kurukṣetra (not the ending the storyteller intends to contrive). As a slave, Yudhiṣṭhira's *dharma* is now to say and do only what he is ordered by his master, and the story is able to proceed to its inevitable conclusion: Yudhiṣṭhira himself later blames his misfortunes on, *inter alia*, his passion for gambling, not on his conduct once he had embarked on the game (3.144.12). The theme of enslavement is not fully explored, but is almost completely overshadowed by the outrage to Draupadī and the debate about her question. Through the rest of the narrative, I repeat, it is on that outrage and the loss of their property that the Pāṇḍavas and Draupadī brood;[13] the brief enslavement must have had some different, more immediate purpose; that purpose was, I propose, to facilitate the outrage upon Draupadī.

A further narrative oddity that betrays the lack of importance the authors attributed to the enslavement theme is their failure to have the Pāṇḍavas' children included in the stakes. It is foolhardy of Śakuni to leave the next generation free to grow up to wage war on the Dhārtarāṣṭras to liberate or avenge their fathers.[14] Only one

---

[12] In a burlesque inversion of this scene in the *Virāṭaparvan*, by contrast, it is Yudhiṣṭhira's refusal to stop talking when ordered that precipitates a crisis; imminent catastrophe is again averted by the quick-thinking Draupadī (4.63.36–64.10). In the *Harivaṃśa*'s pastiche of the *Sabhāparvan* episode Balarāma is unable to maintain his initial sang-froid at being cheated, and soon slaughters his opponent Rukmin (HV 89.17-49).

[13] M. Brockington 2001: 253.

[14] This narrative oddity apparently led the usually careful Edgerton into the subconscious slip of misinterpreting the reference at 58.9 to "princes' ornaments" to mean that Yudhiṣṭhira was now staking his sons (Edgerton 1944: xxv). That these putative sons are not subsequently redeemed would contradict his own assertion (p. xxxii, in a different context) that "such references in the Mbh. always lead to something; they are not left hanging in the air". In an even more puzzling oversight, van Buitenen states baldly "in the fourteenth [play Yudhi-

son is mentioned at all, and then it is not until a telling verse where Draupadī reveals her contempt for her eldest husband's behaviour: she asks Dhṛtarāṣṭra for Yudhiṣṭhira's freedom, not for his own sake, but to save Prativindhya from humiliation (63.29-30).

So much for the text itself, but another factor with an important bearing on this scene is that much neglected factor, performance. The Mbh as we now have it is cast in the form of a series of emboxed performances, and there is every likelihood that at least the narrative core was intended for dissemination by public performance. Whether its composition and initial transmission were oral or written is not in question here. The scene is made up of long passages of dialogue introduced by marginal rubrics, with even Vaiśaṃpāyana's few brief narrative interventions often themselves recording speeches by characters, so that the form lies somewhere between full-scale dramas (intended to be seen as well as heard) and the long narrative epics of a Virgil or a Milton (intended to be read, and read mostly in private).[15] Appreciation of any work of artistic creativity is a two-way process involving originator and recipient: the same picture or story will affect different viewers or readers differently, but the picture or story does not change. In the case of the performing arts a partnership in creativity is introduced by the crucial role of the performer (musician, dancer, actor or reciter) whose responsibility it is to interpret the originator's intentions according to his own insight: the text remains the same, but each performance differs, and each interpretation is equally valid, provided only that basic standards of technical accuracy and fidelity to the received text and the author's overall vision are maintained. Concepts of "right" and "wrong" are not relevant: the only criterion is whether the interpretation is convincing. In the case of

---

ṣṭhira loses] the sons of Draupadī by the five Pāṇḍavas" but translates the verse, correctly, as "Here are the ornaments with which the princes glitter ..." (van Buitenen 1975: 30, 135).

[15] Its nearest modern equivalent is the dramatic monologue that was such a popular feature of music-hall and home entertainment until the latter part of the twentieth century.

written works, the author may leave precise instructions about his intentions (although this is rare), but for works within the oral tradition the performer can rely only on example, memory and his own insight for guidance about how to interpret his mental text.[16] Ironically and regrettably, this accumulated store of tradition is liable to be lost once the text is committed to writing: written words alone cannot convey the variations of tone, speed and pitch by which the skilled reciter will put across his interpretation. Was Yudhiṣṭhira confident, or fearful from the outset as he made his successive wagers? Did he make his stakes with increasing recklessness, or increasing reluctance? or perhaps with a combination, rising to a feverish climax of arrogance just before the dramatic pause in the text where Vidura argues with Duryodhana (tellingly styled a "freeze-frame" by Angelika Malinar),[17] then lapsing back into dereliction and wild despair as he begins to lose things that are far more important to him than mere wealth? Should there be a gradual descent, or a sudden change when he loses the power to pledge his own stakes? Is his paean of praise of Draupadī shouted out with swift defiance, parading her virtues like a pimp trying to sell her to Śakuni? Or is it a barely-audible, heart-rending lament for what he knows he is about to lose, delivered in wistful, faltering tones of disbelief after a long pause by a tortured, broken man? Many interpretations are valid, and can give fresh insights into the text, but they are all interpretations; for my part, I see no compelling reason to view Yudhiṣṭhira's conduct in the *sabhā* in a wholly negative light. At the critical points, he remains the supreme knower and upholder of *dharma*.

---

[16] Bernard Shaw was a notorious exception among dramatists in leaving precise instructions about how he wanted his plays to be performed. Alf Hiltebeitel draws attention to the problems associated with this lack of stage directions in the case of modern chapbook Mbh performances (Hiltebeitel 1988: 163).

[17] In discussion following her paper presented at the third DICSEP, 2002; cf. Malinar 2005: 472.

REFERENCES

BAILEY, Greg 1983. Suffering in the *Mahābhārata*: Draupadī and Yudhiṣṭhira. In: Marie-Claude Porcher (ed.), *Inde et Littérature* (Puruṣārtha, 7): 109-129.

BROCKINGTON, Mary 2001. Husband or king? Yudhiṣṭhira's dilemma in the *Mahābhārata*. *IIJ* 44: 253-263.

BUITENEN, J. A. B. van (trans.) 1975. *The Mahābhārata. Book 2: The Book of the Assembly Hall*. Chicago: University of Chicago Press.

EDGERTON, Franklin (ed.) 1944. *The Mahābhārata. Critically edited by V. S. Sukthankar and others*, II: *The Sabhāparvan*. Poona: BORI.

HILL, Peter 1993. Individual responsibility in the *Mahābhārata*. *South Asia* 16.2: 3-20.

HILTEBEITEL, Alf 1988. *The Cult of Draupadī*, I. Chicago: University of Chicago Press.

—— 2001. *Rethinking the Mahābhārata: A Reader's Guide to the Education of the Dharma King*. Chicago: University of Chicago Press.

LIPNER, Julius 1994. *Hindus: Their Religious Beliefs and Practices*. London: Routledge.

MALINAR, Angelika 2005. How Purāṇas relate the *Mahābhārata*: the case of King Parikṣit. In: Petteri Koskikallio (ed.), *Epics, Khilas, and Purāṇas: Continuities and Ruptures. Proceedings of the Third DICSEP, September 2002*: 465-494. Zagreb: Croatian Academy of Sciences and Arts.

MATILAL, Bimal Krishna 1989. Moral dilemmas: insights from Indian epics. In: B. K. Matilal (ed.), *Moral Dilemmas in the Mahābhārata*: 1-19. Shimla: Indian Institute of Advanced Studies.

MEHENDALE, M. A. 1985. Draupadī's question. *JOIB* 35: 179-194.

—— 1995. Is there only one version of the game of dice in the Mahābhārata? In: Satya Pal Narang (ed.), *Modern Evaluation of the Mahābhārata: Prof. R. K. Sharma Felicitation Volume*: 33-39. Delhi: Nag Publishers.

SÖHNEN-THIEME, Renate 1999. On the composition of the Dyūtaparvan in the Mahābhārata. In: Mary Brockington & Peter Schreiner (eds.), *Composing a Tradition: Concepts, Techniques and Relationships. Proceedings of the First DICSEP, August 1997*: 139-154. Zagreb: Croatian Academy of Sciences and Arts.

SYED, Renate 1996. Yudhiṣṭhira in der sabhā: das akṣadyūta im Mahābhārata. In: Friedrich Wilhelm (ed.), *Festschrift Dieter Schlingloff*: 269-285. Reinbek: Dr Inge Wezler.

—— 1997. Das *akṣadyūta* in epischer Zeit: sowie Anmerkungen zur Verwendung der *akṣa*-s im Ritual, *Studien zur Indologie und Iranistik* 21: 235-291.

Husbands of Earth: Kṣatriyas, Females, and Female Kṣatriyas in the *Strīparvan* of the *Mahābhārata*

SIMON BRODBECK

1. The cosmic reason for the Kurukṣetra war is revealed by Vaiśaṃpāyana to Janamejaya, and hence to the epic's wider audience, in the *Ādiparvan* (Mbh 1.58.25 to 59.6, plus chapter 61 [64-65, 67]).[1] The story – which I shall call the frame story – is given because Janamejaya, having heard in the previous chapter of the births of the epic's main characters, wishes to know *why* they were born (Mbh 1.58.2). The *asura*s, banished from the celestial regions, took birth on earth in various forms, but the resulting havoc oppressed the earth, who sought help from Brahmā; and the celestials, instructed by Brahmā, descended to earth to rescue her by destroying the miscreants on Kurukṣetra. Nārāyaṇa is a crucial

---

[1] I would like to thank: Sîan Hawthorne, for many stimulating conversations that have contributed greatly to the development of this paper; the British Academy, for funding my travel to Helsinki and back; John Brockington, for organising the British Academy bid; Paul Dundas, for bibliographical suggestions; Jim Fitzgerald, for sending me the latest version of his *Strīparvan* translation; James Hegarty, for suggesting the paper's new title; and all those who responded in any way to my presentation in Helsinki, in particular Ashok Aklujkar, Vidyut Aklujkar, Mary Brockington, Alf Hiltebeitel, and Sally Sutherland Goldman. In this paper, chapter and verse references are to the Poona edition of the Mbh (Sukthankar *et al.* 1933-66). References in square brackets are to the chapter numbers of Ganguli's translation (1883-96), where they differ from those of the Poona edition. Unless otherwise indicated, references are to the *Strīparvan*, and translations are my own. In my translations I have elided some of the vocatives.

member of the rescue party, although he does not appear to have been present when Brahmā gave the initial instruction, and his cooperation is ensured independently by the celestials with Indra as their spokesman (Mbh 1.58.48-51). This frame story, which Scheuer calls the Mbh's central myth,[2] is also mentioned during Vaiśampāyana's narration of Yudhiṣṭhira's *rājasūya*: Nārada remembers that many of those assembled have secret celestial identities and a secret celestial mission (Mbh 2.33.11-20 [35]).

The earth was widely mythologised in ancient India,[3] most famously for her maternal beneficence, support and patience (*kṣamā*).[4] In the surviving sources, she is often paired with a celestial male consort. The relation between the two is often understood in terms of the sexual production of the goods of life.[5] In *Atharvaveda* 12.1 the male consort has a protective attitude towards the earth that is then richly elaborated in the epics and Purāṇas. For example, in the *Śāntiparvan* (Mbh 12.248-250 [256-258]) overpopulation causes the earth to seek Brahmā's assistance (249.3c-4d): he initially responds with an accidental holocaust, but is petitioned by Śiva and subsequently creates death instead.[6] At Mbh 12.49.56-79 [50] the earth is fearful and unprotected by Kṣatriyas after the activities of Rāma Jāmadagnya (the prototypical *kṣatra*-slayer, whose story is also told immediately before the *Ādiparvan* passage mentioned above),[7] and she persuades the sage Kaśyapa to

---

[2] Scheuer 1982: 156. For references to Scheuer, Dumézil and Hacker in this connection, see de Jong 1985.

[3] For Vedic references see Macdonell 1897: 21-22, 88, 120-123, 126-127; Macdonell & Keith 1912: 16-17; Kinsley 1986: 8-10. For post-Vedic references, see Hopkins 1915: 78-81; Bailey 1981; Kinsley 1986: 178-184.

[4] On *kṣamā*, see further Paolo Magnone's contribution to this volume.

[5] Through the equation between rain and semen, for example: see Derrett 1959. We must not forget that Vedic literature traditionally functioned in the context of an all-male high-*varṇa* brotherhood. (To call this brotherhood an élite would perhaps be to prejudge the question of how it was viewed by others.)

[6] This story also occurs in various *Droṇaparvan* manuscripts: see Appendix I 8.1-265 [50-52].

[7] On Rāma Jāmadagnya, see Biardeau 1970; Goldman 1970; Fitzgerald 2002a.

find the surviving Kṣatriyas and install them as kings. The Mbh's frame story differs from these two examples in that it incorporates the recurring *deva/asura* battle (between two inimical military-male groups): the victory of the *deva*s rescues the earth. The *prādurbhāva* (later *avatāra*) idea, as presented at Mbh 12.337.28-36 [350], follows this pattern: unruly superhuman beings must repeatedly be curbed by means of divine interventions in order that the earth thrive.[8]

The story of the five former Indras (Mbh 1.189 [199]) appears to be a version of the frame story (it is also a justification of sorts for Draupadī's polyandry). Indra is lured by an unnamed weeping woman to Śiva's Himalayan abode where, to make good their sins of pride, he and four previous Indras are sentenced to rebirth as human beings, in which guise they are to perform great feats of slaughter. They become the five Pāṇḍavas. Given what has already been revealed concerning the reason for the descent of the celestials, it is natural for us to identify the weeping woman as the earth. This identification is reinforced by the fact that before he is lured away, Indra is in attendance at a *satra* where Yama is officiating, and we are told that while Yama is thus occupied earthly creatures do not die and the population rises.[9] In the *Śāntiparvan* overpopulation story it is the earth who suffers, so by implication the suffering woman here is also the earth. This interpretation differs from that

---

[8] The boar is the most obvious earth-rescuer, raising her from the waters: see Prasad 1989. At *Taittirīyasaṃhitā* 7.1.5 Prajāpati, in boar form, consorts with the waters and fathers the world. This story is redolent of the cosmogony of the golden egg emerging from the waters (ṚV 10.121; at *Manusmṛti* 1.12-13 the egg splits into earth and sky; see also *Chāndogya-upaniṣad* 3.19.1-2). For Mbh references to the boar, see Sutton 2000: 160-162; Prasad 1989: 100. Earth also features in accounts of the deluge and the fish. In the Mbh's account at 3.185 [186] she is submerged then re-emerges, but in several Purāṇa accounts she is independently afloat, being the boat on which the survivor is towed. For a discussion of correlations between the boar and fish *avatāra*s, see Magnone 2000: 239-242. Both use one horn or tusk, and neither is initially associated with demon-destruction.

[9] On connections with Yima in the *Avesta*, see Prasad 1989: 125-129; Jackson 1896.

of Hiltebeitel (1976: 81, 96-97, 169-191; see also 2001: 120, 186), whose arguments for identifying the woman as Śrī nonetheless seem sound. Van Buitenen is thus both correct and incorrect in saying that "it does not become clear who she is" (van Buitenen 1973: 465): it *is* clear, but her identity is doubled, and thus there are good poetic reasons for not naming her. Śrī and the earth have overlapping attributes in any case: both consort with the king.[10]

It is important that Śiva be involved in an earth-rescue frame story, since he is closely associated with the full extent of the Kurukṣetra slaughter, through Aśvatthāman and the night attack as well as through his rewarding the *tapas* of Arjuna and Ambā.[11] It is not always clear that the night attack is necessary in order that the earth be fully rescued and *dharma* restored,[12] but there are at least some indications that it was considered to be so. The Mbh's references to the celestial purpose of the Kurukṣetra war often depart in their details from the first *Ādiparvan* presentation, and sometimes the purpose of the celestial mission is said simply to be the destruction of the *kṣatra*.[13] This ties in again with the figure of Rāma Jāmadagnya, and may be a commentary on the Kṣatriya values portrayed by the epic's main characters. But it would also demand the extermination of both sides in the war; this is not necessary if the Pāṇḍava and Kaurava armies are seen to represent the *deva*s and the *asura*s. Tension between these two ideas is evident in the textual discrepancies over which of the celestials is primarily re-

---

[10] On the differences between them in this regard, see Hara 1996-97.

[11] For Arjuna see Mbh 3.38-42 [37-41]; for Ambā see 5.188 [190]. See also 3.240.6 [250].

[12] For the idea that the celestial mission re-establishes *dharma*, see Mbh 3.187.26-28 [188]; 6.26.6-8 [28, = *Bhagavadgītā* 4]; 7.156.28 [181]; 14.53.11-15 [54].

[13] See Mbh 1.155.44-45 [169]; 2.33:19 [35]; 3.42.19 [41]. Ganguli, seeing the problem, sometimes tries to minimise the damage. Mbh 11.8:27 gives the purpose of the mission as the destruction of the world (*lokasaṃhāra*): this may be hyperbole, and/or it may tie in with the myth of *pralaya*, particularly given the mention of Kali in the same verse. On the *pralaya* myth, see Johnson 1998: xxviii-xxxv; on the Mbh and the *yuga* system, see González-Reimann 2002.

sponsible for the mission,[14] and over which human characters are incarnations of which celestials.[15]

The celestial mission serves in part as a discursive expansion of the sheer unavoidability which is repeatedly asserted of many of the epic's upsetting events.[16] Whether it was introduced into an existing *Bhārata* epic, for this purpose or some other, as suggested by van Buitenen (1973: xix-xxi),[17] or whether it was always an integral feature, as suggested by Vassilkov (1995), will not be discussed here.[18] Such discussions, the like of which have raged now for well over a hundred years, are, in my view, a poor substi-

---

[14] Brahmā is usually the coordinator of the rescue mission, Viṣṇu's involvement being ensured by a supplementary request. Whether this request indicates dependence or authority seems to vary from passage to passage. Some of the text's cosmic rescue stories involve Śiva in place of Viṣṇu; some involve Śiva in place of Brahmā. For references and discussion of the cosmic roles of these three deities, see Hill 2001: 124-164; see also John Brockington 1998: 249-256.

[15] Primarily in the case of the Pāṇḍavas (Yudhiṣṭhira incarnates Dharma and a former Indra, Bhīma Vāyu and a former Indra, Arjuna Indra and Nara, etc.). Some accommodation may be attained here by differentiating between the character's father and the figure whom the character incarnates. We may also differentiate, as Hill points out (2001: 158), between full and partial incarnations.

[16] By means of the ideas of *kāla, diṣṭa, daiva, svabhāva, dhātṛ* and *vidhātṛ*. The emphasis tends to be on the reduction of the suffering caused by known (and hence usually past) events, rather than the production of a *laissez-faire* attitude to the future. In the extensive literature, see particularly Bedekar 1992; Bharadwaj 1992; Hill 2001; Long 1980; Modhey 1983; Vassilkov 1999; Woods 1999. See also *Kaṭha-upaniṣad* 2.20, 23. It is noteworthy that the Mbh and its commentators are keener to explain unavoidability in mythical than in philosophical terms; but see Brodbeck 2004a; 2004b. See Solomon 2003 for the distinction between fatalism (narrative necessity) and determinism (causal necessity), a distinction which however is hard to maintain in the face of the Mbh's myriad approaches.

[17] Differentiable text-layers are compatible with a short compositional period: see Hiltebeitel 2001: 29.

[18] For comparison with Greek epic literature, see de Jong 1985. I will also not discuss here the thematic links between the *deva/asura* frame story, with its struggle between two parties over the possession of fertile goods, and other Mbh stories such as the churning of the ocean (Mbh 1.15-17 [17-19]) and the passage of Śrī from various *asura*s to Indra (Mbh 12.216-221 [223-228]). On this theme, see Johnsen 1965-66. The theme recurs beyond India, especially in old Irish and Welsh texts, and even in Shakespeare: an explanation in terms of nature mythology seems sensible. For a bold approach, see Knight 1987.

tute for study of the text itself. Hiltebeitel (2001: 20) asserts that "the *Mahābhārata* must have been written over a much shorter period than is usually advanced ... by 'committee' ... or 'team' ... and at most through a couple of generations"; I view this claim as a complement to his view that "the largest inadequacy in *Mahābhārata* scholarship ... is simply the failure to appreciate the epic as a work of literature" (Hiltebeitel 1999: 156). The more the conditions of authorship approximate to those in which other more conventional works of literature were and are produced, the more a literary approach seems appropriate.

The Mbh's central characters are ignorant of the frame story, and so do not know that the war is cosmically necessary. But the audience do know this, and so they may stand aloof from the characters' various diplomatic and existential negotiations. Without this cosmic perspective, it would seem as if the war were fought because certain Kṣatriyas could not find any solution to their petty jealousies apart from wholesale massacre. With the cosmic perspective, the war is a noble sacrifice, in which many lay down their lives to renew the earth. They do not know that that is what they are doing, but all the same that is what they are doing. They are heroes, protectors of the earth, rewarded in heaven.

Here we have two levels of explanation for the war, a higher and a lower. But these different levels have different outcomes. Before the war, the poets may easily combine Draupadī and the earth: both are offended, and their offence drives the narrative towards the war.[19] On the lower level of explanation the Pāṇḍavas are being good Kṣatriyas, protecting their wife and avenging the insults heaped upon her at the dicing match. The war makes the earth

[19] For Draupadī as a symbolic representation of the earth, see Hiltebeitel 1980: 102 ff. Draupadī is usually said to be an incarnation of Śrī (Mbh 1.61.95-97 [67], 189.29 [199]). This ambiguity matches that of the aforementioned weeping woman, and may aid our understanding of Draupadī's complex character. Biardeau has suggested that Ambā – whose name means "mother" – is also "a symbol of the earth" (Biardeau 1981: 82, see also p. 87). The sometimes striking parallels between their stories, which show once again how important the frame story was to the epic poets, will not be detailed here.

happy again,[20] and might have been expected to have the same effect on Draupadī, since it involves the deaths of her erstwhile abusers. But her sons and brothers have also been killed, and so the end of the war finds her in mourning. Here there is considerable friction between the two levels of explanation. But we may also see the incompleteness of the earth-Draupadī equation as an expression of the tension, mentioned above, between the idea that the Kauravas and their allies must die, and the idea that all the armies must die.

Immediately after the war, at the beginning of the *Strīparvan*, Dhṛtarāṣṭra, in his grief, voices suicidal intentions. The advice of Saṃjaya and Vidura is of no avail, and so Vyāsa steps in to tell Dhṛtarāṣṭra a reasonably full version of the *deva/asura* frame story (11.8.20-26), which he calls an "eternal secret of the gods" (*devaguhyaṃ sanātanam*, 8.34d).[21] The report that Vyāsa gives here seems to be of an occasion subsequent to the earth's initial complaint: she goes to Indra's abode to remind the celestials of their task, and is reassured by Viṣṇu that it is in hand. Vyāsa's narration puts recent events into a new perspective for Dhṛtarāṣṭra, who cheers up momentarily (his frequent claims that *daiva* is the cause of the war are now vindicated),[22] but the reappearance of the frame

[20] It is notable that the earth is not credited with any sense of loss upon the destruction of so many of her children. There is a sense in which we might then interpret her as the ideal Kṣatriya mother, accepting with good humour that all her children are born to die. See Kṛṣṇa's *triṣṭubh* Mbh 11.26.5, quoted below (footnote 42).

[21] This reappearance of the frame story occurs at the end of the traditional *Viśoka(upa)parvan*. However, since Gāndhārī's vision of the battlefield only begins in the eighth chapter of the succeeding *Strī(upa)parvan*, we might consider the prelude to this vision as a fifteen-chapter block, the central chapter of which contains the frame story. For the structure of the *Strīparvan*, and a discussion of its *upaparvan*s, see Paranjpe 1956: xxii-xxvi. For a discussion of the *Viśoka(upa)parvan*, see Bailey 1993: 11 ff. Bailey states that "being told he is like a pawn in the games of the gods is not a salve for [Dhṛtarāṣṭra]" (p. 19), but nonetheless Dumézil is right to highlight the importance of Vyāsa's revelation (Dumézil 1968: 167-168).

[22] We may connect Dhṛtarāṣṭra's appeals to *daiva*, his receipt of the frame story, and his physical blindness. Here I am understanding *daiva* literally, a sense often elided by the use of "fate" to translate a variety of concepts.

story serves (as indeed, one might argue, do those frequent claims) primarily to remind the audience of the higher level explanation. The effect of this reminder is to re-present Kṣatriya responsibility in the cosmic perspective. The responsibility of Kṣatriyas to protect people has been replaced by their responsibility to protect the earth, whose satisfaction takes precedence over that of any human females.

The *Strīparvan* version of the frame story differs from that of the *Ādiparvan* in its stress on Duryodhana's role in the affair: here he is portrayed as the primary agent of the earth's satisfaction. Never did winning the war count so little: it was the death count that mattered. We remember that Duryodhana refused to allow the war to be averted, and was extremely effective in drumming up large armies.[23] When told by Bhīṣma during the war that he cannot win due to the true identities of Kṛṣṇa and Arjuna, Duryodhana seems to take no notice.[24] Dhṛtarāṣṭra is the addressee in the *Strīparvan*'s version of the frame story, and this may force the stress on Duryodhana to some extent, but the point made is a good one.

It is notable that Vyāsa says the secret has previously been told to Dhṛtarāṣṭra and the Pāṇḍavas by Nārada, and to Yudhiṣṭhira by Vyāsa himself (8.32-38). Here we might surmise that the secret is in two parts: first, the massacre's unavoidability, and second, its cosmic rationale. The previous revelations mentioned by Vyāsa were only of the first part. Dhṛtarāṣṭra has now heard *all* of the *devaguhyaṃ sanātanam* (34cd); what Yudhiṣṭhira heard[25] was just the *guhyaṃ*, with no mention of *deva*s (37b: Fitzgerald's translation here is unnecessarily interpretive). Another approach, which however would deal only with Nārada's revelation, would be to collapse the distinction between saying something to oneself (as Nāra-

---

[23] Pāṇḍavas 7, Kauravas 11: see Mbh 6.16.44.

[24] Mbh 6.61.26-64.18 [65-68]; see also 5.48.2-24 [49]. Duryodhana is convinced he will win because he has been told by the Dānavas (in what he thinks was a dream) that he will win, and that his allies are incarnated Dānavas, *asura*s, Daityas and *rākṣasa*s (Mbh 3.240.1-30 [250]).

[25] See *Sabhāparvan* Appendix I 30 [45]; see also footnote 55 below.

da does at the *rājasūya*) and saying something out loud. This would throw up a host of interesting questions about textual genre, but would nonetheless be in line with the text's tendency to deny its characters a private arena of self-narrative.[26]

2. The lamentations of the warriors' wives and mothers are graphically described by Gāndhārī in chapters sixteen to twenty-five of the *Strīparvan*.[27] Gāndhārī, voluntarily blindfolded since her marriage, has been given the divine eye by Vyāsa for the occasion:[28] dismembered bodies and wailing women are the first things she has seen for decades.[29] While the women mourn, the audience knows that the Kṣatriya husbands have effectively reneged on their marital responsibilities in order collectively to look after another. The women are the defeated rivals of the earth. With this in mind, let us look at how the earth is used by the *Strīparvan*'s poets.[30]

---

[26] See Brodbeck 2004b: 88-89.

[27] On the question of female input to the authorial process, see Hiltebeitel 2001: 165-167. Hiltebeitel, following van Buitenen, refuses to speculate in detail: it is difficult to imagine what might count as hard evidence of female or part-female authorship. Moreover, it is difficult to imagine what the claim of female authorship might legitimately involve, given that, unless more Sanskrit texts have this feature than previously supposed, any idea of what an ancient Indian woman might be like is gleaned almost entirely from male-authored texts.

[28] In this she is the female counterpart of Saṃjaya. These two narrators employ a particular type of narration distinguished by its immediacy: the scenes are described as contemporaneously visible. Gāndhārī repeatedly tells Kṛṣṇa to look (*paśya*) at what she is currently seeing, in contrast to most of the epic's narrators, who tell their interlocutors to hear (*śṛṇu*) something that has been previously heard and remembered. For this observation I am indebted to an article (anonymous to me) which may appear in the *Journal of the Royal Asiatic Society*, and which attempts to apply to the Mbh the Greek distinction between *aoidós* and *rhapsōidós*, two types of bard.

[29] We may perhaps interpret the dulling of Gāndhārī's senses as a comment upon what it was like to be married to Dhṛtarāṣṭra in particular, or to an orthoprax Kṣatriya in general.

[30] Many of the ideas dealt with in the following paragraphs have already been extensively treated: I merely apply the findings of others to a specific textual situation. See in particular Hara 1973; Derrett 1959.

The *Strīparvan* often refers to kings as lords, husbands, protectors or governors of the earth, using the compounds *mahīpati*, *pṛthivīpati*, *mahīpāla*, *pṛthivīpāla* and *mahīkṣit*.[31] These common terms are uncommonly significant in the context of the Mbh's singular example of earth-husbandry. If we ask which kings are most appropriately described in this way, that is, which kings are most responsible for the war taking place, the standard answers will be Dhṛtarāṣṭra (for his spineless acquiescence) and Duryodhana (for his aggressive imperialism). Sure enough we find that, of the thirteen uses of these compounds in the *Strīparvan*, seven refer to Dhṛtarāṣṭra, and three to Duryodhana.[32]

On twelve occasions in the *Strīparvan* we hear of people so overcome by grief that they fall upon the earth.[33] Although this is a standard image, it has added significance in the current context because the object fallen upon is the intermediate cause of the grief in question. The warriors have died on account of the earth, so a bodily assault upon the earth by the mourners is particularly appropriate.

---

[31] *Mahīpati*: 1.4d, 8.5b, 9.1b, 12.10d [13], 16.9b (Dhṛtarāṣṭra); 8.10 f. (Janamejaya); 10.3d [11] (Duryodhana). *Pṛthivīpati*: 8.21b, 8.30b (Dhṛtarāṣṭra); 17.19d (Duryodhana). *Mahīpāla*: 8.24e (Duryodhana). *Pṛthivīpāla*: 8.25a (all those kings who gather to fight at Kurukṣetra). *Mahīkṣit*: 17.12b (kings who used to wait upon Duryodhana).

[32] A question may immediately be raised as to whether or not the uncommon contextual significance of these terms, and of their specific application to Dhṛtarāṣṭra and Duryodhana, was intended or anticipated by the poet or poets. I ask that the question be held in abeyance. The juxtaposition of the idioms of kingship and the Mbh's frame story is, from the reader's point of view, a feature of the text, and may be discussed as such in some depth without any hypothesis arising concerning the text's authors. In any case, it is difficult to know how such a hypothesis might be verified. The assumption that poetry must by definition be the deliberate creation of a conscious being impoverishes the concept of poetry, as well as the possibility of meaningful agnosticism or atheism. A tentative hypothesis concerning authorial attitude will be made towards the end of this paper, but is only possible after taking a wide range of textual subtleties into account.

[33] 1.9, 8.1, 8.2 (Dhṛtarāṣṭra); 15.12 (Draupadī); 16.14, 16.56 (the Bhārata women); 17.1, 25.34 (Gāndhārī); 21.10, 21.14 (Karṇa's wife); 24.12 (Bhūriśravas's wives); 25.9 (the women of Māgadha).

The dead warriors are also lying on the earth. We are told this on eighteen occasions, six of which refer to the earth as "the bed of heroes".[34] In the context of the suggestion that earth-husbandry implies marital infidelity, we may note that lying on the earth is also lying with the earth. A sexual connection between the warriors and the earth is suggested by the imagery used on occasion in the *Śalyaparvan*:[35]

> The earth, speckled by the hooves of the war-horses, was decorated like a woman marked by fingernail scratches.[36]
>
> Thus [Śalya], all his limbs broken, covered with blood, was met by the earth as if through love, like a husband met by his dear wife and falling upon her breast. Having enjoyed the dear earth for a long time, he embraced her with all his limbs like a lord his wife, and was as if asleep.[37]

On the whole, though, in the *Strīparvan* celestial *apsaras*es are the new objects of the warriors' sexual attentions, and are mentioned

---

[34] These six are 17.9, 17.11 (Duryodhana); 22.2, 22.4 (a warrior from Avanti); 23.9 (Śalya); 23.17 (Bhīṣma). The other twelve are 16.31, 18.7 (various warriors); 17.12, 17.19 (Duryodhana); 19.1 (Vikarṇa); 19.11 (Citrasena); 20.10, 20.11 (Abhimanyu); 21.2, 21.9 (Karṇa); 23.10 (Bhagadatta); 23.30 (Droṇa). Apart from the text-places already listed in the footnotes, the earth is also mentioned in the *Strīparvan* at 1.6, 1.10, 8.21, 8.22, 8.23, 8.29, 8.31, 15.3, 16.49, 16.55, 17.19, 17.20, 18.3, 18.18, 19.6, 21.11, 25.14, 26.14 and 27.10.

[35] For examples from the *Rāmāyaṇa*, see Hara 1973: 107-108; see also Sally Sutherland Goldman's contribution to this volume.

[36] Mbh 9.8.13 [9]:
teṣāṃ tu vājināṃ bhūmiḥ khuraiś citrā viśāṃ pate |
aśobhata yathā nārī karajakṣatavikṣatā || 13 ||
See also Feller Jatavallabhula 1999: 86-87. Fingernail scratches are an integral part of the Indian erotic repertoire, as detailed at *Kāmasūtra* 2.4.

[37] Mbh 9.16.53-54 [17]:
sa tathā bhinnasarvāṅgo rudhireṇa samukṣitaḥ |
pratyudgata iva premṇā bhūmyā sa narapuṃgavaḥ || 53 ||
priyayā kāntayā kāntaḥ patamāna ivorasi |
ciraṃ bhuktvā vasumatīṃ priyāṃ kāntām iva prabhuḥ |
sarvair aṅgaiḥ samāśliṣya prasupta iva so 'bhavat || 54 ||
Like Ganguli, I translate as if the first of these verses had six *pada*s, not the second. Note the juxtaposition of premortem and postmortem earth-enjoyment.

on two occasions by mourning women. Gāndhārī remarks of Viviṃśati:

> Vāsava's ladies attend upon that *vasu* by the thousand, as maidens of the gods upon a playing *gandharva*.[38]

Abhimanyu's widow Uttarā speaks to her husband's corpse:

> What other woman like me will you now meet in the ancestral world and charm with soft smiling speech, tiger of men? With superlative beauty and smiling speech you will immediately stir up the minds of the *apasaras*es in heaven. Having reached the worlds made by merit, having met *apsaras*es, remember my virtues sometimes while roaming for pleasure.[39]

These two mentions of heavenly pleasures are counterbalanced by two mentions of the carnal pleasures that the widows used to enjoy with their husbands. Gāndhārī says of Bhūriśravas's wife:

> This wife of Yūpadhvaja's, her waist no bigger than two hands might measure, having put her husband's [severed] arm in her lap, mourns pitiably. That hand of his would undo her belt, rub her full breasts, caress her navel, her thighs, her bottom, and pull off her skirt.[40]

---

[38] Mbh 11.19.18:
yaṃ sma taṃ paryupāsante vasuṃ vāsavayoṣitaḥ |
krīḍantam iva gandharvaṃ devakanyāḥ sahasraśaḥ || 18 ||
The term *vasu*, translated by Fitzgerald as "good man", is used here in correlation with Indra's nickname "Vāsava".

[39] Mbh 11.20.23-25:
kām idānīṃ naravyāghra ślakṣṇayā smitayā girā |
pitṛloke sametyānyāṃ mām ivāmantrayiṣyasi || 23 ||
nūnam apsarasāṃ svarge manāṃsi pramathiṣyasi |
parameṇa ca rūpeṇa girā ca smitapūrvayā || 24 ||
prāpya puṇyakṛtāṃl lokān apsarobhiḥ sameyivān |
saubhadra viharan kāle smarethāḥ sukṛtāni me || 25 ||

[40] Mbh 11.24.16-17 (translation from Fitzgerald 2004):
bhāryā yūpadhvajasyaiṣā karasaṃmitamadhyamā |
kṛtvotsaṅge bhujaṃ bhartuḥ kṛpaṇaṃ paryadevayat || 16 ||
ayaṃ sa raśanotkarṣī pīnastanavimardanaḥ |
nābhyūrujaghanasparśī nīvīvisraṃsanaḥ karaḥ || 17 ||

Gāndhārī says of the wife of Sudakṣiṇa, the king of Kamboja:

> Helpless, with her relations far away, she says in the sweetest voice, "Delight never left me when I was in the embrace of these two arms the likes of spike-ended iron clubs, with such beautiful fingers and palms. Deprived of you, lord of peoples, what way shall I go now?"[41]

These images emphasise that the warriors have switched their marital allegiance away from their human wives.

It seems natural for us to interpret this battlefield scene as recommending a certain Kṣatriya ideology. If we take this approach, the message is clear: for social and cosmic order to be preserved, a group of highly trained warriors must be ready to lay down their lives in wars against tyrants. Their loyalty to their wives and families must be secondary and provisional. Those wives and families should also realise this. As Kṛṣṇa tells Gāndhārī:

> The brahmin woman conceives a child bound for *tapas*, the cow a beast of burden, the mare a courser, the *śūdra* a slave, and the *vaiśya* a keeper of beasts. A princess the like of you conceives a child bound for the kill.[42]

---

[41] Mbh 11.25.3-4 (translation from Fitzgerald 2004):
imau tau parighaprakhyau bāhū śubhatalāṅgulī |
yayor vivaram āpannāṃ na ratir māṃ purājahat || 3 ||
kāṃ gatiṃ nu gamiṣyāmi tvayā hīnā janeśvara |
dūrabandhur anātheva atīva madhurasvarā || 4 ||

[42] Mbh 11.26.5:
taporthīyaṃ brāhmaṇī dhatta garbhaṃ
gaur voḍhāraṃ dhāvitāraṃ turaṃgī |
śūdrā dāsaṃ paśupālaṃ tu vaiśyā
vadhārthīyaṃ tvadvidhā rājaputrī || 5 ||
We are reminded of Kristeva (1986: 167): "But the pain, [my child's] pain – it comes from inside, never remains apart, other, it inflames me at once, without a second's respite. As if that was what I had given birth to and, not willing to part from me, insisted on coming back, dwelled in me permanently. One does not give birth in pain, one gives birth to pain: the child represents it and henceforth it settles in, it is continuous … a mother is always branded by pain, she yields to it." Whilst it appears to deal with biological motherhood, this account is also a commentary on the process and institutions of authorship: see Edelstein 1992; Hawthorne 2004. Kṛṣṇa portrays Gāndhārī's pain as specific to her *varṇa* and its institutions, as if other types of mothers might be luckier. In recent times general male conscription has devastated families from a wide range of social classes.

Elsewhere, angry women suggest that Yudhiṣṭhira is an adharmic leader:

> O you best of the Bharatas, Yudhiṣṭhira saw there along the river Gaṅgā throngs of women shrieking like ospreys. The king was surrounded by thousands of these tormented women with their arms up in the air, wailing and uttering fair and foul alike. "How can there be a king who knows Meritorious Law and at the same time the unprecedented cruelty that he slew his fathers, brothers, teachers, sons, and friends? How did you keep your mind, strong-armed prince, once you had caused Droṇa's death, and your grandfather Bhīṣma's, or even after you killed Jayadratha? What shall you do with kingship, Bhārata, when you don't see your fathers and your brothers? And the unassailable Abhimanyu? And Draupadī's boys?"[43]

Yudhiṣṭhira is unmoved by these accusations.[44] The suggestion of *adharma* on Yudhiṣṭhira's part is immediately rebutted by Vaiśampāyana's referring to him as *dharmarāja* (11.10d) and reporting his paying homage to his uncle Dhṛtarāṣṭra, an act that is characterised as *dharmeṇa* (11.11b). The frame story also implies that the women's objection, though understandable, is misguided. The Mbh is explicitly addressed to an audience of men *and* women,[45] and so

---

[43] Mbh 11.11.5-9 [12] (translation from Fitzgerald 2004):
sa gaṅgām anu vṛndāni strīṇāṃ bharatasattama |
kurarīṇām ivārtānāṃ krośantīnāṃ dadarśa ha || 5 ||
tābhiḥ parivṛto rājā rudatībhiḥ sahasraśaḥ |
ūrdhvabāhubhir ārtābhir bruvatībhiḥ priyāpriye || 6 ||
kva nu dharmajñatā rājñaḥ kva nu sādyānṛśaṃsatā |
yadāvadhīt pitṝn bhrātṝn gurūn putrān sakhīn api || 7 ||
ghātayitvā kathaṃ droṇaṃ bhīṣmaṃ cāpi pitāmaham |
manas te 'bhūn mahābāho hatvā cāpi jayadratham || 8 ||
kiṃ nu rājyena te kāryaṃ pitṝn bhrātṝn apaśyataḥ |
abhimanyuṃ ca durdharṣaṃ draupadeyāṃś ca bhārata || 9 ||

[44] They are not unexpected: see Mbh 9.58.23 [59] for Yudhiṣṭhira's anticipation of the widows' reaction.

[45] Mbh 18.5.39-40:
jayo nāmetihāso 'yaṃ śrotavyo bhūtim icchatā |
rājñā rājasutaiś cāpi garbhiṇyā caiva yoṣitā || 39 ||
svargakāmo labhet svargaṃ jayakāmo labhej jayam |
garbhiṇī labhate putraṃ kanyāṃ vā bahubhāginīm || 40 ||
"This *itihāsa* called *Jaya* (*Victory*) is to be listened to by the one seeking prosperity, by the king and his children, and also by the pregnant woman. The one

the frame story asks that military action be judged in the widest possible context, not just by the warriors who must participate, but also by their female relatives who must let them.

This ideological agenda is very familiar. Whether or not the Kurukṣetra war ever took place, the interpretive framework which attempts to justify it contains many elements which have recurred throughout the centuries. Large-scale loss of innocent life would perhaps be unacceptable if it were seen to occur due to ambition, or pride, or greed for territory and natural resources. If, however, it can be made to seem that military action is necessary in order to avert a catastrophe, then those who lose their lives or their loved ones may do so stoically and righteously. The notion of sacrifice is still commonly used in connection with death in battle, and has been well explored in connection with the Kurukṣetra war by Feller Jatavallabhula (1999).[46] At first glance it may seem that the Mbh's spin doctors have been particularly ambitious in presenting the Kurukṣetra war as a necessary restoration of the balance of the whole cosmos. On reflection, however, there is nothing particularly unusual here.

The idea of non-attachment is an important philosophical component of the Mbh's Kṣatriya ideology. In the *Bhagavadgītā*, Kṛṣṇa's exposition of non-attached action effectively replaces Arjuna's family loyalty with loyalty to the world as a whole.[47] To be a good Kṣatriya is to act for *lokasaṃgraha*, the holding-together of the world:

---

desiring heaven gets heaven, the one desiring victory gets victory, the pregnant woman gets a son or a well-appointed daughter." See also Fitzgerald 1991: 169-170.

[46] The objection that the word *yajña* denotes a particular type of Indian ritual and has little semantic overlap with the English word "sacrifice" is inappropriate here, for in both cases the concept has expanded beyond its original ritual context, and Mbh 6.25-26 [27-28, = *Bhagavadgītā* 3-4] shows that "*yajña*" has undergone this development by the time of our text. See Brodbeck 2004a: 87-88. A thorough comparison of these two terms would be very useful.

[47] For Arjuna's initial loyalty, see Mbh 6.23.28c-46 [25, = *Bhagavadgītā* 1].

> Janaka *et al.* attained perfection by means of action alone. You must act, attending only to the holding-together of the world.[48]

> As those attached to action, the unknowing ones, act, just so should the knowing, unattached one act, desiring to effect the holding-together of the world.[49]

Though Kṛṣṇa's speech does not mention the *deva/asura* frame story, it has the same theme. *Lokasaṃgraha* has often been interpreted in terms of general ritual theory, as the cosmically sustaining effect of correct ritual action,[50] but in the specific context of the Kurukṣetra war Vaiśaṃpāyana has already explained this sustaining effect in terms of the rescue and renewal of the earth.

Kṛṣṇa's *karmayoga* allows a man to progress soteriologically without leaving his wife and family.[51] This is in contrast to the traditional *śramaṇa* view, in which enlightenment is preceded by the renunciation of family life,[52] and so at first glance it may appear

---

[48] Mbh 6.25.20 [27, = *Bhagavadgītā* 3]:
karmaṇaiva hi saṃsiddhim āsthitā janakādayaḥ |
lokasaṃgraham evāpi sampaśyan kartum arhasi || 20 ||

[49] Mbh 6.25.25:
saktāḥ karmaṇy avidvāṃso yathā kurvanti bhārata |
kuryād vidvāṃs tathāsaktaś cikīṣur lokasaṃgraham || 25 ||

[50] See for example van Buitenen 1981: 14-21. An interpretation of *lokasaṃgraha* in terms of heavenly *loka*s would be contrary to the spirit of Kṛṣṇa's speech: he objects to Arjuna's initial concern for the maintenance of the *pitṛloka*.

[51] Despite Kṛṣṇa's offering his new soteriological path to women (Mbh 6.31.32 [33, = *Bhagavadgītā* 9]), all the actual and hypothetical *karmayogin*s he cites by way of example are nominally or pronominally male, a fact that is reflected (without comment, and thus, I suspect, unthinkingly) by almost all translators. Here I am being deliberately gender-specific in order to emphasise the androcentrism of the discourse.

[52] See, for example, standard biographies of Yājñavalkya (*Bṛhadāraṇyaka-upaniṣad* 2.4, 4.5), Buddha (Aśvaghoṣa's *Buddhacarita* 2-6), and Mahāvīra (Hemacandra's *Triṣaṣṭiśalākāpuruṣacaritra*, *Mahāvīracaritra* 2.125-155). *Buddhacarita* 2.56ab generalises the point:
vanam anupamasattvā bodhisattvās tu sarve
viṣayasukharasajñā jagmur utpannaputrāḥ |
"All the *bodhisattva*s of matchless character, knowing sensual enjoyments, pleasures and affections, went to the forest once a son was born to them." Within Jainism and Buddhism there are various modifications of this paradigm. The

that Kṛṣṇa accommodates marital attachment. However, while the *karmayogin* may be physically present for his wife and family, he is emotionally committed elsewhere, either to the *loka* (that is, the earth), to Kṛṣṇa, or to his own soteriological progress. For Kṣatriyas, as the *Strīparvan* so graphically illustrates, such commitment may result in premature death. Moreover, soteriological progress is presented in gendered terms.[53] *Mokṣa* is conceived as the emancipation of a masculine entity (*ātman* or *puruṣa*) from its prior involvement with the feminine *prakṛti*. Surviving *Sāṃkhya* texts tell of a form of *mokṣa* called *prakṛtilaya* ("dissolution into *prakṛti*"), but emphasise that this is only a temporary deliverance from *saṃsāra*, pursued and attained by those who are unable to comprehend the subtleties of the twenty-fifth *tattva*, *puruṣa*.[54] I would suggest that the gender of these philosophical ideas is not accidental, and that the apparent gynæphobia of the *śramaṇa* view has been carried over into the Mbh's hybrid soteriology.

Digambaras claim that Mahāvīra had neither wife nor child (see Jain 1974: 39-40). In the *Mūlasarvāstivādavinaya* the birth of his son coincides with Buddha's enlightenment; his wife unsuccessfully attempts to bring her husband home, loses the son to the *saṅgha*, fails in a suicide attempt due to Buddha's interference, and finally becomes a nun. See Strong 1997.

[53] Indological literature on this topic is scarce. See Indradeva 1966; Falk 1977: 106-108; Natarajan 2001 (following Chattopadhyaya 1959); Kelkar 2003. For an exploration of similar issues in European philosophy, see Lloyd 1984. It is important that further research in this area be methodologically rigorous: as James Hegarty puts it, "gender-as-sign may be in a complex and non-reflective relationship with extra-textual gender" (personal communication, 8th August 2003). Vanita 2003 sees the dialogue between King Janaka Dharmadhvaja and the female ascetic Sulabhā (Mbh 12.308 [321], on which see also Fitzgerald 2002b) as a charter for female renouncers. The dialogue is subversive in terms of gender, but reverts to *nivṛtti* soteriology against the trend of the *Bhagavadgītā*. Vanita's claim (on p. 81) that *ātman* is gendered neuter is too hasty.

[54] See Jacobsen 1999: 273-320. We must not forget that our reconstructions of ancient Indian thought are based only on surviving texts which are unlikely to be representative. The various conditions for textual survival need to be properly theorised before any such assessment is made: for example, the fact that the Christians were originally a persecuted minority might not be unrelated to the survival of their texts.

3. Despite its ideological value, the cosmic interpretation of the war is used sparingly by the Mbh. The frame story is a "secret of the gods", and the escalating conflict is generally narrated in human terms. I have called this the lower level explanation, but it remains primary. The war is caused in the first instance by the incompatibility of Duryodhana's ambition and Yudhiṣṭhira's, by the outrage of the Pāṇḍavas following Draupadī's treatment at the dicing match, and by Duryodhana's refusal to return the kingdom to the Pāṇḍavas at the end of their exile. This explanation is self-contained and convincing. The cosmic explanation is mentioned only a handful of times, and does not really exonerate anyone but Kṛṣṇa and Vyāsa, since only they understood the "secret of the gods".

We are entitled to wonder why the poets did not integrate the cosmic explanation more thoroughly into the narrative. The *Ādiparvan* frame story suggests that the Mbh is really the story of the celestials rescuing and renewing the earth, but for the most part it does not appear to be this, because most of the characters do not know the frame story. It would have been quite easy to have had the "secret of the gods" explained to the Pāṇḍavas, either before the war (thus making the *udyoga* less painful) or immediately after it (it is after all revealed to Dhṛtarāṣṭra at this time). But this does not happen. Various secrets are received from time to time by various Pāṇḍavas: here we may include Yudhiṣṭhira's receipt of *pratismṛti* knowledge from Vyāsa (which he subsequently passes on to Arjuna);[55] Yudhiṣṭhira's receipt of the "heart of the dice" from Bṛhadaśva;[56] Arjuna's receipt of Kṛṣṇa's "imperishable *yoga*" and "royal knowledge";[57] and various revelations of the true identities of Kṛṣṇa and Arjuna as Nārāyaṇa and Nara. But none of these secrets include the frame story. Once, at Mbh 3.42.17-23 [41], Yama men-

---

[55] Mbh 3.37.20-38.14 [36-37]. On this passage, see Mehta 1990: 107-109; Hiltebeitel 2001: 52-53.

[56] Mbh 3.78.17 [79]. On this secret, see Bowlby 1991; Hegarty 2001.

[57] Mbh 6.26.1-3 [28, = *Bhagavadgītā* 4] and 31.1-3 [33, = *Bhagavadgītā* 9].

tions the earth's plight and the celestial mission to Arjuna, but thereafter Arjuna shows no signs of having received this information, and we may thus assume that Yama's speech is given, like the account of the frame story that Vyāsa gives to Dhṛtarāṣṭra, primarily for the benefit of the audience.

At the beginning of the *Śāntiparvan*, when Yudhiṣṭhira is beside himself with grief and ready to renounce the kingdom, Vyāsa, Kṛṣṇa and Nārada all fail to tell him the true significance of what has just happened. Vyāsa repeats that the war was unavoidable, insists that Yudhiṣṭhira take the throne, and explains that various expiations are available for those who have committed sins (chapters 23-38, with various interruptions and digressions). At Mbh 12.34.13-21 [33] Vyāsa mentions a previous *deva/asura* battle in which the many who took the side of the *asura*s were deservedly slain, and points out that this carnage was to the greater good. He says "You are following the road that was earlier travelled by the *deva*s",[58] but does not expand on this. It is hard not to imagine him winking at the audience here: there seems to be a deliberate authorial policy to keep Yudhiṣṭhira in the dark.

In the *Āśramavāsikaparvan* Yudhiṣṭhira and the court's inner circle, including many war-widows, visit Dhṛtarāṣṭra, Gāndhārī and Kuntī in their sylvan retreat. A roll-call of the visitors is given by Saṃjaya in 15.32 [25]: apart from the five Pāṇḍavas, they are all women, most of whom have lost husbands or children in the war, and so this episode seems to be a deliberate mirror or continuation of the *Strīparvan* scene. On this occasion Vyāsa appears and, hearing that the assembled company are all still troubled by the war, he emphasises that those who died on Kurukṣetra were excellent Kṣatriyas, and then explains that the warriors were incarnations of various species of celestial being, and that the war was necessary according to a celestial agenda – although he does not explain what this was (chapter 39 [31]). He then invites the assembled company

[58] Mbh 12.34.21cd [33]:
devaiḥ pūrvagataṃ mārgam anuyāto 'si bhārata ‖ 21 ‖

to the river Gaṅgā, out of which, once darkness has fallen, the deceased warriors arise. For one night the dead consort with the living, all enmity forgotten, before returning through the Gaṅgā to their respective heavens where, on Vyāsa's beneficent invitation, many of the women join them, having abandoned their human bodies by plunging into the river (chapters 40-41 [32-33]).

In this episode, despite the fact that those who lost loved ones are still so haunted that they are driven to mass suicide, Vyāsa once again withholds the details of the celestial business which required the Kurukṣetra slaughter. The last few books of the epic are concerned to complete the lives of those characters not killed in the war, who are mostly disposed of in blocks: Vidura; these war widows; the older generation (bar Saṃjaya, a significant survivor); the Vṛṣṇis, Andhakas and Bhojas; Draupadī and the Pāṇḍavas.[59] The widows' afterlives begin happily, returning them to the pleasures of their youth, but the filling thus sandwiched has clearly been unsavoury. The Mbh cannot be accused of neglecting the female response to the war, as the *Strīparvan* shows, and after the first flush of hero-mourning has passed its authors are careful not to ignore the widows, but one senses a slight awkwardness at their cauterised femininities, which in the end are made to serve as a trigger for heroic nostalgia.

Returning to the question of how the authors present the war's genesis, it is clear that, even with the "secret of the gods" remaining firmly in the background of the epic, other honourable explanations for the war might easily have been introduced. More (1995) has shown that it is possible to interpret Kṛṣṇa as a principled statesman, whose anti-imperialist political philosophy causes him to enlist the support of the Pāṇḍavas to depose first Jarāsaṃdha and then Duryodhana.[60] But such an agenda is only to be found between

---

[59] See Mbh 15.33.15 ff. [26] for Vidura; 15.45.9-38 [37] for Dhṛtarāṣṭra, Gāndhārī and Kuntī; 16.4-8 [3-7] for the Vṛṣṇis, Andhakas and Bhojas; 17.2 for Draupadī and the younger Pāṇḍavas; 17.3 and 18.1-4 for Yudhiṣṭhira.

[60] For Jarāsaṃdha, see Mbh 2.12-22 [13-24]; John Brockington 2002.

the lines of the text: Kṛṣṇa does not mention anything of it to his allies. Relatedly, it is often argued that the war is justifiable on utilitarian or moral grounds: so Rosen (2002a: 6) claims that "the battle was fought ... for larger issues involving protection of the innocent and the abolition of a tyrannical regime", that "the Kauravas had become infamous as exploitative kings", and that "they wreaked havoc throughout the country, causing hardship for all their subjects" (Rosen 2002b: 15). Such claims seem intended to arouse sympathy for the Pāṇḍavas and their advisor, but gain little support from the text itself, where mention of the oppressed masses is conspicuous by its absence. Duryodhana is in many ways a paradigm of integrity, as Gitomer (1992) has shown. At Mbh 5.60.16-17 he says:

> In my realm there are no fears, no snakes or suchlike; thanks to me agents of terror do not harm creatures in their sleep; the raincloud rains according to the wishes of the realm's inhabitants; all my subjects are highly righteous and there are no calamities.[61]

Attempts to whitewash Kṛṣṇa and the Pāṇḍavas usually emphasise the lengths to which they went in trying to avoid war, yet according to the *deva/asura* frame story the war was not to be avoided. Kṛṣṇa at least knew this, and at Mbh 5.91.4-18 [93] he admits as much to Vidura, saying that he will go through the motions of attempting to find a diplomatic solution in order not to be held responsible for the war.[62] In verse 8d he applies the future participle *vinaśiṣyat-* ("who will be perishing") to the Kurus and Sṛñjayas.

---

[61] Mbh 5.60.16-17 [61]:
bhayāni viṣaye rājan vyālādīni na santi me ।
mattaḥ suptāni bhūtāni na hiṃsanti bhayaṃkarāḥ ॥ 16 ॥
nikāmavarṣī parjanyo rājan viṣayavāsinām ।
dharmiṣṭhāś ca prajāḥ sarvā ītayaś ca na santi me ॥ 17 ॥

[62] Mbh 5.91.16-17:
na māṃ brūyur adharmajñā mūḍhā asuhṛdas tathā ।
śakto nāvārayat kṛṣṇaḥ saṃrabdhān kurupāṇḍavān ॥ 16 ॥

4. If there are "goodies" and "baddies" in the Mbh, they are not so in the familiar sense: the poets' justification of the war is relatively inaccessible. In human terms, dharmic justification for the war is given only by the importance of discharging one's vows,[63] and by relentless appeal to *varṇadharma*. We are left with a waste of human life, caused by some of the least praiseworthy aspects of human nature, and sporadically embellished with a cosmic explanation. This explanation might seem – to the credulous – to ennoble the proceedings, but many listeners may well have seen it as utterly mythical and as transparently subservient to an ideological agenda. We are reminded that van Buitenen called the *devalasura* frame story "inept mythification" (van Buitenen 1973: xx).

---

ubhayoḥ sādhayann artham aham āgata ity uta |
tatra yatnam ahaṃ kṛtvā gaccheyaṃ nṛṣv avācyatām || 17 ||

"May those who do not know *dharma*, the ignorant and the unfriendly, not say of me, 'Kṛṣṇa, though able to, did not restrain the angry Kurus and Pāṇḍavas'. I have come to bring about the good of both: having taken pains in this, may I be irreproachable by the people." But Kṛṣṇa *is* reproached, by both Gāndhārī (who curses him, Mbh 11.25.36-42) and Uttaṅka (who is about to, Mbh 14.52.20-22 [53], but who is dissuaded by the revelation of Kṛṣṇa's divine identity and allegedly dharmic purpose). At Mbh 16.9.27 [8] Vyāsa implies (see Hiltebeitel 2001: 89) that Kṛṣṇa would have been able to prevent the slaughter, though this presumably would have involved his refusing to aid the celestials in their mission.

[63] On vows, see Ramankutty 1999: 113-136; Hopkins 1932. The importance of discharging one's vows seems to be a special case of the general necessity not to be a liar, and partially exonerates several of the Pāṇḍavas' – particularly Bhīma's – most unruly deeds. See Mbh 9.57.6-7 [58] and 59.14-15, 21 [60] for Kṛṣṇa's justification of Bhīma's striking Duryodhana below the belt, which justification Saṃjaya at 59.22a calls *dharmacchalam* (Ganguli: "fallacious discourse"; Goldman 1997: 209: "specious righteousness"); see Mbh 11.14.17-18 for Bhīma's justification of his drinking – or pretending to drink – Duḥśāsana's blood, including the claim that vow-fulfilment is part of *kṣatradharma*; but see also Mbh 8.49 [69], where Kṛṣṇa explains how lying can be dharmic, and how Arjuna can fulfil a vow obliquely, in a manner contrary to the original intention. On this last incident, see also Matilal 1989: 7-19. Mehendale (2001: 201-205) argues that several vows are interpolated; see also Dange 1984: 59-88. The authorial attitudes that might lie behind these episodes are obscure and require further study.

The problem here, as so often in our reading of the Mbh, is that we do not know the text's audience. But in view of the foregoing considerations, we should pay heed to the text's description of its own scope:

> Concerning *dharma, artha, kāma* and *mokṣa,* what is here is elsewhere, what is not here is nowhere.[64]

We should also pay heed to recent studies of the Mbh as a dialogic text. Taking their lead from Bakhtin, Gitomer (1992: 223) calls it "obstreperously multivocal", and Hegarty (2001: 55) argues that it "models its internal discourse on the encompassing complexity of all discursive practice". Scholars habitually view the text through the lens of Hinduism, a latter-day ideology,[65] but if we instead imagine that the Mbh was placing many of the ideas we now think of as orthodox before a new and possibly sceptical audience, we can listen more readily for voices from the margins.[66] The *Strīparvan* is a promising text for this, since it presents us with a discourse that is overheard and imported into the textual mainstream through Gāndhārī being given the authorial role usually reserved for men.

Gāndhārī makes several statements that we may quite easily interpret as subversive, ironic, even sarcastic. I shall give two examples. In chapter eighteen she says to Kṛṣṇa:

> I reckon that the sin committed in previous births by these irreproachable women and also by imprudent me was perhaps not trivial, O sinless one!

[64] Mbh 1.56.33 [62] (repeated verbatim at 18.5.38):
dharme cārthe ca kāme ca mokṣe ca bharatarṣabha |
yad ihāsti tad anyatra yan nehāsti na tat kva cit ||

[65] Hinduism as we know it cannot be separated from religious nationalism and the legacy of colonialism: see Sen 1993; Dalmia & von Stietencron 1995.

[66] Here I mean textual margins. To what extent these correspond to social or cultural margins is an open question: see above, footnotes 5 and 54. In conceptualising both of these types of marginality, we may "make a definite distinction between that marginality which is imposed by oppressive structures and that marginality one chooses as a site of resistance – as location of radical openness and possibility" (hooks 1991: 153).

> Then this was arranged for us by the king of *dharma*, for there is no avoiding the consequences of good and bad actions.[67]

In chapter twenty-four, looking upon her dead brother Śakuni, she comments upon a central pillar of the Kṣatriya ideology:

> Just as my sons' heavenly worlds were won by the sword, so indeed the heavenly worlds of even this evil-minded one were won by the sword![68]

The question of how such utterances are to be understood is a difficult one, since there is no simple indicator that would allow us to decide once and for all whether any particular Mbh speech is to be taken at face value or not. Van Buitenen saw this problem as a consequence of preserving an orally operative text in writing:

> A wink, a gesture, an irony of enunciation on [the reciter's] part may convey to the listener a specific meaning closed to the reader ... The same lines might have been read in a tone heavily sarcastic, or pathetic ... Here sides have to be taken. Tone, and, most bewilderingly, humorous tone, depends on the listener's understanding of the speaker's intention ... Here we are in treacherous quicksand ... I am not sure what to do about the problem of tone, except to hope that over the years I have developed a bit of an ear.[69]

---

[67] Mbh 11.18.11-12:
pūrvajātikṛtaṃ pāpaṃ manye nālpam ivānagha ।
etābhir anavadyābhir mayā caivālpamedhayā ॥ 11 ॥
tad idaṃ dharmarājena yātitaṃ no janārdana ।
na hi nāśo 'sti vārṣṇeya karmaṇoḥ śubhapāpayoḥ ॥ 12 ॥
Gāndhārī's use of the name *dharmarāja* here is deliciously ambiguous: in their translations Fitzgerald identifies Yama, Ganguli Yudhiṣṭhira, but both are implied (on the links between them, see Fitzgerald 2001: 85-90). Past-life causation is also hypothesised elsewhere in connection with the war, but there is a sharpness in Gāndhārī's choice of words here which we do not find in her husband's at 1.18, for example, or even in her own at 16.59a-d:
nūnam ācaritaṃ pāpaṃ mayā pūrveṣu janmasu ।
yā paśyāmi hatān putrān pautrān bhrātṝṃś ca keśava ।
"Surely in former births sinful conduct was performed by me, the one who sees sons, grandsons and brothers killed!"

[68] Mbh 11.24.27:
yathaiva mama putrāṇāṃ lokāḥ śastrajitāḥ prabho ।
evam asyāpi durbuddher lokāḥ śastreṇa vai jitāḥ ॥ 27 ॥

It is difficult to think of how van Buitenen's policy of hope might be improved upon, except by the realisation that we cannot just leave our "ears" to their own devices: we must always interrogate them concerning the possibility that they have been trained to hear certain types of things more readily than others. Moreover, we must take note of as many subtle indicators as possible. It is clear, though, that if these statements are taken to be ironic, then Gāndhārī thinks little of the ideology peddled by some of the text's authors. The women of the *Strīparvan* would want to keep their men, even if it costs them the earth.

REFERENCES

BAILEY, Greg 1981. Brahmā, Pṛthu and the theme of the earth-milker in Hindu mythology. *IIJ* 23: 105-116.

—— 1993. Humanistic elements in the *Mahābhārata. South Asia* 16: 1-23.

BEDEKAR, V. M. 1992. The doctrines of *svabhāva* and *kāla* in the *Mahābhārata* and other old Sanskrit works. In: H. S. Prasad (ed.), *Time in Indian Philosophy: A Collection of Essays*: 187-202. Delhi: Sri Satguru Press.

BHARADWAJ, Saroj 1992. *The Concept of 'Daiva' in the Mahābhārata.* Delhi: Nag Publishers.

BIARDEAU, Madeleine 1970. The story of Arjuna Kārtavīrya without reconstruction. *Purāṇa* 12: 286-303.

—— 1981. The salvation of the king in the *Mahābhārata. Contributions to Indian Sociology* (new series) 15: 75-97.

---

[69] Van Buitenen 1973: xl. Compare musical performance, where even a heavily annotated score leaves considerable scope for the musician's interpretation. See also Mary Brockington 2000: 92: "Reading an oral narrative on the page, as we do now, inevitably distorts it, robbing it of those nuances of tone, facial expression and timing by which a skilled performer conveys its meaning; the actual words are only a part of the total performance, and we should not underestimate or ignore the role of the performer in evoking the right mood, and playing his text for laughs when required". In a text written for communal recitation rather than private reading, the idea that any particular passage has a definitive tone may well be illusory in any case: the passage would alter its tone depending on the specifics of performer and audience. Preserving tonal ambiguity in the written text would allow for maximum versatility, a variety of possible "right moods".

BOWLBY, Paul 1991. Kings without authority: the obligation of the ruler to gamble in the *Mahābhārata*. *Studies in Religion / Sciences Religieuses* 20: 3-17.

BROCKINGTON, John 1998. *The Sanskrit Epics*. (Handbuch der Orientalistik, 2.12.) Leiden: Brill.

—— 2002. Jarāsaṃdha of Magadha (MBh 2,15-22). In: M. Brockington (ed.), *Stages and Transitions: Temporal and Historical Frameworks in Epic and Purāṇic Literature. Proceedings of the Second DICSEP, August 1999*: 73-88. Zagreb: Croatian Academy of Sciences and Arts.

BROCKINGTON, Mary 2000. Jarāsaṃdha and the magic mango: causes and consequences in epic and oral tales. In: P. Balcerowicz & M. Mejor (eds.), *On the Understanding of Other Cultures. Proceedings of the International Conference on Sanskrit and Related Studies to Commemorate the Centenary of the Birth of Stanislaw Schayer, Warsaw, October 1999* (Studia Indologiczne, 7): 85-94. Warsaw: Instytut Orientalistyczny, University of Warsaw.

BRODBECK, Simon 2004a. Calling Kṛṣṇa's bluff: non-attached action in the *Bhagavadgītā*. *JIPh* 32: 81-103.

—— 2004b. Kṛṣṇa's action as the paradigm of *asakta karman* in the *Bhagavadgītā*. In: R. Czekalska & H. Marlewicz (eds.), *Second International Conference on Sanskrit and Related Studies, September 19-23, 2001: Proceedings* (Cracow Indological Studies, 4-5): 85-112. Cracow: Księgarnia Akademicka.

BUITENEN, J. A. B. van (trans. & ed.) 1973. *The Mahābhārata*, I: Book 1*; The Book of the Beginning*. Chicago: University of Chicago Press.

—— (trans. & ed.) 1981. *The Bhagavadgītā in the Mahābhārata: A Bilingual Edition*. Chicago: University of Chicago Press.

CHATTOPADHYAYA, Debiprasad 1959. *Lokāyata: A Study in Ancient Indian Materialism*. New Delhi: People's Publishing House.

DALMIA, Vasudha & Heinrich VON STIETENCRON (eds.) 1995. *Representing Hinduism: The Construction of Religious Traditions and National Identity*. New Delhi: Sage.

DANGE, Sindhu S. 1984. *The Bhāgavata Purāṇa: Mytho-social Study*. Delhi: Ajanta Publications.

DERRETT, J. Duncan 1959. *Bhū-bharaṇa, bhū-pālana, bhū-bhojana*: an Indian conundrum. *Bulletin of the School of Oriental and African Studies* 22: 108-123.

DUMÉZIL, Georges 1968. *Mythe et épopée: l'idéologie des trois fonctions dans les épopées des peuples indo-européens*, I. (Bibliothèque des Sciences Humaines.) 2nd edition. Paris: Gallimard.

EDELSTEIN, Marilyn 1992. Metaphor, meta-narrative, and mater-narrative in Kristeva's "Stabat mater". In: David Crownfield (ed.), *Body/text in Julia Kristeva: Religion, Women, and Psychoanalysis*: 27-52. Albany: SUNY Press.

FALK, Nancy 1977. Draupadī and the *dharma*. In: Rita M. Gross (ed.), *Beyond Androcentrism: New Essays on Women and Religion* (American Academy of Religion: Aids for the Study of Religion, 6): 89-114. Missoula, Montana: Scholars Press.

FELLER JATAVALLABHULA, Danielle 1999. *Raṇayajña*: the *Mahābhārata* war as a sacrifice. In: J. E. M. Houben & K. R. van Kooij (eds.), *Violence Denied: Violence, Non-violence and the Rationalization of Violence in South Asian Cultural History* (Brill's Indological Library, 16): 69-103. Leiden: Brill.

FITZGERALD, James L. 1991. India's fifth Veda: the *Mahābhārata*'s presentation of itself. In: Arvind Sharma (ed.), *Essays on the Mahābhārata* (Brill's Indological Library, 1): 150-170. Leiden: Brill.

—— 2001. Making Yudhiṣṭhira the king: the dialectics and the politics of violence in the *Mahābhārata*. *RO* 54: 63-92.

—— 2002a. The Rāma Jāmadagnya 'thread' of the *Mahābhārata*: a new survey of Rāma Jāmadagnya in the Pune text. In: M. Brockington (ed.), *Stages and Transitions: Temporal and Historical Frameworks in Epic and Purāṇic Literature. Proceedings of the Second DICSEP, August 1999*: 89-132. Zagreb: Croatian Academy of Sciences and Arts.

—— 2002b. Nun befuddles king, shows *karmayoga* does not work: Sulabhā's refutation of King Janaka at MBh 12.308. *JIPh* 30: 641-677.

—— (trans., ed. & annot.) 2004. *The Mahābhārata*, VII: Book 11, *The Book of the Women*; Book 12, *The Book of Peace* (part one). Chicago: University of Chicago Press.

GANGULI, Kisari Mohan (trans.) 1883-96. *The Mahabharata of Krishna-Dwaipayana Vyasa*. First published in one hundred fascicules, edited by P. C. and later S. B. Roy. (Reprint: New Delhi: Munshiram Manoharlal, 1993.)

GITOMER, David 1992. King Duryodhana: the *Mahābhārata* discourse of sinning and virtue in epic and drama. *JAOS* 112: 222-232.

GOLDMAN, Robert P. 1970. Akṛtavraṇa and Śrīkṛṣṇa as narrators of the legend of the Bhārgava Rāma. *ABORI* 53: 161-173.

—— 1997. *Eṣa dharmaḥ sanātanaḥ*: shifting moral values and the Indian epics. In: P. Bilimoria and J. N. Mohanty (eds.), *Relativism, Suffering and Beyond: Essays in Memory of Bimal K. Matilal*: 187-223. Delhi: OUP.

GONZÁLEZ-REIMANN, Luis 2002. *The Mahābhārata and the Yugas: India's Great Epic Poem and the Hindu System of World Ages.* (Asian Thought and Culture, 51.) New York: Peter Lang.

HARA, Minoru 1973. The king as a husband of the earth (*mahī-pati*). *AS/ÉA* 27: 97-114.

—— 1996-97. Śrī: mistress of a king. *Orientalia Suecana* 45-46: 33-61.

HAWTHORNE, Sîan 2004. Rethinking subjectivity in the gender-oriented study of religions: Kristeva and the "subject-in-process". In: U. King & T. Beattie (eds.), *Gender, Religion and Diversity: Cross-cultural Perspectives.* New York: Continuum International.

HEGARTY, James M. 2001. An apprenticeship in attentiveness: narrative patterning in the *Dyūtaparvan* and the *Nalopākhyāna* of the *Mahābhārata*. *RO* 54: 33-62.

HILL, Peter 2001. *Fate, Predestination and Human Action in the Mahābhārata: A Study in the History of Ideas.* New Delhi: Munshiram Manoharlal.

HILTEBEITEL, Alf 1976. *The Ritual of Battle: Krishna in the Mahābhārata.* (Symbol, Myth and Ritual.) Ithaca: Cornell University Press.

—— 1980. Draupadī's garments. *IIJ* 22: 97-112.

—— 1999. Reconsidering Bhṛguization. In: M. Brockington & P. Schreiner (eds.), *Composing a Tradition: Concepts, Techniques and Relationships. Proceedings of the First DICSEP, August 1997*: 155-168. Zagreb: Croatian Academy of Sciences and Arts.

—— 2001. *Rethinking the Mahābhārata: A Reader's Guide to the Education of the Dharma King.* Chicago: University of Chicago Press.

HOOKS, bell 1991. Choosing the margin as a space of radical openness. In: b. hooks, *Yearning: Race, Gender, and Cultural Politics*: 145-153. London: Turnaround.

HOPKINS, E. Washburn 1915. *Epic Mythology.* (Encyclopedia of Indo-Aryan Research, 3.1.B.) Strassburg: Karl J. Trübner.

—— 1932. The oath in Hindu epic literature. *JAOS* 52: 316-337.

INDRADEVA, Shrirama 1966. Correspondence between woman and nature in Indian thought. *Philosophy East and West* 16: 161-168.

JACKSON, A. V. Williams 1896. On *Mahābhārata* iii.142.35-45, an echo of an old Hindu-Persian legend. *JAOS* 17: 185-187.

JACOBSEN, Knut A. 1999. *Prakṛti in Sāṃkhya-Yoga: Material Principle, Religious Experience, Ethical Implications.* New York: Peter Lang. (Reprint: Delhi: MLBD, 2002.)

JAIN, Kailash Chand 1974. *Lord Mahāvīra and His Times.* Delhi: MLBD.

JOHNSEN, Gösta 1965-66. Varuṇa and Dhṛtarāṣṭra. *IIJ* 9: 245-265.

JOHNSON, William J. (trans., ed. & annot.) 1998. *The Sauptikaparvan of the Mahābhārata: The Massacre at Night.* (Oxford World's Classics.) Oxford: OUP.

JONG, J. W. de 1985. The over-burdened earth in India and Greece. *JAOS* 105: 397-400.

KELKAR, Meena 2003. Man-woman relationship in Indian philosophy. In: M. Kelkar and D. Gangavane (eds.), *Feminism in Search of an Identity: The Indian Context*: 101-120. Jaipur: Rawat Publications. (First published in *Indian Philosophical Quarterly* 26, 1999.)

KINSLEY, David R. 1986. *Hindu Goddesses: Visions of the Divine Feminine in the Hindu Religious Tradition.* Berkeley: University of California Press.

KNIGHT, Chris 1987. The lunar analogue and the origins of culture. *Cosmos* (the yearbook of the Traditional Cosmology Society) 3: 72-106.

KRISTEVA, Julia 1986. Stabat Mater. In: Toril Moi (ed.), *The Kristeva Reader*: 161-186. Oxford: Blackwell. (First published under the title "Hérethique de l'amour", 1977.) English translation by Léon S. Roudiez.

LLOYD, Genevieve 1984. *The Man of Reason: 'Male' and 'Female' in Western Philosophy.* London: Methuen.

LONG, J. Bruce 1980. The concepts of human action and rebirth in the *Mahābhārata.* In: Wendy Doniger O'Flaherty (ed.), *Karma and Rebirth in Classical Indian Traditions*: 38-60. Berkeley: University of California Press.

MACDONELL, Arthur Anthony 1897. *Vedic Mythology.* (Encyclopedia of Indo-Aryan Research, 3.1.A.) Strassburg: Karl J. Trübner.

MACDONELL, Arthur Anthony & Arthur Berriedale KEITH 1912. *Vedic Index of Names and Subjects*, II. London: John Murray.

MAGNONE, Paolo 2000. Floodlighting the deluge: traditions in comparison. In: P. Balcerowicz & M. Mejor (eds.), *On the Understanding of Other Cultures. Proceedings of the International Conference on Sanskrit and Related Studies to Commemorate the Centenary of the Birth of Stanislaw Schayer, Warsaw, October 1999* (Studia Indologiczne, 7): 233-244. Warsaw: Instytut Orientalistyczny, University of Warsaw.

Mahābhārata: Critical Edition (1933-66). 19 vols. Edited by V. S. Sukthankar *et al.* Poona: BORI.

MATILAL, Bimal Krishna 1989. Moral dilemmas: insights from Indian epics. In: B. K. Matilal (ed.), *Moral Dilemmas in the Mahābhārata*: 1-19. Shimla: Indian Institute of Advanced Study.

MEHENDALE, M. A. 2001. Interpolations in the *Mahābhārata. ABORI* 82: 193-212.

MEHTA, J. L. 1990. Dvaipāyana, poet of being and becoming. In: R. N. Dandekar (ed.), *The Mahābhārata Revisited: Papers Presented at the International*

Seminar on the Mahābhārata Organised by the Sahitya Akademi at New Delhi on February 17-20, 1987: 101-111. New Delhi: Sahitya Akademi.

MODHEY, S. C. 1983. Concept of the god *Dhātṛ* in the Vedas and the Epics. *JOIB* 32: 193-202.

MORE, Sadananda 1995. *Kṛṣṇa: The Man and His Mission. An Enquiry into the Rationale of Inter-relationship between Kṛṣṇa*'s *Life, Mission and Philosophy*. Pune: Gaaj Prakashan.

NATARAJAN, Kanchana 2001. Gendering of early Indian philosophy: a study of *Samkhyakarika*. *Economic and Political Weekly*, April 28: 1398-1404.

PARANJPE, Vasudev Gopal (ed.) 1956. *The Strīparvan, Being the Eleventh Book of the Mahābhārata, the Great Epic of India, for the First Time Critically Edited.* (Poona Critical Edition, XII.2.) Poona: BORI.

PRASAD, Maheshwari 1989. *Some Aspects of the Varāha-kathā in Epics and Purāṇas*. Delhi: Pratibha Prakashan.

RAMANKUTTY, P. V. 1999. *Curse as a Motif in the Mahābhārata*. Delhi: Nag Publishers.

ROSEN, Steven J. 2002a. Introduction. In: S. J. Rosen (ed.), *Holy War: Violence and the Bhagavad Gita*: 1-8. Hampton, Virginia: Deepak Heritage Books.

—— 2002b. Kurukshetra in context: an analysis of violence in the *Bhagavad Gita*. In: S. J. Rosen (ed.), *Holy War: Violence and the Bhagavad Gita*: 9-34. Hampton, Virginia: Deepak Heritage Books.

SCHEUER, Jacques 1982. *Śiva dans le Mahābhārata*. (Bibliothèque de l'École des Hautes Études, Sciences Religieuses, 84.) Paris: Presses Universitaires de France.

SEN, Amiya P. 1993. *Hindu Revivalism in Bengal, 1872-1905: Some Essays in Interpretation*. Delhi: OUP.

SOLOMON, Robert C. 2003. On fate and fatalism. *Philosophy East and West* 53: 435-454.

STRONG, John S. 1997. A family quest: the Buddha, Yaśodharā, and Rāhula in the *Mūlasarvāstivāda Vinaya*. In: Juliane Schober (ed.), *Sacred Biography in the Buddhist Traditions of South and Southeast Asia*: 113-128. Honolulu: University of Hawai'i Press.

SUTTON, Nicholas 2000. *Religious Doctrines in the Mahābhārata*. Delhi: MLBD.

VANITA, Ruth 2003. The self is not gendered: Sulabha's debate with King Janaka. *NWSA Journal* (an official publication of the National Women's Studies Association) 15: 76-93.

VASSILKOV, Yaroslav 1995. The *Mahābhārata*'s typological definition reconsidered. *IIJ* 38: 249-256.

—— 1999. *Kālavāda* (the doctrine of cyclical time) in the *Mahābhārata* and the concept of heroic didactics. In: M. Brockington & P. Schreiner (eds.), *Composing a Tradition: Concepts, Techniques and Relationships. Proceedings of the First DICSEP, August 1997*: 17-33. Zagreb: Croatian Academy of Sciences and Arts.

WOODS, Julian F. 1999. *Destiny and Human Initiative in the Mahābhārata.* Albany: SUNY Press.

Triḥsaptakṛtvaḥ: The Significance of the Number "Thrice Seven" in the Rāma Jāmadagnya Myth of the *Mahābhārata*

NICOLAS DEJENNE

INTRODUCTION

Rāma Jāmadagnya, whose myth is narrated at some length at Mbh 3.115-117 and 12.49, appears as one of the most striking characters of the Sanskrit epic. His greatest feat consists in the twenty-one, or more accurately the "thrice seven" (*triḥsapta*) destructions of the Kṣatriya class to avenge the murder of his father, the *brahmarṣi* Jamadagni at the hands of King Arjuna Kārtavīrya's sons. Two main expressions in the Mbh relate this feat:

> *triḥsaptakṛtvaḥ pṛthivīṃ kṛtvā niḥkṣatriyāṃ prabhuḥ*
> (Mbh 3.117.9; and 1.58.4, 12.49.56)
>
> *triḥsaptakṛtvaḥ pṛthivī kṛtā niḥkṣatriyā purā*
> (Mbh 1.98.3; and 8.22.39, 12.48.10, 13.14.138, 13.83.30)

These annihilations provoke amazement among heroes of the Mbh, especially the Pāṇḍavas, who repeatedly question various narrators (Goldman 1970) about the origin of such a mortal feud between Rāma and the Kṣatriyas and the miracle by which there can still be Kṣatriyas on earth in their own *yuga* after they have been totally destroyed by Rāma. But it is noticeable that the interest displayed by the epic characters in the reason and result of the fight between

Rāma and the Kṣatriyas never concerns the very number of destructions of Kṣatriyas, which is puzzling for us in at least two ways. How can the same group be annihilated – twenty-one times – in a row? And what significance can we ascribe to these precisely thrice seven destructions accomplished by Rāma? I think that an enquiry into the connotations attached to the number twenty-one, especially in its form *triḥsapta*, in ancient Indian culture, in addition to its own import, may help in answering the second of these two questions.

The very fact that the epic heroes do not seem interested in knowing more about these twenty-one destructions may suggest that these were not problematic for them and that the use of the expression *triḥsapta* had an obvious meaning for them and the Mbh redactors. But we can suppose that this original meaning got lost with the passing of time so that some late Purāṇas feel the need to give a justification to these twenty-one fights. At *Brahmāṇḍa-purāṇa* 23.90.28-32, Paraśurāma (the most common name of Rāma Jāmadagnya in the Purāṇas) swears to destroy the Kṣatriyas twenty-one times after seeing his mother Reṇukā beating her chest twenty-one times in despair because of Jamadagni's murder. In the *Reṇukāmāhātmya* 34.35, Reṇukā herself received twenty-one strokes from Arjuna Kārtavīrya in trying to protect Jamadagni.. In these two late versions, the justification seems to me to be too psychological, emotional and superficial to explain the number of destructions given in the Mbh, all the more as they use the far more common word *ekaviṃśa* instead of the canonical epic *triḥsapta*. We are thus impelled to search for more convincing arguments in texts written prior to or contemporary with the Mbh, mainly the Vedic ones.

Before presenting my hypotheses and findings on the significance of the number "thrice seven", I want to make two preliminary remarks on the compound *triḥsaptakṛtvaḥ*: the suffix *-kṛtvas*, even if it is not very common, is a Pāṇinian formation indicating the number of repetitions of an action (Renou 1961: 390); and I will consider that *triḥsapta* unequivocally means "thrice seven", "twenty-one" because it is universally accepted in Indian tradition and because other numbers which are multiples of seven enter, according to Monier-Williams dictionary, in the formation of analogous compounds: *dvisaptadhā* (p. 506), *catuḥsaptātman* (p. 384), *pañcasapta-* (p. 577). Therefore, I will not take into account two other theoretically possible readings: *triḥsapta* as meaning "three and seven" or ten, and *triḥsapta* as meaning "three or seven". My inquiry will be divided into three parts. The first one is an investigation of various series, mainly in the Vedic ritual, of twenty-one elements which can provide some insights into the meaning of the twenty-one destructions of Kṣatriyas. The second one presents a survey of the occurrences of the expression *triḥsapta* in the *Ṛgveda.* The last part tries to show to what extent *triḥsapta* can be considered as the "Bhārgava number" *par excellence* and how the whole enquiry can thus contribute to the debate about the "bhṛguization" of the Mbh.

SERIES OF TWENTY-ONE ELEMENTS IN ANCIENT INDIAN CULTURE AND RITUAL

Investigating the meaning of "thrice seven" implies first that we refuse to consider the use of *triḥsaptakṛtvaḥ* by the composers of the Mbh as a mere literary ornament, a sophisticated phrase to express twenty-one. It also implies that we do not take for granted too easy an explanation, often proposed by scholars, according to which *triḥsapta* is an indirect means to refer to a great indefinite number, a synonym of "hundreds" or "scores".

In trying to find a "realistic" or "down-to-earth" explanation of the twenty-one destructions of the Kṣatriyas, we could argue that Rāma Jāmadagnya's story relates on a legendary scale a great and long historical military feud for power between Brahmins and Kṣatriyas which would have happened in a remote past and have consisted in twenty-one battles. In a rather similar approach, Janaki (1966) relied on ṚV 7.18 to find the historical origin of the Mbh story because in this hymn, King Sudāsa defeats ten kings who, along with their allies, form a group of twenty-one tribes, among which figure the Bhṛgus. But we can doubt the relevance of historicizing explanations to understand the inside dynamics and the specific vocabulary of a myth.

Among the other plausible explanations, found in ancient Indian culture, two series of twenty-one elements, referred to in the laws of Manu, seem more relevant in respect with Rāma Jāmadagnya's story. Manu 4.88-90 enumerates the twenty-one hells (*naraka*), the most common number of hells in the Hindu tradition, which is nevertheless not unanimous in that regard. The similarity of the number of hells and of the Kṣatriyas' destructions could reinforce the meaning of total annihilation or punishment against sinful Kṣatriyas. On the other hand, Manu 4.166 declares that "anyone who dares to aggress against a Brahmin, even with a blade of grass, will be reborn twenty-one times in the womb of a lowly animal." This reference is interesting in that it reminds us of the very beginning of the conflict between Rāma Jāmadagnya and the Kṣatriyas, the attempt of King Arjuna Kārtavīrya to steal the calf or the wish-cow of Jamadagni followed by the killing of the Brahmin. In neither case, of course, do I intend to derive mechanically the number of destructions of Kṣatriyas in the Mbh from another text on the basis of similitude, but I am trying to find out correspondences and discover insights into the cultural background of this number.

Considering the importance of rites and sacrifices in this background, and the ritual reading of the main plot of the Mbh, developed by Biardeau or Hiltebeitel in the analysis of the "ritual of battle", it is only logical to look for series of twenty-one elements in the sacrificial field. Let us note first that the very patronymic, Jāmadagnya, of Rāma is a constant reminder in the Mbh of his filiation, of his being the son of Jamadagni, a Vedic *ṛṣi* whose name contains the central element of Vedic sacrifice, the fire – Agni. I will focus my research on the "king of sacrifices", the *aśvamedha*, whose deep links with the story and structure of the Mbh are well-known (Biardeau 2001) and which offers a great wealth of material, precisely described by Dumont (1927). We meet the number twenty-one several times in the description of the *aśvamedha*. Without any claim to being exhaustive, we can mention a few examples.

1. On the first day of the *dīkṣā*, for the rite of Viṣṇu's steps (*viṣṇu-krāmāḥ*), the sacrificer must wear a necklace with a golden circular plate embossed with twenty-one bumps (Dumont 1927: 67, § 280)
2. At the entrance of the *śālā*, the new *gārhapatya* fire, at the time of extension of the sacrificial area, must be circled by twenty-one stones vertically planted in the ground (Dumont 1927: 75-76, § 295).
3. At the end of the third day of soma-pressing, twenty-one sterile cows (*ānubandhyās*) are sacrificed. This bloody episode of the sacrifice echoes the killing of the twenty-one sacrificial animal victims offered to Agni and Soma earlier in the ceremony. (Dumont 1927: 228, § 656)

This bloodshed can be put in relation with the twenty-one destructions of the Kṣatriyas by Rāma Jāmadagnya which may be seen as so many sacrifices. If we admit the strong analogy between sacrifice and battle in the epics, the Kṣatriyas can be taken as images and substitutes of sacrificial victims.

Regarding the *aśvamedha*, we can even go as far as saying that twenty-one is the symbol of this sacrifice because it plays a decisive role in three important domains. First, the *agnikṣetra* – the place where the sacrificial altar must be built in the shape of a bird – must be composed of twenty-one parts (Dumont 1927: 72-75, § 294). Second, the *aśvamedha* comprehends an *ukthya-ekaviṃśa-stoma* (meaning that the fifteen *stotras* sung on the second day of *soma*-pressing are composed of twenty-one stanzas) (p. 131, § 422). Finally, twenty-one sacrificial posts are to be installed. The posts are all twenty-one *aratnis* tall and a sacrificial victim (*paśu*) is tied to each of them before being immolated (pp. 99-101, §§ 348-354). The conjunction of these three series of twenty-one elements, considered as the three heads of the *aśvamedha*, is declared to be most auspicious for the success of the ceremony (pp. 96-99, §§ 342-347).

If all these elements prove the strong sacrificial overtones of the number twenty-one, it must be noted that in every case, the word used is *ekaviṃśa* or *ekaviṃsati*, not *triḥsapta*, even in a case where we can logically deconstruct the series twenty-one in three groups of seven: the twenty-one parts of the *agnikṣetra* in the *aśvamedha* are obtained by multiplying by three the dimensions of the *agnikṣetra* of the common *soma* sacrifice, which is called *saptapuruṣa* or *saptavidha*, but even there, the *agnikṣetra* in the *aśvamedha* is said to be *ekaviṃśatividha*, not **triḥsaptavidha* (pp. 72-75, § 294). The explanations given by the Brāhmaṇas for these various series of twenty-one elements in the *aśvamedha* never refer to three groups of seven either; the most frequent justifications to account for the auspiciousness of twenty-one consist in an addition of the twelve months, the five seasons, the three worlds and the sun (p. 131, § 422, or pp. 228-229, § 656), or in alluding to the correspondences between the universe and the twenty-one parts of Prajāpati's body (pp. 96-99, §§ 342-347). The right order of the world guaranteed by such a sacrifice is often emphasized. Once we have established the close association of "twenty-one" with the sacrifice, we must keep it in mind because what is valid for *ekaviṃśa* is most likely also relevant for *triḥsapta* as a designation of twenty-one, but we must go back further in the Vedic texts to search for occurrences of the very phrase *triḥsapta*.

TRIḤSAPTA, THE NUMBER OF VEDIC KNOWLEDGE

A survey of the mentions of *triḥsapta* in the ṚV, based on Bloomfield's and Lubotsky's Vedic Concordances and Grassmann's *Wörterbuch zum Ṛgveda*, reveals thirteen occurrences disclosed in twelve hymns (ṚV 1.191 contains *triḥsapta* twice). I refer the reader to the Appendix to see this list of quotations. Even if we never find the very phrase *triḥsaptakṛtvaḥ*, *triḥsapta* appears clearly to be an expression dear to the Vedic seers. We must nevertheless acknowledge that it is often difficult to bridge the gap between the Vedic *triḥsapta* and the phrase of the Mbh, and to elucidate the link between the "thrice seven" rivers of 10.64.8 or "thrice seven" peahens of 1.191.14 and the "thrice seven" destructions of the Kṣatriya class. Most frequently (ṚV 1.72.6, 4.1.16, 7.87.4, 8.46.26, 9.70.1, 9.86.21), *triḥsapta* is more or less closely associated with the cows, which can remind us here again of the episode of the theft of Jamadagni's cow.

If we try to establish a typology of these twelve hymns according to the Vedic *ṛṣi*s who authored them, we cannot draw any conclusion as they have been composed by as many different *ṛṣi*s; we can nevertheless remark that none of these hymns has been authored by Jamadagni or any of the Bhārgavas, the ancestors of Rāma Jāmadagnya. Moreover, the gods to whom these hymns are addressed are various, so that we cannot derive any privileged association between a particular Vedic god and *triḥsapta* from a quantitative point of view. But if we consider the worth or power attached to *triḥsapta* in each hymn, we observe that among the four most important of the twelve hymns, one is devoted to Agni (1.72), one to Varuṇa (7.87), one to Agni and Varuṇa (4.1), one to the Puruṣa (10.90). Being aware of the subjectivity in awarding more significance to one hymn than another, I will say that the superior importance and relevance of these four hymns for me are due to their distant echoes of Rāma Jāmadagnya and his myth, and more decisively to the esoteric or magical power attached to *triḥsapta* therein which may account for its use in the Mbh phrase. Let us highlight some interesting possible connections or reminiscences between these four hymns on the one hand and Rāma Jāmadagnya's story on the other.

ṚV 10.90.15, from the famous *Puruṣasūkta*, provides interesting thematic and phonetic echoes with the Rāma Jāmadagnya myth's canonical sentence: *kṛtāḥ* can remind us of *-kṛtvas* and *kṛtvā* or *kṛtā* of the Mbh phrase, and the association of *triḥsapta* with the word *samidh*, the log used to kindle the sacrificial fire, is echoed in the coming back of Rāma, *samidh* in hand, to the hermitage in 3.116.28 and 12.49.43, when he discovers his father's murder and unleashes his wrath, forsaking the usual daily fire sacrifice to destroy the Kṣatriyas in the sacrificial war. If we are right in trying to link these hymns with Rāma Jāmadagnya's myth, we discern a certain logic in the fact that the three others of these four hymns are addressed either to Agni, whose "etymological" connection with Rāma Jāmadagnya has been mentioned earlier, or to Varuṇa, the tutelary deity and ancestor of the Bhārgavas. The latter indeed plays a direct role in 3.115; moreover, Varuṇa, in his function of god punishing the sinners, is said in AV 4.16.6 to catch them with his "thrice seven" links. But more importantly, in 1.72 and 8.87, *triḥsapta* is a number endowed with great holiness and secrecy, emphasized by the use of "*guhya*" in both hymns. In 7.87 especially, *triḥsapta* is the way by which Varuṇa reveals a secret knowledge to a chosen human. In 4.1 and 7.87, this knowledge – certainly the Vedic knowledge – is closely linked with the cow, the symbol of Vedic Brahman, provider of the products for the sacrifice, which is said to possess "thrice seven" names. This is also true of many words also designating the earth and divine speech, in keeping with the synonymy of Sanskrit words denoting these three categories. We come here closer to the fundamental meaning and worth of the phrase *triḥsapta*: it is a cryptic way to express the totality of Vedic knowledge. This totality must not be confused with the indefiniteness I have rejected earlier; it would rather be the contrary thereof. This meaning of *triḥsapta* as the integrity of Vedic knowledge can be more accurately explained in a few ways: there are three classes of seven Vedic sacrifices each (*pākayajña*s, *haviryajña*s, *somayajña*s), thrice seven types of meters in the ṚV – which thus constitute the entire text – or even the twenty-one sounds of the Sanskrit language.

This last hypothesis was proposed by P. Thieme (1985), at the end of an analysis of the verse which was to be recited by the Vedic student on entering his instruction. This is the first verse of the first hymn of the *Atharvaveda* in the Śaunakīya recension, popularly known as the *triṣaptīyam*, that Thieme translates thus "The thrice seven that go around, wearing all the shapes, let the Lord of Speech put their powers into my body". It is quite remarkable to meet *triḥsapta* as referring to, or even denoting, the whole Vedic science in a verse to be pronounced on such an important occasion as the beginning of Vedic instruction. Not only is thus *triḥsapta* the symbol of Vedic knowledge but it is closely linked with its preservation through its transmission from gurus to disciples and students. AV offers other occurrences of *triḥsapta* (1.27.1, 12.2.29, 13.1.3, 14.6.15, 20.92.4) so that Henry (1904: 76) went as far as writing: "ce nombre 21, qui semble, surtout en tant qu'il égale 7x3, la base de l'arithmétique de l'Atharva-Véda". We may seem to be very far from our starting point, the terrifying and bloody twenty-one destructions of the Kṣatriya class by Rāma Jāmadagnya, but all these Vedic quotations and especially this first verse of the Śaunakīya AV may provide us with a means to bridge this apparently increasing distance – because Śaunaka is also the name of an important Bhārgava figure in the Mbh.

TRIḤSAPTA AS A BHĀRGAVA MARKER

In the Mbh, Śaunaka is a Bhārgava Brahmin who hears the whole epic story from Ugraśravas during a *sattra* sacrifice (Mbh 1.1 ff.). Nothing indicates in the Mbh that this Śaunaka is the author of the AV and he is in a position of a hearer, so to say a "student", rather than a master, but one cannot take this similarity of name and learning situation as incidental or insignificant, especially considering the weight of Bhārgava material in the Mbh. Using the same type of analogy, we can also note that the *Kauśikasūtra* of the AV (which often prescribes the use of the *triṣaptīyam*, as 139.10) rings a remote echo with Rāma's story through the name Kuśika, the powerful king and great grandfather of Jamadagni (Mbh 12.49). The inquiry about *triḥsapta* thus provides some insights for the debate on the theory of the "bhṛguization" of the Mbh, initiated by Sukthankar in his famous article of 1936, enriched and strengthened by Goldman in 1977, and seemingly rejected today by most Western scholars in the field of epic studies (Hiltebeitel 2001; Fitzgerald 2002). In a detailed defense of this theory, Shende (1943) has strongly put forth thematic and ideological arguments in favor of the link between AV and Mbh through their supposed common authorship by the Bhārgavas (or rather the Bhārgavas and Āṅgirasas according to him). It is true that the theory of "bhṛguization" has been partly built on the character of Rāma Jāmadagnya, pervasive in the Mbh, and on the repetition of the canonical formula-motive quoted at the beginning of this article, but, to my knowledge, *triḥsapta* has not been considered as such as a symbol of the Bhṛgus or Bhārgavas, whereas their double nature of custodians of the Vedic sacrificial fire and expounders of the Vedic teachings may have entitled them to such a claim. In the Mbh, twenty-one can be found in other Bhārgava stories: in the *Cyavanakuśika-saṃvāda* (Mbh 13.52-56), for instance, the Bhārgava Cyavana visits King Kuśika to test his forbearance, one of these tests consisting in sleeping twenty-one nights in a row whereas Kuśika and his wife must patiently wait for his waking up. We could also find in the Purāṇas other strange allusions to twenty-one in relation with stories involving Bhārgava characters (e.g. *Padmapurāṇa* 2.85).

But, to rightly confine ourselves to the Mbh, we must recall that *triḥsapta* is found in the whole Mbh only in Rāma Jāmadagnya's story, to denote the destructions of Kṣatriya class. As this phrase is clearly an archaism in the Sanskrit of the epics, it may have been intended, in keeping with the meaning of *triḥsapta* as the symbol of knowledge and teaching, to regularly remind the listeners of the Mbh of its being not only an enthralling story but a *śāstra*, a didactic text. But what does it teach? There is no unequivocal answer but maybe for the epic heroes of the main plot of the Mbh and for its listeners, the genocidal destruction of the Kṣatriyas by Rāma, followed by the regeneration of the *kṣatra*, could be seen as a rehearsal and a model of the great battle of the Mbh, it may teach that destruction can be the necessary condition for a genuine rebirth. Regarding Rāma Jāmadagnya himself, he plays a twofold role as a disciple and teacher in the epic. He is the disciple of his father Jamadagni, but more importantly in this respect, his bloody revenge is stopped after twenty-one destructions by his Bhārgava *pitṛs* who teach him renunciation to violence. On the other hand, in the main story of the Mbh, Rāma is the *guru* and master in weaponry of major epic heroes. Thus the very formula denoting the paroxysm of violence of Rāma Jāmadagnya induces the listener, through the connotation of *triḥsapta* as the number of knowledge, to look for a hidden truth. *Triḥsapta* encapsulates thus the ambiguity of Rāma Jāmadagnya, and that is probably why this phrase has become almost exclusively applied to him in later literature. Even when he is better known as Paraśurāma, the mere mention of *triḥsapta* is enough to remind the reader of his epic origin and of his identity as Bhārgava Rāma in all his complexity, whether in the Purāṇas or in *kāvya* texts.

CONCLUSION

To conclude, I would say that the very phrases *triḥsapta* and *triḥsaptakṛtvaḥ* should be taken into account in the debate on the bhṛguization of the Mbh, even if it is doubtful we can ever be certain about the existence of such a process. The inquiry on *triḥsapta* also offers a significant example of the complex intertextuality between Vedic and epic texts. What was the intent of the epic composers in using this Vedic archaism in so localized a phrase? Once we have identified similarities in vocabulary, what interpretation can be given thereof? There are three possibilities: we can suppose a mere coincidence; but the previous inquiry strongly suggests that such an answer cannot be accepted on serious grounds. The second possibility would be that the epic phrase provides an echo, a reminiscence of the Vedic texts, which implies that at least the composers and perhaps the audience of the epics were very familiar with these texts. The last option, probably an overinterpretation – interesting in its very excess – consists in seeing in *triḥsapta* a deep symbol, a key of understanding of Rāma Jāmadagnya's myth and perhaps of the whole Mbh because it would strengthen its own claim to be seen as the fifth Veda (Fitzgerald 1991). Whatever the answer to this difficult question is, and to sum up my findings, I would say that the main significance of the use of *triḥsaptakṛtvaḥ* as a motif in the Mbh is to recall the number of Vedic knowledge in its close connection with the sacrificial skills, but reasserted and embodied in so puzzling a fashion by the Bhārgava Rāma Jāmadagnya.

APPENDIX:
List of occurrences of *tríḥ saptá* in the ṚV

1.72.6: *tríḥ saptá yád gúhyāni tvé ít padā́vidan níhitā yajñíyāsaḥ* |

1.133.6: *trisaptaíḥ śūra sátvabhiḥ*

1.191.12: *tríḥ saptá viṣpulingakā́ḥ* (and 14:) *tríḥ saptá mayūryàḥ*

4.1.16: *té manvata prathamáṃ nā́ma dhenós tríḥ saptá mātúḥ paramā́ṇi vindan* |

7.87.4: *uvā́ca me váruṇo médhirāya tríḥ saptá nā́māghnyā bibharti* |
vidvā́n padásya gúhyā ná vocad yugā́ya vípra úparāya śíkṣan ||

8.46.26: *tríḥ saptá saptatī́nā́ṃ*

8.69.7: *tríḥ saptá sákhyuḥ padé*

8.96.2: *tríḥ saptá sā́nu sáṃhitā girī́ṇā́ṃ*

9.70.1: *trír asmai saptá dhenávo*

9.86.21: *tríḥ saptá duduhānā́*

10.64.8: *tríḥ saptá sasrā́ nadyò mahī́r apáḥ*

10.90.15: *saptā́syāsan paridháyas tríḥ saptá samídhaḥ kṛtā́ḥ* |
devā́ yád yajñáṃ tanvānā́ ábadhnan púruṣaṃ paśúm ||

In the AV (Śaunakīya recension) 1.1:
yé triṣaptā́ḥ pariyánti víśvā rūpā́ṇi bíbhrataḥ |
vācáspátir bálā teṣāṃ tanvò adyá dadhātu me ||

REFERENCES

Primary Sources

Atharva-Veda Saṃhitā (1855-56). Ed. by W. D. Whitney & G. Roth. Berlin: Ferd. Dümmler's Verlagsbuchhandlung.

Brahmāṇḍapurāṇa (1906-12). 2 vols. Bombay: Veṅkateśvara Press.

The Kauśika Sūtra of the Atharva Veda (1889). Ed. by M. Bloomfield. (Journal of the American Oriental Society, 14.) (Reprint: Delhi: MLBD, 1972.)

Mahābhārata. Critical Edition (1933-72). 26 vols. Ed. by V. S. Sukthankar *et al.* Poona: BORI.

Padmapurāṇa (1893-94). 4 vols. Ed. by Viśvanātha Nārāyaṇa Maṇḍalīka. Ānandāśrama Sanskrit Series, 131.) Bombay: Ānandāśrama.

Reṇukāmāhātmya (1877). In: J. Gerson da Cunha (ed.), *The Sahyādri-Khaṇḍa of the Skanda Purāṇa*. Bombay: Thacker and Vining.

Ṛgveda Saṃhitā (1877). Ed. by T. Aufrecht. Bonn: A. Marcus.

The Çatapatha-Brāhmaṇa in the Mādhyandina-çākhā with Extracts from the Commentaries of Sāyaṇa, Harasvāmin and Dvidevaganga (1855). Ed. by Albrecht Weber. (The White Yajurveda, 2.) Berlin: Ferd. Dümmler's Verlagsbuchhandlung – London: Williams and Norgate.

Secondary Sources

BIARDEAU, M. 2001. *Le* Mahābhārata. *Un texte fondateur du brahmanisme classique et son interprétation.* Paris: Seuil.

BLOOMFIELD, M. 1906. *A Vedic Concordance*. (Harvard Oriental Series, 10.) Cambridge, Mass.: Harvard University.

BÜHLER, G. (trans.) 1886. *The Laws of Manu.* (Sacred Books of the East, 25.) Oxford: Clarendon Press.

DUMONT, P.-E. 1927. *L'Aśvamedha. Description du sacrifice solennel du cheval dans le culte védique d'après les textes du Yajurveda blanc.* Paris: P. Geuthner.

EGGELING, Julius (trans.) 1882-1900. The Śatapatha Brāhmaṇa according to the text of the Mādhyandina school, I-V. (Sacred Books of the East, 12, 26, 41, 43, 44.) Oxford: Clarendon Press.

FITZGERALD, J. 1991. India's Fifth Veda: The *Mahābhārata*'s presentation of itself. In: A. Sharma (ed.), *Essays on the* Mahābhārata. Leiden: E.J. Brill.

—— 2002. The Rāma Jāmadagnya "thread" of the *Mahābhārata*: a new survey of Rāma Jāmadagnya in the Pune text. In: M. Brockington (ed.), *Stages and Transitions. Temporal and Historical Frameworks in Epic and Purāṇic Literature. Proceedings of the Second DICSEP, August 1999*: 89-132. Zagreb: Croatian Academy of Sciences and Arts.

GOLDMAN, R. 1970. Akṛtavraṇa vs Śrīkṛṣṇa as narrators of the legend of the Bhārgava Rāma. *ABORI* 53: 161-173.

—— 1977. *Gods, Priests and Warriors: The Bhṛgus of the Mahābhārata*. (Studies in Oriental Culture, 12.) New York: Columbia University Press.

GRASSMANN, H. 1955. *Wörterbuch zum Rig-Veda*. 3rd edition. Wiesbaden: Harrassowitz. (1st edition: Leipzig: F.A. Brockhaus, 1873.)

HENRY, V. 1904. *La magie dans l'Inde antique*. Paris: Dujarric.

HILTEBEITEL, A. 2001. *Rethinking the Mahābhārata. A Reader's Guide to the Education of the Dharma King*. Chicago: The University of Chicago Press.

JANAKI, K. S. S. 1966. Paraśurāma. *Purāṇa* 8: 52-82.

LUBOTSKY, Alexander 1997. *A Ṛgvedic Word Concordance*.(American Oriental Series, 82-83.) New Haven: American Oriental Society.

MONIER WILLIAMS, Monier 1981. *A Sanskrit-English Dictionary*. Delhi: MLBD. (1st edition: Oxford: Clarendon Press, 1872.)

RENOU, Louis. *Grammaire sanscrite*, I-II. Paris: Adrien-Maisonneuve.

SHENDE, N. J. 1943. The Authorship of the Mahābhārata. *ABORI* 24: 67-82.

SUKTHANKAR, V. S. 1936. The Bhṛgus and the Bhārata: a text-historical study. *ABORI* 18: 1-76.

THIEME, P. 1985. The first verse of the *Triṣaptīyam* (AV, Ś 1. 1 ~ AV, P 1. 6) and the beginnings of Sanskrit linguistics. *JAOS* 105.3: 559-565.

WHITNEY, W. D. (trans.) 1905. *Atharva-Veda Saṃhitā*. (Harvard Oriental Series, 7-8.) Cambridge, Mass.: Harvard University.

The Story of Asita Devala and Jaigīṣavya in *Mahābhārata* 9.49

DANIELLE FELLER

INTRODUCTION

In this paper, I will try to examine in some detail a peripheral story told in Mbh 9.49[1], concerning two *ṛṣis*, Asita Devala and Jaigīṣavya. The story is interesting because it illustrates some of the tensions that prevailed in epic times between two different sets of values, those of *pravṛtti*, exemplified by the sacrificial world-view leading to heaven, and those of *nivṛtti*, exemplified by asceticism and *sannyāsa* leading to *mokṣa*. But over and above these two fundamental values, it also stresses the importance of yoga as an essential means to obtain salvation.

The story of Asita Devala and Jaigīṣavya is narrated in the context of Balarāma's *tīrthayātrā* (pilgrimage) on the river Sarasvatī. In the course of his peregrinations, Balarāma reaches the Āditya-*tīrtha*, or *tīrtha* of the sun (9.48.16), where many notable events took place in ancient times. The sun obtained kingship over all the other luminaries (9.48.17). Viṣṇu slew the Asuras Madhu and Kaiṭabha and then performed his ablutions at that spot (9.48.21). Vyāsa himself, after plunging in the waters of the river, obtained the highest yoga and went to the final liberation (9.48.22). And, most importantly for our present concern, this is the *tīrtha* where the *ṛṣi* Asita Devala of great austerities had his hermitage.

---

[1] All the references are to the Critical Edition of the Mbh.

SUMMARY OF THE STORY

In this story, Asita Devala, who is described as a householder and a noble and perfected man, receives very hospitably a wandering ascetic named Jaigīṣavya in his *āśrama* and devotedly watches over him while Jaigīṣavya practises rigid austerities and yoga. One day, Jaigīṣavya suddenly disappears, and when he comes back, Asita is extremely pleased and welcomes him. Up to now, the story resembles so many other stories of ascetics who put to the test the patience and devotion of certain people.[2] After many years of this, Devala realizes one day not without some bitterness that Jaigīṣavya has never once spoken a word to him. Thus reflecting, Asita Devala flies to the shore of the ocean to perform his ablutions.[3] There, to his great surprise, he sees Jaigīṣavya whom he had just left at home, already plunged in the ocean. After performing his ritual ablutions, Devala flies back home, and again to his surprise, he sees Jaigīṣavya, whom he had left in the ocean, already sitting in deep meditation in his hermitage. Finding this somewhat astonishing, Devala decides to enquire so to say with the higher authorities about the identity of this Jaigīṣavya. He flies up to the sky, and there sees a group of Siddhas, who are worshipping none else than Jaigīṣavya. Then Jaigīṣavya goes up, moving from one world to the other: to the *pitṛloka*, from there to Yama's world, hence to that of Soma. Then he goes through a series of worlds which are reserved for those who have performed various types of sacrifices, and then through some more worlds of the gods. Then on to the world of cows, and hence to the world of *pativratā*s, or devoted wives.

Then suddenly Jaigīṣavya vanishes, and Devala, who has been following him all the while, is unable to see him anywhere. He enquires about his whereabouts with the Siddhas, who tell him that

---

[2] See, for instance, Mbh 3.246, where Durvāsas puts to the test the sage Mudgala.

[3] The fact that he flies through the air to reach the ocean – which comes somewhat as a surprise in this context – shows that Asita Devala himself has acquired some *siddhi*s or supernatural powers.

Jaigīṣavya has gone to the "eternal and imperishable world of Brahman/Brahmā": *jaigīṣavyo gato lokaṃ śāśvataṃ brahmaṇo 'vyayam* (9.49.46). Devala tries to fly up there, but falls down again, as if held back by an invisible ceiling, and the Siddhas tell him that there is no way he can go to the abode of Brahman/ Brahmā: *brahmaṇaḥ sadanam* (9.49.48). So Devala goes home to his hermitage, where of course he finds Jaigīṣavya still practising *tapas* as if nothing had happened, and humbly asks him to teach him the *mokṣadharma* (9.49.52), a term translated by Schreiner (1999: 775) as: "a doctrine and method to reach salvific liberation". Accordingly Jaigīṣavya initiates him to *sannyāsa.*

Then, seeing Devala firmly set on adopting *sannyāsa*, all the creatures and the *pitṛ*s start to cry out loud. "Who will give us a share?": *ko 'smān saṃvibhajiṣyati* (9.49.55). Shaken by this piteous wail, Devala again resolves to give up mokṣa: *mokṣaṃ tyaktuṃ mano dadhe* (9.49.56). Then all the roots and fruit, flowers and herbs, start weeping in thousands, saying: "Alas, he had promised us absence of fear (*abhaya*)[4], and now that wicked Devala will again pluck us!" Then Devala filled with doubt reflects for a while. "Which leads to a greater good, *mokṣa* or the *dharma* of a *gṛhastha*?": *mokṣe gārhasthyadharme vā kiṃ nu śreyaskaraṃ bhavet* (9.49.59) and opts for *mokṣa.* After that he obtains the supreme success or emancipation (*siddhi*) and the highest yoga.

Then the gods come along with Bṛhaspati at their head and praise Jaigīṣavya's *tapas*. Only the *ṛṣi* Nārada somewhat slyly remarks that "there is no *tapas* in Jaigīṣavya because he amazes Asita!": *jaigīṣavye tapo nāsti vismāpayati yo 'sitam* (9.49.63). But the gods hush him up: *mā evam*! (9.49.64) and continue to applaud Jaigīṣavya.

---

[4] As Olivelle (1992: 95) notes, "the new renouncer gives safety (abhaya, lit. 'freedom from fear') to all beings."

THE CHARACTERS

Asita Devala is perhaps best known from the context of Buddhism, where he predicts the young Siddhārtha Gautama's future.[5] The *ṛṣis* Asita Devala[6] and Jaigīṣavya also appear in other passages of the Mbh, though they are by no means very prominent personages. Sometimes, both simply appear in lists of sages, often along with Nārada.[7] Jaigīṣavya[8] and Asita Devala can also appear as teachers of the *sāṃkhya* philosophy, especially in the context of the *Mokṣadharmaparvan* (Mbh 12.168-353). In one passage, 12.222, Jaigīṣavya is again Asita Devala's teacher and expounds on equanimity and on the virtue of being despised (*avamāna*). In the *Nāradadevalasaṃvāda* (Mbh 12.267), again in a context of *sāṃkhya* philosophy, Devala "propounds a cosmological view in which the five *mahābhūta*s evolve out of *kāla* in a scheme which is otherwise similar to others in a Sāṃkhya context". (Brockington 1999: 476). In Mbh 12.306.57, Jaigīṣavya's name features as the first, and Asita Devala's as the second, in a list of teachers of yoga and *sāṃkhya.*[9] Jaigīṣavya in particular is closely connected with yoga. Thus a view of Jaigīṣavya is cited in the *Yogabhāṣya ad Yogasūtra* 2.55, and a story is told of Jaigīṣavya's perception of his former births in the *Yogabhāṣya ad Yogasūtra* 3.18.

---

[5] See e.g. *Lalitavistara* 7 or *Buddhacarita* 7.49-81. In both texts he is also said to fly on the path of wind.

[6] Asita Devala is sometimes mentioned only by one of either names, sometimes by both, but according to Brockington (1999: 476) these varying denominations refer to one and the same person.

[7] Thus in 12.1.4, Asita Devala, Jaigīṣavya, and Nārada visit Yudhiṣṭhira after he has performed the funeral ceremonies for the dead. In Mbh 12.200 we find an enumeration of sages, including Asita Devala and Nārada in verses 3-4.

[8] In the *Skandapurāṇa*, Jaigīṣavya is connected with the Pāśupata tradition, and is represented as a Pāśupata ascetic. See Bisschop 2002: 239. Most of the references to Jaigīṣavya were very kindly provided to me by Peter Bisschop, whom I wish to thank here.

[9] Jaigīṣavya is also mentioned in Aśvaghoṣa's *Buddhacarita* 12.67 by Ārāḍa as one of those who attained release by following a sort of proto-*sāṃkhya* path.

Sometimes, Asita Devala appears as a *bhakta* of Viṣṇu and sings the praise of that god. Thus in Mbh 12.281.15, he is one of a group of *mahārṣi*s (including also Nārada) who praise Viṣṇu by means of verses and obtain success by his favour. In Mbh 12.326.110, Asita also tells the *pitṛ*s the story of Viṣṇu's greatness and of his *avatāra*s, as Nārada had heard it first from Viṣṇu's own mouth.

And last, but certainly not least, Asita Devala is one of Vyāsa's students: he is the one who recites the Mbh to the *pitṛ*s (1.1.64), a fact which will prove of some importance for our present purpose.

PRAVṚTTI AND *NIVṚTTI*

The central part of this passage (9.49.24-41) is taken up by a long list of the various worlds through which both Jaigīṣavya and Asita Devala ascend. According to verse 9.49.49, these worlds seem to be situated one above the other, for when Asita Devala returns to his hermitage, "he climbed down all these worlds in due order": *ānupūrvyeṇa lokāṃs tān sarvān avatatāra ha.* Clearly, in this description – at least as far as Asita Devala is concerned – there is an opposition between:

1) the various worlds of the gods and especially those reserved for sacrificers (practically each sacrifice leads to a world of its own), to which Asita Devala is able to go presumably because his life-style as a *gṛhastha* has "won him these worlds", as the phrase goes, and:
2) the highest world, that of Brahman/Brahmā, to which he does not have access, for reasons we shall subsequently examine.

The chart on the next page represents the worlds through which Jaigīṣavya and Asita Devala travel, starting from the *āśrama* (bottom) and going up to the world of Brahman/Brahmā (top). The left-hand column shows the worlds of gods (or similar). Thus "Yama" means: "the world of Yama". The central column shows the worlds reserved for those who have performed certain sacrifices. Thus for "*agnihotra*", read: "the world of those who have performed an *agnihotra* sacrifice". The right-hand column gives the reference to the text. This long list of worlds reserved for sacrificers is rather unusual in the context of a list of heavenly worlds, and could probably be considered as an interpolation. Made, perhaps, by a redactor attached to ritualistic values?

Brahman/Brahmā		9.49.46 & 48
*pativratā*s		9.49.41
"three other worlds"		9.49.41
	brahmasattra	9.49.40
cows		9.49.40
Bṛhaspati		9.49.39
Vasus		9.49.39
Rudras		9.49.39
Ādityas		9.49.38
Mitra and Varuṇa		9.49.38
	12-day *sattra*s	9.49.37
	sautrāmaṇi	9.49.36
	sarvamedha	9.49.36
	naramedha	9.49.35
	aśvamedha	9.49.35
	rājasūya	9.49.34
	puṇḍarīka	9.49.34
	vājapeya	9.49.33
	agniṣṭut(*a*)	9.49.32
	agniṣṭoma	9.49.31
	cāturmāsya	9.49.31
gods		9.49.30
	paśuyāga	9.49.30
	darśapaurṇamāsa	9.49.30
	agnihotra	9.49.29
	ekāntayāga	9.49.29
Soma		9.49.28
Yama		9.49.27
pitṛs		9.49.27
Dyaus		9.49.26
antarikṣa		9.49.24
āśrama		9.49.24

The designation of the highest world: *brahmaṇo lokaḥ* or *brahmaṇaḥ sadanam* is ambiguous. What is meant here? Is it the world of Brahmā, the personified god, or is it the world of the neuter Brahman? In the genitive case ending, there is of course no distinction between masculine or neuter. Both arguments can be supported: the world of the god Brahmā would be just one more heaven, a little higher than the others, and more difficult to reach, which indeed currently figures in heaven-enumerations, and where the highly perfected souls of *ṛṣis* were thought to go. Since this world in the story does not seem to be categorically different from the other heavenly worlds – Jaigīṣavya goes from them to it, and back again[10] – we might feel inclined to say that it is the world of the god Brahmā. On the other hand, Asita Devala, who is unable to reach it, requests Jaigīṣavya to teach him the *mokṣadharma*, in order that he may eventually reach it. This makes us think that what is meant here is the neuter Brahman, which one indeed reaches on final release. The latter choice also seems to be supported by the adjectives *śāśvata* and *avyaya* (9.49.46): it is eternal and imperishable. However, Holtzmann (1884: 178) already makes us attentive to the fact that these epithets are very frequently attributed to the god Brahmā himself, who was originally conceived of as eternal, without origin or end. From the god, these epithets naturally came to be attributed also to his world, although there are indications, in the epic itself, that the sojourn of the dead in this world of Brahmā is no more permanent than in any other heavenly world.[11] Thus the situation seems to be quite entangled. But this state of affairs where the neuter and the personal Brahman/Brahmā are not clearly separated or indeed separable is common in the epics and earlier in some Upaniṣads.[12] As Bailey (1983: 6) puts it:

---

[10] However, there are indications that some really perfected beings (like Śuka for instance) can reach the state of *mokṣa* and then return into the world at their wish. See Hiltebeitel 2001: 283.

[11] See the references given in Holtzmann 1884: 205.

[12] In the *Kauṣītaki-upaniṣad* (ed. Renou 1948), we find the same wavering between Brahmā, the personified god, and Brahman, the absolute and neuter

> Making a clear distinction between personal and impersonal in relation to a concept like *brahma* was not the Indian way of doing things."[13]

Thus at a first glance, it would appear that the main thrust of this story is to oppose the sacrificial life-style to that of the *sannyāsin*. In the Mbh both ways of life are frequently represented, and usually, depending on the passage, one or the other is held to be superior. As Brockington (1998: 246) remarks: "Indeed in later passages, different approaches are deliberately contrasted." In this passage, we would feel tempted to say that it is obviously the *mokṣa* way of life which is preferred: only the knowledge of the *mokṣadharma* through *sannyāsa* can grant access to the highest world of Brahman/Brahmā, whereas sacrifice only leads to one of the lower worlds.

TAPAS AND YOGA

However, the distinction between Asita Devala and Jaigīṣavya is not just that between sacrificer-householder and ascetic-renouncer, especially because the character of Asita Devala cannot be so neatly classified. While Jaigīṣavya is clearly a renouncer or wandering ascetic (he is called *bhikṣuka*[14] or *parivrāṭ*), though one of above-the-average powers,[15] Asita Devala does not seem to conform to the

---

principle. The first *adhyāya* of this Upaniṣad describes how the liberated soul goes through the worlds of many gods and finally reaches that of Brahmā (3). The soul enters into that world which is described in its physical characteristics (4-5) and is received very hospitably by the god Brahmā himself. Questioned by Brahmā (5): *ko 'si*? "Who are you?", the soul must answer, in a variant of the famous formulas (6): ... *yas tvam asi so 'ham asmi*. "What (who) you are, that I am." Here clearly the personal god Brahmā merges with the highest principle Brahman.

[13] Or, as Hopkins (1915: 189) notes about Brahmā: "He [...] tends to pass back into the universal world-power out of which he emerged, the neuter [...] brahman."

[14] This term is synonymous with *sannyāsin*. See for instance the enumeration of the stages of life in Mbh 12.321.1a-b: *gṛhastho brahmacārī vā vānaprastho 'tha bhikṣukaḥ*.

norm of a *gṛhastha* so clearly. In the first verse of the passage, it is said that Asita Devala has adopted the life-style of a *gṛhastha*: *gārhasthyadharmam āsthāya* (9.49.1). And indeed, he worships the gods and the hosts, along with the brahmins (9.49.4), he feeds Jaigīṣavya and looks after him during many years while the latter is engaged in austerities, and he is also thoroughly conversant with the Vedas: *mantrapāraga* (9.49.24). But the state of *gṛhastha* normally implies living in the world, having a wife and children and engaging in some profession and worldly pursuits. This is apparently not the case for Asita Devala: this particular passage at least mentions no wife or children.[16] On the contrary, verse 9.49.4 describes him as "always dedicated to celibacy": *brahmacaryarato nityam*. Usually, *brahmacarya* is strictly incompatible with the state of householder. Then, to complicate matters further, it is clear that Asita Devala does not live in a village or town: he lives in an *āśrama* on a *tīrtha* (9.49.6), rather like a *vānaprastha*. And finally, the way in which he is described reminds us of a *sannyāsin*. He is righteous, *dharmātmā*, and his treasure is asceticism, *tapodhana* (9.49.1). He is also endowed with perfect equanimity of mind. In this respect, verses two and three are highly revealing:

dharmanityaḥ śucir dānto nyastadaṇḍo mahātapāḥ |
karmaṇā manasā vācā samaḥ sarveṣu jantuṣu || 2 ||
akrodhano mahārāja tulyanindāpriyāpriyaḥ |
kāñcane loṣṭake caiva samadarśī mahātapāḥ || 3 ||

---

[15] He spends his time meditating, "having become like a piece of wood": *kāṣṭhabhūta* (9.49.20) and dedicated to *tapas* and yoga. He lives from begging, and apparently keeps a strict vow of silence: he never talks to Asita Devala. Besides, through his practice of *tapas* and yoga, he has obtained supernatural powers which allow him to move with the speed of the wind (one of the *siddhis*, see e.g. Mbh 12.232.21). Most importantly, he must be a liberated soul, since he can enter the supreme world of Brahman/Brahmā and come back at will.

[16] However, in *Harivaṃśa* 18, it is said that Jaigīṣavya marries Ekapāṭalā and Devala marries Ekaparṇā, both daughters of Himavat and Menā. They are thus the brothers-in-law of Śiva, who marries the third daughter Umā (Aparṇā). (Similarly in *Skandapurāṇa* 11.24).

> Always virtuous, pure and restrained, having abandoned the stick (never harming anyone) and endowed with great asceticism, equal towards all creatures in deed, mind and speech. Without anger, o King, indifferent to blame, and to what is agreeable and disagreeable, he looks on evenly at gold and at a clod of earth.[17] (Mbh 9.49.2-3)

Besides, Asita Devala has evidently gained great power by his *tapas*, such as flying through the air like a bird: *pataṅgavat* (9.49.50), and, as we have seen, he is able to fly up through all the worlds and heavens (except of course that of Brahman/Brahmā). Such powers and qualities, which are by all accounts difficult to obtain, are usually the characteristics of ascetics rather that those of a *gṛhapati*. On the whole, Asita Devala does not conform to the model of a *gṛhapati* at all, and his life-style rather seems to be a mixture of all the *āśrama*s kept together. Most strikingly, he can boast of all the accomplishments of a *sannyāsin*.

So, apart from formally adopting the mode of life of a *sannyāsin*, what is it that distinguishes Asita Devala from Jaigīṣavya, and which allows the latter to go to the world of Brahman/Brahmā – in other words to obtain *mokṣa* – and not Asita Devala? The key word here seems to be yoga. For if both Asita Devala and Jaigīṣavya are said to be endowed with great *tapas*, only Jaigīṣavya, and not Asita Devala, is said to practise yoga. The yoga of Jaigīṣavya is emphasized from the start. Thus the first word which characterizes Jaigīṣavya, before even his name is mentioned, is yoga: *yogam āsthāya*, and he is said to be *samāhita* (9.49.5): concentrated and *yoganitya* (9.49.6): always practising yoga. What impresses Asita Devala most is "the power born of yoga of Jaigīṣavya's penance": *prabhāvaṃ tapaso jaigīṣavyasya yogajam* (a phrase which occurs twice in 9.49.22cd = 51cd). Thus Jaigīṣavya's power is not just the power of *tapas*, but the power of *tapas* "born of yoga". When Jaigīṣavya accepts to initiate Asita Devala in the *mokṣadharma*, he teaches him, among other things, "the precepts or method of yoga": *vidhim ... yogasya* (9.49.53). The phrase which concludes the story

[17] Cf. *Bhagavadgītā* 6.8cd: *yukta ity ucyate yogī samaloṣṭāsmakāñcanaḥ.*

of Asita Devala is "he obtained supreme liberation and the highest yoga": *prāptavān paramāṃ siddhiṃ paraṃ yogaṃ ca* (9.49.61). Likewise, the verse which introduces the story of Asita Devala at the end of the preceding *adhyāya* is:

> *asito devalaś caiva tasminn eva mahātapāḥ* ।
> *paramaṃ yogam āsthāya ṛṣir yogam avāptavān* ॥ 23 ॥
>
> At this very spot, the *ṛṣi* Asita Devala of great austerities, after practising the highest yoga, obtained yoga. (Mbh 8.48.23)[18]

As we can see, Asita Devala is associated with yoga only after receiving his initiation from Jaigīṣavya. Thus in this passage, although yoga is at all times combined with *tapas*[19] and not described in any kind of detail, it is undoubtedly something more than *tapas* and can be considered as the clinching element when it comes to obtaining liberation. *Tapas* alone can only produce something akin to magical powers, such as flying through the air.[20] Thus the fundamental contrast between Asita Devala and Jaigīṣavya is probably not only that between sacrificer and renouncer, but also that between non-*yogin* and *yogin*.

THE ULTIMATELY UNSATISFACTORY CHOICE

Ultimately, however, Asita Devala's choice of mokṣa is unsatisfactory, because it turns out that he cannot please everyone by choosing liberation. When they see Devala intent upon *sannyāsa*, the despairing *pitṛ*s (Manes) and the *bhūta*s (creatures) cry out piteously: "Who will give us a share?" As we know, the householder

[18] In this verse, the term *yoga* seems to apply first to the technique, and then to the desired result.

[19] This is striking in a phrase like *yoganityo ... mahātapāḥ* (6), which describes Jaigīṣavya.

[20] In many passages of the epics, yoga and *tapas* are virtually synonymous. See Brockington 1998: 309. But usually, as in this passage, the difference between the two is that *tapas*, at least originally, did not have a religious aim and was used for personal ends, to get power, whereas yoga is used to obtain liberation. See Brockington 1998: 239.

upholds the world with his sacrifices and feeds all the creatures, who entirely depend on him for their food. Thus we find the following statement in the *Mārkaṇḍeyapurāṇa*:

> O child, the man who has accepted the householder status nourishes all the universe. The fathers, sages, gods, living beings and mankind, worms, insects and flying creatures, birds, cattle and demons subsist upon the householder and thereby become satisfied. And looking at his face, they wonder, "what will he give us". (MkP 29.3-5, trans. Bailey 1983: 49.)

On the other hand, the *dharma* of a *gṛhastha* also involves injury to many creatures for the sake of sacrifice. We may notice that the creatures who lament in thousands when Asita Devala decides to "abandon *mokṣa*" are the plants, the fruit and roots, the Kuśa grass (*pavitrāṇi*), the flowers and the herbs (9.49.57):

> *tatas tu phalamūlāni pavitrāṇi ca bhārata* |
> *puṣpāṇy oṣadhayaś caiva rorūyante sahasraśaḥ* || 57 ||

The passage from the *Mārkaṇḍeyapurāṇa* quoted above shows that the plants are missing on the list of the beings who are fed by the householder. On the contrary, they serve as food to most creatures: they are eaten, but do not eat. In other words, they are at the bottom of the food-chain, and do not benefit from the system. Thus, as is so often happens in Indian mythology, one of the problems raised by this narrative concerns food, the distribution of food, and one's place in the universal food-chain.[21]

Asita Devala is caught in a double-bind: whatever path he chooses, he will harm somebody. In the end, he decides to ignore the wailing *pitṛ*s and to favour *sannyāsa*, but we do not know why he prefers *sannyāsa*. No reason is given. This would have been a

[21] What about the gods, we may ask? The gods are certainly at the top of the food-chain, and are obviously fed by the householder's sacrifices, like the *pitṛ*s. But the gods applaud Asita Devala's decision and Jaigīṣavya's prowess in converting him to *mokṣadharma*, as if it were to their own advantage, which it really is not. Here the gods are obviously used as ploys by the propounders of the *mokṣadharma*, who depict them as endorsing a world-view which is actually deleterious to their very survival.

perfect place to insert a tag like *ahiṃsā paramo dharmaḥ*, to explain his choice of giving absence of fear – *abhaya* – to all the creatures, but this is not the case. The tension between the two modes of life is left as it is with no satisfactory solution, nor is there a third way out proposed anywhere, as for instance *bhakti* associated with renouncing the fruit of one's actions (*karmaphalatyāga*) which could mediate (as it often does) between the two sets of value – ascetic and ritualistic – and ultimately set everyone at peace.[22] Thus in its final lack of a satisfactory resolution the tone of this passage is rather pessimistic.

THE FINAL DILEMMA

At the end of the story, when the gods praise Jaigīṣavya, the *ṛṣi* Nārada tells them: "There is no *tapas* in Jaigīṣavya, since he amazes Asita". This remark is astonishing, because up to then, the text has loaded upon Jaigīṣavya epithets to the effect that he is a great *yogin*, and a great ascetic. Thus, according to Nārada, Jaigīṣavya's primary aim was to dazzle Asita Devala with his ascetic power – and Asita is indeed described as *savismaya* (astonished) in verse 16, when he sees Jaigīṣavya, whom he has just left at his hermitage, already bathing in the ocean.

The dig here might be directed at pseudo-ascetics, or rather illusionists and magicians, who trick their amazed audience into believing that they are endowed with supernatural powers. We know that *yogin*s were not supposed to use thus the *siddhi*s (magical powers) supposedly derived as side-effects from their practise of

---

[22] O'Flaherty (1980: 27) (talking of the Purāṇas) distinguishes four temporal stages advocating different means to escape from rebirth: 1) giving gifts to Brahmins; 2) yoga; 3) *tīrthayātrās*; 4) *bhakti*. *Bhakti* seems to play no role in the passage which concerns us here: Viṣṇu or Kṛṣṇa, the principal *bhakti* god, is never mentioned. Indeed, if we go by the list of heavens, the highest god seems to be Brahmā. There is some evidence that Brahmā was worshipped by some as the supreme god in the north of India for a few centuries before and after the beginning of our era. See Bailey 1983: 33; Brockington 1998: 236. But here he does not get involved personally in the story at all, only his world is mentioned.

yoga.[23] Nārada is perhaps implying that Jaigīṣavya is a fake, somewhat like one of those pseudo-gurus of modern ages, who abuse the gullible crowd. On the other hand, we do not know how trustworthy Nārada himself is, for of course Nārada is the prime gossipmonger among celestials, and he loves nothing more than sowing dissent and trouble. When they hear his words, the gods seem to be shocked and hush him up. But note that they do not say: *na evam* "It's not like that!" They say: *mā evam*! "Don't say like that!" Therefore they do not necessarily question the truth of Nārada's assertion. So ultimately, the doubt lingers. Who is right? Is Jaigīṣavya a fraud, and is the *mokṣadharma* therefore but a fake doctrine? Or should we trust what the text tells us concerning Asita Devala, that "he obtained the supreme emancipation and the highest yoga"? (9.49.61). Perhaps we should do so, especially considering that these events take place at the Āditya-*tīrtha*: for the sun is ever a symbol of eternity and immortality, for instance in some passages of the Upaniṣads, where the liberated soul goes to the sun. But on the whole, here again, the text offers no clear resolution and leaves us to doubt.

EPILOGUE

Thus the story of Asita Devala is a story of double-binds, of unsatisfactory choices and ultimately of doubts. If we now return to the immediate context in which it is told, we remember that it is inserted in another tale of indecision: that of Balarāma's *tīrthayātrā*, which Balarāma undertakes precisely because of his incapacity to choose sides in the war. And the story of Balarāma's *tīrthayātrā* is of course a part of the Mbh, which is – if ever there was one – a story of unsatisfactory choices and disastrous results. And it is this story of the Mbh (in which of course his own is contained) which Asita Devala, as Vyāsa's student, recites to the *pitṛ*s whom his choice of *mokṣa* has deprived of their share. We

---

[23] See Patañjali's *Yogasūtra* 3.39 and Mbh 12.232.21-22.

might first surmise that Asita Devala recites the Mbh, with its awful description of the bloody war, as an apology for his own final choice of *abhaya*. But the ultimate result of his recitation might be more satisfactory than this. For we find the following statement in the *phala-śruti* of the Mbh:

> *yaś cedaṃ śrāvayec chrāddhe brāhmaṇān pādam antataḥ* |
> *akṣayyam annapānaṃ vai pitṝṃs tasyopatiṣṭhate* || 36 ||
>
> And if someone makes brahmins listen to this [Mahābhārata] at a *śrāddha*-ceremony, at least to one chapter (or: one fourth) of it, [then] his Manes get an inexhaustible supply of food and drink. (Mbh 18.5.36)

We can see from this that the redactors of the Mbh have tried at many levels to impose their text as authoritative: not only is the Mbh repeatedly said to be a Veda, the fifth Veda, and to be more effectual than all the Vedas put together,[24] but – judging from the above-cited verse – its recitation is even regarded as an efficient replacement of certain sacrificial offerings. Thus Asita Devala's recitation of the Mbh to the *pitṛ*s turns out to be much more satisfying than an apology: it is an effectual replacement of the food and drink offered to the dead ancestors at the *śrāddha*-ceremonies. But obviously, this more optimistic conclusion cannot be gathered from the passage under discussion itself, but only from the wider context of the Mbh.

REFERENCES

BAILEY, Greg 1983. *The Mythology of Brahmā*. Delhi: OUP.

BISSCHOP, Peter 2002. On a quotation of the *Skandapurāṇa* in the *Tīrthavivecanakāṇḍa* of Lakṣmīdhara's *Kṛtyakalpataru*. Studies in the Skandapurāṇa V / *IIJ* 45: 231-243.

BROCKINGTON, John 1998. *The Sanskrit Epics*. (Handbuch der Orientalistik, 2.12.) Leiden: Brill.

—— 1999. Epic Sāṃkhya: texts, teachers, terminology. *AS/ÉA* 53.3: 473-490.

[24] See Mbh 1.1.205, 1.1.208-209, 1.56.17, 1.57.74.

HILTEBEITEL, Alf 2001. *Rethinking the Mahābhārata. A Reader's Guide to the Education of the Dharma King.* Chicago: The University of Chicago Press.

HOLTZMANN, Adolf 1884. Brahman im Mahābhārata. *ZDMG* 38: 167-234.

HOPKINS, E. Washburn 1915. *Epic Mythology.* (Encyclopedia of Indo-Aryan research, 3.1.B.) Strassburg: Karl J. Trübner. (Reprint: Delhi: MLBD, 1974.)

Kauṣītaki Upaniṣad. Publiée et traduite par Louis Renou. Paris: Librairie d'Amérique et d'Orient, Adrien-Maisonneuve, 1948.

Mbh = *The Mahābhārata for the First Time Critically Edited.* 19 vols. Ed. by Vishnu Sitaram Sukthankar *et al.* Poona: BORI, 1933-59.

O'FLAHERTY, Wendy Doniger 1980. Karma and Rebirth in the Vedas and Purāṇas. In: Wendy Doniger O'Flaherty (ed.), *Karma and Rebirth in Classical Indian Traditions*: 3-37. Berkeley: University of California Press.

OLIVELLE, Patrick 1992. *Sannyāsa Upaniṣads.* New York: OUP.

SCHREINER, Peter 1999. What comes first (in the Mahābhārata): Sāṃkhya or Yoga? *AS/ÉA* 53.3: 755-777.

A Preliminary Study of the 681 *Triṣṭubh* Passages of the *Mahābhārata*

JAMES L. FITZGERALD

INTRODUCTION

This paper is a preliminary report on the 681 discrete *triṣṭubh* passages found in the *Mahābhārata.* (I use the term "passage" as a technical term which I will clarify shortly.)

Table 1 gives a quantitative overview of the different prosodic elements of the entire epic. It lists the counts of lines, stanzas, and passages for the Mbh as a whole; for prose in contrast to verse; for *anuṣṭubh* verse in contrast to non-*anuṣṭubh*; for *triṣṭubh-jagatī* in contrast to fancy non-*anuṣṭubh.* For each of these counts an adjacent column gives corresponding percentages. These same prosodic elements are also counted in terms of the 95 *upaparvan*s and 1,995 *adhyāya*s of the entire text.

As you can see from Table 1, if we look at the non-*anuṣṭubh* elements, there are 784 discrete non-*anuṣṭubh* passages; 755 of these are verse passages and 29 are prose. Of the 755 verse passages, 74 are passages of the fancy meters, and 681 are *triṣṭubh*s (and unless I am speaking more specifically, I use the term *triṣṭubh* as a generic term that embraces all epic forms of *triṣṭubh*s and *jagatī*s).

The most important reason I am interested in the *triṣṭubh*s of the Mbh is that they contain within them some of the most dramatic and, possibly, scientifically useful variations, of any of the epic's prosodic types. Or at least some of them do. One of the tasks to be accomplished is to survey the extent and types of variation among the epic *triṣṭubh*s. But my basic concern here is not prosody; rather it is the composition, inner structure, and history of the Mbh. I hope ultimately that the study of the epic's *triṣṭubh*s will uncover significant, scientifically grounded – and by this I mean grounded through rigorous statistical study – heterogeneities and homogeneities among the *triṣṭubh-jagatī*s, which groupings may serve as one reliable set of material indicators aiding the study of linguistic and thematic continua in the text. Unlike many earlier scholars who took up the study of *triṣṭubh*s, I am not interested in studying the rhythmic, musical, or psychological aspects of *triṣṭubh*s, nor with their archaic, pre-Indian history.

My study of the epic's *triṣṭubh*s is still in a heuristic phase, and is still philological, not statistical. That is, I am still reconnoitering the text and its non-*anuṣṭubh* passages basically in terms of the categories of Sanskrit studies and *Mahābhārata* studies – using concepts like "*syllaba anceps*", "fancy meters", and "*adhyāya*" to organize my study. I am still some way short of being able legitimately to single out sample passages and perform statistical tests to verify homogeneity or the lack of it among those samples. There are, of course, plenty of data to throw against lots of other data, but which are the key independent variables that should be used to define samples? And how do we best construct samples?

What I present to you today are, first of all, two sets of measures I see as promising variables for the eventual scientific comparison and contrast of *triṣṭubh* samples. Secondly, I will put up a side by side comparison of a very basic division of the *triṣṭubh*s into two sets: single-passage *triṣṭubh* instances and multi-passage instances.

PASSAGES, PROSODIC "INTERVENTIONS", PASSAGE-CLUSTERS

Let me call your attention to footnote 1 of Table 1: It defines the technical term "passage". While the *pāda*s and stanzas enumerated on Table 1 correspond to familiar elements of our experience, the "passages" enumerated there are not so straightforward. For purposes of my work, "passage" is a technical term that refers to a continuous run of text of a single prosodic type: *śloka*, prose, *triṣṭubh-jagatī*, or one of the fancy Sanskrit meters. A switch in the text's prosodic treatment (e.g., a switch from *śloka*s to *rucirā*s, or a switch from *rucirā* to *praharṣiṇī*), or the end of an *adhyāya*, constitutes the end of one passage and the beginning of the next one.

Now such switches of prosodic treatment are very interesting from a literary and historical view, because a switch is a deliberate interruption of the material surface of the text – a "prosodic intervention", to coin another technical term. The initial presumption is that a "passage" – as defined above – was composed simultaneously by its authorial agency;[1] a change in prosody is an always potentially interesting break in continuity. A new passage of a different prosodic type necessarily reflects some kind of interrupting literary or editorial act, even if it is only a particular author's decision to switch into a different voice or register. Of course I suspect that such a switch means something other than that in most cases, basically someone splicing in an addition to the pre-existing text; either his own composition, or something old or new from someone else, a splicing done either contemporaneously with the composition of the original or at some later time. If we look at the text of the Mbh in terms of these switches, the *triṣṭubh*s seem more important to the text than they do if we consider only the quantity of their *pāda*s in the surrounding sea of *śloka*s. In terms of lines of

[1] Obviously, a prosodically homogenous run of *pāda*s may not have been composed by a single author, may not be the product of a single authorial act; but for the moment I focus only on matters of prosody. Finer analysis of these "passages" depends upon non-prosodic elements of the text.

text,[2] the number of *śloka*s is 88% of the Mbh, but in terms of passages only 75% of the epic is *śloka* passages. For every three times the epic initiates a *śloka* passage there is a non-*śloka* passage, and the great majority of these alternative passages are *triṣṭubh-jagatī* passages. This matter is not as simple and straightforward as these numbers make it sound, but it is a topic worth investigating further.

One necessary and important qualification of this line of thought is the fact that many of the *triṣṭubh-jagatī* passages occur in obviously related clusters of non-*anuṣṭubh* passages. And it is also true, that a number of these non-*śloka* clusters are amalgamations of *triṣṭubh*s with fancier verses, as happens prominently, for example, in the *Āstīkaparvan* of the *Ādiparvan.* While a mechanical definition of a cluster of non-contiguous, prosodically differentiated passages can be given and a computer programmed to locate and enumerate such clusters on principles of proximity and material similarity, I have preferred, at this stage of the study, to identify non-*śloka* clusters manually. To make a long story short, my very preliminary and rough analysis of the 681 non-*śloka* verse passages of the epic distinguishes those passages into 293 separate "instances" of *triṣṭubh-jagatī*s. 179 of those instances are single *triṣṭubh* passages, 114 of those instances are multi-passage clusters that comprise among them 502 of the 681 passages.

THE MAIN VARIATIONS OF EPIC *TRIṢṬUBHS*: CLASSICAL UNIFORMITY VS. NON-CLASSICAL VARIABILITY

The *triṣṭubh*s of the Mbh constitute an extremely interesting and important population of Indian verse. Mbh *triṣṭubh* stanzas range from a variability that is reminiscent of Vedic *triṣṭubh*s, on the one hand, all the way to the rigidly uniform *upajāti*, *śālinī*, and *vātormī* stanzas of classical Sanskrit poetry, on the other. Since the general

[2] Of course "lines" compares quatrain *pāda*s to the double-*pāda ardhaśloka*.

trend of Sanskrit poetry between 1000 BC and 1000 AD was to move from rather variable verse forms to rather invariable verse forms (the development of *mātrā* and *gaṇa* meters is an interesting sideline that argues for this trend, not against it), it seems plausible to me to hypothesize – and I emphasize the word hypothesize – that, in general, the more variable a *triṣṭubh* passage of the Mbh is, the older it is likely to be; and the more uniform it is, the younger it is likely to be. That is, that we have in the Mbh numerous *triṣṭubh* passages that represent the broad diachronic trend of prosodic development in Sanskrit. But even if there were some way to prove that the more variable *triṣṭubh*s of the Mbh are generally older than its more uniform *triṣṭubh*s, we would still need always to be circumspect and cautious. Even as we would then be justified to judge all uniform stanzas to be relatively late (since uniform stanzas virtually do not exist in the known older literature), we would not be able to say the opposite, that all non-uniform stanzas are relatively early. There is no reason to think that the general literary impulse behind the overall prosodic trend operated uniformly and consistently across the entire spectrum of *triṣṭubh* poets who contributed to the creation and growth of the Mbh. We cannot assume that all aspects of *triṣṭubh*s that came eventually to be more or less rigidly prescribed became subject to the process of homogenization at the same times and at the same rates. Nor can we rule out the operation of special factors – some kind of deliberate archaization, certain authors' attachment to a freer prosodic style, the connection of a freer prosodic style to certain types of content such as dialog – that might have operated to prevent the freer style's being displaced only because of the march of time. Like other traditions of India, the Mbh is simultaneously very conservative and very inventive.

Now to the two measurable variables I mentioned earlier: The first is the relative degree of uniformity among the *pāda*s of *triṣṭubh* stanzas; the second is the set of major *triṣṭubh* features that were eliminated in the creation of the classical *triṣṭubh* standard.

Stanzaic uniformity

As my earlier remarks about the general trend of Indian versification indicate, stanzaic uniformity is one of the most important variables of epic *triṣṭubh*s. I have developed a consistent way to rate *triṣṭubh* stanzas on a scale of uniformity that starts at 0 and ends at 200. For now, this rating system looks only at the "opens" and "breaks" of a stanza's *pāda*s. I employ this distinction of "opens" and "breaks" only for descriptive purposes. See Table 3: By the "open" I refer of course to syllables 2, 3, and 4 of the *pāda*, and by "break" I refer to syllables 5, 6, and 7. This scheme ignores the initial and final syllables, the cadences (that is, syllables 8 through 10, or 8 through 11 for *jagatī*s), and the caesura.

With regard to these currently ignored elements, let me interrupt to make the following observations. In a classical verse, the cadences are, of course, uniform for either the *triṣṭubh* or the *jagatī* type; of the 1,808 classically uniform stanzas of the epic, about 2/3 of them might show some evidence of deliberate patterning of the *pāda* finals or initials or both (slightly under 10% of them [167 such stanzas] are completely classical, that is they have either the initial *and* final syllables all the same or have them occurring in alternation, as with *indravajra* and *upendravajra* forms of *upajāti triṣṭubh*s). Finally, the caesuras are relatively variable too. For the more than 7,000 *upajāti triṣṭubh*s in the classical stanzas, by Professor Tokunaga's specifications of caesuras, 2,550 have the caesura after the fourth syllable, 3,642 have it after the 5th, and more than 800 *pāda*s have the caesura after syllables 2, 3, 6, 7, or 8. Interestingly, for the 161 stanzas that have uniform or patterned initial and final syllables, the rates of the caesuras are almost identical. It would be interesting to have a few thousand stanzas of indisputably classical *upajāti*s to measure the classical standard precisely.

To resume with my system of scoring *pāda*s according to the uniformity of their opens and breaks: A stanza is rated as "uniform", that is it scores 200, if all its "opens" match and if all its "breaks" match. It is "classically uniform" if there are no "anti-classical" elements (which are taken up just below) in it. All but four such classically uniform stanzas form *upajāti*s, *śālinī*s, or *vātormī*s, three forms of the *triṣṭubh* with their own careers in classical poetry. The other four uniform *triṣṭubh* stanzas found in the Mbh seem not to have survived as classical *triṣṭubh* forms.[3] Sliding down from 200 points, a stanza is rated 175, 150, etc., down to 0, depending upon the number of matches among its opens and its breaks. A stanza in which the four *pāda*s fall into two matching pairs – ABAB, AABB, ABBA – , a 50-50 match, scores 100 points. Table 5 gives the frequencies for the ratings of the 4,426 *triṣṭubh* stanzas of the epic. Table 6 graphically charts those frequencies against the frequencies of anti-classical elements at the same uniformity values – I will come to these "anti-classical" elements shortly.

What these ratings reveal about the epic's *triṣṭubh*s is that almost half of the epic's *triṣṭubh* stanzas, 46%, are uniform in the terms just described. This trend toward classical uniformity is made even more definite when we put it together with the fact that among the 17,928[4] *triṣṭubh pāda*s of the Mbh, almost 61% are *upajāti pāda*s, while 2,076 (11.6%) of them are *śālinī pāda*s, and 1,093 (6.1%) are *vātormī pāda*s. If we restrict ourselves to the 1,808 classical *triṣṭubh* stanzas, the trend toward classical *upajāti*s is overwhelming.[5]

---

[3] These are three stanzas (at 5.36.12, 5.47.35, and 12.288.38) that have the open-break sequence RaRa and one (5.45.27) with MaBha. There are three other uniform stanzas in the Mbh which are not "classical" because they contain the "anti-classical" elements of highly unusual opens or breaks. Their locations are quite interesting when they are looked at together with the four classically uniform stanzas listed earlier in this note. Two of them (at 12.288.41-2) have the combination YaSa and another (3.134.19) has RaSa.

[4] I leave out of consideration here five *triṣṭubh pāda*s that occur within fancy-meter stanzas.

[5] 4 * 1746 [pure *upajāti* stanzas] + 74 [extra *pāda*s from 6-*pāda* stanzas] = 7,058 *upajāti pāda*s; 1,808 [classically uniform *triṣṭubh*s] * 4 + 74 [extra *pāda*s from 6-*pāda* stanzas] = 7,306 *pāda*s in uniform stanzas. *Upajāti* preponderance = 96.6%.

Obviously, the more uniformity there is among the *triṣṭubh*s, the less interesting the *triṣṭubh*s are as possible indicators of different authorial hands or voices. It is not the case, however, that half of the epic's *triṣṭubh*s are simply classical verses with no more value as distinct textual features than the epic's fancy verses. Three quarters of these classical stanzas occur in multi-passage clusters and three quarters of them in passages that are not uniformly classical passages. So, what we have in the epic *triṣṭubh*s is a pronounced trend toward classical *upajāti triṣṭubh*s, but it is only a trend; it is a phenomenon with a widely varied distribution. Only 20% of the classical stanzas occur in stand-alone, homogenous instances.[6] The other 80% occur in more complex, more varied settings, and these more complex settings are what will ultimately interest us most.

Non-classical variability

Having defined one end of the *triṣṭubh* continuum, let me say something about those that are not uniform. As many of you know well, these verses often mix *jagatī*s and *triṣṭubh*s in the same stanza: Dhṛtarāṣṭra's long *yadāśrauṣam* lament near the beginning of the epic has 54 of its 57 *triṣṭubh* stanzas close with the *jagatī* refrain *tadā nāśaṃse vijayāya saṃjaya.* As a second major kind of pre-classical trait, they often have hypermetric *triṣṭubh*s and occasionally even double hypermeters, hypometers, and *triṣṭubh*s with defective cadences. Thirdly, there are various, relatively "uncommon" "open" and "break" sequences. There are altogether 437 such "uncommon" *pāda*s among the 17,928, and the more uniform a stanza is, the rarer these "uncommon" *pāda*s are.[7] Fourthly, there are a number of other "open" and "break" combinations that occur

[6] 128 individual passages comprising 357 stanzas. Another 21 passages, comprising 55 stanzas, are homogenous passages of classically uniform stanzas in multi-passage clusters.

[7] They occur in 358 stanzas; 3 in stanzas rated 200; 27 in stanzas at 175+; 65 in stanzas at 150+.

commonly in the Mbh, but these are far outnumbered by the *upajāti*s, and these do not survive as classical Sanskrit verse forms, as do *upajāti*s, *śālinī*s, and *vātormī*s. These "common, but not classical" *pāda* types constitute another significant variable with which to chart the epic *triṣṭubh*s. In Table 2 columns 4, 7-8, 11-12, and 24 show the quantities and relative frequencies, as percentages, for these variables across the entire Mbh. (Table 2 also lists a number of other variables of *triṣṭubh* passages the discussion of which must be deferred to another occasion.)

ISOLATED *TRIṢṬUBHS* VS. MULTI-PASSAGE *TRIṢṬUBH* CLUSTERS

Table 7 juxtaposes two broad groups of epic *triṣṭubh*s in terms of the measures I have enumerated (and a couple of others about which I was curious, as well), and both these groups are put up against the all-Mbh values in addition. The two groups of *triṣṭubh*s are based upon a distinction which strikes me as potentially historically significant, and also important for constructing samples for statistical testing. I distinguish between *triṣṭubh* passages that occur more or less in isolation from other *triṣṭubh* passages, on the one hand, and, on the other, *triṣṭubh* passages that occur adjacently to others, or which occur in the same narrative, though perhaps separated by an *adhyāya* or two. I have applied these principles of proximity and thematic similarity very roughly, and these two categories are quite provisional.

This distinction is grounded in the hypothesis that one likely way that "*triṣṭubh*-interventions" were made was to splice a series of existing *triṣṭubh* passages into a *śloka* narrative, or to fill out in *śloka*s a narrative implicit in a set of old *triṣṭubh* passages. Both scenarios postulate a set of *triṣṭubh* passages forming some kind of larger text. Hypotheses based on this principle are worth testing and the basis of such testing is a preliminary segmentation of the *triṣṭubh* clusters. On the other hand, the relatively isolated, single-passage *triṣṭubh*s obviously represent a different history, a different pattern of "*triṣṭubh*-intervention;" of course it is quite possible that these instances represent several different patterns of "*triṣṭubh*-intervention". I have added a few surface observations regarding the comparison of the two groups to the table itself, and added, in Table 8 a comparison of the frequencies of different passage-lengths in the 179 single-passage *triṣṭubh* instances with the passage-length frequencies of all *triṣṭubh* instances in the Mbh.

Table 9 is a listing of the twenty *triṣṭubh* clusters that consist of the largest numbers of component passages, basically six passages and up. The table lists the initial *pāda* of the instance, its size, its contents, the average of the uniformity rating of all its component stanzas (labeled the "instance uniformity rate"), and a composite score for its "anti-classical" features. A tabular listing of all the "anti-classical" measures would be awkward and hard to read, so I have devised a synthesized score to stand in the stead of such a listing. The bottom rows of Table 9, the totals and percentages, show that in terms of bulk, these twenty passages make up 40% of all of the epic's *triṣṭubh*s, 4.5% of the entire Mbh. These 1,800 stanzas are not Mary Carroll Smith's archaic core of the warrior song, but they do represent an extremely interesting mix of old literature, epic or otherwise. I call your attention to the way in which Dhṛtarāṣṭra and his weakness for his son is so very prominent in many of these clusters, and so too then, Vidura and Saṃjaya. Nor is it just in the *Udyogaparvan* that we find Vidura wrangling wisdom with Dhṛtarāṣṭra. In cluster #9, row 4 on Table 9, which is focused upon the narrative of the dicing, much of the *triṣṭubh* material is actually wrangling among Dhṛtarāṣṭra, Vidura, and Duryodhana.

A FINAL SUGGESTION REGARDING DRAUPADĪ'S RIDDLE IN THE SABHĀ

I will close by posing this suggestion for a future discussion: It seems clear that more than one hand was at work in the 28 passages of cluster 9. I have laid them out in Table 10. Row 22 stands out in particular, whereas rows 4, 7, 11, 12, and 13 seem to stand out by their general resemblance to each other. When Franklin Edgerton used the *Sabhāparvan triṣṭubhs* to typify the least uniform and irregular Mbh *triṣṭubhs*, he overlooked how very different was the prosody of Draupadī's posing her riddle in 2.60 (row 22 of Table 10). Whereas the entirety of cluster 9 has a uniformity rating of 135.5 across its 148 stanzas, this component of it has the much higher rating of 186.7 across its 32 stanzas. The contrast is even more pronounced if we calculate the uniformity rating of the cluster apart from the passage of row 22 and then compare row 22 to the remainder of the cluster. Against row 22's almost classical rating of 186.7 the rest of the cluster has the decidedly pre-classical uniformity rating of 121.4. The other measures – particularly the rates of the non-regular *pāda*s and of the classical *pāda*s and then the *upajāti* rate – strongly suggest a different hand for Draupadī's speech. But when? Under what circumstances? By whom? For what reasons?[8]

[8] I presented a comprehensive analysis of the passage beginning at Mbh 2.60.16 (describing the abuse of Draupadī and her subsequent protests; row 22 of Table 10) and I contrasted this passage with the other passages of cluster #9 at the 214th meeting of the American Oriental Society in San Diego, California, in 2004.

TABLE 1: Overview of Prosody in the *Mahābhārata*

	All lines or *pādas*	% of all lines or *pādas*	Stanzas or numbered units	% of all stanzas or numbered units	Number of discrete passages[1]	% of all discrete passages	Average number of lines per passage	*Upa-parvans*[2]	*Adhyāyas*
All Mbh	161,587	100%	73,821	100%	3,112	100%		95	1995
Prose	1,111	0.69%	385	0.52%	29	0.93%	38.31	6	12
All verse	160,476	99.31%	73,436	99.48%	3,082	99.07%		95	1995[3]
Anuṣṭubh	141,940[4]	87.84%	68,858	93.28%	2,328	74.81%	60.97[5]	95	1941
Non-*anuṣṭubh*	18,536	11.47%	4,578	6.20%	755	24.26%		69	509
Fancy	608	0.38%	152	0.21%	74	2.38%	8.22	18	59
Triṣṭubh-Jagatī	17,928	11.09%	4,426	6.00%	681	21.88%	26.32[6]	66	450

[1] A "passage" is defined mechanically as an instance of one or several contiguous "units" of a given prosodic type within an *adhyāya.*

[2] The numbers in this column and the *adhyāya* column give the count of *upaparvans* and *adhyāyas* that contain at least one line/*pāda* of the given prosodic type.

[3] There are no *adhyāyas* consisting of 100% prose. All *adhyāyas* containing prose (12) also have *ślokas*, and 5 of the 12 have *triṣṭubhs* as well.

[4] *Anuṣṭubhs* are counted in *ardhaślokas*.

[5] *Arhaślokas*; so approximately 30½ *ślokas* per passage.

[6] Quatrain *pādas*; so, approximately 6½ stanzas per passage.

TABLE 2: *Triṣṭubh* Profile of the Whole *Mahābhārata*

1.			Passage start	
2.	4426		Stanzas	4426
3.	17928		*Pādas*	17928
4.	840	5%	Non-regular *pāda* (Hypermetric or irregular)	840
5.	14792	83%	*Ttriṣṭubh pāda*	14792
6.	2296	13%	*Jagatī pāda*	2296
7.	413	2%	Uncommon *triṣṭubh*	413
8.	24	0%	Uncommon *jagatī*	24
9.	14379	80%	Common *triṣṭubh*	14379
10.	2272	13%	Common *jagatī*	2272
11.	2489	14%	Common non-classical *triṣṭubh*	2489
12.	132	1%	Common non-classical *jagatī*	132
13.	11890	66%	Classical *triṣṭubh*	11890
14.	2140	12%	Classical *jagatī*	2140
15.	2061	11%	*Śālinī triṣṭubh*	2061
16.	10	0%	*Śālinī jagatī*	10
17.	1071	6%	*Vātormī triṣṭubh*	1071
18.	19	0%	*Vātormī jagatī*	19
19.	8758	49%	*Upajāti triṣṭubh*	8758
20.	2111	12%	*Upajāti jagatī*	2111
21.	0		% of (strict) *upajātis* (*triṣṭubh* or *jagatī*) in passages	59.95%
22.	1808	41%	Classical stanzas	1808
23.	0		% of classical stanzas	40.9%
24.	315	2%	*Triṣṭubh-jagatī* mixed stanzas	315
25.	4211	23%	All anti-classical elements	4211
26.	158.2		Average stanza uniformity	158.2
27.	-29.78		Average anti-classical rating	-29.78
28.	166.3		Average classical rating	166.3
29.	136.5		Average stanza rating	136.5

TABLE 3: Basic Terms and Definitions

Triṣṭubh-Jagatī description

("–" or "g" = "guru," heavy syllable; "∪" or "l" or "la" = "laghu," light syllable)

Saṃjñā	**Initial anceps**	**Opening** (syllables 2,3,4)	**Break** (syllables 5, 6, 7)	**Cadence** (syllables 8, 9, 10 [& 11])	**Final "anceps"**
Triṣṭubh	X	Usually Ra or Ma	Usually Bha, Ra, Sa	– ∪ – (Ra)	X
Jagatī	X	Usually Ra	Usually Bha	– ∪ – ∪ (Rala)	X
Upajāti	X	– ∪ – (Ra)	– ∪ ∪ (Bha)	– ∪ – (Ra)	X
Śālinī	g	– – – (Ma)	– ∪ – (Ra)	– ∪ – (Ra)	g
Vātormī	g	– – – (Ma)	∪ ∪ – (Sa)	– ∪ – (Ra)	g

TABLE 4: The Elements of *Triṣṭubh Pādas* and their Frequencies throughout the *Mahābhārata*

	∪∪∪ **Na**	∪∪– **Sa**	∪–– **Ya**	––– **Ma**	––∪ **Ta**	–∪∪ **Bha**	–∪– **Ra**	∪–∪ **Ja**
Triṣṭubh opens	0	1	175	3,777	111	8	10,720	2
Triṣṭubh breaks	101	1,899	2	2	12	9,415	3,362	1
Jagatī opens	0	0	4	139	1	1	2,164	1
Jagatī breaks	17	27	0	0	0	2,238	28	0

TABLE 5:
Frequencies of Uniformity Rates for all 4426 *Triṣṭubh* Stanzas of Mbh

Stanza uniformity rates	Number of stanzas
0	4
5	0
10	0
15	0
20	0
25	8
30	0
35	0
40	0
45	0
50	117
55	0
60	1
65	4
70	2
75	279
80	2
85	5
90	1
95	5
100	536
105	3
110	3
115	0
120	4
125	459
130	3
135	4
140	2
145	3
150	470
155	5
160	1
165	0
170	7
175	535
180	0
185	13
190	0
195	0
200	1950

TABLE 6:
Frequency of Uniformity Rates & "Anti-Classical" Elements

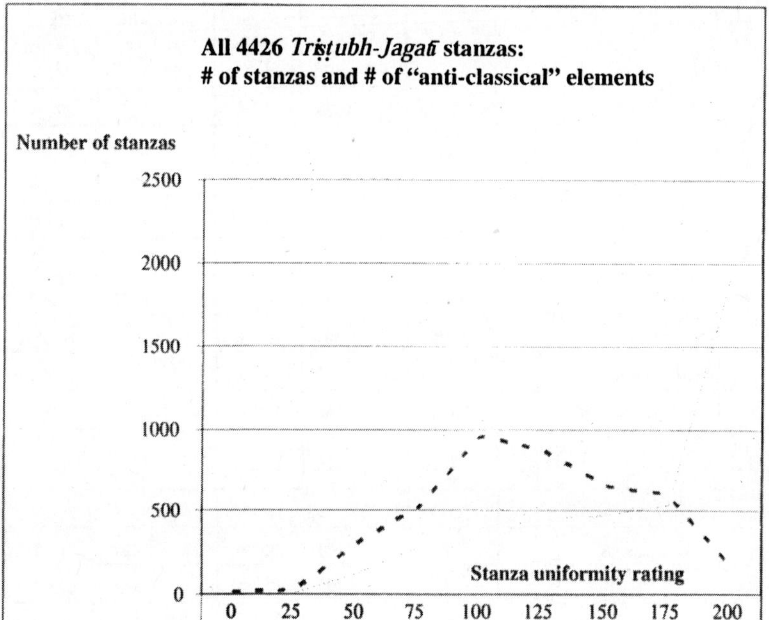

	0	25	50	75	100	125	150	175	200
- - · "anti-classical" element count	4	25	293	509	956	872	650	597	158
# of stanzas	4	8	117	279	536	459	470	535	1950

TABLE 7:
Comparisons of Single-passage Instances and Multi-passage Instances

		All Mbh	179 individual passages	Rates for the 179	114 multi-passage clusters	Rates for the 114
1.	*Triṣṭubh pādas*	**17928**	**4,036**	22.5%	**13,892**	77.5%
2.	*Triṣṭubh* stanzas	**4426**	**996**	22.5%	**3,430**	77.5%
3.	Anti-classical stanzas	**2346**	**476**	20.3%	**1870**	79.7%
4.	Classical stanzas	**1808**	**469**	25.9%	**1339**	74.1%
5.	*Upajāti jagatī* stanzas	**407**	**77**	18.9%	**330**	81.1%
6.	*Upajāti pādas*	**10869**	**2672**	24.6%	**8197**	75.4%
7.	*Śālinī pādas*	**2061**	**402**	19.5%	**1659**	80.5%
8.	*Śālinī* stanzas	**59**	**8**	13.6%	**51**	86.4%
9.	Anti-classical elements	**4213**	**880**	20.9%	**3333**	79.1%
10.	Common non-classical *pādas*	**2620**	**570**	21.8%	**2050**	78.2%
11.	Uncommon *pādas*	**437**	**72**	16.5%	**365**	83.5%
12.	Mixed stanzas	**315**	**91**	28.9%	**224**	71.1%
13.	IRG/HYP *pāda*	**840**	**146**	17.4%	**694**	82.6%
14.	Average uniformity rating of stanzas	**158.38**	**163.74**		**156.82**	

The 179 single-passage instances are somewhat closer to classical sorts of verse than are the multi-passage instances, but the differences are not terribly dramatic. The single-passage instances tend to be shorter passages than is the average in the Mbh as a whole (as can be seen on the frequency table to the right, 51.7% of all Mbh passages are one or two stanzas in length, but 61.4% of the single-passage instances are one or two stanzas long), but again the difference points to a trend, not to a clear black and white difference. In the chart just above the noticeably lower levels of the uncommon *pāda*s and the irregular *pāda*s may just be due to chance, or it may be significant. These rates will have to be probed with the appropriate statistical tests. One thing is quite striking, however: the rather elevated rate for mixed *triṣṭubh-jagatī* stanzas in the 179 singles. This elevation runs counter to my naïve expectation and is thus interesting. Finally, notice how close are the uniformity ratings of line 14 above.

TABLE 8:
Passage size of single-passage instances compared to general passage size throughout Mbh

Number of stanzas in a passage	Frequency in all Mbh	Percentage of all passages	Frequency in 179 singles	Percentage of the 179 passages
1	222	32.6%	70	39.1%
2	123	18.1%	40	22.3%
3	58	8.5%	14	7.8%
4	34	5.0%	9	5.0%
5	38	5.6%	6	3.4%
6	19	2.8%	5	2.8%
7	22	3.2%	3	1.7%
8	14	2.1%	1	0.6%
9	14	2.1%	3	1.7%
10	16	2.3%	1	0.6%
11	8	1.2%	2	1.1%
12	6	0.9%	3	1.7%
13	6	0.9%	2	1.1%
14	9	1.3%	3	1.7%
15	7	1.0%	1	0.6%
16	8	1.2%	2	1.1%
17	3	0.4%	0	0.0%
18	9	1.3%	1	0.6%
19	1	0.1%	0	0.0%
20	5	0.7%	1	0.6%
21	4	0.6%	1	0.6%
22	4	0.6%	2	1.1%
23	3	0.4%	1	0.6%
24	6	0.9%	1	0.6%
25	6	0.9%	0	0.0%
26	2	0.3%	1	0.6%
27	3	0.4%	0	0.0%
28	5	0.7%	0	0.0%
29	3	0.4%	1	0.6%
30	1	0.1%	0	0.0%
31	1	0.1%	1	0.6%
32	2	0.3%	0	0.0%
33	3	0.4%	0	0.0%
34	2	0.3%	0	0.0%
35	0	0.0%	0	0.0%

TABLE 9: Overview of the 20 Largest *Triṣṭubh* Clusters of the *Mahābhārata*

Row #	First *pāda* of passage	Cluster #	# of passages in instance	# of stanzas in instance	# of *pādas* in instance	Instance uniformity rate	"Anti-classical" rating of instance	Indication of contents
1.	01.050.001.a	3	6	32	128	131.25	-26.56	Āstīka praises Janamejaya's sacrifice. Janamejaya & the brahmins talk of Āstīka's mission. They both want Takṣaka. The priests claim Takṣaka to be in their power. Janamejaya grants Āstīka his boon. Āstīka saves Takṣaka. *Phalaśruti*.
2.	01.082.004.a	6	14	103	418	124.51	-21.65	Uttarayayāta
3.	01.176.034.a	7	15	170	688	172.59	-7.41	Draupadisvayamvara & marriage
4.	02.049.025.a	9	28	148	594	135.47	-20.27	Dicing match & its sequel. Much discussion between Dhṛtarāṣṭra and Vidura.
5.	03.132.001.a	16	8	71	284	114.72	-29.30	Aṣṭāvakra
6.	04.006.001.a	21	8	58	234	196.98	-3.36	Disguises of the Pāṇḍavas
7.	05.022.001.a	27	10	280	1142	115.98	-21.73	Saṃjayayāna
8.	05.033.012.a	28	36	123	492	137.40	-14.51	Prajāgara: Dhṛtarāṣṭra's anxiety after the Saṃjayayāna. Vidura counsels him at length with generalities about kingship & virtue and specific advice to settle with the Pāṇḍavas without resorting to war.
9.	05.042.001.a	29	20	53	206	100.00	-39.15	Sanatsujāta

10.	05.050.061.a	30	9	50	200	157.50	-13.10	Yānasaṃdhi: Dhṛtarastra's fear of Bhīma's club and Arjuna's fury. Saṃjaya describes in loving detail Arjuna's flag and Arjuna's and other Pāṇḍavas' horses. Saṃjaya quotes Dhṛṣṭadyumna urging that Bhīṣma make peace with Yudhiṣṭhira. Karṇa boasts; Bhīṣma criticizes him; Karṇa vows not to fight til Bhīṣma is down and stalks out. More from Bhīṣma. Saṃjaya quotes Arjuna's threats. Private discussion between Saṃjaya & Dhṛtarāstra. Vyāsa joins them & instructs Saṃjaya to tell Dhṛtarāstra fully about Arjuna & Kṛṣṇa. Dhṛtarāstra expresses *bhakti* for Kṛṣṇa.
11.	07.115.009.a	46	6	30	120	181.67	-6.50	Sātyaki slays Alambusa, then the horses of Duḥśāsana. Arjuna the Kirīṭin fighting splendidly.
12.	08.046.031.a	56	9	137	562	149.64	-16.09	Violent conflict between Arjuna & Yudhiṣṭhira; Kṛṣṇa mediates.
13.	08.062.036.a	59	10	219	900	189.63	-4.45	The battle of Arjuna & Karṇa; the death of Karṇa; Śalya takes over. End.
14.	09.016.007.a	60	7	90	362	188.06	-4.17	Deaths of Śalya & Śakuni.
15.	09.047.061.a	61	7	18	72	198.61	-2.50	Rāma's *yātrā*.
16.	12.048.015.a	64	6	13	52	200.00	0.00	Focus on Kṛṣṇa. Miscellaneous tags. Kṛṣṇa urges Bhīṣma to teach Yudhiṣṭhira.
17.	12.063.004.a	67	6	35	140	145.71	-8.86	Varṇadharma
18.	12.288.005.a	89	6	15	[illegible]0	113.33	-16.33	Saṃvāda of Sādhyas & haṃsa.
19.	13.106.008.a	112	6	13	52	130.77	-42.69	Bhagīratha lists his gifts to brahmins & his sacrifices. The vow of the fast, which Indra knew but kep secret, was discovered by Bhṛgu and transmitted to the rest by Uśanas. Bhagīratha's summation; he has recited this at the command of God [presumably Brahmā, to whom he has been speaking]; asks for good treatment from Brahmā.
20.	13.143.004.a	113	8	111	452	109.77	-25.86	Bhīṣma says he will die soon & tells Yudhiṣṭhira to start asking Kṛṣṇa what he wants to know (in this instance, another question about the value of brahmins). High *bhakti* toward Kṛṣṇa.
Totals			225	1769	7158			
% of all Mbh			28.8%	40.0%	39.9%			

TABLE 10: The 28 Passages of Cluster 9 (all but two of the *triṣṭubh* passages of the *Sabhāparvan*)

0.	1.		2.	3.	4.	5.	6.	7.	8.	9.	10.
			148	594	53	23	126	381	254	120.56	53.86
	Rates against all *pāda*s in passages				8.9%	3.9%	21.2%	64.1%	42.8%		
	Rates against all Mbh *pāda*s				4.7%	2.4%	14.6%	78.2%	60.6%	158.24	29.777
Row	Passage start	Brief indication of thematic content	Stanzas	*Pādas*	Non-regular *pāda* (Hypermetric or irregular)	Uncommon rate	Common non-classical rate	Classical rate	*Upajāti* rate	Average stanza uni-formity	Average anti-classical rating
3.	02.049.025	Duryodhana sums up his grief at Yudhiṣṭhira's opulent *rājasūya*.	1	4	0.0%	0.0%	0.0%	100%	75.0%	150.0	-5.0
4.	**02.051.011**	**Duryodhana & Dhṛtarāṣṭra disagree over *dyūta*; Dhṛtarāṣṭra acquiesces.**	**11**	**44**	**9.1%**	**4.5%**	**20.5%**	**65.9%**	**15.9%**	**127.3**	**-51.8**
5.	02.051.024	Vidura demurs to Dhṛtarāṣṭra, Dhṛtarāṣṭra's reply.	2	8	12.5%	0.0%	25.0%	62.5%	25.0%	75.0	-82.5
6.	02.052.001	Narrative: Vidura to the Pāṇḍavas.	1	4	25.0%	0.0%	50.0%	25.0%	0.0%	100.0	-55.0
7.	**02.052.004**	**Vidura issues the invitation; Yudhiṣṭhira demurs.**	**14**	**56**	**10.7%**	**1.8%**	**32.1%**	**55.4%**	**14.3%**	**132.1**	**-46.8**
8.	02.053.004	Śakuni on the gambler's art.	2	8	12.5%	0.0%	0.0%	87.5%	62.5%	150.0	-32.5
9.	02.055.002	Vidura censures the ongoing match, addressing Dhṛtarāṣṭra. Recalls Duryodhana's jackal-like birth;the line will die!	1	4	0.0%	0.0%	75.0%	25.0%	0.0%	150.0	-35.0
10.	02.056.001	Vidura continues his harangue; points out Duryodhana is creating a tremendous rift or causing war.	1	4	50.0%	0.0%	25.0%	25.0%	0.0%	75.0	125.0
11.	**02.056.004**	**Vidura continues, advising Dhṛtarāṣṭra of the great dangers at hand. Advises Śakuni be sent packing.**	**7**	**28**	**10.7%**	**17.9%**	**21.4%**	**50.0%**	**25.0%**	**114.3**	**-77.9**
12.	**02.057.001**	**Duryodhana accuses Vidura of being a traitor, tells him stop his criticism & leave. God is the only Ruler for him.**	**8**	**32**	**28.1%**	**3.1%**	**15.6%**	**53.1%**	**12.5%**	**121.9**	**-90.0**

13.	**02.057.012**	**Vidura touts loyalty and berates Duryodhana.**	**5**	**20**	**15.0%**	**5.0%**	**20.0%**	**60.0%**	**45.0%**	**110.0**	**-59.0**
14.	02.057.019	Vidura exhorts Duryodhana to quell his anger and drink the bitter draft drunk by the sat and eschewed by the asat. Vidura pronounces a wish for Duryodhana's wealth & fame; asks that the brahmins bless him. [Does not take leave!]	2	8	0.0%	0.0%	50.0%	50.0%	50.0%	150.0	-20.0
15.	02.058.014	The wager of Sahadeva.	1	4	0.0%	0.0%	50.0%	50.0%	0.0%	100.0	-30.0
16.	02.058.020	The wager of Arjuna.	1	4	25.0%	0.0%	75.0%	0.0%	0.0%	75.0	110.0
17.	02.058.022	The wager of Bhīma.	3	12	8.3%	0.0%	58.3%	33.3%	8.3%	133.3	-60.0
18.	02.059.001	Duryodhana orders Vidura to bring Draupadī; Vidura expresses amazement.	2	8	0.0%	12.5%	0.0%	87.5%	37.5%	75.0	-35.0
19.	02.059.005	Vidura criticizes Duryodhana for needlessly injuring the Pāṇḍavas; more amazement at Duryodhana's dancing over a chasm!	8	32	3.1%	3.1%	25.0%	68.8%	46.9%	131.3	-30.6
20.	02.060.001	Duryodhana replies and orders a servant to bring Draupadī. Servant approaches Draupadī. She disputes with him and learns what has happened.	6	24	12.5%	4.2%	41.7%	41.7%	12.5%	104.2	-62.5
21.	02.060.012	Usher to Draupadī; Draupadī on the *dhātṛ*.	2	8	12.5%	0.0%	25.0%	62.5%	25.0%	112.5	-57.5
22.	**02.060.016**	**Gross abuse of Draupadī; Draupadī protests; her riddle/*praśna***	**32**	**128**	**0.0%**	**0.8%**	**5.5%**	**93.8%**	**88.3%**	**186.7**	**-5.8**
23.	02.062.022	Silence of kings vis-à-vis Draupadī; Duryodhana puts the responsibility on the Pāṇḍavas to repudiate Yudhiṣṭhira; focus on *dharma*-idea.	7	30	3.3%	0.0%	30.0%	66.7%	23.3%	146.4	-33.6
24.	02.063.001	Karṇa taunts Draupadī. Bhīma expresses frustration toward Yudhiṣṭhira.	7	28	17.9%	10.7%	25.0%	46.4%	17.9%	92.9	-89.3
25.	02.063.016	Vidura censures the outrage and argues Draupadī was not properly staked. An exchange on the point between Duryodhana and Arjuna. The omens. Dhṛtarāṣṭra laments his son and relents to pacify the Pāṇḍavas.	11	44	15.9%	6.8%	15.9%	61.4%	22.7%	104.5	-70.9
26.	02.066.035	Gāndhārī cites wisdom against riches gained by cruelty.	1	4	0.0%	0.0%	25.0%	75.0%	50.0%	125.0	-15.0
27.	02.068.007	Duḥśāsana taunts the Pāṇḍavas cruelly as they depart for the forest	6	24	8.3%	4.2%	12.5%	75.0%	33.3%	145.8	-41.7
28.	02.068.014	Conclusion of last; narrative; Bhīma confronts Duḥśāsana.	2	8	0.0%	0.0%	12.5%	87.5%	50.0%	137.5	-12.5
29.	02.068.019	Narrative of Duḥśāsana taunting Bhīma as "cow".	1	4	25.0%	25.0%	25.0%	25.0%	25.0%	100.0	140.0
30.	02.068.023	Duryodhana taunts Bhīma. Bhīma restrains his actions, responding only with words, out of deference to Yudhiṣṭhira.	3	12	0.0%	8.3%	33.3%	58.3%	41.7%	150.0	-33.3

To Wake a Sleeping Giant: Vālmīki's Account(s) of the Life and Death of Kumbhakarṇa

ROBERT P. GOLDMAN

Anyone familiar with the story of the *Rāmāyaṇa* in any detail through any of its innumerable versions will immediately recognize the name and character of Kumbhakarṇa, surely the largest and most grotesque of the epic's many larger than life characters. For the gargantuan *rākṣasa* prince, as described by Vālmīki at least, is surely one of the First Poet's, and indeed the entire literature's most extraordinary and colorful characters. Indeed, in the *Yuddhakāṇḍa* of the *Vālmīki Rāmāyaṇa* Kumbhakarṇa is characterized through the poet's grand indulgence in *atiśayokti* as a caricature, even a parody of the already hyperbolic monsters that people his masterpiece.

In Kumbhakarṇa we find a warrior so enormous that he towers over the lofty ramparts of the citadel of Laṅkā.[1] His deep, somnolent breathing is so forceful that it literally blows other powerful *rākṣasa*s out of his cave.[2] The fleshly appetites of this monster are so vast that he breakfasts on piles of deer, buffalo and boar washing this Brobdignagian repast down with a thousand jars of strong drink.[3] And, when he is finally slain by Rāma, his enormous head

---

[1] Ram 6.49.1-6. (All references, unless otherwise specified, are to the critical edition of the text produced and published by the Rāmāyaṇa Department of the Oriental Institute of Baroda, 1960-75.)

[2] Ram 6.48.18-19, 34.

[3] Ram 6.48.26-26, 82.

smashes the gates of the buildings on Laṅkā's main thoroughfares and knocks down its towering walls while his headless trunk falls into the sea crushing crocodiles, shoals of huge fish, and serpents before entering the earth.[4]

But this fearsome giant, so voracious that there is a real danger that he will devour every living thing in the universe,[5] is not just a monolithic monster. Surprisingly, it turns out that for all his mindless violence and gluttony, he is an accomplished student of *dharma* and *nītiśāstra*, capable of lecturing his older brother Rāvaṇa at length on the finer points of law and statecraft.[6] Indeed he is the only one among all of the demon-king's counselors who is capable of eliciting from him an acknowledgement of the catastrophic nature of his decision to abduct Sītā.[7]

But despite the rhetorical exuberance with which the gargantuan *rākṣasa* is portrayed, the interesting complexity of his character and the evident fascination he had for a poet who devotes some nine complete *sarga*s comprising some 450 *śloka*s to his history and actions in the *Yuddhakāṇḍa* alone, Kumbhakarṇa has received surprisingly little attention on the part of epic scholars. Indeed, with the exception of Dr. von Simson's interesting attempt to trace the names (and to some degree the characters) of the important *Mahābhārata* figures of Droṇa and Karṇa to the dissolution of the name Kumbhakarṇa,[8] there appears to be relatively little critical scholarship devoted centrally to this striking and entertaining figure.

This lack I believe unfortunate. For one thing the character of Kumbhakarṇa is intrinsically interesting in terms of his role in the epic narrative and as an object of comparative study in folklore and epic studies. Even more interestingly, however as I hope to suggest,

---

[4] Ram 6.55.124-5.

[5] Ram 6.49.19-20.

[6] Ram 6.51.1-20.

[7] Ram 6.51.25-26.

[8] von Simson 1968.

the varying accounts of his history that the epics present and the ways in which pre-modern commentators and modern Indologists respectively attempt to rationalize and explain this kind of variance may give us some additional information on the receptive and genetic histories of the *Rāmāyaṇa*. Moreover, they may perhaps shed an additional modest beam of light on the question of the relationship between the *Vālmīki Rāmāyaṇa* and the *Rāmopākhyāna* of the Mbh.

Of all the extraordinary things the *Rāmāyaṇa* tells us about Kumbhakarṇa, by far the most striking and the most widely recognized is the prodigious nature – both in terms of duration and of profundity – of his sleep. The depth of his slumber is, like everything else about this interesting figure, prodigious. The heroic efforts required of the *rākṣasa*s to wake him – the blaring of trumpets, the beating of drums, the assault with fists, feet and various weapons and the trampling with herds of elephants etc. – are elaborately and amusingly described at length by Vālmīki.[9] However, it is the epic's varying accounts of the etiology and duration of Kumbhakarṇa's sleep that will concern me in the present paper.

The first mention of Kumbhakarṇa in the critically edited text of the *Yuddhakāṇḍa*,[10] at least in connection with his sleep, occurs

---

[9] Ram 6.48.28-48.

[10] The southern recension includes Kumbhakarṇa among the *rākṣasa*s who counsel Rāvaṇa near the beginning of the *Yuddhakāṇḍa* (Critical Edition, Appendix I, No. 3 (= Vulgate 6.12.28 ff.) There, as in *sarga* 51 of the critical edition, Kumbhakarṇa rebukes his brother for his violation of *dharma* and *nīti*. The passage is contextually awkward, however, precisely because it does not explain how Kumbhakarṇa could be awake at that moment. Following 6.48.12ab, D5-7, 10-11, T, G1, 2, and M insert a passage of one line (1029*) in an apparent attempt to explain this seeming contradiction: "For, having given his counsel, he fell asleep on the ninth day from now."

This half verse is ambiguous and somewhat controversial in that it raises once again the complex issue of how long Kumbhakarṇa sleeps at a stretch, discussed in the preceding note. Commentators and translators differ considerably over such issues as the point from which to count the nine days, whether one should count back or forward in time, or whether, indeed the term, day (*ahani*), here, refers by metonymy (*lakṣaṇa*) to months. Nāgeśa quotes the opinion, elsewhere stated by Govindarāja, that Kumbhakarṇa falls asleep on the ninth day before the day on which the battle starts, but claims that this is not consistent with the text, since it appears to contradict Rāvaṇa's statement at 6.50.12 that Kumbhakarṇa has been asleep "for a very long time" (*sumahān kālaḥ*). For, since according to the commentators we are now at the sixth day of battle, this would mean that Kumbhakarṇa would have been sleeping for only some fifteen days, hardly a very long time by his standards. Moreover, such a reading raises the problem of how, indeed, Kumbhakarṇa, who through the power of Brahmā's curse appears to be forced to sleep for a minimum of six months, could be awakened after such a brief span of time. Nāgeśa proposes, as an alternative, that we understand the word *ahan*, "day", by *lakṣaṇa*, or secondary meaning, to stand for *māsa*, "month". Thus, according to this interpretation, Kumbhakarṇa would have been asleep for nine months and so could be awakened. Nāgeśa concludes by stating that this will all be made clear later on. Among the translators consulted, only M. N. Dutt (1892: 1288) follows this interpretation, translating, "he hath slept for nine months". This interpretation is, however, difficult to accept, since the counsel to which Rāvaṇa alludes must be the frank advice given to Rāvaṇa in the assembly described in lines 195-229 of Appendix 1, No. 3 (= Vulgate 6.12.28-40), which follows *sarga* nine in the critical edition. (See note to 6.9.22.) This assembly, according to Govindarāja would have taken place eleven days before the start of the battle, or seventeen days before the present moment.

Śivasahāya takes a completely different approach, claiming that we should understand that, having given his counsel, Kumbhakarṇa fell asleep, but will awaken on the ninth day and that he will have reached the limit for the time set for his sleeping on this very day (*jāgariteti śeṣaḥ*).

Satyatīrtha quotes Śivasahāya in full on this point, but disagrees with him, finding his argument to be contradicted by the text and claiming that his recourse to *lakṣaṇa* is pointless. As an alternative, Satyatīrtha proposes that, in stating later on that Kumbhakarṇa has slept for a very long time (6.50.12), Rāvaṇa is merely giving an example of the way in which people who are in misery consider a short period of time as very long (*duḥkhasamayatvenālpakālasyāpi bāhulyoktiḥ*). As another example of this he cites *Bhāgavatapurāṇa* 1.14.7, where Yudhiṣthira in his anxiety over Arjuna's failure to return, claims that he has been gone for seven months.

Satyatīrtha, Maheśvaratīrtha, and to a very elaborate extent, Govindarāja take this line as the starting point for a day by day chronology of the campaign in Laṅkā. Starting from the day of Kumbhakarṇa's counsel to Rāvaṇa and Vibhīṣaṇa's defection they attempt to fit the various events and battles into the framework of nine days posited by Rāvaṇa. They justify this chronology by quoting specific verses from the earlier portions of the *Yuddhakāṇḍa* which give indications of the passage of time. Govindarāja takes this task particularly seriously dating the epic's events by the lunar calendar retrospectively from the abduction of Sītā and prospectively until the death of Rāvaṇa. Govindarāja is also concerned with reconciling his chronology (in which the events from Hanumān's meeting with Sītā in Laṅkā to the death of Rāvaṇa span only a little more than a fortnight) with Sitā's statement to Hanumān and Rāvaṇa's to Sītā, in the in the forty-eighth *sarga* of the book. There Rāvaṇa, having been humiliatingly defeated and then dismissed from the battlefield by Rāma, tells his attendants that Kumbhakarṇa – whom he describes as being overcome by Brahmā's curse (*brahmaśāpābhibhūtaḥ*)[11] – must be awakened as he is the only warrior seemingly capable of defeating the demon-king's enemies. He remarks that Kumbhakarṇa sleeps for "six, seven, eight or even nine months at a time" (*nava ṣaṭ sapta cāṣṭau ca māsān svapiti rākṣasaḥ*).[12] He goes on to add that, addicted to this vulgar pleasure (i.e. sleep) his brother lies in a stupor all the time. (*kumbhakarṇah sadā śete mūḍho grāmyasukhe ratah.*)[13]

Rāvaṇa's comments, in which he mentions but does not describe in any detail, a curse on the part of Brahmā thus appear upon a first reading to indicate that the periods of Kumbhakarṇa's sleep are not fixed but are, in fact, variable.

Rāvaṇa's indeterminacy in this matter, however, seems to be at odds with the account of the history and terms of the curse as they are related to Rāma by Kumbhakarṇa's other brother Vibhīṣaṇa in the very next chapter (*sarga* 49).

There we learn that when Indra, having been defeated by Kumbhakarṇa, appealed to Brahmā for help, the latter, fearing that the monster represented a threat of universal destruction, cursed him to suffer immediate and perpetual sleep so that he would be as good as dead (*tasmāt tvam adyaprabhṛti mṛtakalpaḥ śayiṣyasi*).[14] But at this point, so Vibhīṣaṇa's tale goes, Rāvaṇa intervened arguing that it would be wrong of Brahmā to – in effect – put his own grandson to death. Acknowledging that the word of Brahmā can never prove false and that the curse of somnolence is inevitable for his brother, the *rākṣasa* lord nevertheless urged the Creator to set

---

Sundarakāṇḍa concerning the amount of Sītā's year of captivity that remains before she must either submit to him or be killed.

[11] Ram 6.48.9.

[12] Ram 6.48.12.

[13] Ram 6.48.14.

[14] Ram 6.49.23.

some specific time limits on Kumbhakarṇa's sleeping and waking (*kālas tu kriyatām asya śayane jāgare tathā*).[15] Moved by Rāvaṇa's appeal, Brahmā modifies his curse, ordaining that the voracious Kumbhakarṇa shall sleep for periods of precisely six months waking only for a single day between these periods to indulge his ferocious appetite by consuming all the worlds like a raging fire (*śayitā hy eṣa ṣaṇmāsān ekāhaṃ jāgariṣyati* | *ekenāhnā tv asau vīraś caran bhūmiṃ bubhukṣitaḥ* | *vyāttāsyo bhakṣayel lokān saṃkruddha iva pāvakaḥ*).[16]

These two slight but puzzling differences in the calculation of the duration of Kumbhakarṇa's periods of dormancy, however, do not exhaust the *Vālmīki Rāmāyaṇa*'s varying formulations of the story. For in the *Uttarakāṇḍa* we find yet two more accounts of this seemingly simple tale according to which the *rākṣasa*'s epic slumbers are to be reckoned not in months but in years or even millennia.

One of these additional explanations of Kumbhakarṇa's sleep, narrated at 7.10.31-41, is of particular interest. For it is here that we find what is perhaps the best known account of how Kumbhakarṇa came to sleep for so long. For here his prolonged slumber is not the result of a curse, but instead of what is supposed to be a boon. In this passage, the sage Agastya tells Rāma the following story. The gods fear that, if Brahmā were to grant Kumbhakarṇa the same kind of boon in compensation for his heroic austerities as his brothers Rāvaṇa and Vibhīṣaṇa have earned through theirs, he will become a still greater terror than before. They beg the god to delude the *rākṣasa* under the pretext of granting him a boon. In this way, they argue, the Creator can bring the monster down and so save the worlds from his ravages (*varavyājena moho 'smai dīyatām amitaprabha* | *lokānāṃ svasti caiva syāt bhaved asya ca saṃnatiḥ*).[17] Brahmā agrees and summons Sarasvatī, the goddess of speech, in-

[15] Ram 6.49.25.

[16] Ram 6.49.26-27.

[17] Ram 7.10.34. Cf. the Vulgate's *saṃmatiḥ*, honor, satisfaction.

structing her to enter Kumbhakarṇa and, in effect, speak through him to choose his "boon" for him. Thus, when Brahmā asks Kumbhakarṇa to select his reward the latter replies, "O god of gods, what I desire is to sleep for many years" (*svaptuṃ varṣāṇy anekāni devadeva mamepsitam*).[18] The deluded demon is then left wondering what sort of strange request has come out of his mouth.[19]

The final reference to the duration of Kumbhakarṇa's sleep in the *Rāmāyaṇa* occurs three *sarga*s after this last one as a sequel to Agastya's account of the history of the principal *rākṣasa*s. Here, unlike in the *Yuddhakāṇḍa* version of Vibhīṣaṇa, where Kumbhakarṇa collapses in a stupor the moment Brahmā utters his curse, some time elapses between the deception perpetrated by Brahmā and Sarasvatī and Kumbhakarṇa's succumbing to his drowsiness. At *Uttarakāṇḍa* 13.1-7, the irresistible urge to sleep only gradually comes upon the giant. He informs Rāvaṇa of this and the *rākṣasa*-lord has time to have his artisans construct a grand and ornate sleeping chamber for his brother. Only when the building is complete does Kumbhakarṇa succumb to his somnolence and fall into a profound slumber that – in this variant – continues without his waking for "many thousands of years" (*bahūny abdasahasrāṇi śayāno nāvabudhyate*).[20]

As the preceding discussion has demonstrated, it appears that there are basically two separate and ultimately irreconcilable accounts of how Kumbhakarṇa came to sleep for so long: the *Yuddhakāṇḍa* version in which he is cursed as a result of his rapacity and the *Uttarakāṇḍa* version in which he is "rewarded" for his austerities with a fraudulent "boon" that has the same purpose and much the same effect as the curse. Each version has two subvariants, narrated in close textual proximity to each other, each with a slightly different account of the duration of Kumbhakarṇa's

---

[18] Ram 7.10.39.

[19] Ram 7.10.41.

[20] Ram 7.13.7.

period of dormancy. As a result, it appears that in regard to this fairly minor and seemingly simple point of fact, as it were, the text of the *Vālmīki Rāmāyaṇa*, as it has come down to us has four different calculations of the duration of Kumbhakarṇa's slumber.

Now what, if anything, are we to make of all this? Has the poet nodded? Is this a genuine text-historical issue than can shed light on the genetic history of the epic?

One thing is certain. From the point of view of the poem's receptive history it is clear that the principal custodians, editors and interpreters of the work – by which I mean in a word, its Sanskrit commentators – have always found the apparent discrepancies just noted – at least those concerning the duration of Kumbhakarṇa's sleep – significant, troubling and fully worthy of their learned attempts at reconciliation.

As an example of this let us revisit for a moment Rāvaṇa's statement that his brother sleeps "for six, seven, eight, even nine months at a time" (*nava ṣaṭ sapta cāṣṭau ca māsān*). This reading of the critical edition which can also be understood to mean "for nine, six, seven, *and* eight months" that is to say for thirty months, appears to be shared and discussed by only one commentator, Govindarāja.[21]

Govindarāja understands the passage, as do I, to indicate that Kumbhakarṇa may, on different occasions, sleep for nine months, seven months, etc. He sees this as in keeping with the non-specific boon request of Kumbhakarṇa (at *Uttarakāṇḍa* 10.39) to sleep for many years (*varṣāṇy anekāni*). He then refers to the other two interpretations, suggesting that the curse of sleeping for precisely six months at 6.49.26 either refers by synecdoche (*upalakṣana*) to the *rākṣasa*'s other, longer periods of sleep or represents only the *minimum* time during which Kumbhakarṇa must remain asleep (*anyūnābhiprāyaṃ vā*). Finally, Govindarāja provides a lengthy

[21] The verse upon which Govindarāja is commenting (Critical Edition 6.48.12) is found in the so-called Vulgate at 6.60.17. For the text of Govindarāja's remarks see *Śrīmadvālmīkirāmāyaṇam* (1935). See this texts also for the commentaries of Nāgeśa Bhaṭṭa and Śivasahāya.

quotation from the *Taittirīyasaṃhitā* (7.5.6.1), where in the context of the *gavāmayana* rite, it is stated that the ritual officiants reckon as a month (*māsa*) a period of six days (*ṣaḍahaḥ*). If, Govindarāja argues, we then add up the number of such "months" indicated in the verse, we get a total of thirty months (i.e., 6+7+8+9=30) of six days each, or 180 days. This calculation then agrees with the passage at 6.49.26, at which the *rākṣasa* sleeps for six (lunar) months reckoned at 30 days each.

A variety of manuscripts collated for the critical edition as well as the widely published "Vulgate" text of the southern commentators Nāgojī Bhaṭṭa, Mādhavayogin and Śivasahāya as well as the printed northern texts of Lahore and Gorresio do not read with the critical edition and Govindarāja. They read instead that Kumbhakarṇa sleeps "for, nine, seven, ten, and eight months, (*nava sapta daśāṣṭau ca māsān*), i.e. for thirty-four months. This reading is mentioned as a variant and commented upon by Govindarāja as well. Nāgojī attempts to reconcile the three different passages by arguing that the verse does not specify a precise period of time for Kumbhakarṇa to sleep, but simply indicates that the duration of his dormancy has no upper limit. He further states that the reference at 6.49.26 indicates only that six months is the *minimum* period that he must sleep, but that after any period of sleep, regardless of its length, his waking is restricted to a single day. In other words, Nāgojī argues that "the boon" of Brahmā specifies only how long Kumbhakarṇa can be awake, not how long he sleeps. This, he argues, is confirmed by the other two passages mentioned above where Kumbhakarṇa is said to sleep for many years or for thousands of years. The commentator Śivasahāya extends this argument by claiming that although Brahmā's boon compels Kumbhakarṇa to sleep for at least six months, "there is nothing to prevent him from sleeping naturally beyond that term" (*taduttaraṃ svabhāvika-nidrayā niṣedhābhavāc ca*). Nāgojī then quotes yet another line of interpretation, which he attributes to unnamed "others". According to this interpretation, the word *aṣṭau* is not to be understood in the sense of the number eight, but as the locative of a noun *aṣṭi*, (pervasion, eating) whose range of meaning he extends to include the sense of "to leave aside" (*tyāge*). According to this interpretation the compound *daśāṣṭau*, has the sense of "leaving out ten". If then, as Nāgojī suggests, we add up the nine and seven months mentioned in the verse, we get a period of sixteen months, which, with ten months subtracted, leaves the six months of sleep referred to in 6.49.26. Although Nāgojī does not specify his sources, this ingenious interpretation is offered by several other commentators, who differ only in their derivation and lexical identification of *aṣṭau*. Thus, Govindarāja, who notes this variant, derives the word from the root √*aś*, in the sense of "eat" (*aśanam*), whose meaning he extends to "loss or destruction" (*nāśaḥ*). Similarly Śivasahāya glosses, "swallowing" (*nirgaraṇa*) in the sense of "casting out" (*niḥsāraṇe*) and takes the word in the sense of "eating" (*bhakṣaṇārthakāśadhātuprakṛtikatinantaḥ*). Lokanātha, quoted by Gorresio (*Rāmāyaṇa* 1856, IX, p. 377), perhaps deriving the word from the root √*as*, "throw, toss", glosses "casting out ten" (*daśaprakṣepe sati*).

Interestingly, Śivasahāya, who accepts Nāgojī's ingenious suggestion that we must cast out ten to achieve the total number of months, balks at his idea that the passage indicates merely a minimum period during which the giant must sleep. In his comments on Vulgate 7.10.45 (= critical edition 7.10.39) He quotes Nāgojī but indicates that the latter's point here is doubtful (*cintyā*) since, according to him, there are two separate "boons" at issue: the one referred to in the *Yuddhakāṇḍa* and the one in the *Uttara*. Śivasahāya adds a new dimension to the problem of the duration here by interpreting the boon Kumbhakarṇa solicits against his will while under the influence of Sarasvatī as specifying a period of slumber of three years. (*anekāny ekabhinnāni kapiñjalādhikaraṇanyāyena trīṇītyartho varṣāni*). He claims that the *Uttarakāṇḍa* account makes no allusion to any such condition. So far as I have been able to discover Śivasahāya is the only commentator to directly address the issue of there being two separate and complementary explanations for Kumbhakarṇa's sleep quite apart from the question of the different lengths of time during which he is supposed to sleep. Other commentators concern themselves exclusively with reconciling the numbers.[22]

The only additional light that the epic literature seems to shed on this perhaps yawn-inducing question is to be found in the terse narration of Kumbhakarṇa's curse found in the *Rāmopākhyāna* of the Mbh. There (3.259.28)[23] when the *rākṣasa* is told by Brahmā to select a boon as a reward for his austerities the text simply says, "He chose long sleep, his mind being seized by darkness" (*sa vavre mahatīṃ nidrāṃ tamasā grastacetanaḥ*). On this, the influential 17th century commentator Nīlakaṇṭha explains, "The expression 'by darkness' means that it was out of delusion that he chose sleep, which he did not desire" (*tamasety aniṣṭām api nidrāṃ mohād vṛtavān ity arthaḥ*).[24]

Now what, if anything, can this odd textual and commentarial data tell us about the genetic and receptive histories of Vālmīki's poem?

First, briefly, the genetic history. The learned and prolific student of the *Rāmāyaṇa*, John Brockington has argued, that on the basis of the relative ornateness of its poetry, the length of some of its relevant *sarga*s and its use of certain verbal forms much of the *Yuddhakāṇḍa*'s account of the history, awakening, exploits and death of Kumbhakarṇa shows signs of relative lateness within his schematization that assigns this book to "stage 2" of the epic's growth (dated roughly from the 3rd century BCE to the 1st century

---

[22] See for example the elaborate commentary of Satyatīrtha who expends considerable effort on the problem. See *Śrīmadvālmīkirāmāyaṇam* (1911-13). Keep in mind that it is a commonplace of the epic texts to provide two or more complementary explanations for a single event or phenomenon: Well-known examples would be the three explanations for Draupadī's polyandrous marriage and the two causes of Kalmāṣapāda's becoming a *rākṣasa*.

[23] *Mahābhārata: Critical Edition* (1933-70).

[24] Vulgate 3.275.28 (*Mahābhārata* [1929]).

CE).[25] If Brockington's model and his dating are correct, then we must understand that the Kumbhakarṇa episode, or at least the portion with which we are dealing, probably derives from the end of this period. According to the same formulation, the entire *Uttarakāṇḍa* belongs to the next stage, stage 3 (1st to 3rd centuries CE). Thus the two accounts of how Kumbhakarṇa came to sleep for so long and the length of his slumbers would appear to originate from adjacent if not identical periods in the poem's development. Thus it does not seem that a compelling argument for the discrepancy between the two books can be made on the grounds that many centuries during which the tale mutated intervened between their composition. Rather, it seems likely that, as appears to be the case with many variant versions of stories in the epic, the details of a given version are governed more by the immediate rhetorical and contextual needs of the author(s) than by any "lapse" on the part of the composers of one or the other version.[26]

This kind of argument can also work to help us understand certain differences between the two great epics. Thus, for example, instead of arguing that the *Rāmopākhyāna*'s lack of any reference to Rāma's abandonment of Sītā is testimony to that text's having condensed the *Rāmāyaṇa* before the composition of the *Uttarakāṇḍa*, we might well stand back and ask how such an episode would fit in with Mārkaṇḍeya's efforts to reassure Yudhiṣṭhira after the loss of his kingdom and the outrages perpetrated upon Draupadī. For surely, the ostensible purpose of the *upākhyāna*, is the consolation of Yudhiṣṭhira and his dependents. A discussion of Rāma's rejection of Sītā would be highly inapposite from the point of view of narrative parallelism and, needless to say, far from comforting to the exiled Pāṇḍavas and their long-suffering wife.

It thus seems likely that the authors of the *Uttarakāṇḍa* versions of the legend of Kumbhakarṇa too were operating under the influence of their local context. In the present case this was the narrative

---

[25] Brockington 1984: 329.

[26] Goldman 1973; 1984: 37.

of the fearsome austerities practiced by the three principal *rākṣasa* descendants of Pulastya and the boons that they extract from Brahmā in compensation for them. The critical factors for the authors would most probably have been Rāvaṇa's boon of invulnerability to all superhuman beings (as opposed to mere men) and Vibhīṣana's gift of eternal righteousness, both critically important to the story of the *Rāmāyaṇa*. The details of how Kumbhakarṇa came to suffer from his peculiar condition of permanent narcolepsy could, I believe, in this larger context easily become subordinated to the common epic-purāṇic technique of attributing a single effect to multiple causes that are not mutually exclusive and may even be complementary.

In other words, it is not that the *Uttarakāṇḍa* authors were either unaware of the version in the *Yuddha* or careless in recalling its details; it is just that they may well have tailored the circumstances leading to Kumbhakarṇa's sleep to suit their different context.

What then of the *Rāmopākhyāna*'s brief account of the curse of Kumbhakarṇa? It is true that, as Brockington[27] and other scholars have noted, the *Rāmopākhyāna* devotes a disproportionate amount of its text to what corresponds to the *Yuddhakāṇḍa* of Vālmīki and has, in effect, no epilogic *Uttarakāṇḍa*. Nonetheless, its account of the false boon of Kumbhakarṇa (along with the boons of his brothers Rāvaṇa and Vibhīṣaṇa) – placed here at the beginning of the *upākhyāna* – is clearly akin to and in fact evidently derived from the *Uttarakāṇḍa*'s account.

Indeed it is difficult to think of any source other than the *Uttarakāṇḍa*[28] for the Mbh's version because it not only follows the *Uttarakāṇḍa* version's logic but it is yet another of those narrative elements of the *Rāmopākhyāna*, such as those noted by Raghavan and myself[29] among others, that are in fact largely unintelligible without knowledge of Vālmīki.

---

[27] Brockington 1998: 476.

[28] Other than some purely hypothetical common source such as proposed by van Buitenen (1975: 213-214).

Consider the *Rāmopākhyāna*'s laconic phrase that in choosing his reward for his austerities, Kumbhakarṇa was *tamasā grasta-cetanaḥ*. The Mbh text gives us no explanation at all for the *rākṣa-sa*'s sudden mental confusion and we are at a loss to understand what has happened unless we have in mind the *Uttarakāṇḍa* version in which Brahmā, through the instrumentality of Sarasvatī carries out the gods' plea *varavyājena moho 'smai dīyatām*.

On this basis it would seem reasonable to suppose that the author of the *Rāmopākhyāna*, which most scholars after Jacobi have taken to be a *nachdichtung* and condensation of Vālmīki, had clearly in mind the account of the delusion and false boon of Kumbhakarṇa recorded in the 10th *sarga* of the *Uttarakāṇḍa*, and not the story as it appears in the *Yuddha*.

Then too what are we to make of the heroic struggles of the *Rāmāyaṇa* commentators to rationalize the two accounts of the curse/boon of Kumbhakarṇa and of modern scholars' efforts to explain the kind of variation we have seen at work here?[30]

If the authors of the *Uttarakāṇḍa* version – which we will have to assume is at the very least somewhat posterior to that of the *Yuddhakāṇḍa* – were as cavalier as all epic bards and poets about the consistency of multiple versions of a given story, the same is clearly not the case with later students of the poems, including the epic commentators and modern Indologists.

The former are in effect part of a large and complex cultural, literary, and theological project to interpret and represent the epic as history. Thus for them, differences in the details of a narrative – especially if they involve significant characters and events – are

---

[29] Raghavan 1973; Goldman 1984: 37-39.

[30] Perhaps the epic poets had something of the attitude expressed to V. Narayana Rao by brahman women in Andhra regarding *Rāmāyaṇa* variations across versions. "Like most of the participants in the tradition, these women believe the *Rāmāyaṇa* to be fact and not fiction, and its many different versions are precisely in keeping with this belief. Contrary to the usual opinion, it is fiction that has only one version; a factual event will inevitably have various versions, depending on the attitude, point of view, intent, and social position of the teller." (Narayana Rao 1991: 115.)

potentially critical problems requiring the investment of considerable ingenuity, learning, and intellectual capital by way of rationalization and remediation. How else are we to understand, for example, the detailed concern and deep division of opinion expressed by several *Rāmāyaṇa* commentators at 6.62.4 (= Vulgate 6.75.4) over the actual airspeed of Hanumān during his two round trip flights between Laṅkā and the Himālayas to fetch and replace the mountain of healing herbs or their continual obsession with and disagreements over the actual calendar dates of the various events, battles etc. described in the poem?

Thus a primary concern of the commentators who exert considerable influence on the textual and interpretive history of the poem from around the 12th century to the 17th is to validate the work as a basically unitary and internally consistent narrative of real events that, even if they took place in the most remote antiquity (the *tretāyuga*), nonetheless played out in real and calculable time in real geographic locations. This is not to say that they accepted everything in their received manuscripts as belonging to the authentic composition of the First Poet or, in consequence, as correct history. On the contrary they argue among themselves about many matters both philological and hermeneutic, declaring one passage or another to be either authentic (*pāṅkta*) or interpolated (*prakṣipta*) and engaging in interpretive disputation – often violent or mocking – with their predecessors. Although they may thus disagree – even sharply, on occasion[31] – with each other in these matters, the common goal of each is to edit, and explain the *Rāmāyaṇa* as a clear, unitary and internally consistent narrative of an exemplary and theologically significant history.

Like their traditionalist counterparts, western and western-trained Indologists have been alert to and interested in variants and

---

[31] Compare for example Mādhava Yogin's mocking critique of "Yaḍvābhaṭṭa" (apparently Govindarāja) and Satyatīrtha's constant and cutting refutation of the opinions of Maheśvaratīrtha and Nāgeśa Bhaṭṭa. For the commentary of Mādhava Yogin see the *Śrīmadvālmīkirāmāyaṇam* with *Amṛtakataka* of Mādhavayogi (1960-).

especially apparent contradictions in the epic narratives. However, unlike the *Rāmāyaṇa* commentators whose project leads them to rationalize and erase such differences, modern scholarship has tended to stress their importance even to the point of occasionally overstating it. This is because the philological goal has been to use these narrative differences as evidence for the position that instead of being the unitary and internally consistent historical narratives of single authors, the *Rāmāyaṇa* and the Mbh are instead complex, digressive and often carelessly compiled products of many bards, redactors and scribes living and working in different times and places.

Thus, for western scholars, apparent contradictions such as the one concerning the reason for Kumbhakarṇa's sleep can be read as the result of the complex and even chaotic textual history of these works with multiple variants being added in the absence of any single author or even any consistent and alert editorial agency that could prevent, eliminate or rationalize them. In keeping with this understanding, western students of the epic have often proposed the excision of passages on the grounds that their narratives conflicted with similar ones that were or appeared to be earlier or more authentic. This sort of variation, in Jacobi's terminology, could be used to demonstrate the *unechtheit* of a passage. In this way, for example Jacobi attempted to reject as ungenuine much of the central portion of the *Sundarakāṇḍa*.[32] In many cases, however, these excisions were subsequently shown to have no demonstrable basis in the critical editions of the poems produced by the scholars at the Oriental Institute in Vadodara and the Bhandarkar Oriental Research Institute in Pune respectively.

Both of these approaches to textual variance in the epics have yielded interesting results. The first has left us with a fascinating and useful corpus of textual exegesis that shows us how deeply imbedded the epics were in the complex cultural and intellectual universe of pre-modern Sanskrit scholarship. It demonstrates the

[32] For a discussion of this see Goldman 1998-99.

extraordinary intellectual and linguistic resources traditional scholars had at their disposal in pursuit of their hermeneutic project and it shows us with tremendous clarity how deeply important the understanding of what some might think of as extravagantly mythological tales as in fact consistent, genuine and verifiable history was and to a great extent still is, to Indian audiences.

By the same token, modern text-critical studies of the epics, many dealing with the kind of variation discussed above, has, despite its occasional excesses, of course contributed enormously to our scientific knowledge of both the genetic and receptive history of these endlessly fascinating texts.

But what the case of Kumbhakarṇa may well suggest to us is that both of these approaches may be reading too much into this type of variation. We should perhaps be neither overly concerned, as are the Sanskrit commentators, to rationalize such difference though ingenious *explication de texte* nor too quick, like some western students of the epic, to see them as the result of authorial carelessness, editorial inattention or disparate and isolated moments of production.

Instead, we may see them as contained within the rhetorical and performative parameters of epic composition and performance in which stories are repeated and revised in keeping with the specific local textual contexts in which they are embedded. Thus, although they may, in the end, tell us less than we would like about the textual history of the poems, they may encourage us to read them more carefully with our eyes now – like Kumbhakarṇa's – more fully awakened to the narrative and rhetorical strategies of their authors.

REFERENCES

Primary Sources

Mahābhārata (1929). 6 vols. With the commentary of Nīlakaṇṭha. Poona: Chitrashala Press.

Mahābhārata: Critical Edition (1933-70). 24 vols. With *Harivaṃśa* (1969-73). Critically edited by V. S. Sukthankar *et al.* Poona: BORI.

Ramayana, poema indiano di Valmici (1843-67). Edited by Gaspare Gorresio. Paris: Stamperia Reale.

The Ramayana of Valmeeki (1806-10). 3 vols. Serampore: Baptist Mission Press. Translated and edited by William Carey and Joshua Marshman.

The Rāmāyaṇa of Vālmīki (1930). With the commentary (*Tilaka*) of Rāma. Edited by Wāsudeva Laxmaṇ Śāstrī Paṇaśīkar. 4th rev. ed. Bombay: Nirṇayasāgar Press.

Rāmāyaṇ of Vālmīki (1914-20). With three commentaries called *Tilaka*, *Shiromani*, and *Bhooshana.* 7 vols. Edited by Shastri Shrinivas Katti Mudholkar. Bombay: Gujarati Printing Press.

Śrīmadvālmīkirāmāyaṇam with *Amṛtakataka* of Mādhavayogi (1960-). Vols. 1-4 and vol. 5 (unpublished). Vidvan K. S Varadacharya. Mysore. Oriental Research Institute.

Śrīmad Vālmīki-Rāmāyaṇa (1969). 3 vols. Gorakhpur: Gita Press.

Śrīmadvālmīkirāmāyaṇam (1911-13). (Also called the Kumbakonam Edition.) 7 vols. Edited by T. R. Krishnacharya and T. R. Vyasacharya. Bombay: Nirṇayasāgar Press.

Śrīmadvālmīkirāmāyaṇam (1935). 3 vols. With the commentaries of Govindarāja, Rāmānuja, and Maheśvaratīrtha and the commentary known as *Taniślokī.* Edited by Gaṅgāviṣṇu Śrīkṛṣṇadāsa. Bombay: Lakṣmīveṅkaṭeśvara Mudraṇālaya.

The Vālmīki Rāmāyaṇa: Critical Edition (1960-75). 7 vols. General editors: G. H. Bhatt and U. P. Shah. Baroda: Oriental Institute.

Secondary Sources

BUITENEN, J. A. B. van 1975. *The Mahābhārata: Books 2 and 3.* Chicago: The University of Chicago Press, 1975, pp. 213-214.

DUTT, M. N. (trans.) 1892. *The Ramayana.* Calcutta: Girish Chandra Chackravarti

BROCKINGTON, John L. 1984. *Righteous Rāma: The Evolution of an Epic.* Delhi: OUP.

BROCKINGTON, John 1998. *The Sanskrit Epics*. (Handbuch der Orientalistik, 2.12.) Leiden: E.J. Brill.

GOLDMAN, Robert P. (ed. & trans.) 1984. *The Rāmāyaṇa of Vālmīki: An Epic of Ancient India*, I: *Bālakāṇḍa*. Introduction by Robert P. Goldman. Annotation by Robert P. Goldman and Sally J. Sutherland. Princeton: Princeton University Press.

—— 1973. Akṛtavraṇa vs. Śrīkṛṣṇa as narrators of the legend of the Bhārgava Rāma *à propos* some observations of Dr. V. S. Sukthankar. *ABORI* 53: 161-173.

—— 1998-99. *Sundare kiṃ na sundaram*? The genetic and receptive histories of the *Sundarakāṇḍa* of the *Vālmīki Rāmāyaṇa*. *JOIB* 48.1-4: 83-106.

GOLDMAN, Robert P. & Sally J. Sutherland GOLDMAN (eds. & trans.) 1996. *The Rāmāyaṇa of Vālmīki: An Epic of Ancient India*, V: *Sundarakāṇḍa*. Introduction and annotation by Robert P. Goldman and Sally J. Sutherland Goldman. Princeton: Princeton University Press.

NARAYANA RAO, Velcheru 1991. A Rāmāyaṇa of their own: Women's oral tradition in Telugu. In: Paula Richman (ed.), *Many Rāmāyaṇas: The Diversity of a Narrative Tradition in South Asia*: 114-136. Berkeley: University of California Press.

RAGHAVAN, V. 1973. *The Greater Ramayana*. Varanasi: All India Kashiraj Trust.

SIMSON, Georg von 1968. The mythic origin of Droṇa and Karṇa. *Journal of the Bihar Research Society* 54: 40-44.

Sītā's War:
Gender and Narrative in the *Yuddhakāṇḍa* of Vālmīki's *Rāmāyaṇa*

SALLY J. SUTHERLAND GOLDMAN

The *Yuddhakāṇḍa* of Vālmīki's *Rāmāyaṇa* can be understood as a series of masculine struggles both physical and verbal (in the form of dialogues, debates, threats, boasts, and the like) between and among its male characters. These struggles reflect a multiplicity of ethical, familial, ethnic, and political dilemmas and stances played out in numerous embedded and interconnected narratives. The battles and dialogues of the *kāṇḍa* are largely controlled by the male characters of the epic, the former, though frequently quite graphic and gory, are generally mechanical – with their long lists of weapons and military paraphernalia – and somewhat repetitive, while the latter could be considered mind-numbingly technical and presuppose a deep familiarity with a broad range of śāstraic knowledge.

Nevertheless, at a number of junctures throughout this masculine narrative of violence and war, the feminine emerges, and it is these ruptures in the narrative on which this paper will focus. The female characters of the *Yuddhakāṇḍa* are limited to the *rākṣasīs*, either as individuals or as a group, and Sītā. Three named *rākṣasa* women are given voice (Saramā, Trijaṭā, and Mandodarī) and two in dialogue with Sītā (Saramā, Trijaṭā). Mandodarī, the wife of Rāvaṇa, is only given voice to lament her husband's death (*sarga*

99) and the *rākṣasī*s *en masse* are given voice to lament the death of their respective husbands (*sarga* 82), as are the wives of Rāvaṇa (*sarga* 98).[1]

Unquestionably, the most important and prevalent female presence in the *Yuddhakāṇḍa* is the heroine of the epic, Sītā. While there are numerous references in passing to the epic's heroine, Sītā is the subject (or perhaps more appropriately the object) of one *sarga* (5) and as a real or imagined figure, as it were, directly participates in five distinct episodes in the book (22-25; 37-38; 68; 80.41-49; 101-106) and is given voice in four of them (22-25; 37-38; 80.41-49; 101-106). It is my contention that these episodes rupture the main narrative of the *Yuddhakāṇḍa* marking crucial transitions and provide a feminine frame within which the masculine functions.

The *Yuddhakāṇḍa*'s narrative makes clear that both the protagonist Rāma and the antagonist Rāvaṇa have identified Sītā as the sole object of their respective desire. The opening *sarga*s of the narrative, however, although frequently referring to her, have as their primary focus not her male defenders. For example, Rāma, having heard from Hanumān of his adventures in Laṅkā and the discovery of the abducted Sītā (at the end of the *Sundarakāṇḍa* 63-66), praises Hanumān's accomplishments. The praise focuses not on the discovery of the princess as much as the protection of his lineage:

ahaṃ ca raghuvaṃśaś ca lakṣmaṇaś ca mahābalaḥ ǀ
vaidehyā darśanenādya dharmataḥ parirakṣitāḥ ǁ 10 ǁ

The discovery of Vaidehī has preserved powerful Lakṣmaṇa, the house of Raghu, and myself from unrighteousness. (6.1.10)

---

[1] The lament of the *rākṣasī*s *en masse* offers a fascinating critique of the epic's antagonist and the events of the epic as viewed through the eyes of women who have suffered the loss of sons, husbands, and relatives as well as a rare opportunity to hear women's voices. At one point in the *sarga* (verse 30), it appears as if only one voice is heard, as the word, *manye*, "I think", is introduced. In any case, these women, although allowed voice, are not given names or further marks of individuality.

Sītā is not forgotten, but rather redefined or perhaps reconstructed to address male concerns. Given the situation and company, such a contextualization is not only desirable, but expected.[2] As the story shifts from individuals to the forces of the monkeys, the narrative becomes even more masculine in its concerns. Led by Rāma and Lakṣmaṇa, who are carried on the shoulders of Aṅgada and Hanumān, the army, looking no less fearsome than the surge of a mighty ocean (6.4.11), begins its march to the shores of the ocean. References to Sītā become sparse to nonexistent, and with good reason, this is neither the time nor place for such thoughts. The narrative is dense in its description of the journey to the sea and once there, the fierce, seemingly impassible, ocean that must be crossed is described as awesome, fear-inspiring, and powerful. Thus the narrative of the *kāṇḍa*, with its surge of military might, opens by defining itself as masculine. The feminine, is introduced only as a mechanism through which to articulate fidelity, friendship, devotion, and patronage among Rāma's allies and friends.

After this theme of male bonding – physically marked by the fact that Rāma and Lakṣmaṇa ride on the backs of the monkeys – is firmly established, the narrative then takes a moment to expose a more emotionally vulnerable hero, one who cares deeply about his abducted wife. This switch in the tenor of the story is marked by Rāma now entering into conversation with his brother. Lakṣmaṇa, as he has earlier in the epic, serves here as a foil for Rāma's emotional outburst[3] and continues to do so here and throughout the *kāṇḍa*.[4] The placement of this pause in the narrative is significant. Not only have the masculine concerns of the narrative been firmly established, but the primacy and importance of the relationships between and among males has been foregrounded. That Lakṣmaṇa

---

[2] To focus on male concerns, in the company of males and on a march to battle is not surprising, in fact, I would argue that it is both culturally and contextually appropriate. See Goldman & Goldman 1996: 26-28.

[3] See R. Goldman 1980.

[4] See, for example, *sarga* 70.

is privy to Rāma's poignant outburst becomes, as we shall see, more meaningful as the *kāṇḍa* develops. In his soliloquy, which is really more of a lament, Rāma presents himself as very human, an emotional man, who is deeply in love with his wife. His profound and moving grief over her loss and his separation from her leave little room to doubt his love.

Vālmīki uses the physical boundary encountered by the army, that is the ocean, to provide a moment's respite from the intense preparations for war and the marshalling of the troops. He pauses to meditate for a moment on Rāma's plight as a lover separated from his beloved. The locus of Rāma's words, the ocean's edge, heightens the sense of physical separation between the two lovers. The passage, a beautifully constructed early example of *vipralambhaśṛṅgārarasa*, leaves little doubt that Rāma has a deep, all-consuming attachment to Sītā. From the beginning of the passage, we witness both the intense longing of the hero and the poet's creativity at work:

> *śokaś ca kila kālena gacchatā hy apagacchati* |
> *mama cāpaśyataḥ kāntām ahany ahani vardhate* || 4 ||
>
> They say that grief diminishes with the passage of time. But bereft as I am of the sight of my beloved, mine only increases day by day. (6.5.4)
>
> *vāhi vāta yataḥ kāntā tāṃ spṛṣṭvā mām api spṛśa*
> *tvayi me gātrasaṃsparśaś candre dṛṣṭisamāgamaḥ* || 6 ||
>
> Blow, breeze, where my beloved stays. Touch her, and then touch me. For the touching of our limbs now depends on you, as on the moon depends the meeting of our glances. (6.5.6)

Rāma professes that, because his love for Sītā is so great and his anguish at separation from her so profound, he would be willing to abandon his life. Without question, the poetry of the verses is intense and calls upon the heat of passion to be quenched by the waters, not of life, but death:

> *tadviyogendhanavatā taccintāvipulārciṣā* |
> *rātriṃdivaṃ śarīraṃ me dahyate madanāgninā* || 8 ||

avagāhyārṇavaṃ svapsye saumitre bhavatā vinā |
kathaṃcit prajvalan kāmaḥ samāsuptaṃ jale dahet || 9 ||

Night and day my body is consumed by the fire of love, whose fuel is my separation from her and whose towering flames are my constant brooding on her. (6.5.8)

I shall plunge into the ocean without you, Saumitri, and rest there. For it would be hard for the flame of desire to burn me were I to sleep in its waters. (6.5.9)

The words of these *śloka*s hark back to the *Sundarakāṇḍa*, where Hanumān, having given up hope for discovering Sītā, reflects on self-destruction (5.11.20-51). But the passage here, as laden with emotion as it is, also reminds the audience that Rāma's feelings for Sītā could also act as a barrier, like the ocean, to his ability to do what is right.

The passage also reminds us that Rāma's love is, to a great extent, based on the physical. Rāma laments not only the fact that the abducted Sītā is far away but that her youth is escaping during her long absence (6.5.5). He refers to her as the "lady of lovely thighs" (10), as "the fair-hipped one" (12), she, whose eyes are like "hundred-petaled lotuses" (12), her mouth is "lotus-like" and her breasts are "full and closely pressed" like "ripe palmyra fruit" (14). Her beauty is compared to that of Śrī, and looking upon her is like a tonic to an invalid. She is "dark-eyed" (15) and "naturally slender" (17). Though many of these are stock descriptions, their sheer number and density, and the corresponding lack of descriptive phrases emphasizing other qualities, gives precedence to the sensual, visual[5], and physical.

Rāma concludes his lament by making reference to Rāvaṇa and how he will slay him.

kadā nu rākṣasendrasya nidhāyorasi sāyakān |
sītāṃ pratyāhariṣyāmi śokam utsṛjya mānasam || 18 ||

[5] Note that the idea of being able to visualize or gaze upon one's beloved is a mark of ownership (S. Goldman 1997).

> When shall I bury my arrows in the breast of the lord of the *rākṣasa*s, so that I may bring Sītā back and thus banish the anguish in my heart? (6.5.18)

The *śloka*, with its direct reference to the demon king, can be understood both as a transition to the next *sarga*, where the scene switches to the court of Rāvaṇa and a fantasized revenge on the male who has deprived him of the sight of his wife. In the following *śloka*, Rama fantasizes about his reunion with his beloved:

> *kadā nu khalu māṃ sādhvī sītāmarasutopamā* |
> *sotkaṇṭhā kaṇṭham ālambya mokṣyaty ānandajaṃ jalam* || 19 ||

> When will virtuous Sītā, who is like a daughter of the immortal gods, clasp her arms eagerly about my neck, shedding tears of joy? (6.5.19)

The verse provides an ironic and emotional contrast to the reality of the harshness Rāma will inflict upon Sītā at the end of the *kāṇḍa*.

The *sarga*, which might seem somewhat out of place in the war-focused tale of the *Yuddhakāṇḍa*, is, I believe, structurally crucial to the narrative. Through its poetry of *vipralambhaśṛṅgāra-rasa* and obsession with the physical details of Sītā's body it provides, the *sarga* introduces the feminine world into the narrative.[6] This rupture of feminine difference leads us into the world of the *rākṣasa*s, as it does in the *Sundarakāṇḍa*.[7] In addition, the *sarga* has as its locus the ocean's shores while the language of the passage employs the ocean as metaphor. The narrative, reinforced by the poetic phrasing, uses the ocean to mark a transition into the *rākṣasa* realm, the realm of the other.[8] The dark, dreadful, unknown ocean surges between Rāma on one side and Rāvaṇa on the other, much as Sītā stands between the two rivals, rupturing, as it were, into the text. Finally Rāma's heart-felt musings over his beloved and fantasizing of their reunion, not only allow an opening

---

[6] Note both the feminization of the Other and of poetry here.

[7] See S. Goldman 2003.

[8] Note that the *Sundara*, too, uses the ocean as a transition (S. Goldman 2003).

frame for Sītā to emerge in the *kāṇḍa*, but reveal Rāma's emotional obsession with Sītā, an obsession that will find resolution in the closing *sarga*s of the *Yuddhakāṇḍa* in a manner that the audience least expects, given the tenor of this passage.

Immediately upon the conclusion of Rāma's lament, the scene changes to the court of the *rākṣasa*s; and the masculine concerns of the text are once more placed in the forefront. One of the more ironic juxtapositions of the *Yuddhakāṇḍa* occurs in this context, for we have just left a lamenting Rāma filled with anguish over the loss of his beloved Sītā and are next introduced to Rāvaṇa in his court, expounding the virtues of wise counsel and careful deliberation (6.6). Certainly the audience little expects the hero to have fallen under the sway of uncontrollable emotions, while the antagonist is the voice of calm reason.[9]

The following seventeen *sarga*s (including *sarga* 6) of the critical edition, and somewhat more in the vulgate[10], detail proceedings in the court of Rāvaṇa, including the advice of Vibhīṣaṇa to return Sītā and his defection to the camp of Rāma and the monkeys, the building and crossing of the bridge, and the reports of the spies Śuka, Sāraṇa, and Śārdūla concerning the arrival, encampment, and numbers of the monkey forces. The information provided by Rāvaṇa's spies and the advice given by the majority of his ministers cause the *rākṣasa* king some disquiet, and, in *sarga* 22, we are told that Rāvaṇa, having taken counsel, has become somewhat agitated (6.22.2: *jātodvego 'bhavat kiṃcit*).

It is at this juncture in the text that the feminine again ruptures the narrative. The scene is one of the better-known episodes of the *kāṇḍa*. It is here that Rāvaṇa, seemingly desperate to avoid the upcoming confrontation with Rāma and equally desperate to possess Sītā, attempts to delude her by means of magical powers into think-

---

[9] In the vulgate, at the resolution of the *kāṇḍa*, the inverse is true: Rāma is the voice of reason and Rāvaṇa falls victim to his emotions (GPP 6.92).

[10] Note here that the vulgate includes one *sarga* where Rāvaṇa's own lovesick state is described (GPP 6.11).

ing that Rāma has been already killed, before the battle has even begun.

The context of the passage is as important as its content to our understanding of how the narrative makes use of the feminine to mark critical junctures in the story. The detailed enumeration of the monkey forces has seemingly a twofold effect on Rāvaṇa: on one level it has agitated him, but on another he sees it as an opportunity to force Sītā finally to submit to him. Dismissing his ministers and counselors, Rāvaṇa summons Vidyujjihva, a *rākṣasa* skilled *māyā*, "magical illusion". Rāvaṇa orders Vidyujjihva to create through his magical powers an illusory replica of Rāma's severed head, as well as an illusory replica of Rāma's bow and arrows. With these, Rāvaṇa hopes to delude Sītā into thinking that Rāma has been slain. Rāvaṇa then approaches Sītā and, in "feigned delight" (*praharṣan nāma*)[11], tells her of the night attack that his forces directed against the army of the monkeys in which all of the latter were slaughtered along with Rāma and Lakṣmaṇa. The passage is made convincing by its specificity. Rāvaṇa describes in great detail the various monkey leaders – mostly the ones he had been so recently informed of – and the manners of their respective, but imaginary, deaths.

Ravaṇa's words here reflect a bit of poetic irony, in that earlier Rāma had fantasized the death of Rāvaṇa, and now Rāvaṇa fantasizes his. At the end of his description of the imaginary engagement, Rāvaṇa calls in Vidyujjihva, who enters bearing the illusory rep-

[11] In this phrase, found at 6.22.12, the particle *nāma* is understood in its sense of a marker of falsehood (*aparamārthe*). (See Mallinātha's comments on *Kumārasambhava* 5.32 for a similar usage.) The text of the southern commentators as well as a number of other northern and southern manuscripts, read the variant, *praharṣaṃ nāma*, which, if it is not taken as a *sandhi* variant of the critical reading, would make *praharṣam* the object of the verbal participle *kīrtayan*. Nāgojī and Kataka read *nāma* as we have done and explain that Rāvaṇa is falsely proclaiming his joy that is a result of his feigned victory over Rāma. Śivasahāya reads the accusative *praharṣam* adverbially and takes *nāma* then nominally as the object of the participle *kīrtayan*. He thus understands the clause to mean, "joyfully proclaiming his name". Govindarāja understands *praharṣam* metonymically for *praharṣavarttām*, and understands, "falsely proclaiming the joyful news". Maheśvaratīrtha understands, "joyfully calling out Sītā's name".

licas of Rāma's head and bow. The objects, with all their phallic imagery, mark Rāvaṇa as the possessor of the phallus, as it were, and by extension the possessor of the desired object Sītā. But, of course, such possession is merely illusory. During the *sarga*, Sītā is physically present but silent. Only the masculine voice is heard, deconstructing, as it were, the presence of the hero. Rāvaṇa's intention is clear:

> *chinnaṃ te sarvato mūlaṃ darpas te nihato mayā* |
> *vyasanenātmanaḥ sīte mama bhāryā bhaviṣyasi* || 14 ||
>
> I have completely undermined your grounds for refusing me and crushed your pride. As a result of you catastrophic loss, Sītā, you will have to become my wife. (6.22.14)

Rāvaṇa's harsh words bring the *sarga* to a close: *bhava me vaśānugā*, "You must be under my control (6.22.43). For the *Yuddhakāṇḍa*, the passage is significant, in that it is the first time that the magical arts have been employed. The *rākṣasas*' skills in the use of *māyā*, or magical illusion, have been in evidence earlier in the epic[12] and Sītā's inability to distinguish *māyā* from "reality", was early witnessed in the *Araṇyakāṇḍa* (3.40.31-32). *Māyā*, as we will discover, is intimately, but not exclusively, connected to the scenes in the *kāṇḍa* where Sītā, real or imagined, is present. Neither Rāvaṇa's resorting to such trickery nor Sītā's response to it are a surprise. The art of *māyā*, as we can see, permeates the world of the *rākṣasas*, and thus, the *kāṇḍa*. Outside of the *Rāmāyaṇa* tradition, the notion of *māyā* is well documented, both as a practical tool of "illusion" and a religious/philosophical concept. Generally *māyā per se* is conceived of as a neutral term; one that can and does belong to gods, demons, and even humans. However, it is most pervasively used with reference to the divinities and rather more rarely with the demonic world. The use of the term can be traced to the *Ṛgveda* where we find it associated with both Indra and with the

---

[12] Mārīca, for example, is commonly said to possess *māyā* (see 3.38.16, 3.40.31, 3.41.6, etc.)

demon Vṛtra.[13] According to Hopkins,[14] outside of the *Gītā*, where we see the term employed more as a philosophical concept in line with its use in the *Śvetāśvatara-upaniṣad*,[15] *māyā* in the *Mahābhārata* "is merely a trick of delusion indulged in by the gods (especially by the chief of illusion-gods Kṛṣṇa) for overcoming the enemy".[16] What is interesting in the context of the *Rāmāyaṇa* is that, unlike in the *Mahābhārata*, *māyā* is seemingly exclusively possessed, mastered, and employed by *rākṣasa*s and apparently only used in the sense of its older (Vedic) meaning of magical trick or illusion.

Note, too, the fact that the introduction into the text of *māyā* coincides with the first real appearance of a female character in the *kāṇḍa* is more than fortuitous. The word itself is feminine and is elsewhere personified as a feminine figure.[17] Rāvaṇa, though apparently skilled in its use, calls upon the services of another *rākṣasa* to create the illusion here, as he called upon Mārīca earlier. Later it is his son Indrajit who employs *māyā*.[18]

Sītā, upon seeing the head of her beloved Rāma and not able to tell that it is a mere illusion, collapses to the ground. Regaining consciousness after a moment (6.23.7: *muhūrtāt samāśvasya*), Sītā thinks that her lord is dead, and for the first time in the *sarga*, is given voice in order to express her sorrow. Note that the last time Rāma spoke was to lament his separation from her.[19] But before

---

[13] See ṚV 10.54.2, where Indra's battles are called illusions; ṚV 3.53.8 and 6.47.18 which ascribe Indra's taking on forms to his *māyās*. See, too, Goudriaan 1978: 5-15; Radhakrishnan 1952: 43, 45.

[14] Hopkins 1901: 138 ff.

[15] The term is found in the *Śvetāśvatara-upaniṣad* (4.10) and used in the sense of "illusion", where the Lord of all beings is called *māyāvin*.

[16] Radhakrishnan 1952: 105, n. 3; Hopkins 1901: 138.

[17] Māyā is, of course, the name of the Buddha's mother, and is also used as an epithet of Lakṣmī and Durgā (see *Bhāgavatapurāṇa* 2.3.3: *devīṃ māyāṃ tu*). Compare, too, Yogamāyā in *Bhāgavatapurāṇa* 10.4.

[18] It is probably no accident that the conqueror of Indra (*indra-jit*), would, like that god himself, be in possession of *māyā*.

voicing her grief, in a fervent, Salome type gesture, she kisses the severed head of Rāma. The lament is passionate and in full keeping with the tenor of Sītā's soliloquies found in the *Sundarakāṇḍa* and of those of others in the epic.[20] Of course, Sītā's grief arises from her delusion. At this juncture, before Rāvaṇa is provided an opportunity to reply, the scene is interrupted by the entrance of a messenger telling him that his general Prahasta has arrived on an urgent matter. The *sarga* ends as Rāvaṇa, departing in haste, gives the orders to assemble the troops for battle. As soon as Rāvaṇa leaves the grove, the head and bow vanish (6.23.38). While the illusory images conjured up by the demon have disappeared, Sītā's delusion has not.

The following two *sarga*s (24-25), both of which have as one of their main characters, Saramā, Sītā's *rākṣasī* friend and companion, continue the feminine rupture of the narrative. Both *sarga*s appear very similar on the surface, as Saramā comforts Sītā and heralds the victory of Rāma. In the first (24), the action continues in the *aśoka* grove, where Sītā is described as utterly confused. The adjective used by the text is *mohitām*, literally, "deluded, confused". Saramā's role is somewhat similar to that of Trijaṭā in the *Sundarakāṇḍa*, where the elderly *rākṣasī* provides comfort and foretells Rāvaṇa's defeat (5.25.4-39). Here Saramā has resorted to old-fashion eavesdropping: she has spied on Rāvaṇa and has overheard the conversation between Rāvaṇa and Sītā (6.24.4-5). Comforting Sītā, she assures her that "it would be impossible" to actually slay Rāma or Lakṣmaṇa (6.24.7) and that all this was a trick of Rāvaṇa's (6.24.12). Sītā is given no voice whatsoever in

---

[19] Note, too, that the other female characters of the *kāṇḍa* are primarily given voice to lament (see above, and footnote 1).

[20] S. Goldman 2001. Of particular note is that she, as a good wife (see, too, Sutherland 1991), blames herself for his death, grieving,

tathā tvaṃ saṃpariṣvajya raudrayātinṛśaṃsayā |
kālarātryā mayācchidya hṛtaḥ kamalalocanaḥ ||

"Having fallen into my clutches – I whom am the fierce and pitiless Kālarātrī, the dark night of universal destruction – you, a lotus-eyed hero, have been thus cut down and carried off." (6.23.15)

this first *sarga.* Saramā, the *rākṣasī*, possesses the knowledge and the voice with which the *māyā* of Vidyujjihva, and by extension Rāvaṇa, can be dispelled.

Saramā's speech consists of two distinct parts. The first (verses 4-17) takes the form of a panegyric to Rāma [and Lakṣmaṇa], letting Sītā know that her husband is alive and well and that he and his troops have crossed the ocean and arrived in Laṅkā. These verses are interrupted when the two women hear the sounds of troops making preparations for war. In the second half (verses 20-36) Saramā tells Sītā what the noises she has heard mean and points out to Sītā the various signs of the *rākṣasa*s' preparations for war. Vālmīki has cleverly crafted the passage. While on the one hand Saramā's direct discourse brings the sounds of the troops marshalling to our attention and makes more immediate the preparations for war, these descriptions of the most masculine of activities are articulated through a feminine voice. Saramā's closing words anticipate the union between the separated lovers. Much as Rāma had fantasized his joyous meeting with Sītā, so Saramā reminds Sītā of what the future will hold when Rāma is victorious.

avajitya jitakrodhas tam acintyaparākramaḥ I
rāvaṇaṃ samare hatvā bhartā tvādhigamiṣyati II 28 II
vikramiṣyati rakṣaḥsu bhartā te sahalakṣmaṇaḥ I
yathā śatruṣu śatrughno viṣṇunā saha vāsavaḥ II 29 II
āgatasya hi rāmasya kṣipram aṅkagatāṃ satīm I
ahaṃ drakṣyāmi siddhārthāṃ tvāṃ śatrau vinipātite II 30 II
aśrūṇy ānandajāni tvaṃ vartayiṣyasi śobhane I
samāgamya pariṣvaktā tasyorasi mahorasaḥ II 31 II
acirān mokṣyate sīte devi te jaghanaṃ gatām I
dhṛtām etāṃ bahūn māsān veṇīṃ rāmo mahābalaḥ II 32 II
tasya dṛṣṭvā mukhaṃ devi pūrṇacandram ivoditam I
mokṣyase śokajaṃ vāri nirmokam iva pannagī II 33 II
rāvaṇaṃ samare hatvā nacirād eva maithili I ...
samāgatā tvaṃ rāmeṇa modiṣyasi mahātmanā I
suvarṣeṇa samāyuktā yathā sasyena medanī II 35 II

When your inconceivably valorous husband, who has subdued his anger, has defeated and slain Rāvaṇa in battle, he will surely take you back. (6.24.28.)

Together with Lakṣmaṇa, your husband will defeat the *rākṣasas* just as that slayer of his foes, Vāsava, together with Viṣṇu, did his enemies. (29)

Soon Rāma will come, and I shall see you seated upon his lap, your enemy slain and all your wishes fulfilled. (30)

Lovely lady, once you are reunited and in his tight embrace, you will shed tears of joy on the chest of that broad-chested hero. (31)

Soon, Sītā, my lady, mighty Rāma will unbind the braid – falling to your waist – that you have worn these many months. (32)

Once you see his face, my lady, which is like the full moon newly risen, you will abandon these tears born of your sorrow, as a female serpent sheds her skin. (33)

Very soon, Maithilī, Rāma will slay Rāvaṇa in battle. (34ab)

Once you are reunited with Rāma, you will rejoice with that great man, just as the earth does with its ample crops when watered with copious rains (35)

Saramā paints a picture of the reunion of the hapless couple – joyous, with tears of happiness flowing and with tight embraces, imagined renewal, and fecundity – echoing Rāma's own earlier feelings. The words of both Sītā and Saramā parallel those of Rāma. Here, Sītā's all-consuming passion is reinforced. Nevertheless, deluded, she cannot see the possibility of reunion, while Saramā, who is able to see through the *māyā*, must remind her of that very possibility.

The last *sarga* of the episode appears to be largely a continuation of the former one, but here Sītā, who had been "deluded", again the word used is *mohitām*,[21] and is suffering (*jātasaṃtāpāḥ*), is revitalized (*prahlādayāmāsa*) by the *rākṣasī*'s words that call to mind Rāma. No longer "deluded", and again given voice, she is further comforted and aided by the *rākṣasī*. Sītā blames her delusion on the *rākṣasa*,

sa hi māyābalaḥ krūro rāvaṇaḥ śatrurāvaṇaḥ |
māṃ mohayati duṣṭātmā pītamātreva vāruṇī || 8 ||

For cruel and wicked Rāvaṇa, who makes his enemies cry out, is a master of illusion. He robbed me of my senses, as does wine the moment you drink it. (6.25.8)

---

[21] Cf. *Bhagavadgītā* 7.13-15 where Kṛṣṇa says the whole world is *mohita*.

The spell that entranced Sītā is now broken, and she can now function in a manner that will best aid her lord and sends Saramā to spy on Rāvaṇa. Returning, the *rākṣasī* tells the princess of the events, especially the preparations for war, taking place in Rāvaṇa's court. This passage parallels the structure of the preceding *sarga*. For here, too, Saramā spies on Rāvaṇa and then comforts Sītā. The two *sarga*s, however, serve different purposes. The goal of the first is to dissipate Sītā's confusion or delusion. In aid of this, Saramā reassures Sītā that Rāma will be victorious, reflects on the glory, power, and strength of Rāma, and predicts Sītā's longed for reunion with Rāma. Even though Saramā says that she has spied on Rāvaṇa, we are told little of the events in the *rākṣasa*'s court.[22] This latter *sarga*, on the other hand, has a far more practical goal. Here, Saramā actually reports on Rāvaṇa and what she has observed in the court, information potentially valuable for Rāma's forces. Here, too, Saramā cautions Sītā that Rāvaṇa is himself so "befuddled by his impending doom (*mṛtyulobhāt*)" that he is not capable of returning her (6.25.25). The *sarga* ends with the sound of the *bherī* drums and conches of the monkeys blasting forth so loudly, that the *rākṣasa*s, on hearing it, sink into depression, as "they foresaw no good arising from the crimes of their king" (25.27-28).

Note the transformation in the episode: The passage starts with a confident and proud Rāvaṇa, who intimidates and "deludes" Sītā, but as the passage continues, Rāvaṇa becomes agitated, and is finally, described as "befuddled". Sītā, who is at first, "deluded", slowly awakens from her confusion, and sees once again that her husband will rescue her and defeat the forces of evil. Clear-headed, she can, by the end of the episode, even participate in a plan that will aid her lord's efforts. The insertion of this episode has marked movement in the narrative from the siege of Laṅkā to the onset of the battle and marked transition in the character primarily of

---

[22] Mention is made of Rāvaṇa's own mother and his counselor Aviddha who are said to urge the return of Sītā (25.20-22).

Rāvaṇa but also of Sītā. Moreover, the passage introduces Sītā's emotional dependency on Rāma, her susceptibility to *māyā*, and the mechanism, here in the form of advice from a good *rākṣasī*, through which *māyā* can be dispelled.

At this point the narrative shifts first back to the court of Rāvaṇa, then to Rāma's camp, the siege of Laṅkā, and finally to the beginning of the hostilities – that is back to a "masculine narrative". The battle is bloody, so much so that it cannot be compared to any other (GPP 6.42.47). Eventually, Aṅgada battles Indrajit, who, finally resorting to *māyā*, makes himself invisible and is thus able to strike down for the first time Rāma and Lakṣmaṇa, covering them in a net of arrows. Indrajit, who is here called *mahāmāya*,[23] thinking that he has killed the two heroes, victoriously returns to the city of Laṅkā. The monkeys, in turn, sink into corresponding depression and dejection (6.36.24-25), only to be comforted and reassured by the *rākṣasa* Vibhīṣaṇa (6.36.26-37). That Rāma and Lakṣmaṇa have fallen under the spell of *māyā* once they have entered into the *rākṣasa* realm has been foreshadowed by Sītā's own succumbing to its power earlier.

It is at this juncture (*sarga* 37) that we once again see the feminine reinsert itself into the narrative. As the monkeys stand guard over the two brothers, Rāvaṇa, delighted and thinking that they lie slain on the battlefield, summons the *rākṣasa* women guarding Sītā, including Trijaṭā. He commands them to take Sītā in his flying palace, the Puṣpaka, and show her the bodies of Rāma and Lakṣmaṇa lying inert on the field.

yadāśrayād avaṣṭabdhā neyaṃ mām upatiṣṭhati ।
so 'syā bhartā saha bhrātrā nirasto raṇamūrdhani ॥ 8 ॥
nirviśaṅkā nirudvignā nirapekṣā ca maithilī ।
mām upasthāsyate sītā sarvābharaṇabhūṣitā ॥ 9 ॥

[23] GPP 6.46.45 as is Viṣṇu at Mbh 12.325.4 – *mahāmāyādhāraḥ*. Note to that a similar epithet is used of Kumbhakarṇa in the *Rāmopākhyāna* by Māyāvī at 3.259.11.

> That husband of hers relying on whom she stubbornly spurned me, has been destroyed along with his brother in the vanguard of battle. (6.37.8)
>
> Now Sītā Maithilī, free from anxiety, longing, and hope, and adorned with all manner of jewelry will surely come to me. (6.37.9)

Rāvaṇa, still intent on possessing Sītā, appears himself to be under a misapprehension, or perhaps a bit deluded, for the heroes are alive, and Sītā, as we know, would rather die than come under his sway.

As Sītā is reintroduced into the narrative, and delusion once again permeates the text. Not only have Rāma and Lakṣmaṇa fallen under the power of Indrajit's *māyā* and are lying unconscious, but both Indrajit and Rāvaṇa are under the misapprehension that the two heroes are dead. Sītā, too, once again is convinced that her lord has been slain, for, upon seeing them, "she assumes that they were dead" (6.37.21: *vitarkayantī nidhanaṃ tayoḥ*).

Here the structure of the episode parallels that of the earlier one, where first Sītā speaks, and then is reassured by her confidant, here the *rākṣasī* Trijaṭā, that her husband is not dead. Sītā once again begins to lament her situation, but here, rather than focus on her lord directly, she focuses on herself, literally.

As the *sarga* opens, the princess questions the veracity of those scholars who know the science of bodily signs:

> *ūcur lakṣaṇikā ye māṃ putriṇy avidhaveti ca* |
> *te 'dya sarve hate rāme 'jñānino*[24] *'nṛtavādinaḥ* ‖ 2 ‖
>
> Those scholars who know the science of bodily signs said that I would bear sons and never be a widow. Now that Rāma has been slain, it is clear that all those wise men spoke falsely. (6.38.2)

The attack on tradition continues in the next two *śloka*s as Sītā further accuses the prognosticators of [falsely] telling her that she would be a chief queen (3), and the fortunate wife of a heroic king (4). She feels that their words are completely fallacious and mean-

---

[24] The critical text has been emended here. See Goldman, Goldman & van Nooten 2008, note to 6.38.2.

ingless (7, 8). Sītā then details her various body parts and complains that the prognosticators [falsely] claimed that they were auspicious:

> *keśāḥ sūkṣmāḥ samā nīlā bhruvau cāsaṃgate mama* |
> *vṛtte cālomaśe jaṅghe dantāś cāviralā mama* || 9 ||
> *śaṅkhe netre karau pādau gulphāv ūrū ca me citau* |
> *anuvṛttā nakhāḥ snigdhāḥ samāś cāṅgulayo mama* || 10 ||
> *stanau cāviralau pīnau mamemau magnacūcukau* |
> *magnā cotsaṅginī nābhiḥ pārśvoraskaṃ ca me citam* || 11 ||

> My hair is fine, even, and dark. My eyebrows do not meet. My legs are smooth and tapering, and my teeth are closely set. (6.38.9)
>
> My temples, eyes, hands, feet, ankles, and thighs are nicely developed. My nails are rounded and glossy; my fingers and toes are well proportioned. (10)
>
> My breasts, their nipples sunken, are full and closely set. My navel is deep with sloping sides. My chest and sides are nicely developed. (11)

Even as Sītā mentions her beloved Rāma at the conclusion of her lament, the focus of her concern is still herself, not her husband:

> *adṛśyamānena raṇe māyayā* [*vāsavopamau*] |
> *mama nāthāv anāthāyā nihatau rāmalakṣmaṇau* || 17 ||

> My two protectors, Rāma and Lakṣmaṇa ... have been slain in battle through the power of illusion by an invisible force. Now there is no one to protect me. (6.38.17)

Sītā in her despair, finally giving up all hope says:

> *na kālasyātibhāro 'sti kṛtāntaś ca sudurjayaḥ* |

> I see that nothing is beyond the power of Kāla and it is impossible to avert one's destiny. (6.38.19ab)

The detail and nature of the bodily description are quite remarkable and have parallels elsewhere in the epic.[25] The passage provides a clear articulation of the ideal woman, and, of course, marks Sītā as that woman. Sītā's disavowal of the reliability of the *śāstra* and its practitioners is recognized as misguided by the audience, who

---

[25] It parallels similar *sarga*s of the *Sundarakāṇḍa* (5.33.15-19), where Rāma is described, and Mbh 4.8.9-14 where Draupadī's body is detailed.

know the eventual outcome of the story. Her lack of faith is yet another effect of the *māyā* under which Sītā has fallen. Rhetorically then, these words, as a sort of *via negativa*, highlight once again Sītā's inability to perceive "what really is", even though the means to that truth, i.e., her own bodily signs, are not just right before her but, in fact, part of her. That this inability is associated with the heroine who is here "human" and "female" is probably no accident. Then again, the character of Sītā is one with which the audience can identify, a person lost, unable to discern truth from falsehood, while others – prognosticators and friends – can. Sītā's earlier soliloquy focuses on the heroine's attachment to and dependence on her husband. Here, however, it focuses outward and challenges the very structure of her social/political universe.

Once again, the misconception or misunderstanding of reality by Sītā is deconstructed by a *rākṣasī* confidant. Urging Sītā not to despair and reassuring her that her husband lives (6.38.22-23), the *rākṣasī* proceeds to point out to Sītā the various signs that mark the heroes as still living.[26] Noting that the two have only been "defeated in battle by the power of illusion" (6.38.27), Trijaṭā calls to Sītā's attention the most important sign of all, viz., "their vital glow has not left them" (6.38.31). Finally, Trijaṭā urges:

> *tyaja śokaṃ ca duḥkhaṃ ca mohaṃ ca janakātmaje* |
> *rāmalakṣmaṇayor arthe nādya śakyam ajīvitum* || 33 ||
>
> So, daughter of Janaka, you must give up your grieving, pain, and delusion on account of Rāma and Lakṣmaṇa. For it is not possible that they could have been killed this day. (6.38.33)

Trijaṭā, like Sītā, resorts to physical signs to indicate that the heroes are not slain but, in fact, temporarily *māyayā nirjitau* "defeated by the power of illusion". The *rākṣasī* refers to both the two brothers and Sītā as being "deluded". While this episode is similar to the previous one in its structure and narrative disruption, it differs

[26] For example, that their troops are animated and angry (6.38.24), rather than confused or despondent (6.38.27).

significantly in a number of aspects. Earlier, the episode depicts an "illusory" Rāma (the real Rāma never participates in the episode), while here Rāma and Lakṣmaṇa are physically present, but not conscious, being themselves under the power of *māyā*. In both episodes Sītā is given voice, and is present, although unable on her own to see past the *rākṣasa*'s *māyā*.

Sītā's final words and gestures indicate hope rather than conviction:

> *kṛtāñjalir uvācedam evam astv iti* [*maithilī*] ॥ 34 ॥
>
> ... she cupped her hands in reverence and said this, "May it be so." (6.38.34cd)

The *sarga* ends with the ladies returning to the *aśokavana* and Sītā sinking again into "profound despair" (6.38.37). This episode presents to us a heroine who has lost her faith. The confidence of the heroine displayed at the end of the preceding episode has faded. Sītā remains vulnerable to the power of *māyā*, while her *rākṣasī* confidant has the power to dispel its effects. Much like his beloved wife, Rāma (and Lakṣmaṇa) is literally "unconscious" under the power of *māyā*. The *sarga* again marks a transition, functioning as a harbinger of Rāma's own emotional struggles.

The narrative of the following *sarga* (39) reverts to the battlefield where Rāma awakes, finds Lakṣmaṇa laid low on the field, and grieves over his condition. The *sarga* functions as a transition back to the male narrative and is reminiscent of Rāma's earlier lament (*sarga* 5) as well as Sītā's more recent words (*sarga* 38). It is only in the context of the larger masculine narrative that we are able to understand how Vālmīki has carefully constructed his story to make use of the feminine voice so effectively. As the narrative reveals the object of Rāma's affection is not his wife, but rather his brother. Much as Sītā thinks that Rāma and Lakṣmaṇa have been slain, so, too, does Rāma think that Lakṣmaṇa lies dead on the battlefield. Under this misconception, the hero gives way to hopelessness and despondency. Important to our concerns in this passage is Rama's well-known valuation of Lakṣmaṇa's life over Sītā's that is so fully articulated at this juncture in the narrative.

kiṃ nu me sītayā kāryaṃ kiṃ kāryaṃ jīvitena vā I
śayānaṃ yo 'dya paśyāmi bhrātaraṃ yudhi nirjitam II 5 II
śakyā sītāsamā nārī prāptuṃ loke vicinvatā I
na lakṣmaṇasamo bhrātā sacivaḥ sāṃparāyikaḥ II 6 II

What do I care for Sītā or even for my life itself now that I see my brother lying defeated in battle? (6.39.5)
Were I to search the world, I could find another woman like Sītā, but never a brother, a counselor, or a warrior equal to Lakṣmaṇa. (6.39.6)

Rāma, in words very reminiscent of Sītā's, vows not to continue living if Lakṣmaṇa is indeed dead:

parityakṣyāmy ahaṃ prāṇān vānarāṇāṃ tu paśyatām I
yadi pañcatvam āpannaḥ [*sumitrānandavardhanaḥ*] II 7 II

If Lakṣmaṇa ... has indeed returned to the elements, then I shall abandon my life breaths right before the eyes of the monkeys. (6.39.7)

But note the change we see in Rāma. At the opening of the *kāṇḍa* these were the very sentiments that he expressed at the thought of loss or separation from Sītā. Here the focus of his affections has changed. Finally, having praised the heroic efforts of the monkeys Rāma tells them,

mitrakāryaṃ kṛtam idaṃ bhavadbhir vānararṣabhāḥ I
anujñātā mayā sarve yatheṣṭaṃ gantum arhatha II 29 II

Bulls among monkeys! You have discharged the obligations of friendship. I therefore give you all leave. You may go as you please. (6.39.29)

In an attempt to prevent this, Vibhīṣaṇa approaches, but the monkeys all flee in terror of Rāma's demonic ally, misidentifying him as Indrajit.

Much as Sītā has given up hope for Rāma, so has Rāma given up hope for his brother Lakṣmaṇa. Sītā's own emotional state has set the tone for Rāma's. Important, too, for the narrative structure is that we witness yet another critical juncture in the text. The introduction of the feminine into the narrative at this juncture has marked a crucial transition: We have moved from the first frenzy and excitement of battle, to the realities of conflict and the seeming hopelessness of the project. Rāma realizes that without his brother Lakṣmaṇa, Sītā has no value for him, and that the war and even his life are not worth continuing. Rāma's dejection is so complete that it will take a *deus* [*avis*?] *ex machina*, in the form of Garuḍa, to literally rescue the mission. Rāma's words are eerily reminiscent of those he used to lament his lost Sītā at the opening of the *kāṇḍa* and a haunting premonition of those he will use later to reject Sītā in the *kāṇḍa*'s closing moments. This episode presents to us a heroine who has lost her faith and trust in her world. And this depiction of Sītā is not haphazard on the part of Vālmīki but signals once again a transition in the masculine narrative. Additionally the episode presents Rāma gaining consciousness, but still bound by the "snake-arrows" of Indrajit's *māyā*, confronting for the first time the true hazards of sending friends and relatives to battle for the sake of a woman. The audience is well prepared for the despondency and despair of Rāma and the monkeys, for it is the hopelessness of which Sītā's own rupture into the narrative has warned.

The next *sarga*s, indeed, reflect the darkest moments of the battle that Vālmīki presents to his audience. One by one, Rāvaṇa sends forth his great generals, brothers, and son to fight the monkey forces. Each time the monkeys are victorious, but only after great struggle and loss. Each time a *rākṣasa* is defeated, a stronger and more powerful one is ordered out to fight. Finally, Rāvaṇa sends forth Indrajit once again. The latter wreaks havoc on the monkey forces, laying low once again the two heroes (this time revivified by Hanumān who fetches the mountain of herbs) and the entire army with the exception of Jāmbavān, Vibhīṣaṇa, Hanumān, and Sugrīva. Revivified for a second time, the army continues its assault, but the magical power of Indrajit, through which he is made invisible in battle, proves too great for the monkey forces.

Rāghava, realizing this, begins to contemplate a method whereby Indrajit can be defeated, a mechanism whereby he can neutralize Indrajit's magical powers (6.67.37-42). Once again the figure of Sītā ruptures the narrative; the feminine source of the very battle, emerges on to the most masculine of sites, the battlefield. Indrajit creates an "illusory" Sītā (6.68.4: *sītāṃ māyāmayīm*) and in front of the entire monkey army, led by Hanumān:

> *tad vānarabalaṃ dṛṣṭvā rāvaṇiḥ krodhamūrchitaḥ* |
> *kṛtvā vikośaṃ nistriṃśaṃ mūrdhni sītāṃ parāmṛśat* || 14 ||
> *tāṃ striyāṃ paśyatāṃ teṣāṃ tāḍayāmāsa rāvaṇiḥ* |
> *krośantīṃ rāma rāmeti māyayā yojitāṃ rathe* || 15 ||
>
> But when Indrajit Rāvaṇi spied the monkey hosts, he was beside himself with rage. Unsheathing his sword, he seized Sītā by the head. (6.68.14)
>
> Then right before their eyes, Indrajit Rāvaṇi struck that woman, whom he had conjured up in his chariot through his power of magical illusion, as she cried, "Rāma, Rāma". (6.68.15)

and finally,

> *tam evam uktvā rudatīṃ sītāṃ māyāmayīṃ tataḥ* |
> *śitadhāreṇa khaḍgena nijaghānendrajit svayam* || 28 ||
> *yajñopavītamārgeṇa chinnā tena tapasvinī* |
> *sā pṛthivyāṃ pṛthuśroṇī papāta priyadarśanā* || 29 ||
>
> Indrajit himself slew the wailing, illusory Sītā, with his sharp-edged sword. (6.68.28)
>
> Hacked in two from her shoulder to her waist, the poor woman, so beautiful and broad-hipped, fell to the ground. (6.68.29)

Unable to discern that the figure slain was only a magical illusion, Hanumān and the monkeys sink into profound despair. Enraged at the heinous act, Hanumān rallies the monkey troops (who had once again fled the battle) and they savagely attack the *rākṣasa* forces and seem ready to defeat them, when Hanumān orders a retreat, declaring further fighting unnecessary since Janaka's daughter has been slain. Hanumān returns to tell Rāma what he had seen, and Rāma, upon hearing the news, loses consciousness, eventually to be revived not by his brother but the *rākṣasa* Vibhīṣaṇa, who convinces him that Indrajit could not have slain Sītā and that the slaying was merely an illusion.

The episode is an inversion of the earlier passage, where Sītā, seeing Rāma's severed head, was "tricked" into thinking that he had been slain. In both passages, however, it is a *rākṣasa* who must finally dispel the *māyā*. Only Vibhīṣaṇa's words bring Rāma out of his swoon and reassure him that Sītā lives, and it is only the *rākṣasa* who knows the secret of Indrajit's power of *māyā* and how to defeat it. Following this incident, with the aid of Vibhīṣaṇa, Rāma and Lakṣmaṇa are able to devise a plan to block Indrajit from accessing his power of magical illusion. Once this is accomplished, Indrajit and then Rāvaṇa can be defeated. Like the earlier episodes, this appearance of Sītā, albeit here in an illusory form, marks a crucial transition in the text, wherein Rāma, unable heretofore to defeat the forces of evil that control the power of *māyā*, can now break their hold over him. While the use of *māyā* in the *kāṇḍa* has been linked to the feminine narrative, here *māyā* is literally mapped onto the female body.[27] Only when Rāma has overcome his "delusion" about Sītā, and the control that that delusion has held over him, can the battle with the enemies of righteousness, who possess the powers of *māyā*, be won.

Sītā appears and is given voice only once more in the narrative while still in the hands of Rāvaṇa. The *rākṣasa*s have suffered numerous defeats, and finally their most crippling blow has come with the slaying of Rāvaṇa's son Indrajit. His death at the hands of Lakṣmaṇa (78) has caused Rāvaṇa to sink into profound dismay, followed by unequalled rage (16-22). At *sarga* 80 he turns his wrath on Sītā, resolving to kill her to avenge his son's death (29). Swearing to turn Indrajit's hoax into reality (31-32), he races through the palace, sword drawn, in order to slay Sītā (34). Sītā, seeing the enraged Rāvaṇa approaching her with upraised sword, laments her

---

[27] Earlier, of course, it was mapped onto Rāma's body, or at least his head. This is logical within the narrative, since Rāma was at that juncture in the narrative still susceptible to the power of *māyā*.

fate once more, reflecting upon her helpless condition and the possibility of her death or, more significantly, her husband's. Her concern turns outward, toward her husband's mother.

> *manye tu hṛdayaṃ tasyāḥ kausalyāyāḥ phaliṣyati* ।
> *ekaputrā yadā putraṃ vinaṣṭaṃ śroṣyate yudhi* ॥ 46 ॥
> *sā hi janma ca bālyaṃ ca yauvanaṃ ca mahātmanaḥ* ।
> *dharmakāryāṇi rūpaṃ ca rudatī saṃsmariṣyati* ॥ 47 ॥

> I think that the heart of Kausalyā will burst when she, who has only one son, hears that her son has been slain in battle. (6.80.46)
> Weeping, she will remember the birth, childhood, and youth of that great man, as well as his beauty and his righteous deeds. (6.80.47)

The passage is brief, but remarkable given the heroine's character in the earlier passages. There is no *rākṣasī* attendant to provide her support, nor is she merely an illusory figure or deluded. Here, too, she is given voice, although she speaks only to herself. The *sarga* is notable in that it is the first appearance of Sītā in the epic wherein the presence of *māyā*, although mentioned, is not employed, having apparently lost all of its power with the demise of Indrajit. Rāvaṇa's uncontrollable anger focused on Sītā depicts the complete change in emotional tenor of the *kāṇḍa*. Rāvaṇa, who is overwhelmed with grief for his son and whose grief has turned to unprecedented rage at Sītā, is completely unfit for battle. Sītā's depiction as free from delusion and free from the illusory effects of the *rākṣasa* world, prefigures Rāma's own newfound release from delusion that allows him to finally meet and defeat Rāvaṇa in battle. Sītā, resigned to death, focuses not inward on herself, but outward toward the patriarchy, and once again on her husband's family.

With this understanding, the harsh treatment of Sītā at the end of the *kāṇḍa*, the final locus of her appearance in the narrative, which constitutes the last feminine rupture of the *kāṇḍa*, becomes logical and necessary. The longed-for reunion of the two lovers is anything but the joyous one prophesied by her two *rākṣasī* confidants and fantasized by Rāma and Sītā. But the audience has been prepared for this, as the sequence of feminine ruptures of the narrative has marked transitional moments in the text. This series of ruptures has marked both Sītā and Rāma as mutually obsessed, deluded, as it were, with the other. But Sītā, during her unwilling sojourn in the world of the *rākṣasas*, has been caught up in their illusory world, and is released from it only when it is destroyed. Rāma, on the other hand, who at the outset of the *kāṇḍa* is depicted as completely focused on Sītā, is able to move from that obsession to understanding the potentially destructive nature of his longing and finally to overcoming it.

The final rupture in the narrative by the feminine voice occurs in *sargas* 101-106, where we finally see the couple reunited. The narrative clearly places the political above the emotional, following the fall of Rāvaṇa, and prior even to mentioning Sītā. Rāma installs Vibhīṣaṇa on the throne in Laṅkā. Only after Vibhīṣaṇa's coronation (*sarga* 100), does Rāma instruct Hanumān to inquire after Sītā and to take her a message of the good tidings (6.100.22).[28] Her words to husband, like those of her husband's to her, are first mediated through the figure of Hanumān and then that of Vibhīṣaṇa. Overjoyed at the news brought by Hanumān, Sītā becomes momentarily speechless (6.101.15: *nirvakyāsmi kṣaṇāntaram*) and finally responds that there is nothing in the world that is as great as the news he has brought. Finally Hanumān begs Sītā for a message that he might give to Rāma (39), and she responds:

> ... *draṣṭum icchāmi bhartāraṃ vānarottama* || 40 ||
>
> I wish to see my lord, o best of monkeys. (6.101.40)

Hanumān returns with her message, and a graphic description of the forlorn Sītā (6.101.1-5). However, rather than first rushing to see his beloved, Rāma,

[28] Of course, the choice of Hanumān as his messenger to Sītā is not unexpected given the fact that the monkey undertook the same role in the *Sundarakāṇḍa*.

> *dīrgham uṣṇaṃ ca niśvasya medinīm avalokayan* ।
>
> having heaved a deep, anguished (hot) sigh, looking at the ground (6.102.6ab),

orders Vibhīṣaṇa to tell Sītā to wash her hair (*śiraḥsnātām*) and adorn herself, before being brought before him (6.101.7). Vibhīṣaṇa does so (6.101.9), but Sītā rejects her lord's request, wishing to see her husband without having bathed (6.101.10: *asnātā*). Vibhīṣaṇa convinces her to do Rāma's bidding. The incident is important for a number of reasons. Rāma's reaction, his deep, hot sigh, marks a hesitation that is not lost on the audience. Moreover, Rāma's demand that Sītā bathe before coming into his presence conveys a specific meaning. For without a bath, Rāma considers Sītā impure, dirty. Sītā insists that she be allowed to come into his presence *asnātā*, unbathed, indicating her lack of need to be cleansed or purified. This mediated dialogue is the first indication that the reunion between the two will be less than ideal. Finally Vibhīṣaṇa escorts Sītā to the gathering of monkeys and *rākṣasa*s, in front of which the two are at last reunited. But as he first looks upon his wife, he is clearly a man of mixed emotions.[29]

> *tām āgatām upaśrutya rakṣogṛhaciroṣitām* ।
> *harṣo dainyaṃ ca roṣaś ca trayaṃ rāghavam āviśat* ॥ 16 ॥
>
> Having heard that she, who had lived so long in the home of the *rākṣasa* had arrived, Three emotions gripped Rāghava: anger, joy, and despondency. (6.102.16 = GPP 6.114.17)

Rāma insists that all the monkeys and *rākṣasa*s, much to their distress, be present[30] and able to gaze upon Sītā. He then, speaks harsh words to her,[31]

---

[29] The commentators are concerned about the passage and the words and comment upon it at length. See the *Yuddhakāṇḍa* (Goldman, Goldman & van Nooten 2008, *sarga* 102.16 and notes; GPP 6.114.17).

[30] 6.102.25. This also indicates that Rāma's feelings about Sītā have dramatically changed. See S. Goldman 1997.

[31] See S. Goldman, forthcoming.

tad gaccha hy abhyanujñātā yatheṣṭaṃ janakātmaje |
etā daśa diśo bhadre kāryam asti na me tvayā || 18 ||
kaḥ pumān hi kule jātaḥ striyaṃ paragṛhoṣitām |
tejasvī punar ādadyāt suhṛllekhena cetasā || 19 ||

Go, therefore, as you please, daughter of Janaka. You have my permission. Here are the ten directions. I have no further use for you, my good woman. (6.103.18)

For what powerful man born in a respectable family – his heart tinged with affection – would take back a woman who had lived in the house of another man? (6.103.19)

The harshness of these words is real but not unexpected. In light of Rāma's own emotional development throughout the *kāṇḍa* – clearly indicated by the feminine ruptures discussed above – his cold treatment of Sītā has been anticipated and is contextually apposite. Once Rāma sees through his own obsession with Sītā, the very source of his delusion, he can reprioritize his relationship with Lakṣmaṇa and the masculine world.[32] He is now able to publicly acknowledge, through his harsh rejection of Sītā, this change. Rāma's public rejection of his wife assures the priority of the masculine concerns of the narrative and the patriarchy it defends. After the public prioritization of his commitment to the patriarchy, Rāma can accept his wife back (after, of course, the very public display of her purity in the *agniparīkṣā*)[33] and, his delusion thoroughly dispelled, return to his kingdom. It is these episodes wherein Sītā is placed in the forefront of the text that provide a narrative space in which these transitions can occur, never letting us forget the danger in which the feminine places the masculine.

The *ādikavi*'s use of rupture and the feminine voice – primarily that of Sītā and her two *rākṣasī* confidants in the *Yuddhakāṇḍa*'s narrative – is intentional and provides a site through which the emotional movement of the narrative is foreshadowed while the

[32] Something his father, Daśaratha, and other males of the epic, have not been able to do (Goldman & Goldman 1996: 68-74).

[33] 6.104. Of course, there are really two public displays of her purity. See Sutherland 1989; S. Goldman 2004.

emotional development of the hero, and to a much lesser extent the heroine, is revealed. That this space is marked by the feminine voice aligns the emotional world and dependency on it as feminine and negative. Moreover, in what could be considered a type of over-determination, the fact that the action of the narrative and the location of the feminine is situated in the māyic world of the *rākṣasa*s serves to further reinforce the *kāṇḍa*'s negative valuation of the feminine. Those that succumb to the power of that world come under the sway of *māyā*, the power of illusion. For the patriarchal world of Vālmīki's heroes, such dependency leads to potential disaster, and only by recognizing and overcoming the delusional world of the feminine, as has Rāma, can a man participate uncompromised in the patriarchy.

REFERENCES

Primary Sources

The Bhagavad-Gita (1935). With eleven commentaries. Edited by Shastri Gajanana Shambhu Sadhale. Bombay: Gujarati Printing Press.

Bhāgavatapurāṇam (1983). With the commentary *Bhāvārthabodhinī* of Srīdhara Svāmin. Delhi: MLBD. (Reprint: 1988.)

GPP = *Rāmāyan of Vālmīki* (1914-20). 7 vols. With three commentaries called *Tilaka*, *Shiromani*, and *Bhooshana*. Edited by Shastri Shrinivas Katti Mudholkar. Bombay: Gujarati Printing Press.

Mahābhārata: Critical Edition (1933-70). 24 vols. With *Harivaṃśa* (1969-73). Critically edited by V. S. Sukthankar *et al.* Poona: BORI.

Ṛgveda-Samhitā (1933). 5 vols. With the commentary of Sāyaṇāchārya. Poona: Vaidic Samshodhan Mandal.

Śrīmadvālmīkirāmāyaṇam (1911-13). (Also called the Kumbakonam Edition.) 7 vols. Edited by T. R. Krishnacharya and T. R. Vyasacharya. Bombay: Nirṇayasāgar Press.

Śrīmadvālmīkirāmāyaṇam (1935). 3 vols. With the commentaries of Govindarāja, Rāmānuja, and Maheśvaratīrtha and the commentary known as *Taniślokī*. Edited by Gaṅgāviṣṇu Śrīkṛṣṇadāsa. Bombay: Lakṣmīveṅkaṭeśvara Mudraṇālaya.

Śvetāśvatara Upaniṣad (1966). Ed. with the commentaries of Śaṅkara, Nandagiri, Śaṅkarānanda, and Nārāyaṇa. (Ānandāśrama Sanskrit Series, 17.) Poona: Ānandāśrama.

The Vālmīki Rāmāyaṇa: Critical Edition (1960-75). 7 vols. General editors: G. H. Bhatt and U. P. Shah. Baroda: Oriental Institute.

Secondary Sources

GOLDMAN, Robert P. 1980. Rāmaḥ sahalakṣmaṇaḥ: Psychological and literary aspects of the composite hero of Vālmīki's Rāmāyaṇa. *JIPh* 8: 149-89.

—— (trans.) 1984. *The Rāmāyaṇa of Vālmīki: An Epic of Ancient India*, I: *Bālakāṇḍa: Boyhood*. Introduction and translation by R. P. Goldman. Annotation by Robert Goldman and Sally Sutherland. Princeton: Princeton University Press.

GOLDMAN, Robert P. & Sally J. Sutherland GOLDMAN (trans.) 1996. *The Rāmāyaṇa of Vālmīki: An Epic of Ancient India*, V: *Sundarakāṇḍa*. Introduction, translation, and annotation by Sally J. Sutherland Goldman and R. P. Goldman. Princeton: Princeton University Press.

GOLDMAN, Robert P., Sally J. Sutherland GOLDMAN & Barend VAN NOOTEN (trans.) 2008. *The Rāmāyaṇa of Vālmīki: An Epic of Ancient India*, VI: *Yuddhakāṇḍa*. Annotation by Robert P. Goldman, Sally J. Sutherland Goldman and Barend van Nooten. Introduction by R. P. Goldman and Sally J. Sutherland Goldman. Princeton: Princeton University Press.

GOLDMAN, Sally J. Sutherland 1997. The power of the gaze: Scopophilic behavior in Sanskrit narrative. Paper Delivered at "Re-Presenting Women: Workshop on Women in the Literary, Performing, and Visual Arts of India", International Workshop and Conference, University of California at Berkeley, April 25-27, 1997.

—— 2001. Sītā speaks: The voice of the heroine in the *Sundarakāṇḍa* of the *Vālmīki Rāmāyaṇa*. In: Paula Richman (ed.), *Questioning Ramayanas: A South Asian Tradition*: 223-238. Berkeley: University of California Press.

—— 2003. Re-siting Sītā: Gender and narrative in *Vālmīki's Sundarakāṇḍa*. *Purāṇa* 45.2: 115-135.

—— 2004. Gendered narratives: Gender, space, and narrative structures in Vālmīki's *Bālakāṇḍa*. In: Mandakranta Bose (ed.), *The Rāmāyaṇa Revisited*: 47-85. New York: OUP.

—— forthcoming. Suttee, satī, and sahagamana: An epic misunderstanding. In: R. Sharma (ed.), *Women, Power, and Cultural Difference: Negotiating Gender in South Asia*. Delhi: Indian Books Centre.

GOUDRIAAN, Teun 1978. *Māyā Divine and Human: A Study of Magic and its Religious Foundations in Sanskrit Texts, with Particular Attention to a Fragment on Viṣṇu's Māyā as Preserved in Bali*. Delhi: MLBD.

HOPKINS, E. W. 1901. *The Great Epic of India: Its Character and Origin*. New York: Charles Scribner's Sons. (Reprint: Calcutta: Punthi Pustak, 1969.)

RADHAKRISHNAN, Sarvepalli (ed.) 1952. *History of Philosophy Eastern and Western*, I. London: George Allen and Unwin Ltd.

SUTHERLAND, Sally J. (Goldman) 1991. The bad seed: Senior wives and elder sons. In: S. J. Sutherland (ed.), *Bridging Worlds: Studies on Women in South Asia*: 24-52. Berkeley: Centers for South and Southeast Asia Studies, U. C. Berkeley.

Authorial Paths Through the Two Sanskrit Epics, Via the *Rāmopākhyāna*

ALF HILTEBEITEL

In advancing the arguments of this article, I want to acknowledge at the outset that I am emboldened to make them because I have been persuaded that Madeleine Biardeau has recently cleared up some basic and satisfactory working premises for scholarship on the two Sanskrit epics. To the point: I agree with her chronological positioning of the *Mahābhārata* as older than the *Rāmāyaṇa* (Biardeau 2002, I: 700-701 and ff., 726; 1999: xxxiii-xxxv), though with some differences between us as to relative dating, manner, and timespan of composition that I need not go into fully here.[1] I also agree with her that each epic received its basic contents and design in the process of its first composition, and that there is nothing to be gained by excavating or surgically peeling back from their "extant" texts to uncover cores, interpolations, and strata – here again with some further differences as to the merits and implications of the Mbh's Critical Edition, on which I am more positive than Biardeau and some others.[2] Further, as Biardeau sees, one must

---

[1] See Hiltebeitel 2001a: 15-31, 165; 2004c.

[2] See Hiltebeitel 2004c on the distinction between excavation and surgery, for which Fitzgerald (2003) is an advocate, and Hiltebeitel 2005 for some discussion of the merits of the Critical Edition. Fitzgerald's negative remarks on the "unsuccessful effort to arrive at a critical edition" (Fitzgerald 2002: 89, n. 1) would

address not only the relation between the two epics as provisional wholes but as provisional wholes including parts. For this paper, that is especially relevant to the *Rāmopākhyāna*, the Mbh's main version of the Rāma story, which Biardeau regards as an integral part of the Mbh, and thus in principle earlier than the Ram. Moreover, to theorize this relation, it should be pertinent, she says, that the *Rāmopākhyāna*, along with the *Bhagavadgītā*, the *Nārāyaṇīya*, and the *Sauptikaparvan*, is one of the units of the eighteen-*parvan* Mbh to have eighteen *adhyāya*s: that is, it has an eighteen-to-eighteen part-to-whole relation.[3] This numerology suggests that each of these units can be viewed as one or another kind of epitome. Further, in Biardeau's terms, the *Rāmopākhyāna* is one of three "mirror stories" in the Mbh's Forest Book that the Pāṇḍavas and Draupadī hear (the other two being "Nala" and "Sāvitrī").[4] From an inside-out perspective, the Mbh's Forest Book is thus the *Rāmopākhyāna*'s frame story.

This means that I now take a position on the priority of these two texts. Before this recent turn, I regarded the *Rāmopākhyāna* as to some extent intelligible simply as being first and foremost the Mbh's main version of the Rāma story, and considered the question of priority between it and the Ram to be inconclusive. But I now believe there are good reasons to accept the view (if not all the arguments) of scholars who have considered the *Rāmopākhyāna* to be prior: notably, in the most recent discussions, P. L. Vaidya

---

seem connected to his view that the recovery of the political intent of the first written Mbh requires surgical excision to remove *bhakti* segments that would have been among the features added as late as the Gupta period (see also Fitzgerald 2001). But the attempt to defer epic *bhakti* to a vague lateness that extends to the Guptas is an old ploy of epic "analysts" that has no external, and thus no internal, evidence to support it; see Hiltebeitel 2001a; 2004c; 2006; and indeed Fitzgerald 2004: 141.

[3] Biardeau 2002, I: 700. Vaidya (1971: xxxi) notes the *Rāmopākhyāna* count without comment on it, though perhaps as prelude to his view that it is "a genuine part of the Mahābhārata" (p. xxxii). On the *Nārāyaṇīya*, see Hiltebeitel 2006.

[4] As "Nala" is a mirror story recalling primarily the dice match and anticipating primarily the Pāṇḍavas' year in disguise, "Rāma" is a mirror story recalling the abduction of Draupadī and anticipating primarily the war.

(1971: xxxi-xxxvi), J. A. B. van Buitenen (1975: 207-214), and Biardeau.[5] But let us see what this priority might mean.

A. AUTHORS, HEROINES AND THE ENDS OF THE PATHS

There has been some interest over recent decades in similarities in design between the two Sanskrit epics,[6] perhaps enough to begin noticing how the similarities relate to differences. I will argue that one of the areas of tension by which the two epics betray significant differences is in their respective treatments of the way the "author" of each epic is positioned in relation to other *ṛṣi*s and to the lead heroine, and that this positioning can be traced through notions of a path through each of the two texts. I will try to establish at the outset that this is a potent configuration, and then demonstrate some of the particulars by which it can be traced.

A provocative first difference is this: Whereas in the Mbh the author appears in person to introduce the heroes to the heroine by showing the path that leads to her before they meet her at the debut scene where she will "choose" a husband, in the Ram the author appears in person only in the last stages of the heroine's path from the point where he receives her at his hermitage to the final scene where she calls on the earth to engulf her. More specifically, in the Mbh Vyāsa makes three of his forty-one appearances in a row to advance Draupadī's story. First, he tells the youthful forest-wandering Pāṇḍavas the Overanxious Maiden story that introduces Draupadī as destined from her previous life to marry five husbands (Mbh 1.157.6-16); then he shows up again to keep them "on the

[5] Disagreeing with criticism of Vaidya and, after Raghavan's study (1973: 2-31), of van Buitenen, see Goldman 1984: 33-39, and Brockington 1998: 473-477. Of the older discussions mentioned by these authors, I have reviewed (the English translation of) Jacobi [1893] 1960: 69-84; Hopkins 1901: 58-84, alone here in favoring the priority of the *Rāmopākhyāna*; Winternitz 1927, I: 500-507; and Sukthankar 1939 and 1941: 472-487.

[6] See Hiltebeitel 2001a: 6, n. 27, citing Pollock 1986: 38-42 and Biardeau 1997: 77-119.

path" (*pathi*) to Pāñcāla (176.2-3); and third, he shows up in time to narrate the stories that explain how Draupadī's polyandry is virtuous, dharmic (187.32-190.4). And in the Ram, Vālmīki not only receives Sītā after Rāma has banished her (Ram 7.44-48), but receives her pregnant with the twins Lava and Kuśa, helps her raise these boys, teaches them the Ram and brings them to Rāma's *aśvamedha* (7.84.5) to sing it – whereupon Rāma realizes their song is about him and wishes to be reunited with Sītā; Vālmīki then brings Sītā before Rāma, attests to her purity as a *dharmacāriṇī*, one who "fares in *dharma*" (7.87.14-20), and tells Rāma that "she will give proof of her fidelity" (*pratyayaṃ dāsyate*; 87.15c and 20d) by the act of truth that then ends her life (88.10).[7]

I would propose that the two texts work this configuration along with a common design and a largely overlapping vocabulary. When we realize that Vyāsa makes no further appearances in the main story that concern Draupadī as the person most directly affected,[8] and that Vālmīki makes no appearances in the main story at all until the events just described, we may say, in brief, that not only do the "authors'" stories follow paths defined by their heroines, but that the authors appear at these two decisive *doubtful* end-points precisely to vouch for the purity, fidelity, and chastity of the heroines on whose paths their narratives proceed. Along the way, each epic will be full of reminders, with words like *mārga*, *patha*, *pantha*, *vartman*, *adhvan*, *padam*, and in the Mbh the additional word *padavī*, that the heroines' movements define such a "path", and that she walks it as a *dharmacāriṇī*, a vibrant phrase, at least when used in narrative contexts, that I believe could be well gloss-

[7] See Hiltebeitel 2001a: 318-322.

[8] Two of Vyāsa's forty-one other appearances affect Draupadī immediately, but are not primarily concerned with her: When he appears with Nārada between the weapons of Arjuna and Aśvatthāman, he changes the terms that affect Draupadī's revenge against Aśvatthāman for slaying her children – terms that leave Draupadī barren (see Hiltebeitel 2001a: 62-64); and she is among those whom Vyāsa enables to see her slain sons when he brings forth a vision of the slain warriors from the Gaṅgā (Hiltebeitel 2001a: 81).

ed as "one who moves gracefully in *dharma*".[9] Moreover, if Vālmīki appears only at the end of his story, vouchsafing for Sītā there by this very phrase, there is also the indication at its beginning, where his poem is introduced, that the composition he imparted to Kuśa and Lava to sing to Rāma is called *sītāyāścaritaṃ mahat* (1.4.6b) – that is, if I may translate it in the same vein, literally "The Great Course of Sītā".[10]

Pivotal to making the case for such a path through each epic will be the Forest Books, with their preludes and sequels. For it is there that the heroines' paths take them and the heroes on their longest and profoundest journeys.

B. WALKING THE PATH OF DRAUPADĪ

In the Mbh, it is in and around the forest that we meet that epic's distinctive use of the term *padavī*, "footstep, path, way", used with the roots *car* or *gam*, "move" or "go", and modified by *draupadyāḥ*, "Draupadī's", or, if Draupadī is speaking herself, by *mama*, "my", to describe "walking on the path of Draupadī" (as I will translate it). Although the Mbh is, of course, a text of many criss-crossing paths and doors,[11] I will let this idiom suffice to make my

[9] In the Mbh, it has the following uses for Draupadī. Vidura (who incarnates *dharma*) establishes after the dice match in words to Yudhiṣṭhira: "And Draupadī walks in the Law and is wise both in Law and Profit" (*dharmārthakuśalā caiva draupadī dharmacāriṇī*) (2.69.9cd; van Buitenen 1978: 163). And just after this, once the Pāṇḍavas and Draupadī have left for the forest, Dhṛtarāṣṭra reveals his anxieties to Saṃjaya, and Saṃjaya replies: "Though warned by Bhīṣma, Droṇa, and Vidura, [not] to bring in Draupadī, the Pāṇḍavas' beloved wife, who walked in the Law (*draupadīṃ dharmacāraṇīm*), your foolish son Duryodhana sent the son of a sūta as an usher" (2.72.6-7; van Buitenen 1978: 167). See also 3.222.58; 4.15.35; 18.1.9 and 18.2.11 (as described by Yudhiṣṭhira, not finding Draupadī in heaven). For the Ram as designating Sītā, see 1.72.17 (*dharmacārī*, a short form, as described by her father to Rāma at their wedding); 2.23.19; 2.109.21 (as perceived by Anasūyā); 7.87.14 (as attested to by Vālmīki at the end of her road, as already cited).

[10] As others have taken the term *Sītāyana*.

[11] See Hiltebeitel 2001a: 1, n. 3 on "forking paths", and p. 20, citing 12.342 – the end of the *Śāntiparvan* on the many doors to heaven. At the beginning of the

case that Draupadī's path is the one that the Mbh marks the most carefully. On the verge of entering the forest, the first occurrence comes with Nakula's oath of revenge after the dice match:

> At the command of Dharmarāja, walking the path of Draupadī (*nideśād dharmarājasya draupadyāḥ padavīṃ caran*) I shall soon empty the earth of the Dhārtarāṣṭras (2.68.45).

Then, most tellingly, Draupadī uses these terms twice herself in the Forest Book in the episode of her abduction by Jayadratha, just before he grabs her:

> I am very strong (*mahābalā*), but here it is as if the Sauvīra king thinks me powerless – that, convinced by subjugation, I would speak here pitifully to the Sauvīra king, (I) whose path the two Kṛṣṇas will surely walk (*yasyā hi kṛṣṇau padavīm caretām*), the two companions stationed on a single chariot – not even Indra could carry her (*tām*) off, how then a mere miserable man? When Kirīṭin, the slayer of enemy heroes, stationed on the chariot, shattering the foes' minds, pervades your army on my account, burning deadwood like a summer fire, Janārdana's heroic Vṛṣṇi followers and all the great Kekaya bowmen too, indeed, all these princes of pleasing form will walk my path (*ete hi sarve mama rājaputrāḥ | prahṛṣṭarūpāḥ padavīṃ careyuḥ*; 3.252.13-16).

Note that Draupadī is describing how Jayadratha will be killed in the Mahābhārata war, not how her husbands will rescue her now from his grasp, which the immediate sequel does not fail to describe in related terms. For as Indrasena, Yudhiṣṭhira's charioteer, says on learning with the Pāṇḍavas of her abduction,

> Even if the queen has entered the earth, ascended to heaven or plunged in the sea, the sons of Pṛthā will follow her path, for so surely tortured is Dharmarāja (*tasyā gamiṣyanti padaṃ hi pārthās | tathā hi saṃtapyati dharmarājaḥ*)... . She's the walking heart of the Pāṇḍavas! (*bahiścaraṃ hṛdayam pāṇḍavānām*) (3.253.12 and 13f).[12]

Śāntiparvan, consider the play on contending "roads" and "paths" (12.8.37–12.9 and 11) in the disagreement between Arjuna, who has just had Kṛṣṇa to set his course (i.e., drive his chariot) through the eighteen days of war, and Yudhiṣṭhira, who now has some decisions to make on his own.

Next, such terms occur twice in Book Five on occasions when Kuntī tells Kṛṣṇa to remind Arjuna that, with the war still ahead, "the path of Draupadī" has a ways yet to go (5.66.79; 135.19):

> Having gone, strong-armed one, say to the best of all weapon-bearers, the hero Arjuna Pāṇḍava, "Walk the path of Draupadī" (*draupadyāḥ padavīṃ cara*) (5.88.79);

and again,

> Strong-armed one, say to that best of all weapon-bearers, the tiger among men Arjuna, "Walk the path of Draupadī" (*draupadyāḥ padavīṃ cara*) (135.19).

And the terms last occur at the end of the war when Bhīma describes Duryodhana's death to Yudhiṣṭhira as a resolution toward which Draupadī's path has led:

> By good luck, the sinful Duryodhana has been slain with his followers in battle. By good luck, you have gone the path of Draupadī's mass of hair (*draupadyāḥ keśapakṣasya diṣṭyā tvam padavīm gataḥ*; 12.16.25).[13]

Draupadī's path is a dark one, foreseen by the incorporeal voice that announces at her birth that she will be the destruction of the Kṣatriyas.[14] As the passages further indicate, though the "two Kṛṣṇas"[15] and indeed "all the princes" follow this path, it is espe-

---

[12] Slightly modifying van Buitenen 1978: 715, but keeping his translation "tortured", which elegantly conveys the sentiment behind what would be a more literal "for so surely does Dharmarāja burn ..." Among further iterations of the path theme in this passage, the Pāṇḍavas "take to the path (*padavīm*) at once" (17d) and are thrice said to follow Jayadratha and Draupadī's tracks (*vartmāṇi*: 256.16a, 20e, 22b).

[13] See Hiltebeitel 1981: 200-201.

[14] 1.155.41-46; see Hiltebeitel 2001a: 187.

[15] See Hiltebeitel 1984. As these passages remind us, it is also a path defined by the interwoven threads that link the actions of all the epic's Kṛṣṇas: the "two Kṛṣṇas", Arjuna and Kṛṣṇa; Draupadī Kṛṣṇā (her name at birth); and the author Kṛṣṇa Dvaipāyana, "the Island-born Kṛṣṇa", who set the Pāṇḍavas on this path in the first place, as earlier noted.

cially Dharmarāja who keeps them all to it with his indestructible yet "tortured" love for this woman. And finally, just because that is the case, it means that the text follows the path of Draupadī until the very end, when Yudhiṣṭhira asks to question Draupadī even when he is in heaven,[16] that is, even when she is no more.

C. THE SEVEN *ṚṢI*S AND AGASTYA

In the Ram, the term *padavī* is very rarely used, and never with the same meanings or with reference to Sītā.[17] Rather, the path theme is developed in two phases divided by Sītā's abduction: the first defined primarily by *ṛṣi*s; the second traced mainly by animals. As we approach the first, we must get our bearings on the contrasting treatments of *ṛṣi*s in the two epics.[18]

As E. W. Hopkins has shown, as a class *ṛṣi*s form a rather elastic grouping; I quote him because he permits us to narrow things down rather quickly:

> Among Ṛṣis some are Devarṣis and Dānavarṣis; some are Maharṣis, some are Paramarṣis (the *arciṣmantaḥ* or very bright stars around the polar star); others, like Triśaṅku, are Rājarṣis, of kingly extraction; or Brahmarṣis (Viprarṣis), of priestly origin. The most famous group is that of the Seven Seers of the North) (Hopkins 1915: 177).

Now, in both epics there are times when the *ṛṣi*s appear in all their variety to witness some great event. But there are also moments and situations where they are, as it were, represented by those "most famous" Seven, or by some significant variation thereof.

---

[16] 18.3.8; see Hiltebeitel 2001a: 276-277.

[17] I find only three usages of *padavī* in the Ram, with different verbs and meanings: "come to the aid of" (*padavīm āgatān* [3.19.4d]; *padavīm prāptā* [3.20.12c], on which see Pollock 1991: 128, 131); the "region of the gods, etc." (*padavīṃ devatānām … gamiṣyasi*) that, according to Aṅgada, Rāvaṇa will attain when he is slain (6.31.41).

[18] The gist of §§ C.-E. of this essay was presented in 1979 at an American Academy of Religion panel I organized on the two epics, with Madeleine Biardeau, Wendy Doniger O'Flaherty, and Robert P. Goldman as co-speakers. Twenty-five years later, perhaps it will be more timely. See Hiltebeitel 1979.

These Seven have three major traits, all of which are functional and interrelated in the two epics.

First, they represent the religious authority of Veda; five of them have names that can be given to the "family books" of the *Ṛgveda* (Viśvāmitra [Book 3], Gotama [4], Atri [5], Bharadvāja [6], Vasiṣṭha [7]), and the other two (Kaśyapa[19] and Jamadagni) are known as poets of various hymns as well, as is Agastya, whom we must begin to keep track of along with the Seven. Jamadagni is the only one who has minimal association with the Vedic corpus (ṚV 9.65 being attributed to him or Bhṛgu), but he is of course a descendent of Bhṛgu, this latter being mentioned in a number of *Ṛgveda* hymns (8.43.13; 10.14.6; 92.12) and associated still more closely with the *Atharvaveda*. One may thus say that the Seven *ṛṣi*s (who are themselves credited as co-authors of two hymns [ṚV 9.67; 10.137[20]]) and Agastya are *the* Vedic *ṛṣi*s par excellence. Their importance here is related to their identity as the eight *pravararṣi*s, the eponymous ancestors of the eight Brahman *gotra*s – that is, the ones to whom all Brahman families make invocation (*pravara*), and to whom they trace their line of descent. These eight gotras were the basis for the system of sept-exogamy, or marriage outside one's "eponymous clan". By classical times, the Seven *ṛṣi*s plus Agastya thus represent not only the authority of Veda, but the very human tissue of Brahmandom.

Second, both epics regard these *ṛṣi*s as having *āśrama*s in the forest, where they live as *vānaprastha*s, still sometimes in the company of their wives where the texts take in interest in such matters.

---

[19] Some would add him as well to the short list of five as the *ṛṣi* of Book 9.

[20] On these hymns I thank T. P. Mahadevan for the following information and quoted comments: ṚV 9.67.1-21 has contributions from the Seven "amounting to three *gāyatri* verses [each] except Jamadagni's three *dvipadā gāyatri*. The order of the *ṛṣi*s is: Bharadvāja, Kaśyapa, Gotama, Atri, Viśvāmitra, Jamadagni, and Vasiṣṭha. This order, if it is a sign of the relative importance or prestige of the clans at redaction of the *Ṛgveda*, changes by post-Vedic times to the order [found here in this essay]. That order dates from the sūtra period and the subsequent purāṇa period ..." The tenth book *ṛṣi* hymn is "a seven-verse hymn with each *ṛṣi* getting one *anuṣṭubh* verse. The order of *ṛṣi*s is the same" as in Book 9.

But there is a difference. In the Ram, these *ṛṣi*s, or important members of their lines, are still living relatively earthly lives, and can thus readily interact with the hero and heroine. But in the Mbh their stories belong largely to the past – a past not so long distant in terms of generational time, though long in terms of ordinary human years. Their interactions with the heroes are thus more indirect.

Third, in the cosmological domain that epic scholars mostly ignore or shuttle aside, the Seven *ṛṣi*s and Agastya are important stars: the Seven form the Great Bear or Big Dipper, which moves around the Pole Star (*dhruva*, the Fixed) and is identified with the *devayāna*, the soteriological path to *mokṣa*. Agastya, however, is the star Canopus, second brightest star in the southern skies which are associated with the *pitṛyāna*,[21] the path of reincarnation, and with Yama, god of the dead and lord of the southern region.

D. THE SEVEN *ṚṢIS* AND AGASTYA IN THE Mbh

Before we consider the treatment of these Seven *ṛṣi*s plus Agastya in the Ram, we can thus expect to learn something from their contrasting treatment in the Mbh. Unlike the Ram, the Mbh does not present them as living concurrently with the heroes of the main story. The Seven *ṛṣi*s and Agastya's involvements with the main narrative of the Mbh are limited to visits from the heavens where they have already attained their stellar status (a partial exception may be Vasiṣṭha, who has a rather low-profile identity as a guru of Bhīṣma [1.44.32; 12.46.15]; but considering that Bhīṣma has spent time with his celestial mother Gaṅgā, we have no guarantee that this discipleship occurred on earth).[22] The Seven *ṛṣi*s do occasionally visit Mbh events en masse from above, as at the birth of Arjuna:

> The Seven Seers Bharadvāja, Kaśyapa, Gautama, Viśvāmitra, Jamadagni, Vasiṣṭha, and he who rises as the sun goes down, the blessed lord Atri came there too (1.114.41).

---

[21] See Hiltebeitel 1977: 347-350.

[22] See Hiltebeitel 2001b.

But they do not structure the Pāṇḍavas' itinerary during their forest exile or elsewhere, and are not their major Brahman interlocutors there or anywhere else.

Yet they have another importance in this epic. Although we find stories about them widely dispersed, they repeatedly make signal contributions to the dynastic past, contributing to the great confluences of cosmic and societal forces, including mixture of caste, that recur through the lunar dynasty down to and into the Mahābhārata crisis. They do this over a long period, but with a seeming incremental intensity that marks their connection with the line at its major turning points or crises. According to a tradition that is found largely in post-epic texts, Atri, as the father of Soma, is the progenitor of the Lunar Dynasty itself. The epithet "he who rises as the sun goes down" is, however, surely connected with these lunar associations, which the Mbh knows (see Hopkins 1915: 90-91). As a group, the Seven *ṛṣis* and Agastya all appear in the story of Nahuṣa, father of Yayāti, who, when he becomes king of heaven at the fall of Indra, makes the Seven pull his carriage, until he arrogantly touches Agastya's head with his foot.[23] The Bhārgavas then intermarry into the line through Yayāti when the latter marries the Bhārgava Śukra's daughter Devayānī; their son Yadu is not an ancestor of the central branch of the dynasty, which descends from his younger brother Pūru, the first of the line's eponymous ancestors, but Yadu's descendants – the Yādavas – twice recombine with the central branch in the epic's main narrative: first, when Kṛṣṇa's aunt Kuntī, a Yādava, marries Pāṇḍu and becomes the mother of the eldest three Pāṇḍavas (1.71-78); and second, when Kṛṣṇa's sister Subhadrā marries Arjuna, with their recombinant Paurava-Yādava descendants providing the dynasty's sole heirs.[24] Mean-

---

[23] See 5.11-17, 12.329.29-41 (*Nārāyaṇīya*), and 13.101.44–103.37; Hiltebeitel 1977.

[24] See Defourny 1978. There is, of course, much more extensive Bhārgava material in the Mbh, one major upshot of which is that Bhārgava Rāma is still hanging around to teach weaponry to various heroes. See most recently Fitzgerald 2002.

while, Viśvāmitra and the Apsaras Menakā were then the parents of Śakuntalā, who bears with King Duḥṣanta another famous eponym of the line, Bharata (1.65-69). And drawing still closer in time to the events of the epic, Vasiṣṭha is the father of Śakti, grandfather of Parāśara (1.169.1-8), and thus great grandfather of Vyāsa, who is the father of Dhṛtarāṣṭra, Pāṇḍu, and Vidura, not to mention their non-dynastic elder half-brother Śuka. Meanwhile, off-center from the dynastic line but still contributory to the Kaurava camp and the build-up of the main epic crisis, one finds Bharadvāja directly siring Droṇa, and Gautama as either the grandfather, or a more distant ancestor, of Kṛpa and Kṛpī (1.120-21), with Aśvatthāman being the outcome of the marriage of Droṇa and Kṛpī – all these fighting Brahmans contributing to the crisis by siding with the Kauravas.

The only one of the Seven *ṛṣi*s, or *ṛṣi* families, not contributing genealogically to the crisis is Kaśyapa. But then this most highly generative *ṛṣi* has a hand in the regeneration of all the Kṣatriyas after their destruction by Bhārgava Rāma (12.49). He is also a still more primordial progenitor: partner of Aditi in bearing the Ādityas and, in other contexts, of incarnations of Viṣṇu. He is also, as the husband of Kadrū and Vinatā (1.14.5-7), the father of all snakes and birds. Thus if, as it seems, there is a connection between the Kauravas and snakes, Kaśyapa's progeny may have taken another route into the lineage. Perhaps it is thus fitting that one of his descendants should make the effort to cure the Pāṇḍavas' heir Parikṣit of snakebite, without however succeeding (1.46.38-39). And it is curious that the two somewhat disreputable Brahman brothers Yāja and Upayāja who officiate at the sacrifice that produces the births of Dhṛṣṭadyumna and Draupadī are both Kāśyapas (1.155.7). Thus while Kaśyapa and the Kāśyapas present the largest exceptions to the main pattern by which the Seven *ṛṣi*s and Agastya are treated, we find them marked by traits that still contribute to the pattern: those of primordiality, generativity, and willingness to use that generativity in the performance of an unusual but vital sacrifice.

Two more contrasts thus emerge. In the Ram, the Ikṣvākus' solar line is without such repeated Brahman interventions as these, which include several Brahman adulterations of the Kṣatriya stock. All this will allow us to say, secondly, that whereas in the Mbh the Seven *ṛṣis* and Agastya mainly map time, in the Ram they mainly map space.

E. THE FIRST PART OF THE *RĀMĀYAṆA* PATH: THE SEVEN *ṚṢIS* AND AGASTYA

With these themes in mind, we can now look at these *ṛṣis* as a relay system in the Ram, for it will be my contention that Vālmīki defines the first part of Rāma and Sītā's path precisely by this group of seven plus one, allowing in two cases, already anticipated by what we have just culled from the Mbh, for replacements by their descendants. More specifically, Vālmīki maps these *ṛṣis* onto the story as the main representatives and spokesmen for *all* the *ṛṣis*, who are to be the beneficiaries of the divine plan to have Rāma eradicate the *rākṣasa* nuisance that disturbs their forest *āśrama*s – a mission for which the abduction of Sītā will be necessary and a cause for the *ṛṣis* to rejoice.[25]

This pattern begins somewhat inconspicuously with two Brahmans who provide the *ṛṣis* with their generative "home base" in Rāma's family, in effect suspending their *vānaprastha* mode of life while they serve the royal line. Thus, most importantly, Vasiṣṭha and Ṛśyaśṛṅga Kāśyapa (descendent of Kaśyapa) oversee the rites of Rāma and his brothers' births (Ram 1.9-16),[26] along with several other Brahmans named. After this, both Vasiṣṭha and *a* Kāśyapa (it is doubtful this would still be Ṛśyaśṛṅga, but the continued

[25] The moment Rāvaṇa lifts Sītā off, all the *paramarṣis* of the immediate Daṇḍaka Forest are "thrilled and agitated" – *prahṛṣṭā vyathitāścāsan* (3.50.11a). I believe Shastri's "filled with joy" (1969: 110) and Raghunathan's "glad" (1981: 112) are closer to the sense of *prahṛṣṭa* than Pollock's "*shuddered*" (1991: 196).

[26] On the pair in combination, see notably 1.12.33-34; 13.42.

home-base presence of a Kāśyapa is still of interest) accompany Rāma's wedding party to Mithilā (68.4), where Vasiṣṭha recites the Ikṣvāku lineage (69.14-15) to which Ṛśyaśṛṅga has so crucially contributed in the case of Rāma and his brothers. A Kāśyapa is then also among the Brahmans advising Vasiṣṭha at Ayodhyā, along with others named (2.61.2). Vasiṣṭha and a Kāśyapa are then in attendance, along with five other *ṛṣi*s,[27] at Rāma's enthronement (6.116.55), and finally they are among the first four of the seventeen (in the Critical Edition) *ṛṣi*s named when Rāma invites "all the ṛṣis"[28] to his *aśvamedha* to witness what he believes will be Sītā's conclusive oath of chastity, but which will instead be the end of her life and her earthly path. Vasiṣṭha is a fixture in his role as *purohita* of the Ikṣvākus under Daśaratha, Bharata, and Rāma (e.g., 1.11.6c; 2.61.3d), as is probably also implied in the *Rāmopākhyāna*, as we shall see below. This thread of Kāśyapas, beginning with Ṛśyaśṛṅga, seems to be a theme launched by Vālmīki.[29] Let me just suggest that in mapping the Seven *ṛṣi*s, the Ram handles the Kāśyapas much as the Mbh does by having them contribute to the pattern but from the greatest remove. Vālmīki thus solves his most difficult problem adroitly and at the beginning by replacing Kaśyapa – the primordiality of whose stories perhaps dates him beyond the range of Vālmīki's Ram history – *primarily* by Ṛśyaśṛṅga, who is also a Kāśyapa in the Mbh (3.110.2b etc.) but without any connection there to the Rāma story, or more particularly with the *Rāmopākhyāna*, and who shares with Kaśyapa the traits one finds among Kāśyapas in the Mbh of extraordinary generativity and the availability to use it in an unusual but vital sacrifice.

[27] Vāmadeva, Jābāli, Kātyāyana, Gautama, and Vijaya.

[28] *ṛṣīn sarvān* – the others named in the Critical Edition being Vāmadeva, Jābāli, Viśvāmitra, Dīrghatapas, Durvāsas, Agastya, Śakti, Bhārgava, Vāmana, the "long-lived Mārkaṇḍeya", Maudgalya, Cyavana, Śatānanda, Bharadvāja, and Agniputra (7.87.1-4).

[29] As noted above and explored further below, it is not found in the *Rāmopākhyāna*.

For the other five of the Seven *ṛṣi*s, however, their *Rāmāyaṇa* life is in the forest. While Rāma is but a youth, Viśvāmitra appears to demand his aid in slaying the *rākṣasa*s who disturb his hermitage. There this *ṛṣi*, the Kṣatriya who had become a Brahman, becomes Rāma and Lakṣmaṇa's guru, "initiating" the boys into the mastery of weapons that unite the *brahman* and *kṣatra* powers and testing them with their use against the youngsters' first *rākṣasa* opponents – including the female *rākṣasī* Tāṭakā, whom Rāma kills at Viśvāmitra's instruction. Then, just as Vyāsa does in directing the Pāṇḍavas to Draupadī, Viśvāmitra, now satisfied, informs the young men about the forthcoming marriage ceremony of Sītā and leads them to Mithilā, where, "protected by the son of Kuśika" (*guptaḥ kuśikaputreṇa*; 1.67.15), Rāma wins Sītā's hand. Along the way, Viśvāmitra has facilitated the transition between Rāma's killing of Tāṭakā and his marriage to Sītā by imparting instruction about the dangers of female sexuality,[30] and this has culminated, just before reaching Mithilā, with their passage through the hermitage of Gautama. There Rāma learns that this *ṛṣi* has long abandoned this retreat after cursing his wife Ahalyā for her affair there with Indra: she would remain there immobile and invisible, doing penance until she should be freed from the curse and purified by the presence of Rāma. Once Ahalyā is restored, she is rejoined by Gautama, who bestows "great homage" on Rāma before the latter "proceeded on to Mithilā" (1.47.11-48.22; Goldman 1984: 218). Probably Rāma thus restores the marriage relation between this *ṛṣi* and his wife in anticipation of his marriage with Sītā, with it likely foreshadowed that his own marriage will also be one to suffer from long separations and a question of infidelity.

Upon the conclusion of the wedding,[31] Viśvāmitra takes leave of Rāma (1.73.1), or – more exactly – yields way, just as Rāma is

---

[30] Thanks to Sally Sutherland on this point, which she discusses in S. J. S. Goldman 2004: 55-76.

[31] It is to be noted that Gautama's son Śatānanda is King Janaka's *purohita*. (1.69.1), and officiates, along with Vasiṣṭha and Viśvāmitra, at Rāma and Sītā's wedding.

confronted by Rāma Jāmadagnya (Bhārgava Rāma, Paraśurāma) in a terrifying apparition. Concerning Rāma's meetings with the Seven *ṛṣi*s, this is Vālmīki's only other adjustment after his handling of the Kāśyapas.[32] Vālmīki places Ram events in the aftermath not only of Jamadagni's killing, but the slaughters by Rāma Jāmadagnya that avenge it (see footnote 32). This Rāma Jāmadagnya has thus now *already* – that is, long before the Mbh,[33] which makes so much of it – slain the earth's Kṣatriyas twenty-one times over, and now he threatens Rāma with the same extermination. He has heard Rāma has won Sītā by breaking the bow of Śiva; he now appears with the bow of Jamadagni himself, which had descended to Jamadagni from Viṣṇu. If Rāma can string it without breaking it, the two can then fight. Rāma strings the bow without breaking it, and with the arrow destroys the worlds that Rāma Jāmadagnya has won with his *tapas*. Rāma Jāmadagnya is thus defeated without a fight, and gracefully accepts his eclipse by Rāma Dāśarathi (1.73.16–76.3).

The fact that it is the mastery of the bow of the *ṛṣi* Jamadagni as well as that of Śiva makes this encounter all the more significant. For it was Jamadagni who had the restraint that checked, for one generation, the fateful combination of Brahman energy with Kṣatriya inclinations that appeared in his son Rāma Jāmadagnya. That Rāma Dāśarathi should destroy the worlds of asceticism of Rāma Jāmadagnya with the bow of Jamadagni is thus an indication of this

[32] Indeed, the two adjustments bear a temporal correlation – at least in the Mbh. For in the *Śāntiparvan* account of the Jamadagni-Rāma Jāmadagnya story, Kaśyapa figures as the *ṛṣi* who enables the Kṣatriyas' regeneration after Rāma Jāmadagnya has slaughtered them in revenge for his father's slaying. While Vālmīki could allow Rāma to meet Kaśyapa under these conditions, he is not willing to let Rāma meet Jamadagni, whose earthly career has been terminated too early in this episode, which, at least in this version, has Kaśyapa's intervention in its conclusion. Vālmīki thus leaves the matter of Rāma's status as a regenerate Kṣatriya to be worked out, without reference to Kaśyapa, in Rāma's face-off with Rāma Jāmadagnya, who now appears before Rāma to challenge him.

[33] Which could suggest the Ram's knowledge of the Mbh.

restoration of restraint over the power of destruction.[34] Rāma holds the combination of *brahman* and *kṣatra* powers as the disciple of Viśvāmitra (Rāma Jāmadagnya's great uncle, the two being the recipients of opposing destinies). That is, he is the disciple of the exemplary Kṣatriya who is oriented toward the *brahman* power; not of Rāma Jāmadagnya, the exemplary Brahman who is oriented toward the *kṣatra*.[35] Rāma thus shows his mastery of the two bows differentially and correctively. In one case, it is not only Śiva's bow but a Kṣatriya's, Janaka's, and he breaks it, still under the tutelage of Viśvāmitra, the Kṣatriya who had become a Brahman. In the other, it is not only Viṣṇu's bow but a Brahman's (Jamadagni's), and he leaves it unbroken, destroying the worlds of the Brahman with too much of the Kṣatriya in him.

After this encounter, Rāma returns home and faces the circumstances that lead to his banishment: a series of affairs again highlighting Vasiṣṭha. As he is about to depart, his mother Kausalyā says to him, with suggestive transparency,

> May the Seven *ṛṣi*s and Nārada guard you everywhere, my wise son, may all the constellations, and all the planets with their presiding deities, as you wander in a *muni*'s garb through the great forest (2.22.5).

Kausalyā's words effectively bring out the Seven *ṛṣi*s' (and Nārada's) double link with the stars (constellations and planets) above and the forests that loom ahead, and also bridge Rāma's movements from his princely upbringing (to which Ṛśyaśṛṅga Kāśyapa, Vasiṣṭha, Viśvāmitra, Gautama and Ahalyā, and Rāma Jāmadagnya

---

[34] See further Biardeau 1976: 190-197, appreciating these and other interrelated themes in this episode: an affirmation of the complementarity of Śiva and Viṣṇu, Rāma now having strung both their bows; further indications of the superiority of Viṣṇu over Śiva (the episode invokes a myth to this effect), and of restraint over the power of destruction; and more particularly the eclipse of the destructive avatāric role of Paraśurāma by the restorative avatāric role of Rāma Dāśarathi. Cf. Thomas 1996 on Paraśurāma's durability.

[35] A description that also befits Droṇa, Rāma Jāmadagnya's most prominent Brahman disciple in the Mbh.

have all contributed) to his banishment to the forest, where the meetings with the rest of the great *ṛṣi*s will continue.

First, shortly after having set out, Rāma, Sītā, and Lakṣmaṇa encounter Bharadvāja, who, at Rāma's request that he "think of some good site for an ashram in a secluded place" (2.48.23; Pollock 1986: 188), directs them to go ten *krośa*s ahead to Mount Citrakūṭa, "a meritorious (*puṇyaḥ*) place frequented by *maharṣi*s" (2.48.25 [22-36]), where they will make their first real residence in the forest. But Bharadvāja's main contribution soon follows when Bharata passes through his hermitage on the way to his meeting with Rāma to ask Rāma to return to Ayodhyā. Bharadvāja conjures up a sumptuous feast and a royal palace for Bharata, but Bharata rejects the royal seat, thus anticipating his stewardship of Rāma's throne (2.84-85). Once Bharata has proved his worthiness, Bharadvāja again gives the directions to Citrakūṭa (2.86.8-13), this time so that Bharata can find Rāma there.

Second, when Rāma, Sītā, and Lakṣmaṇa leave Citrakūṭa, it is by way of the hermitage of Atri. There the main interaction is between Sītā and Atri's now aged wife Anasūyā, who informs Sītā about the duties of a faithful wife or *pativratā*, and then bestows on her the apparel that Sītā will wear henceforth in the forest (2.109.5-111.20) – adding to the jewels that Daśaratha gave Sītā on her departure (2.33.14; 34.15-18). Again Rāma receives directions. Just as Bharadvāja directs him and his companions on the path to Citrakūṭa, the ascetics at Atri's hermitage now direct him on "the path through the forest which the *maharṣi*s use when they go to gather fruits" (*eṣa panthā maharṣīṇāṃ phalānyāharatāṃ vane*; 2.111.19) – all other routes, they say, being treacherous, as if the fruits to be gathered by Rāma will not be treacherous too. The trio is, in fact, directed toward the dangerous, *rākṣasa*-infested Daṇḍaka Forest. There they will spend ten years visiting hermitages, including those of two rather extreme ascetics named Śarabhaṅga (a Gautama; 3.6.14d), who *is* mentioned in the *Rāmopākhyāna* unlike the second, Sutīkṣṇa, who finally tells them the way they should proceed southward (3.10.36) through this forest to the hermitage of Agastya.

Rāma has thus encountered the Seven *ṛṣi*s, five directly and two through their descendants, in the following order: Vasiṣṭha, Ṛśyaśṛṅga (for Kaśyapa), Viśvāmitra, Gautama, Rāma Jāmadagnya (for Jamadagni), Bharadvāja, and Atri.[36] At last he is directed on to Agastya, who, added to the Seven, completes the list of the eight *pravararṣi*s. Upon seeing Agastya's hermitage, Rāma says,

> This must be the ashram of that seer whose power made the *rākṣasas* look on this southern region with terror and give up their hold on it. From the moment the virtuous sage set foot in this region, the nightstalkers ceased hostilities and grew peaceable. (3.10.80-81; Pollock 1986: 109-110)

Agastya is, of course, *the ṛṣi* of South India, regarded as the bringer of Brahmanical civilization to the south, and supposedly still resident on Mount Podiyil in Tirunelveli District, Tamilnadu. When Rāma asks him where he and his companions can find a peaceful spot, Agastya reflects for a moment and then directs them toward Pañcavaṭī, near the Godāvarī River (3.12.15-18). When they take up this "path by which the great seer had directed them",[37] they are going into an uncharted territory in which, from here on, their path will no longer be pointed out by great or lesser intermediary *ṛṣi*s, but by generally inauspicious creatures, beginning with the vulture Jaṭāyus. From Pañcavaṭī Rāma will begin in earnest his extermination of the *rākṣasa*s at Janasthāna, and it will be at Pañcavaṭī that Sītā will be abducted. Indeed, Agastya has directed them into a southern realm filled with inauspiciousness and death where, once Sītā is soon abducted, the first help available in recovering the path

---

[36] Durvāsas, a son of Atri, will also mark the end of Rāma and his brothers' lives, urgently demanding food in circumstances that prematurely end Rāma's sequestered conversation with Time (or Death, Kāla; 7.93-95). The episode begins describing Rāma as "firm on the path of *dharma*" (*rāme dharmapathe sthite*; 93.1b).

[37] Pollock 1986: 115; Ram. 3.12.25cd: *yathopadiṣṭena pathā maharṣiṇā prajagmatuḥ pañcavaṭīṃ samāhitau.*

– which will now be the broken path of Sītā's abduction – comes from deer, a headless trunk, vultures, monkeys and so-called "bears", plus a strange cavewoman. For present purposes, it will suffice to recover this track through the directions of the vulture Jaṭāyus and the headless trunk.

F. THE SECOND PART OF THE *RĀMĀYAṆA* PATH: THE UNCHARTED TERRITORY

After Rāma and Lakṣmaṇa learn from the dying vulture Jaṭāyus of Sītā's abduction, they proceed, as the bird has directed them, in a southerly direction on an "untrodden path" (*aviprahatam ... panthānam*; 3.65.2).[38] Having exhausted their visits to the hermitages of all the famous Vedic *ṛṣi*s down to the southernmost and last, Agastya, they now go into uncharted forest that is, if one may so put it, Vedically unmapped. Passing through several thick woods, they meet Kabandha, the "Headless Trunk", a Dānava suffering from a curse who guards the way past him (3.65.15-24).[39] Once Rāma has helped him to regain his beauty by cremating him, he tells Rāma that Rāvaṇa's abode may be found if Rāma forms an alliance with Sugrīva (68.10-22; cf. 67.20). Kabandha then provides them with an itinerary to Sugrīva's haunt on Mount Ṛṣyamūka near Lake Pampā, and on the way they must pass Mataṅga's Wood (*mataṅgāraṇya*; 3.69.27c; *mataṅgavanam*; 3.70.17c), where the non-Vedic *ṛṣi* Mataṅga had his hermitage (*mataṅgasyāśramam*; 4.11.41d).[40] Within that hermitage all the *ṛṣi*s (including Mataṅga)

[38] Some of what follows in this paragraph is modified or summarized from Hiltebeitel 1980: 200-211.

[39] As does the *rākṣasa* Kirmīra when the Pāṇḍavas first enter the forest (Mbh 3.11.23, 12.7-15). Moreover, at the beginning of Book 3, after the Pāṇḍāvas have killed Kirmīra, they realign themselves along their implied path by "placing Kṛṣṇā first" (*kṛṣṇāṃ puraskṛtya*) as they enter the Dvaita Forest (3.12.68).

[40] The "safe path" (*śivaḥ panthā*; 69.2) Kabandha recommends for their approach will be remarkable, past flowering trees and lotuses that make unfading garlands but which no man has ever picked. Explains Kabandha: "The disciples of Mataṅga there were well-adorned *ṛṣi*s. When they were overheated (*abhi-*

have passed away – all but one: a "mendicant woman" (*śramaṇī*, 3.69.19; also a *siddhā*, 3.70.6 and 9) named Śabarī – in whose name we may read "the Tribal Woman".[41] The rest of them, Mataṅga and his other disciples, as Śabarī will soon corroborate, ascended to heaven just when Rāma and company had reached Citrakūṭa.

Rāma and Lakṣmaṇa thus "set out in the forest on the path to Pampā shown them by Kabandha" (*tau kabandhena taṃ mārgaṃ pampāyā darśitaṃ vane*; 70.1ab). They head toward Mount Ṛṣyamūka by way of Mataṅga's hermitage, where they find Śabarī still there, awaiting Rāma's arrival so that, as Mataṅga had promised her, the sight of him would bring her heaven. This she soon enough obtains, rejoining her *maharṣi* preceptors there after Rāma gives her permission to enter fire (*hutvātmānaṃ hutāśane*; 3.70.26) – thereby indexing an association between fire-entry and purification that will later apply also, implicitly, to Vālmīki's Sītā. Rāma and Lakṣmaṇa then leave Mataṅga's hermitage itself, and with a sense of a favorable turn, meet Sugrīva and company on Mount Ṛṣyamūka.

Yet however favorable the turn, the story of Mataṅga's vacating of his hermitage still defines this place, for in Mataṅga's name and story lie enigmatic references to untouchability, buffalo sacrifice, and, as already noted, impurity. Sugrīva can find asylum there because Mataṅga, before dying, cursed Vālin, Sugrīva's brother and enemy, for befouling the *āśrama* with the blood drops of a huge buffalo named Dundubhi, whom Vālin had slain. Although Rāma has thus arrived too late to meet this "untouchable" *ṛṣi*, the place remains one where Rāma can show his grace and prowess with respect to the residues of such impure presences, blessing the "Tribal", Śabarī, and kicking away Dundubhi's buffalo bones with

---

tapta) by the burden of fetching forest produce for their guru, the drops of sweat from their bodies that fell to the ground quickly were born as flowers from the *munis*' *tapas*. Produced from their drops of sweat, they do not die, Rāghava" (3.69.16cd-18).

[41] Śabaras are now the Saoras. See Lutgendorf 2001.

one toe to impress Sugrīva that he, Rāma, will be up to the task of dispatching Vālin (4.3-12). Rāma thus forges his "friendship" with Sugrīva[42] in this portent-ridden place, which, beyond the range of the Vedic *ṛṣi*s, now marks the end of the trail as defined by *ṛṣi*s of any kind. Henceforth the path must be divined from the signs left by Sītā; the words of another vulture, Saṃpāti; the cavewoman Svayaṃprabhā; and the reconnoitering of the monkeys and bears, which the friendship with Sugrīva has made possible. Through all this, though, the path is defined primarily by Sītā: the quest for her, begun when Rāma learns from the monkeys that she had dropped her garment and jewels to mark her trail as she passed over the monkeys on Mount Ṛśyamūka.

G. THE *RĀMOPĀKHYĀNA*

As noted, it is the Forest Books of the two epics that bring the path theme to central stage. The Mbh, however, goes further in providing a touchstone for this theme: one that I have already signalled as the most salient moment in that epic's use of the distinctive phrase "following the path of Draupadī" – Draupadī's abduction by Jayadratha Saindhava. It is this episode that elicits the *Rāmopākhyāna*: a narrative in which the heroes and heroine of the one epic take consolation from hearing the story of the hero and heroine of the other – or, to put it, I think, more accurately, a narrative in which the Mbh auditors hear a story that Vālmīki will soon make the subject of that other epic.

As noted at the beginning of this paper, from an inside-out perspective, the Mbh's Forest Book is the *Rāmopākhyāna*'s frame story. And indeed, it is a rather beautifully designed frame in which our path theme is one of the major linking threads. Here is how the Mbh author gets into the eighteen-*adhyāya Rāmopākhyāna* and out of it. First, from the Mbh's own inner frame, Janamejaya begins a short connective *adhyāya* asking Vaiśampāyana: What did the

---

[42] I discuss the differing treatments of this friendship in the *Rāmopākhyāna* and Vālmīki in Hiltebeitel 2004a and 2004b.

Pāṇḍavas do "after they had incurred incomparable trouble because of Kṛṣṇā's abduction" (*evaṃ hṛtāyāṃ kṛṣṇāyāṃ prāpya kleśam anuttamam*; 3.257.1). Vaiśampāyana describes the scene. As "Dharmarāja Yudhiṣṭhira sat with the throngs of *muni*s" who attend the Pāṇḍavas' forest travels, he asks, "in the midst" of those "listening and commiserating great *ṛṣi*s" (*teṣāṃ madhye mahaṛṣīṇāṃ śṛṇvatām anuśocatām*): Unless it is the workings of time, fate, or predestination (*kāla*, *daivam*, *vidhi*, *bhavitavya*),

> how indeed could such a happening touch (*bhāva ... saṃspṛśed*) our *dharma*-knowing wife, one who fares in *dharma* (*dharmacāriṇī*), as a false charge of theft (might touch) a pure man? Surely no sin is committed, not a blameworthy deed anywhere; even among Brahmans the great *dharma* is well fared (*sucarito*) by Draupadī.(3.257.1-6)

Be it noted that Yudhiṣṭhira starts out with the question "how could this happen to Draupadī", fully defending her, and not "how could this happen to me?" Even though he turns shortly to this second question, it is the subordinated one. Yudhiṣṭhira begins with a question and a defense that are not, I think, typical of Rāma-or at least of Vālmīki's Rāma. Now addressing Mārkaṇḍeya among the throng of *ṛṣi*s, Yudhiṣṭhira observes further that having one's wife abducted is miserable, as is this forest life caused by lying kinsmen, and asks, "Is there indeed a man less fortunate than I, have you ever seen or heard of one before?" (7-10).

In response to this, Mārkaṇḍeya begins the *Rāmopākhyāna in medias res*:

> Immeasurable misery (*apratimaṃ duḥkham*) was obtained by Rāma, O Bharata bull. His wife Jānakī was abducted by a powerful *rākṣasa* ... (3.258.1).

Then, eighteen *adhyāya*s later, Mārkaṇḍeya has another short *adhyāya* to wrap things up and move on to the Forest Book's third "mirror story", "Sāvitrī" (3.277-83). Mentioning first that Rāma too met with "exceedingly terrible calamity" (*vyasanam atyugram*) during his *vanavāsa* ("forest residence") (276.1), he brings the focus back to our theme:

> Do not grieve, tiger among men, you are a Kṣatriya, enemy-burner; you are traversing a path of blazing resolve that relies on heroism of arms (*bāhu-vīryāśraye mārge vartase dīptanirṇaye*); indeed, not the slightest bit of guile (*vṛjinam*) is seen in you. On that path (*asmin mārge*) even the gods and *asura*s with Indra might despair (2-3).

As is the case elsewhere, the main path through the Mbh relies on Yudhiṣṭhira's guileless or uncrooked resolve to follow it, but also on maintaining the force of arms that comes from keeping his brothers together, as Mārkaṇḍaya continues to emphasize (4-7) while thus turning to the heart of the matter:

> And now look at her (*itaśca tvamimāṃ paśya*)! Abducted by the ill-souled Saindhava, strong and drunk with heroism, Draupadī Kṛṣṇā was recovered by those great-souled ones [your brothers], having accomplished a very difficult feat ... Rāma recovered Vaidehī without such companions ... His allies were monkeys[43] and black-faced bears, creatures of a different species (*jātyantaragatā*), king – think that over in your mind (7-11).

Both sides of the *Rāmopākhyāna*'s frame thus have the same structure, moving in from Draupadī to Dharmarāja, and out from Dharmarāja to Draupadī: it is Yudhiṣṭhira's guileless questions[44] and his resolve that keep things to the path, but it is "looking at her" – something he has done from its beginning[45] – that defines it. As an eighteen-*adhyāya* epitome, one might thus consider the *Rāmopākhyāna* as a model lesson on sticking to the path not only in the face of adversity, but when the path is broken.

Now within the *Rāmopākhyāna* itself, while it allows one to trace a path theme that is sometimes explicit and more often implicit, it is, in Ram terms, only the second part of the path – from

---

[43] Literally "deer of the trees", *śākhāmṛga* (3.276.11a).

[44] This is an important strain (or trope) that carries through the *Śāntiparvan*: e.g., Yudhiṣṭhira's reflections on the dashed "hopes" that he had for Duryodhana (12.125.1-7); his horrified and stunned reaction to the "robber morality" (*dasyu-maryādā*) that Bhīṣma has unveiled as law for times of distress (140.1); his claim not to "understand those who are cruel and their action" (*nṛśaṃsān na vijānāmi teṣāṃ karma ca*; 158.1cd).

[45] See 1.182.11-15 on first seeing her; 2.58.33-37 describing her as he is about to wager and lose her.

Kabandha on – that can be traced with any consistency. For the first part, there is to begin with no Vālmīki, and of course a different frame story. And from there on, of the Seven *ṛṣi*s, the only one to make an appearance is Vasiṣṭha, who, as hinted earlier, is probably already a fixture in the *Rāmopākhyāna* when Daśaratha hails his *purohita*, without naming him, in announcing his determination to make Rāma his successor (Mbh 3.261.14), and who thereafter appears by name twice.[46] We may note that the *Rāmopākhyāna* thus has no earlier roles for Vasiṣṭha. And for the rest of the *ṛṣi*s, next to nothing. There is no Ṛśyaśṛṅga, or for that matter Vasiṣṭha, at the boys' birth; instead, just this from Brahmā: "For that purpose the four-armed Viṣṇu has descended at my command" (*tadartham avatīrṇo 'sau manniyogāc caturbhujaḥ* I *viṣṇuḥ*; 260.5). There is no Viśvāmitra, Atri, Rāma Jāmadagnya,[47] or for that matter Vasiṣṭha involved in the stories of youth and marriage; just this: "In the course of time his sons grew up very vigorous, and became fledged in the Vedas and their mysteries and in the art of archery. They completed their student years, and took wives" (261.4-5b; van Buitenen 1978: 731). There is no Bharadvāja; just this of Bharata: "He found Rāma and Lakṣmaṇa on Mount Citrakūṭa" (216.63cd). From Citrakūṭa to Pañcavaṭī (which is not named) there is not a peep from Atri or Agastya. Sītā drops her jewels over the monkeys when she is abducted (263.7), but there is no mention that she might have gotten some of them from Atri and Anasūyā. Nor does Atri give any directions to the Daṇḍaka Forest, which Rāma enters via the hermitage of Śarabhaṅga, the only forest *ṛṣi* mentioned (261.39), to settle down by the Godāvarī (40). And from there his movements continue with no Sutīkṣṇa or Agastya to give directions until the battle at Janasthāna has left Khara and

---

[46] Where the Ram would lead one to expect him: attending Bharata into the forest to find Rāma (261.43) and performing Rāma's coronation after his return from Laṅkā (275.65) – both times with Vāmadeva.

[47] The Mbh knows a clear departure from or variant of this story only in a clear interpolation (3, Appendix I, no. 14), on which see Sukthankar 1936: 20-21; Fitzgerald 2002: 94, n. 12; Magnone 2004.

Dūṣaṇa killed and Śūrpaṇakhā disfigured (41-44) – it does not say by whom. Further on, as we now see, there is no Mataṅga *ṛṣi* either.

Once Rāma has "made this *dharma*-forest by the Godāvarī safe again" (*cakre kṣemaṃ punar ... dharmāraṇyam*; 3.261.43cd), it doesn't stay safe for long, since it is there that Sītā is soon abducted (262.40). Whereupon the path theme blooms openly. First, by reading the head gesture of the dying Jaṭāyus, Rāma gleans that Sītā has gone south (263.20c-21b). And then comes Kabandha, of whom Vālmīki tells quite a different, more attenuated story and revelation: that Rāma may find Rāvaṇa's abode if he forms an alliance with Sugrīva, though Vālmīki also gives Kabandha the role of being the first to mention Mataṅga's Wood. In the *Rāmopākhyāna*, the killing of Kabandha sets free a *puruṣa* that not only reveals Kabandha's prior identity to have been that of the *gandharva* Viśvāvasu cursed by Brahmā to pass through a *rākṣasa* womb (34-38), but the following priceless, if partly erroneous, information:

> Sītā has been abducted by King Rāvaṇa, who dwells in Laṅkā. Go to Sugrīva, he will render you help. Close by Mount Ṛṣyamūka there is a Lake Pampā ... Sugrīva lives there with four councillors; he is the brother of the monkey king Vālin, of the golden garlands. This much I can tell you: you shall see Jānakī. The monkey king surely knows Rāvaṇa's seat. (3.263.39-42; van Buitenen 1978: 737.)

Of course Sugrīva turns out not to know Rāvaṇa's seat, and soon enough sends the monkeys out to the four directions to find not only Sītā but, one must presume, Laṅkā (266.15-19). But for the rest Kabandha gives reliable information that does not complicate Rāma's path to Sugrīva with a forest or hermitage of Mataṅga or anything having to do with it such as meeting with Śabarī, or hearing the stories of Vālin's fights with Māyavin and the buffalo demon Dundubhi.[48] Indeed, Kabandha's words seem to remain continually useful beyond Kiṣkindhā. Rāma is reminded of them

[48] Curiously, the *Rāmopākhyāna* gives this name in the feminine as that of the Gandharvī who takes birth as Mantharā to carry forward the gods' mission and the plan of Brahmā (see 3.260.7-10).

before he learns that Sugrīva has sent out the monkey search parties (266.4cd), and, after some explicit input on the path (*pathā*; 3.266.41d) from a female ascetic named Prabhāvatī rather than Svayaṃprabhā, they would seem to have been recalled when Jaṭāyus's vulture brother Saṃpāti finally tells that he knows where Laṅkā and Rāvaṇa are, giving specifics that Hanumān uses to jump the ocean (266.54). Thereafter, the Ocean allows Rāma to extend the "path" (*mārga*; 267.31a, 36a, 37a) to Laṅkā by a bridge.

And where does the path end up? Not of course with Vālmīki at Sītā's second ordeal, of which the *Rāmopākhyāna* is silent. It ends up at the only ordeal for Sītā that the *Rāmopākhyāna* knows. "Putting Sītā in front, who was put before Vibhīṣaṇa" (*sītāṃ puraskṛtya vibhīṣaṇapuraskṛtām*; 275.6ab), the kindly *rākṣasa* Avindhya[49] invites Rāma, "Receive your queen Jānakī of good conduct" (*sadvṛttām*; 7). But seeing "her body caked with dirt, wearing a black robe" (*śokakarśitām* | *malopacita ... kṛṣṇavāsasam*; 9), Rāma suspects her of having been touched and spurns their reunion with the meanest words. It may be that having her come forth in black was a bad idea; Vālmīki has her emerge in costly jewels and "wearing a very costly robe" (*mahārhāmbaradhāriṇīm*; Ram 6.102.13d), though with no better results. So I think it more revealing to note that her appearance provides one of several reminders that Draupadī, who will soon begin her period in disguise entering the kingdom of Matsya "wrapped in a single large black garment that was very dirty" (*vāsaśca ... kṛṣṇaṃ sumalinaṃ mahat*; Mbh 4.8.2), is listening – and that Sītā's path here overlaps with hers. Indeed, perhaps Draupadī has taken the cue from Sītā on this element of her disguise[50] in the hope that it will turn men off. In any case, it is now

[49] There is no Avindhya in this role in the Ram. See van Buitenen 1975: 212 and Vaidya 1971, who make this an argument for the priority of the *Rāmopākhyāna*, one which I believe still weighs in their favor despite Goldman's dismissal of it, drawing on Raghavan, that an Avindhya has lesser roles in the Ram (Goldman 1984: 37; Raghavan 1973: 18).

[50] On Draupadī and the Pāṇḍavas' taking cues for their disguises from "Nala", see Hiltebeitel 2001a: 237-239.

that Brahmā appears along with Indra, Agni, Vāyu, Yama, Varuṇa, Kubera, Bhagavat, the spotless Seven *ṛṣi*s, and Daśaratha, along with other gods and *gandharva*s, crowding the heavens "like the autumn sky dotted with stars" (3.275.18-20). Agni, Vāyu, and Varuṇa come to vouch for Sītā's innocence; Brahmā and Daśaratha for other stated reasons;[51] Bhagavat, rather unexpectedly;[52] and the Seven *ṛṣi*s – for what? They would seem to be among the stars here. But perhaps they are also an inspiration for Vālmīki to bring them down to earth into the life of the hero and heroine. In isolation, the point is frivolous, but it is in their company, following the attestations by the elemental gods, that Brahmā tells Rāma,

> Son, for you to act here like this is not strange in you who obey the *dharma* of the royal *ṛṣis* (*rājarṣidharmiṇi*) and are strict in staying on the path of good conduct (*sādho sadvṛttamārgasthe*) (275.29a-c).

Brahmā is in effect saying that Rāma's behavior is up to code for one who strictly follows the royal *ṛṣi*s' path, but that, now knowing Sītā to be innocent, he should (in the imperative) "Take her back" (*pratīcchemām*; 34b). Rāma should be accompanied on his "path of good conduct" by his wife "of good conduct" – both *sadvṛtta* (274.7 and 29), a term with some similarity to *dharmacārin*.

H. *BHAKTI*, *DHARMA*, AND *KĀVYA*

In treating how author, heroine, *ṛṣi*s, and "path" are positioned, I have shown that the *Rāmopākhyāna* and Ram differ widely. But do the differences reveal anything significant? Some scholars have noted the absence in the *Rāmopākhyāna* of some, but not all, of the *ṛṣi*s threaded through the Ram,[53] but none have seen a pattern there

---

[51] Brahmā, among other things, to tell Rāma that he protected Sītā against Rāvaṇa's touch by Nalakūbara's curse; Daśaratha to hail his son and confirm him as heir.

[52] This usage could just refer back to Kubera, but more likely, in my opinion, it refers to someone additional, leaving Viṣṇu among the more surprising possibilities.

and none even mention the absence of Vālmīki in this connection, although van Buitenen makes a good point about him when he says that the *Rāmopākhyāna* authors either did not know the Ram or knew that their own story was different from it, for

> [o]therwise it is hard to explain why they should not simply have placed the narrative in Vālmīki's mouth; *The Book of the Forest* does not hesitate to recruit a sage out of the blue to tell a story, witness Bṛhadaśva and the story of *Nala*. The Mbh does know Vālmīki as a sage. (van Buitenen 1975: 214)

For most treatments of the relation between the two epic Rāma texts, it has been as if such features were secondary to the development of "real" *Rāmakathā*: that is, a heroic story about a king. With the exception of Biardeau, both scholars who have advanced the argument for the priority of the *Rāmopākhyāna* and those who have made good points while advancing the opposite position have weighed the discussion down with notions about source-dependence relations[54] and, above all, arguments about stages of growth, with the assumption that one or, better, both texts can be dissected to align portions of each along the timeline of a hero-story becom-

---

[53] Biardeau (2002, I: 724) observes the absence of Viśvāmitra, Ātreya and Anasūyā, and Agastya, but not the others; Vaidya (1971: xxxii) notes the absences of Viśvāmitra and "the episode of Ahalyā", which figures Gotama; Goldman (1984: 36), while criticizing Vaidya, remarks only on the absence of Viśvāmitra. For van Buitenen (1975: 211), without mentioning the *ṛṣis* at all, "*Rāma* and *Rām.* are wholly parallel till the death of Jaṭāyu"! For Brockington, "the Ṛśyaśṛṅga episode probably has an independent origin", and the Bhārgava Rāma encounter is an "interpolated" "grotesque story" (appreciatively quoting Sukthankar 1936: 21 to the latter effect) (Brockington 1998: 478-479). In another Brockington study, the Bharadvāja and Agastya episodes are "examples of interpolated episodes completely lacking in the Rāmopākhyāna" (Brockington 2000: 299). Curiously, the only serious attention I know of to the related Ram themes of "Encounter holy hermit" and "Description of route through forest to goal" is Richard Gombrich's very suggestive comparison of the Ram with the *Vessantara-jātaka*, whose verse portions he dates to no "later than the 3rd century B.C." (Gombrich 1985: 428, 433 and *passim*). But the comparison goes only so far into the Ram as the Bharadvāja episodes, and concerns only that one *Rāmāyaṇa ṛṣi*.

[54] See Sukthankar 1939: 300-303; 1941: 487; van Buitenen 1975: 208. Goldman (1984: 34) starts his argument with Vaidya and van Buitenen's "revival of the theory that the Ram is not the source of the *Rāmopākhyāna*".

ing mythologized by Rāma's divinization[55] to which John Brockington adds an argument about recensional variation.[56] While I do think Vālmīki has the *Rāmopākhyāna* as *a* source, I believe the evidence of an archetype for both epics nullifies arguments for textual strata, for the hero-to-god timeline, and for recensional variation as a measure of early growth rather than simply *just* recensional variation. Yet when I say I believe that Vālmīki has the *Rāmopākhyāna* as *a* source, it must also be said that he almost certainly knew a variety of *Rāmakathā* sources,[57] as would the *Rāmopākhyāna* author as well, if from nothing else than from the dispersal of varied Rāma story material in the Mbh. Indeed, as Brockington observes, the number of similes drawn on the Rāma story in the *Āraṇyakaparvan* and the battle books "implies considerable familiarity with the story on the part of the audience as well as the performer" (Brockington 1998: 472). As the *Rāmopākhyāna* itself says, "Even now 'Nala's Bridge' is famous on earth" (*nalasetur iti khyāto yo 'dyāpi prathito bhuvi*; Mbh 3.267.45ab). It is thus not necessary to rely on van Buitenen's notion of an "improbable proto-*Rāmacarita*" (Goldman 1984: 39) that the *Rāmopākhyāna* first summarizes before it grows further and "becomes known as the original poem *(ādikāvya)* of Vālmīki" (van Buitenen 1975: 211). We are surely not dealing with a linear cumulative development.

But yes, I do think the differences reveal something significant, and limit myself to three areas of more than a little consequence for Vālmīki: *bhakti*, *dharma*, and *kāvya*.

With regard to the first, the *Rāmopākhyāna*, like the *Nalopākhyāna*, keeps its story focused on the human plane of the hero and

---

[55] This is now mainly Brockington's project (1998: 476-477; 2000: 297-300), which goes back to Jacobi [1893] 1960 and Hopkins 1930. But see also van Buitenen 1975: 209, 213; Goldman 1984: 38.

[56] See Brockington 1998: 474-476; 2000: 290-291.

[57] See Hiltebeitel 2005 for a discussion of non-epic genres in which the Rāma story was probably known before Vālmīki. See also Hopkins' not implausible argument that Rāma is originally a golden age king of legend whose story is only secondarily put to epic purposes (Hopkins 1930: 88-92).

heroine, which is appropriate to their context as "mirror stories" for the Pāṇḍavas and Draupadī. But like the *Nalopākhyāna*, it also makes a bare but sufficient allusion to its context amid the epic's wider *bhakti* idioms or conventions. Thus in the *Nalopākhyāna* Nala is accompanied by a superfluous charioteer named Vārṣṇeya described as *avatīrya vārṣṇeyo*, "Vārṣṇeya descending" (3.71.18), when he "descends" from the chariot, suggesting his role as a double for Vārṣṇeya Kṛṣṇa, avatar and chariot-driver for Arjuna.[58] And in the *Rāmopākhyāna*, Brahmā tells the gods and *ṛṣis* how Rāvaṇa will be killed: "For that purpose the four-armed Viṣṇu has descended (*avatīrṇo ... viṣṇuḥ*) at my command" (260.5) – as already quoted, with Brahmā going on to command the hosts of gods to take birth on earth as "Viṣṇu's companions" (*viṣṇoḥ sahāyān*; 260.6-7).[59] The chief difference is that whereas the *Nalopākhyāna* is intentionally cryptic (as it is frequently) in evoking an incarnation who is superfluous to its story, the *Rāmopākhyāna* can only be straightforward since it is introducing the hero as an incarnation. These are *bare* references, but the *Rāmopākhyāna* ones are not isolated, as has been argued by Brockington.[60] There is also, as we have seen, the strange appearance by "Bhagavat among those who reunite Rāma and Sītā" (275.18); and when Vasiṣṭha and Vāmadeva consecrate Rāma, he is called "the *Vaiṣṇava* hero" (*taṃ vaiṣṇa-*

[58] See Biardeau 1985: 5-6, 8-9, 16-17, 31-32; Hiltebeitel 2001a: 219, 232; and further, the discussion of a "descent convention" in Hiltebeitel 2004c.

[59] The same term is used by Vaiśampāyana in the *Rāmopākhyāna*'s "frame story" to describe the monkeys, bears, Pāṇḍavas, and allies of Indra (276.5-10 – four times).

[60] Brockington 1998: 476: "The sole exception" [= Brockington 2000: 300: "the only exception"] to Rāma being mainly a human and exemplary figure, "the position reached in the middle of the second stage of growth of the Rāmāyaṇa", "is the brief *adhyāya* 260 where Viṣṇu incarnates as Rāma, and the other gods beget" monkey and bear sons. Brockington finds it "the more significant that the *Rāmopākhyāna* does not allude to Rāma's divinity in its closing chapter", but it is hard not to read Brahmā's closing words as just such an allusion: "Like an immortal, you have accomplished a great feat of the gods" (*kṛtaṃ tvayā mahatkāryaṃ devānām amaraprabha*; 3.275.34cd). In any case, as quoted just below, it is in the same closing *adhyāya* that Rāma is consecrated "the *Vaiṣṇava* hero" (65).

vaṃ śūram; 275.65). If Vālmīki had the *Rāmopākhyāna* among his sources, he would have been able to recognize a *bhakti* strain to improve upon, and also a model for restricting obvious *bhakti* references to scenes at the beginning and end of Rāma's story. The reasons for this economy in explicit reference to Rāma's divinity, which are especially pertinent in *Vālmīki* but also implicit in the *Rāmopākhyāna*, have been made clear by Pollock (1984).

As regards *dharma*, that is surely the primary subject that Vālmīki has enriched by introducing the Seven *ṛṣi*s plus Agastya, and by inversion the *ṛṣi* Mataṅga, as guides and signposts along the hero and heroine's path. For as representatives of Veda, the Seven and Agastya are the highest authorities on *dharma*, which is, in one way or another, what they and their wives communicate to Rāma and Sītā along that path. The striking thing, however, is that whereas the *Rāmopākhyāna* keeps the Rāma-Sītā story within the ambiguous, problematic, and somewhat forgiving (that is all Rāma has to do at its end) *dharma* of the Mbh, Vālmīki – it would almost seem – seizes on the Rāma story to present *dharma* as a much more rigorous and uncompromising affair: monogamy as the model; a *dharma* of the limit situation (*maryādā*) – a term never used in the *Rāmopākhyāna* but vital to Vālmīki's portrayal of Rāma.[61] One of the other personages absent from the *Rāmopākhyāna* but emphasized by Vālmīki is the *śūdra* Śambūka, killed by Rāma for the offense of practicing *tapas* (Ram 7.66-67).[62] The *Rāmopākhyāna*'s Kiṣkindhā is uncomplicated by stories of impure buffalo blood and implications of untouchability contaminating a nearby Mataṅgavanam. The *Rāmopākhyāna* gives Sītā only one ordeal, the first, and

[61] See Ram 2.103.3 (Rāma speaking on "the man who is beyond the limit" (*nirmaryādas ... puruṣaḥ*, pointing toward his post-epic title of Maryādā Puruṣottama); 4.18.25 (Rāma's new excuse for killing Vālin is the latter's "transgression of the limit"); 5.33.11 (Hanumān to Sītā: "Lovely lady, Rāma is the guardian of the four classes of society and enforcer of the norms of social behavior" [*maryādānāṃ ca lokasya kartā kārayitā ca saḥ*]; Goldman & Goldman 1996: 201).

[62] Cf. Biardeau 2002, I: 275; Hopkins 1930: 101: The Rāma-Śambuka (*sic*) story *is* mentioned at Mbh 12.149.62.

it is not by purifying fire as it is in Vālmīki; and thereafter Rāma has no second thoughts about her – the story is over. Yet in the Ram it is precisely at the second ordeal, not found in the *Rāmopākhyāna*, and "crucial", as Shulman says, "to any understanding of the poetics of the work as a completed whole" (Shulman 2001: 34), that Vālmīki makes himself present at the end of the road to introduce his own final twist on the problematic character of *dharma* and Rāma's strict adherence to it: that it cost Rāma his wife.

As to *kāvya*, there are two ideas that have tied debate over these matters in knots. The first is that either the *Rāmopākhyāna* is some kind of résumé or abridgment of the Ram[63] or that the *Rāmāyāṇa* is some kind of embellishment of the *Rāmopākhyāna*. The issue has seemed inconclusive precisely because so much ingenuity has been expended in nuancing and making good arguments for both positions. The best argument for abridgment is that there certainly are passages in the *Rāmopākhyāna* that look like they need some fuller version to unpack them, and that the Ram, being a text one can cite in such cases, is a more convincing candidate than some "improbable proto-Rāmacarita". That is Goldman's argument (1984: 38-39). But I am no longer convinced that it levels the playing field.[64] For

---

[63] Recently, this is Shulman's view: "Western scholarship has laboured valiantly to make the relationship between this *resumé* and the text of the *Rāmāyaṇa* intelligible – but there is still no consensus" – that is, while there is no consensus on intelligibility, the *Rāmopākhyāna is* a "resumé", to which Shulman adds, "the *significant fact* remains that one epic *cites* at length *the story of the other*" (my italics). Shulman speaks of "certain minor but interesting divergences" between the two Rāma narratives without saying what they are (Shulman 2001: 22).

[64] Recognizing that this is a vulnerable point in my argument, I would, at least at this point, recommend that we approach individual cases from one or the other of two angles. Either the *Rāmopākhyāna* would probably be drawing on a *Rāmakathā* tradition that later makes it into the *Rāmāyana*, as in the crow story discussed by Goldman (1984: 38), or it may only appear as an ellipsis because we know the *Rāmāyaṇa*, but actually makes sense on its own – as when Śūrpaṇakhā is defaced without it being told how (Mbh 3.262.44), which looks like a fragment, but, in its context, could have taken place while fighting alongside her brothers Khara and Dūṣaṇa – like Tāṭakā. Similarly, Hanumān only faces (and kills) one marine *rākṣasī* (266.57).

one thing, too much weight has been put on the claim that differences are "easily explainable as examples of the *Rāmopākyāna*'s somewhat awkward and often pedestrian condensation of the tale as told by Vālmīki" (Goldman 1984: 37; cf. Brockington 1998, 474: "a rather careless abridgement"). The differences are not so easily dismissed and the *Rāmopākhyāna* is perhaps not so awkward or careless. More than this, those maintaining the priority of the Ram have never answered why a poem condensing or abridging that text would persist in eliminating so many of the scenes and characters for which it is famous, many already mentioned, such as Sītā's *agniparīkṣā*, banishment, and final ordeal; Śambūka, Kuśa, Lava, Vālmīki himself and the creation and transmission of the poem; others not yet mentioned, such as Sītā's birth in a furrow; Hanumān "bringing the mount Droṇācala (*sic*) with its medicinal plants to revive Lakṣmaṇa hit by Indrajit's missile" (Vaidya 1971: xxxii);[65] and indeed, some of which are among those that best exemplify the Ram as *kāvya*: Rāma's madness upon Sītā's abduction; Hanumān's viewing of Rāvaṇa's harem and his telling Sītā her husband's story; all the scenes of grief upon Rāma's departure from Ayodhyā – grief being the Ram's underlying *sthāyibhāva* or "stable aesthetic emotion" in relation to *karuṇā*, "pity" as its predominant aesthetic flavor (*aṅgī rasa*).[66]

The second idea to have tied up debate is that the Ram as *kāvya* – indeed *ādikāvya*, "the first poem" – is to be differentiated from the Mbh as *itihāsa*, something like "history". This idea has been

---

[65] See Biardeau 2002, I: 725.

[66] Ram 1.2.17; cf. 4.8. See Goldman 1984: 71-72; Tubb 1991: 174-179. There are only four uses of the word *śoka* in the *Rāmopākhyāna*, all at telling points but centered only on Rāma and Sītā: Rāma's grief at Sītā's abduction (Mbh 3.263.23); Sītā's "grief for her husband" in Rāvaṇa's *aśoka* grove (264.48); a description of Sītā as "thin from grief" as she is surrounded there by *rākṣasīs* (265.30); and finally another as Rāma sees her "drawn with grief" just as he is about to repudiate her (275.9). There are no scenes of grief in "*Ayodhyā*" paralleling those in the Ram's second book. Vālmīki also emotionally deepens *Rāmopākhyāna* relationships in this direction, such as his construal of Rāma and Sugrīva's "friendship" as one of commiseration (see Hiltebeitel 2004a; 2004b).

advanced along with different arguments. Vaidya, for instance, picking up on the "history" connotation of *itihāsa*, argues that

> the poet Vālmīki introduced into his epic poem an innovation of Sītā's test by fire against the epic and historical background of Vāyu assuring Rāma of Sītā's purity (Vaidya 1971: xxxv).

That is, since the *Rāmopākhyāna* is "a part and parcel of a work called Itihāsa", its account featuring Vāyu makes a "historical statement" (p. xxxv). As Goldman says, Vaidya's point can be counted among the "absurdities" to have arisen in this debate, since the *itihāsa/kāvya* genre distinction is useless in claiming one or the other to be "more or less valid historically".[67] On the other hand, stressing the *kāvya* side of the distinction, Shulman calls on the opposition to remind us that India provides no genre term for both works that would cover over the felt differences between them in the manner of the Western term "epic" (Shulman 2001: 39).

My working premise for this article has been a simple one: that the Ram poet knowingly develops his poem as a single-genre work out of, and over against, the multi-genre precedent of the Mbh, which characterizes itself not only as *itihāsa* but *purāṇa*, *ākhyāna*, *upākhyāna*, *saṃvāda*, *śāstra*, *upaniṣad*, *saṃhitā*, great *jñāna*, and fifth Veda. I believe that the selection of *itihāsa* as the genre term for the Mbh could only have arisen once classifying minds selected that term out of this welter of genre terms, and that such a reduction could only have been made once it became a matter of aesthetic interest to distinguish the Mbh from the Ram and the latter's reputation as *kāvya.* As with his narrowed down articulations of *dharma*, Vālmīki invents a purer model, that of single-genre poetry.

Yet no one would say there are not fine poetic moments in the Mbh, or even in the *Rāmopākhyāna*. Moreover, the epic has some interesting things to say about *kavi*s, poets. Near the beginning of

[67] Goldman 1984: 35. On the genre issue, see further Goldman 1995: 75-76; Hiltebeitel 2001a: 6 and n. 27.

its very first *adhyāya*, before the bard Ugraśravas opens his story-telling, he announces to the Naimiṣa Forest sages,

> I will proclaim the thought entire of the infinitely splendid Vyāsa *(pravakṣyāmi matam kṛtsnam vyāsasyāmitatejasaḥ)*. Some poets *(kavayaḥ)* have told it before, others tell it now, and others too will tell this history *(itihāsa)* on earth. It is indeed a great erudition (*mahaj jñānam*) established in the three worlds that is held (or "possessed": *dhāryate*) by the twiceborn in its particulars and totalities (*vistaraiś ca samāsaiḥ*). (Mbh 1.1.23-25)

Then, a little further along, toward the end of the second *adhyāya*, the bard adds,

> Having heard this *upākhyāna* so worthy of being heard no other will please him, just as the crow sounds harsh after hearing the male cuckoo. From this supreme *itihāsa* arise the inspirations of poets (*jāyante kavibuddhayaḥ*), just as the three dispositions of the world[68] arise from the five elements. Purāṇa turns in the compass of this *ākhyāna*, O twiceborns, just as the four classes of creatures (turn) in the compass of space. Works of every quality resort to this *ākhyāna* even as the interacting senses resort to the manifold workings of the mind. There is no story (*kathā*) on earth that hasn't resorted to this *ākhyāna*, even as support for the body comes from resorting to food. This *ākhyāna* is lived on by all the best poets (*idaṃ sarvaiḥ kavivarair ākhyānam upajīvyate*) even as a lord is born with servants wishing for promotion (*udayaprepsubhir bhṛtyair abhijāta iveśvaraḥ*).[69]

---

[68] According to the Vedanticizing construal of Nīlakaṇṭha, *ādhyātmādhibhūtādhidaivānāṃ samyagvidhayo racanāḥ* (Kinjawadekar 1929-33, I: 39). Van Buitenen (1973: 43) translates "the configurations of the three worlds"; Ganguli & Roy 1884-96, I: 35: "the formation of the three worlds".

[69] Mbh 1.2.236-241:
śrutvā tvidam upākhyānaṃ śrāvyam anyan na rocate |
puṃskokilarutaṃ śrutvā rūkṣā dhvāṅkṣasya vāg iva || 236 ||
itihāsottamād asmāj jāyante kavibuddhayaḥ |
pañcabhya iva bhūtebhyo lokasaṃvidhayas trayaḥ || 237 ||
asyākhyānasya viṣaye purāṇaṃ vartate dvijāḥ |
antarikṣasya viṣaye prajā iva caturvidhāḥ || 238 ||
kriyāguṇānāṃ sarveṣāṃ idam ākhyānam āśrayaḥ |
indriyāṇāṃ samastānāṃ citrā iva manaḥkriyāḥ || 239 ||
anāśrityaitad ākhyāṇaṃ kathā bhuvi na vidyate |
āhāram anapāśritya śarīrasyeva dhāraṇam || 240 ||
idaṃ sarvaiḥ kavivarair ākhyānam upajīvyate |
udayaprepsubhir bhṛtyair abhijāta iveśvaraḥ || 241 ||

Taken together in sequence, these two passages first have the bard locate the text as a possession of Brahmans. Then he indicates that now that he has heard it recited by Vaiśampāyana at Janamejaya's Snake Sacrifice, that is, at its debut recital in the world of men, from which he has travelled to the more or less celestial Naimiṣa Forest, domain of the celestial *ṛṣis*,[70] it is now in that world of men for others to tell, and, more than that, for others to be inspired by as they seek to supercede it. Indeed, it is almost as if the bard senses in the second passage that a work such as Vālmīki's is competition coming over the horizon. I believe this possibility should be seriously considered. What is the relation between the Ram poet and the sage Vālmīki mentioned fairly frequently in the Mbh?[71] Con-

[70] See Hiltebeitel 2001a: 92-176.

[71] See 1.50.14 (Vālmīki praised by Āstīka for his gentle firmness), 2.7.14 (among many famous *ṛṣis* in Indra's *sabhā* or hall), 3.83.102 (among select *ṛṣis* waiting for the Pāṇḍavas on pilgrimage), 5.81.27 (among illustrious *ṛṣis* attending Kṛṣṇa's departure for Hāstinapura to confront the Kauravas), 5.99.11 (a son of Garuḍa, and thus probably someone else), 12.200.4 (among *ṛṣis* cited by Bhīṣma regarding Govinda), and 13.18.7 (addressing Yudhiṣṭhira regarding Śiva, who absolved Vālmīki of a charge of Brahmanicide and told him, "Your fame shall be foremost (*yaśas te 'gryaṃ bhaviṣyati*; 8f). One problematic reference, however, is included in the Pune Critical Edition under questionable conditions, since it is not found in one Kāśmīrī manuscript, K4. At 7.118.48ab, Sātyaki, having taken criticism for the manner in which he has dismembered Bhūriśravas, attributes to "Vālmīki" the following "*śloka*" (even though it is only a half-*śloka*, and is referred to otherwise in many mss.): "what causes pain to enemies, that should be done" (*pīḍākaram amitrāṇāṃ yat syāt kartavyam eva tat*; 7.118.48cd = Ram 6.68.27cd). This epigrammatic line gets inflated with further Ram echoes in various mss. by an extra line to make it quotable as a "*śloka*", raising the likelihood that it has been overlaid not only by these echoes but by the attribution to Vālmīki. See Hopkins 1926: 216-217; 1930: 86-87, and Brockington 1998: 480, going over some of the same ground from different angles. Brockington (1998: 480) also mentions an identification by Albrecht Weber of the "Bhārgava" cited at Mbh 12.57.40-41 as Vālmīki, and concurs with Weber that the verses attributed to this "Bhārgava" are "based on" Ram 2.61.1. But given the extensive differences between the two passages, the identification cannot carry much weight. Fitzgerald identifies this Bhārgava as "= (probably) Śukra" (Fitzgerald 2004: 302 and notations).

Curiously, the only other problematic passage I know of implying direct reference to the Ram, one mentioning the work's title rather than its author, is also found in three lines (Mbh 3.147.11c-12d) omitted by the same Kāśmīrī

sidering the largely overlapping reading communities created by these two works, it is not impossible that "Vālmīki" could be a *nom de plume* taken up from the Mbh by a Ram poet highly familiar with that text. Indeed, if the Mbh is a work of composite authorship, "Vālmīki" may have been an apprentice-contributor, or someone at least familiar with the project. To speak of the temporal priority of the Mbh over the Ram is thus not to rule out the possibility that the latter might have been started before the former was finished. We are a long way from making such speculation worthwhile, but I offer it because I believe that it points in a reasonable direction.

Yet this allusion to new ambitious *kavis* coming along, and possibly to Vālmīki as the first among them, was at some point no longer felt to be sufficient to characterize Vyāsa's inspiration of other poets, or indeed the relation of his work to the Ram. Thus the famous interpolation in which Brahmā appears to Vyāsa to recommend that Gaṇeśa be his scribe was introduced between these two passages, though much closer to the first, to make the point that the Mbh is indeed a *kāvya*. For present purposes, what matters is that the whole passage is an interpolation within an interpolation.[72] First there was an interpolation featuring Brahmā's confirmation that Vyāsa has composed a *kāvya*. Says Vyāsa,

> O Blessed one, I have created this highly venerated *kāvya* (*kāvyaṃ paramapūjitam*) in which I have proclaimed the secret of the Vedas (*vedarahasyam*) and other topics (Vulgate 1.1.61-62; Pune Critical Edition 1, App. I, lines 13-14),

---

manuscript that omits the attribution to Vālmīki, K4. Here, quite plausibly interpolated between lines that have Bhīma relate that he and Hanumān are brothers, Bhīma further describes Hanumān as "renowned in the Ram" (*rāmāyaṇe 'tivikhāyātaḥ*: 147.11c) for the leap (already just mentioned by Bhīma at 147.9d) that rescued Sītā. In retaining these passages, the editors (S. K. De for Book 7 and V. S. Sukthankar for Book 3) seem to follow, without comment, Sukthankar's poor evaluation of K4 as "carelessly written" with some noteworthy insertions (Sukthankar 1933: xii, li; Prolegomena to Book 1). But Sukthankar does not address the value of K4's omissions.

[72] See Lüders 1929: 1144-1145.

to which Brahmā replies,

> I know that since your birth you have truthfully given voice to the *brahman*. You have called this a *kāvya*, and therefore a *kāvya* it shall be.[73] No poets (*kavayo*) are equal to the excellence of this *kāvya* (Vulgate 1.1.72-73b; Critical Ed. 1, App. I, lines 33-35)

– more or less repeating what the second of the older passages had said about emerging rival poets, but substituting *kāvya* for the genre-terms *itihāsa* and *ākhyāna*. Second, twenty lines were subsequently inserted into this first interpolation for Brahmā to recommend that Vyāsa call upon Gaṇeśa to be his scribe.[74] While the Brahmā interpolation is concerned with *kāvya*, the Gaṇeśa interpolation within it is concerned with writing and mentions *kāvya* only in its lead-in verse.

Now as Shulman says, the Brahmā interpolation was "clearly composed under the influence of the Ram frame story, [in having] Brahmā visit Vyāsa just as he is said to have come to Vālmīki", adding further that it was "an attempt to bring the *Mahābhārata* in line with the *kāvya* tradition" (Shulman 2001: 33, n. 10). One might assume that at least the Gaṇeśa modification would have been made rather late in the Mbh's manuscript history. Lüders observes that it is clearly a northern interpolation, and mentions references to the Gaṇeśa legend by the 9th century CE as a *terminus ante quem* (Lüders 1929: 1144). More interesting, however, are his remarks on the Brahmā interpolation: Based "not only on its occurrence in all Grantha, Telugu, and Malayālam manuscripts (with the exception of M_1), but also on the mention of Pāśupata philosophy" (Lüders 1929: 1144 [my translation]) in it, Lüders argues that the Brahmā interpolation was almost certainly introduced in South India. Although I doubt that Pāśupata philosophy can identify the passage as South Indian, since Pāśupatas are also mentioned in the *Nārāyaṇīya*

[73] That is, Brahmā treats Vyāsa's word as generating an act of truth.

[74] Vulgate 1.1.74-83; Critical Ed. 1, App. I, *apud* line 36. See Lüders 1929: 1144; Sullivan 1990; Hiltebeitel 2004b.

(Mbh 12.337.59b and 62d), the manuscript evidence for the southern origins of the Brahmā interpolation is certainly sound. It is particularly its occurrence in all but one[75] of the Malayālam (M) manuscripts that is striking. Here I would like to draw on the current work of T. P. Mahadevan (forthcoming), who attempts to link the migrations of two Brahman groups – the Pūrvaśikhas (those with forelocks) and Aparaśikhas (those with topknots to the back) – from North to South India with the north-to-south migrations of the epics. Mahadevan argues that the M version – long recognized as the shortest version in the Southern Recension, and similar in at least that regard to the shortest Northern Recension versions (the Śāradā and Kāśmīrī) – is connected with those who made the first migration, the Pūrvaśikhas, and that the more inflated other manuscript groupings of the Southern Recension (the Telugu and Grantha manuscripts) reflect the overlay upon M that follows from the arrival south of the much later (mainly) Aparaśikha migration. Mahadevan argues that the Pūrvaśikha Brahmans would have brought a Mbh probably close to the Kāśmīrī-Śāradā recension which they fashioned into the oldest Southern archetype and later developed into M in Kerala after (or even during) the so-called Kaḷabhra interregnum of the 4th to 7th centuries AD (Monius 2001: 3). Because the Brahmā story is so widespread in Southern manuscripts, it would be likely to have originated from the pre-Kaḷabhra times when M was establishing the groundwork of the Southern Recension, and to have also traveled north even to be found in *some* of the Kāśmīrī manuscripts. We thus get a quite early pre-4th century date as likely for the Brahmā interpolation, with its concern to establish Vyāsa's Mbh on a par with Vālmīki's Ram as a *kāvya*. And indeed, it would not be an insignificant fact for it to be in a South Indian setting that the two epics would be for the first time

[75] Note that the issue here differs from that raised in footnote 71 above concerning the two omissions from one Kāśmīrī manuscript. This omission only reflects what is clearly an interpolation as a whole, and could suggest a state of things in the south prior to the interpolation's being made there.

felt in India to be of a single genre, for that is what I have heard them called in South India: *irentu kāppiyam*, "the two *kāvya*s".[76] In this regard, Shulman seems to have reached a selective conclusion when he writes in the next-to-last sentence of his essay on the historical poetics of the Sanskrit epics,

> The Indian tradition is, in any case, clearly right to class the two epics separately, in different genres reflecting very distinct visions – even if to us both are surely "epic" (Shulman 2001: 39).

In South India, they can both be *kāvya*.

Finally, what happens if we add the theme I have explored most extensively in this essay – the unfolding of Rāma and Sītā's path by posting the Seven *ṛṣi*s plus Agastya along the way – to our examples of how the Ram as *kāvya* surpasses not only the Mbh but, with it, and more specifically, the *Rāmopākhyāna*? Here Mahadevan's research into the initial Pūrvaśikha migration opens another intriguing angle. Whereas the Pūrvaśikhas, as first to arrive in the south, go by the primary *pravara* names of the Seven *ṛṣi*s plus Agastya (the latter is included, but only barely), the Aparaśikhas, as subsequent arrivals, take on only secondary and tertiary *pravara* names. That is to say, the *pravara* names used by the Pūrvaśikhas as the first Brahmans to migrate to the south are the very same names as those of the Vedic Ram Brahmans who guide Rāma and Sītā to the south. This coincidence would do nothing to discourage the idea that the *Vālmīki* Ram has something to do with "Brahman colonization" of the south. Indeed, in giving these Vedic *ṛṣi*s the trailblazing role in mapping the extension of Rāmrājya to the

---

[76] I have not yet been able to learn how old this usage is – in particular, in relation to that of *kāppiyam* as the genre term for classical Tamil epics. See *Encyclopaedia of Tamil Literature* (1990): 138, 200-211, 342-353. But in harmony with what is said there, the *Tamil Lexicon* (1926-39): 2, 868 gives a definition of *kāppiyam* that certainly accommodates both Sanskrit epics: "kāppiyam, n. < *kāvya*. A narrative poem dealing with *aṟam*, *poruḷ*, *iṉpam*, and *vīṭu* [i.e., and *mutatis mutandis*, with *dharma*, *artha*, *kāma*, and *mokṣa*] and describing the exploits of a hero, being of two kinds, viz., *peru-ṅ-kāppiyam* and *ciṟu-kāppiyam* [i.e., big *kāvya* and small *kāvya*]."

south,[77] Vālmīki, probably reflecting conditions in which that first migration had already begun, may go beyond the *Rāmopākhyāna*, and the Mbh, precisely to create a charter myth for this unfolding process.

In any case, considering how many have overlooked it, the marking of Rāma and Sītā's path by these *ṛṣi*s is clearly not the most memorable or "poetic" of Vālmīki's inspirations. But it is the one by which he sets forth the path of Sītā and Rāma as both a *ṛṣi*'s path *and a poet's path* that leads, in more ways than one, ultimately to him.

REFERENCES

BIARDEAU, Madeleine 1976. Études de mythologie hindoue: 5. Bhakti et avatāra. *Bulletin de l'École Française d'Extrême-Orient* 65: 111-263.

—— 1985. Nala et Damayantī. Héros épiques. Part 2. *IIJ* 28: 1-34.

—— 1997. Some remarks on the links between the Epics, the Purāṇas and their Vedic sources. In: Gerhard Oberhammer (ed.), *Studies in Hinduism. Vedism and Hinduism*: 69-173. Vienna: Verlag der Österreichischen Akademie der Wissenschaften.

—— 1999. *Le Rāmāyaṇa de Vālmīki*. Paris: Gallimard.

—— 2002. *Le Mahābhārata. Un récit fondateur du brahmanisme et son interprétation*, I-II. Paris: Éditions du Seuil.

BROCKINGTON, John 1998. *The Sanskrit Epics*. (Handbuch der Orientalistik, 2.12.) Leiden: E.J. Brill.

—— 2000. *Epic Threads. John Brockington on the Sanskrit Epics*. Edited by Greg Bailey & Mary Brockington. New Delhi: OUP.

BUITENEN, J. A. B. van (trans. & ed.) 1973, 1975, 1978. *The Mahābhārata*, I: 1. *The Book of Beginnings*; II: 2. *The Book of the Assembly Hall*; 3. *The Book of the Forest*; III: 4. *The Book of Virāṭa*; 5. *The Book of the Effort*. Chicago: University of Chicago Press.

DEFOURNY, Michel 1978. *Le mythe de Yayāti dans la littérature épique et purāṇique. Étude de mythologie hindoue*. Paris: Société d'Edition "Les Belles Lettres".

[77] This is the brunt of what Rāma has to tell Vālin at 4.18.6-11 and 23-24: while in exile, Rāma extends the law of Bharata – itself, of course, anchored by Bharata's devotion to Rāmrājya via Rāma's sandals throughout the world.

Encyclopaedia of Tamil Literature (1990). Vol. 1, *Introductory Articles*. Thiruvanmiyur, Madras: Institute of Asian Studies.

FITZGERALD, James L. 2001. Making Yudhiṣṭhira the king: The dialectics and the politics of violence in the *Mahābhārata*. *RO* 54.1: 63-92.

—— 2002. The Rāma Jāmadagnya 'thread' of the *Mahābhārata*: A new survey of Rāma Jāmadagnya in the Pune text. In: Mary Brockington, (ed.), *Stages and Transitions: Temporal and Historical Frameworks in Epic and Purāṇic Literature. Proceedings of the Second DICSEP*: 89-132. Zagreb: Croatian Academy of Sciences and Arts.

—— 2003. The many voices of the *Mahābhārata*. An article reviewing *Rethinking the Mahābhārata: A Reader's Guide to the Education of the Dharma King* by Alf Hiltebeitel. *JAOS* 123.4: 803-818.

—— (trans. & ed.) 2004. *The Mahābhārata*, VII: 11. *The Book of the Women;* 12. *The Book of Peace* (Part One). Chicago: University of Chicago Press.

GANGULI, Kisari Mohan (trans.) & Pratap Chandra ROY (publisher) 1884-96. *The Mahabharata*, I-XIX. (Reprint: New Delhi: Munshiram Manoharlal, 1970.)

GOLDMAN, Robert P. (trans.) 1984. *The Rāmāyaṇa of Vālmīki*, I: *Bālakāṇḍa*. Princeton: Princeton University Press.

—— 1995. Gods in hiding: The Mahābhārata's Virāṭa Parvan and the divinity of the Indian epic hero. In S. P. Narang (ed.), *Modern Evaluation of the Mahābhārata (Prof. P. K. Sharma Felicitation Volume)*: 73-100. Delhi: Nag Publishers.

GOLDMAN, Sally J. Sutherland 2004. Gendered narratives: Gender, space, and narrative structures in Vālmīki's *Bālakāṇḍa*. In: Mandakranta Bose (ed.), *The Rāmāyaṇa Revisited*: 47-85. New York: OUP.

GOLDMAN, Robert P. & Sally J. Sutherland GOLDMAN (trans.) 1996. *The Rāmāyaṇa of Vālmīki: An Epic of Ancient India*, V: *Sundarakāṇḍa*. Princeton: Princeton University Press.

GOMBRICH, Richard 1985. The Vessantara Jātaka, the Rāmāyaṇa and the Dasaratha Jātaka. *JAOS* 105.3 (Ernest Bender (ed.), Special Issue. Indological Studies Dedicated to Daniel H. H. Ingalls): 427-437.

HILTEBEITEL, Alf 1977. Nahuṣa in the skies: A human king of heaven. *History of Religions* 16.4: 329-350.

—— 1979. Ṛṣis and Rākṣasas: At home and abroad in the Indian epics. New York: American Academy of Religion annual meeting.

—— 1980. Rāma and Gilgamesh: The sacrifices of the water buffalo and the Bull of Heaven. *History of Religions* 19: 187-223.

—— 1981. Draupadī's Hair. In: Madeleine Biardeau (ed.), *Autour de la déesse hindoue* (Puruṣārtha, 5): 179-214.

HILTEBEITEL, Alf 1984. The two Kṛṣṇas on one chariot: Upaniṣadic imagery and epic mythology. *History of Religions* 24.3: 1-26.

—— 2001a. *Rethinking the Mahābhārata. A Reader's Guide to the Education of the Dharma King*. Chicago: University of Chicago Press.

—— 2001b. Bhīṣma's Sources. In: Klaus Karttunen & Petteri Koskikallio (eds.), *Vidyārṇavavandanam. Essays in Honour of Asko Parpola* (Studia Orientalia, 94): 261-278. Helsinki: Finnish Oriental Society.

—— 2004a. Mapping bhakti through friendship in the Sanskrit epics. American Oriental Society, San Diego, April 2004.

—— 2004b. The emergence of kāvya out of the two Sanskrit epics. International Seminar on the Origins of Mahākāvya, Università degli Studi di Milano, June 4-5.

—— 2004c. More rethinking the *Mahābhārata*: Toward a politics of bhakti. *IIJ* 47: 203-227. (First presented at the 32nd Annual South Asia Conference, Madison WI, October 2003.)

—— 2005. Weighting orality and writing in the Sanskrit epics. In: Petteri Koskikallio (ed.), *Epics, Khilas and Purāṇas: Continuities and Ruptures. Proceedings of the Third DICSEP September 2002*: 81-111. Zagreb: Croatian Academy of Sciences and Arts.

—— 2006. The *Nārāyaṇīya* and the early reading communities of the *Mahābhārata*. In: Patrick Olivelle (ed.), *Between the Empires. Society in India 300 BCE to 400 CE*: 227-255. New York: OUP.

HOPKINS, Edward Washburn 1901. *The Great Epic of India. Its Character and Origin*. (Reprint: Calcutta: Punthi Pustak, 1969.)

—— 1915. *Epic Mythology*. (Encyclopedia of Indo-Aryan Research, 3.1.B.) Strassburg: Karl J. Trübner. (Reprint: New York: Biblo and Tannen, 1969.)

—— 1926. The original Rāmāyaṇa. *JAOS* 46: 202-219.

—— 1930. Allusions to the Rāma-story in the Mahābhārata. *JAOS* 50: 85-103.

JACOBI, Hermann 1960. *The Rāmāyaṇa: Das Rāmāyaṇa of Dr. Hermann Jacobi*. Trans. by S. N. Ghoshal. Baroda: Oriental Institute. [First German edition: Bonn: Friedrich Cohen, 1893.]

KINJAWADEKAR, Ramachandra (ed.) 1929-33. *Mahābhāratam with the Commentary of Nīlakaṇṭha*, I-VI. Poona: Chitrashala Press.

LÜDERS, Heinrich 1929. Review of *The Mahābhārata for the first time critically edited* by Vishnu S. Sukthankar, vol. 1. *Deutsche Literaturzeitung* 24: 1137-1146.

LUTGENDORF, Philip 2001. Dining out at Lake Pampa: The Shabari episode in multiple Ramayanas. In: Paula Richman (ed.), *Questioning Rāmāyaṇas:*

A South Asian Narrative Tradition: 119-136. Berkeley: University of California Press.

MAGNONE, Paolo 2004. *Rāmo Rāmam udaikṣata*: The encounter of the two Rāmas between *itihāsa* and *kāvya*. International Seminar on the Origins of Mahākāvya, Università degli Studi di Milano, June 4-5, 2004.

MAHADEVAN, T. P., forthcoming. *The Arrival of Vedism in South India: The Aparaśikha and Pūrvaśikha Brahmans* (tentative title).

MONIER-WILLIAMS, Monier 1899. *A Sanskrit-English Dictionary*. Oxford: Clarendon Press.

MONIUS, Anne E. 2001. *Imagining a Place for Buddhism: Literary Culture and Religious Community in Tamil-Speaking South India*. New York: OUP.

POLLOCK, Sheldon I. 1984. Ātmānam mānuṣaṃ manye: Dharmākūtam on the divinity of Rāma. *JOIB* 33: 505-528.

—— (trans.) 1986. *The Rāmāyaṇa of Vālmīki: An Epic of Ancient India*, II: *Ayodhyākāṇḍa*. Ed. by Robert P. Goldman. Introduction and annotation by translator. Princeton: Princeton University Press.

—— (trans.) 1991. *The Rāmāyaṇa of Vālmīki: An Epic of Ancient India*, III: *Araṇyakāṇḍa*. Ed. by Robert P. Goldman. Introduction and annotation by translator. Princeton: Princeton University Press.

RAGHAVAN, V. 1973. *The Greater Ramayana*. Varanasi: All-India Kashiraj Trust.

RAGHUNATHAN, N. (trans.) 1981. *Srimad Vālmīki Ramayana*, II: *Aranya Kānda, Kishkindha Kānda, and Sundara Kānda*. Madras: Vighneswara Publishing House.

SHASTRI, Hari Prasad (trans.) 1969. *The Ramayana of Valmiki*, II: *Aranya Kanda, Kishkindha Kanda, Sundara Kanda*. London: Shanti Sadan.

SHULMAN, David 2001. Toward a historical poetics of the Sanskrit epics. Chapter 1 of: *The Wisdom of Poets: Studies in Tamil, Telugu, and Sanskrit*. Delhi: OUP. [First published in *International Folklore Review* (1991) 11: 9-17.]

SUKTHANKAR, Vishnu S. (ed.) 1933. *The Ādiparvan*. (*Mahābhārata. Critical Edition*, 1.) Poona: BORI.

—— 1936. Epic Studies, 6: The Bhṛgus and the Bhārata: A text-historical study. *ABORI* 18.1: 1-76.

—— 1939. The Nala episode and the Rāmāyaṇa. In: S. M. Katre & P. K. Gode (eds.), *A Volume of Eastern and Indian Studies Presented to Professor F. W. Thomas*: 294-303. Bombay: Karnatak Publishing House.

—— 1941. The Rāma episode (Rāmopākhyāna) and the Rāmāyaṇa. In: S. M. Katre & P. K. Gode (eds.), *A Volume of Studies in Indology Presented to Prof. P. V. Kane*: 472-487. Poona: Oriental Book Agency.

SUKTHANKAR, Vishnu S. *et al.* (eds.) 1933-70. *Mahābhārata. Critical Edition.* 24 vols. with *Harivaṃśa*. Poona: BORI.

SULLIVAN, Bruce M. 1990. *Kṛṣṇa Dvaipāyana Vyāsa and the Mahābhārata: A New Interpretation.* Leiden: Brill.

Tamil Lexicon (1926-39). 6 vols. Madras: University of Madras.

THOMAS, Lynn 1996. Paraśurāma and time. In: Julia Leslie (ed.), *Myth and Myth-making*: 63-85. Richmond, Surrey: Curzon.

TUBB, Gary A. 1991. Śāntarasa in the *Mahābhārata*. In: Arvind Sharma (ed.), *Essays in the Mahābhārata*: 171-203. Leiden: E.J. Brill.

VAIDYA, P. L. (ed.) 1971. *The Yuddhakāṇḍa. The Sixth Book of the Vālmīki Rāmāyaṇa. The National Epic of India. The Vālmīki-Rāmayaṇa Critically Edited for the First Time*, II. Baroda: Oriental Institute.

WINTERNITZ, Moriz 1908-22. *Geschichte der indischen Litteratur*, I-III. Leipzig: C. F. Amelangs Verlag. (English translations: *A History of Indian Literature*. Calcutta: The University of Calcutta, 1927-33; New Delhi: MLBD, rev. ed. 1981-85).

The Relationship between the *Bhagavadgītā* and the Vedic Upaniṣads: Parallels and Relative Chronology

MISLAV JEŽIĆ

INTRODUCTION

The *Bhagavadgītā* has played a well-known and unique role among epic episodes or epic didactic treatises since it was accepted by the *Uttaramīmāṃsādarśana*, along with the Upaniṣads and the basic exposition of the system – the Brahmasūtras, as one of the three basic authorities, *prasthāna*s, of the system. Although it does not belong to *śruti*, but to *smṛti*, it was treated practically on an equal basis with the Upaniṣads. There are well-grounded reasons for such treatment, and this paper will explore those among them that are inherent in the text and its history.

There are a number of passages in the BhG that run parallel to passages in some Vedic Upaniṣads. A list of parallels with older Upaniṣads was collected by George C. O. Haas (1922: 40-43). He checked their exhaustiveness with the help of Colonel Jacob's *Concordance* (1891). However, he includes not only repeated passages and expressions, but also recurrences of ideas, allusions and the like. In this paper I shall restrict the survey of parallels to those of both content and expression. The principal intention of the paper is not to study those parallels from the standpoint of their philosophical interpretation, but from the philological viewpoint of the relationship between the texts.

While Haas (1922) gives only an enumeration of parallel passages, G. V. Devasthali (1953) presents a survey of parallels following their content. He lists six literally parallel passages and several others which contain only similar ideas. The former include the following themes: the metaphor of the *aśvattha* tree, the paths to immortality or to rebirth (*devayāna*, *pitṛyāna*), the creation and absorption of the worlds, the influence of the last thought at the moment of death in determining the future fate, the importance of sacrifice, asceticism and liberality (*yajña*, *tapas*, *dāna*), and the restrictions on imparting of occult knowledge. Devasthali remarks that "since BhG is a metrical work it is but natural that it should have no passages in common with the prose Upaniṣads" and stresses that "it must, however, be observed that even among the older metrical Upaniṣads BhG has parallel passages with only two viz. *Kaṭha* and *Śvetāśvatara*" (Devasthali 1953: 133.). For him it is a natural assumption that it is the BhG that picked up the ideas found in the Upaniṣads.

As is known, Paul Deussen (1906) had already cited passages from the BhG, partly the same as in Devasthali, as parallels to the Upaniṣads, taking it for granted that they were posterior to the Upaniṣads.

A detailed list of the parallels can be also found in Brockington 1997 and 1998.[1] Brockington reasonably estimates that "the number of quotations indicates that the BhG is deliberately using them for their prestige value and that it must have been composed at a period when these Upaniṣads were regarded as authoritative". At the same time he is aware, referring to T. Oberlies 1988 and 1995, that "recently it has been argued that the *Śvetāśvatara-upaniṣad* draws on the *Bhagavadgītā* rather than the other way round" (Brockington 1998: 13).

If we distinguish the basic textual strata of the BhG, it will be equally important to note exactly which parts of the Gītā show parallels with the Upaniṣads. We should also try to find out (in this

[1] Brockington 1997: 47, notes 25 and 27; 1998: 12-13, n. 28.

paper that can be only hinted at) if the textual location of the parallels in the Upaniṣads can reveal to us something about the chronological relationship not only between the whole works but also between their layers.

* * *

Since Wilhelm von Humboldt's essay (1826) various text-historical analyses of the BhG have been undertaken by scholars in the West as well as by some Indian scholars. Good surveys of the history of research are given by A. Malinar (1996: 21-51), J. Brockington (1998: 267-277), and P. Szczurek (2002: 55-72, especially 55-58). In this paper I shall mostly refer to my own analysis, in part published in 1979 and 1986, in which I tried to show that there were four main categories of text in the BhG, three of them (1, 2b, 3) expanding the text inside the Mbh and one (2a; following 1, but parallel with 2b) originally composed as a separate hymn:

1. BhG – epic episode (Mbh): 1.1-47; 2.1-4, 9-10, 31-37

2a. BhG – the hymn (independent text): 2.5-8, (87*); 11.15-50

2b. BhG – the Upaniṣads (Mbh)

3. BhG – the *bhakti* synthesis (Mbh)[2]

---

[2] After the text analysis brought me to this general scheme, I noticed that the traditional colophon of the BhG chapters in practically all mss in a way confirms the scheme. I cite the apparatus from the critical edition: "All MSS. (Ś1 K4 Da2 G1 om.) *śrī* or *śrīmad* (K5 G4 om. *śrī* or *śrīmad*) *bhagavadgītāsu* (K6 *bhagavadgītāyāṃ*) *upaniṣatsu* (K6 D7 om. *upaniṣatsu*). K0.3.5 Ñ1 B3 Da1 Dn D1, 2, 4, 6, 8 Cv cont.: *brahmavidyāyāṃ yogaśāstre śrīkṛṣṇārjunasaṃvāde*. Some mss. have some further modifications.

The epic episode (1) is already *śrīkṛṣṇārjunasaṃvādaḥ;* what follows is first *yogaśāstra* and then *brahmavidyā;* altogether the expanded text are *upaniṣadaḥ* (2b); they are sung by the Lord *bhagavadgītāḥ* as the teacher in the BhG. But the *bhagavadgītā* could be distinguished from the *upaniṣadaḥ*, as in K6, and in that case it could best denote the *triṣṭubh* hymn (2a – which was in fact the "Ur-Bhagavadgītā"!), from which the title could have originated; it also fits very well the layer 3, or the whole BhG as we know it. As a title, it does not fit the Epic layer, nor even the *upaniṣadaḥ* without the theistic *bhakti* redaction.

A closer but still sketchy survey of chapters may help us in recalling the parallels between passages in the BhG and those in older *Vedic* Upaniṣads. They can be found in chapters 2, 3 and 5, as well as 13 and 15, all of them in the Upaniṣadic passages (2b) (from an older and a younger group), and in chapter 8 embedded in the Bhakti layer (but recognizable by the *triṣṭubh* metre)[3]:

BhG 1; 2.1-4, 9-10, 31-37 – **the epic episode**. Setting: the battlefield. Arjuna's dilemma and Kṛṣṇa's first answer concerning *kṣatriyadharma* (the category 1).

BhG 2-6 – **the Upaniṣads** (teaching *sāṃkhya, yoga, saṃnyāsa*) ...
cf. *Kaṭha, Śvetāśvatara*

BhG 2.11-30, 38 – the first Sāṃkhya layer (with some interpolations)

BhG 2.39–4.42 – the first Yoga layer (with a number of interpolations)

BhG 3.9-16; 4.23-(34) – the *yajña* digressions

BhG 7-12 – **the *bhakti* synthesis** (the core of the category 3)

BhG 8 – Vedic topics (Brāhmaṇic and Upaniṣadic: *kiṃ tad brahma kim adhyātmaṃ* ...; 24-25 *agnir, jyotir ... dhūmo rātris* ...)
cf. KaU, ŚvU

BhG 9.16 ff.; 10.20 ff.; cf. *Bāṣkalamantra*

BhG 11 – **the hymn** (*rūpam aiśvaryam*): the *triṣṭubh*s 15 – 50 (the core of the category 2a, to which already 2.5-8 belongs) – awe and grace; the *śloka*s – *bhakti* ... cf. *Bāṣkalamantra*

BhG 12 – *bhakti*

Thus, A. L. Basham (1989: 82) stresses that the "full name, therefore, is *Bhagavad-gītopaniṣad* 'Upaniṣad sung by the Lord'". Peter Schreiner (1991: 10) is more precise: "Die einzelnen Kapitel bezeichnen sich selber als 'die von Bhagavad gesungenen Upaniṣaden'." It is important for us to notice, first, that the BhG is called in Sankrit tradition *upaniṣadaḥ* (pl.!), although it is a part of the great epic, and not of the Vedic corpus. Second, that it is modified by the attribute *bhagavadgītā* (f.), which points to the inclusion of the *triṣṭubh* hymn in it and to its *bhakti* redaction. Third, the title *śrīkṛṣṇārjunasaṃvādaḥ* may refer to its first Epic layer, and certainly does refer to it as its "frame-story" by means of which all these Upaniṣads were gradually embedded into the Mbh.

[3] It is significant that these parallels encompass most of the *triṣṭubh*s outside the hymn (2a): 2.20, 29; 15.2-5 and 8.9-11. They do not include 8.28 (connected with 8.9-11?); 9.20-21 nor 15.15 (which are all interconnected in contents). It poses the question of their mutual relationship: are they, all or some, connected in a separate layer, or do they also belong to the hymn, or are they isolated verses? The stanza 2.70 e.g. looks rather like a floating gnomic verse.

BhG 13, 15 – **the Upaniṣads** (*kṣetra-kṣetrajña*; *mahad brahma – pitā*; *kṣara-/akṣara-/uttama-puruṣa*); cf. KaU, ŚvU

BhG 16 – classifications (*daiva-asurasampad*)

BhG 14, 17–18 – classifications (the three *guṇas*), glosses

BhG 18, (from 41, 49, 54 or) 64 ff. (or 72-73) – conclusion

It is essential for our purpose to note which chapters of the BhG show parallels with the old classical Upaniṣads, mostly the metrical ones – the KaU and the ŚvU. Similarly, it has been important for another purpose to see that the passages in the BhG parallel to those in the *Bāṣkalamantra-upaniṣad* are to be found in chapters 9, 10 and 11 belonging to the Bhakti layer.[4]

The parallels with the Gītā appear in the *Kaṭha-upaniṣad* in chapters 2, 3, 5 and 6; and in the *Śvetāśvatara-upaniṣad* in chapters 3, 4 and 6.

MYTHIC AND HISTORICAL PARALLELS

In a very broad sense there are some formulaic mythic or historical parallels in the Vedic corpus that can be mentioned at the outset.

áhaś ca kṛṣṇ ám áhar árjunaṃ ca

The *Ṛksaṃhitā* stanza 6.9.1 from a hymn to Agni Vaiśvānara uses in a mythic context three words that play a central role (especially in the theological layer) in the BhG: adjectives *kṛṣṇa* "black" and *arjuna* "silvery, bright" attributed to *ahar* "day", and the verb *ava-√tṛ* "to cross down, to descend into (later: to become incarnate)" with the subject Agni Vaiśvānara, who represents a celestial god descended with light into the darkness (and the earthly world). That name of Agni is, in spite of popular interpretations, in fact a patronymic derived from the name of his divine father Viśvānara (an attribute of Savitar or of Indra in the ṚS). Similarly, Vāsudeva is a

[4] See Ježić 2002: 39.

patronymic derived from the name Vasudeva, be it the name of a mortal hero from Mathurā or of a mythic divine figure from the sphere of the Vasus after whom the mortal hero could have been named.

> RS 6.9.1 (Agni Vaisvānara; *kavi* Bharadvāja Bārhaspatya)[5]
> *áhaś ca kṛṣṇám áhar árjunaṃ ca*
> *ví vartete rájasī vediyā́bhiḥ* |
> *vaiśvānaró jáyamāno ná rā́jā*
> *ávātiraj jyótiṣāgnís támāṃsi* || 1 ||[6]

Although I hope to dedicate more space to this subject at some later date, let it suffice in this paper to mention that a mythic or archaic theological model could have (partly) underlain the theological interpretation of Kṛṣṇa (and Arjuna) in the Gītā, in the *Mahābhārata*, and in the Purāṇic tradition. And that we can find traces of that model in the Ṛgvedic and broader Vedic formulaic treasure as well as its reflections in the post-Vedic literature.[7]

---

[5] Edition: van Nooten & Holland 1994.

[6] Translation: "The black and the silvery (bright) "day" revolve, the two (dark) spaces, by (their) skills. Vaiśvānara (son of Viśvānara), as if a king were born, crossed down (descended) into the darkness (pl. dark (spaces) on the Earth without sun) with (his) light." I would propose to understand the metaphors in the following way: The nights of the new and of the full moon (and all those that turn up between them in their time) turn according to the (appropriate) knowledge. Fire, son of the god Viśvānara (one to whom all are sons, or whose son is the Universe), as if a king were born, descended with his light into the darkness (of these nights).

I do not reject Bergaigne's and Geldner's interpretation that the dark and the bright hemisphere of the Sky or of the Sun (representing day and night) can be implied, but I prefer to follow the more specific meaning of "*arjuna*", and apply it also to the interpretation of "*rajasī*" in this passage. Their interpretation does not differ in respect of the possibility that a mythic (Vedic) model could have influenced epic (narrative) structures.

[7] After Jacobi (1924) and Thieme (1985), Utz Podzeit (1994; 1995) paid attention to the mythical (theological) sense of the name Vāsudeva and Devakī. Podzeit (1994: 193-194) showed that the all-embracing conception of Vāsudeva in *Harivaṃśa* App. I, 13.34-43 reflected a similar idea of the correspondence between the Vasus and parts of the cosmos in ŚB 11.6.3. 6, and ultimately the conception of the primeval Puruṣa in ṚS 10.90. On the other hand, he cites Mbh 12.47.18 where Devakī is called *araṇi* "the tinder-stick" (for kindling fire) im-

Kṛṣṇa Devakīputra

On the other hand, the well-known passage of *Chāndogya-upaniṣad* 3.17 mentions a Kṛṣṇa, son of Devakī, as a pupil of Ghora Āṅgirasa, and confronts us with the long-debated question whether it is the same person as Kṛṣṇa who teaches Arjuna in the Gītā.[8]

In that passage Ghora Āṅgirasa teaches Kṛṣṇa that aspects or phases of common life and activity have the same meaning as ritual acts at a sacrifice: hunger and thirst are comparable to *dīkṣā*s (the sacrificial consecrations which include fasting); eating, drinking and enjoying to *upasada*s (preparatory rites); laughing, feasting and having sexual intercourse to recitations and hymns of praise (*stuta-śastra*); austerity, generosity, uprightness, non-injury and truthfulness to *dakṣiṇā*s (gifts to the priests), while death is comparable to *avabhṛtha* (the final ritual "descent" from the sacred sacrificial sphere at the end of a sacrificial rite, opposite to *dīkṣā*, initiation into the sacred sphere of sacrifice at the beginning of a rite). These correspondences remind one directly of the *yajña* passages in BhG 3.9-16 and 4.23-33 (the *yajña* interpolations), and indirectly – and even more significantly – they remind us of the *karmayoga* in general in the Gītā (in the first Yoga layer), where the term *karman* is used in the generalized sense, not only for ritual or sacrificial acts, but for all activity in life, and applied especially to the kind of activity that is regarded as one's duty (*dharma*). ChU 3. 17 passage continues with the words:

---

plying that Kṛṣṇa is Agni, as he is indeed sometimes called in the Mbh (Podzeit 1995: 33). I would only clearly distance myself from Jacobi's reduction of Vāsudeva to Vasudeva.

[8] It seems that Barth, Macdonell and Keith, F. E. Pargiter, S. K. De, A. D. Pulsaker and S. Jaiswal opposed the identification of Kṛṣṇa in the ChU and Kṛṣṇa in the Gītā, but Colebrooke, Weber, Hopkins, Max Müller, Garbe, Winternitz, Jacobi and Raychaudhuri supported it. Podzeit (1995) cites Benjamin Preciado-Solis, *The Kṛṣṇa Cycle in the Purāṇas. Themes and Motifs in a Heroic Saga* (pp. 24-27, Delhi 1984) for a detailed review of discussions.

ChU 3.17.6

... taddhaitad ghora āṅgirasaḥ kṛṣṇāya devakīputrāyoktvovāca | apipāsa eva sa babhūva | so 'ntavelāyām etat trayaṃ pratipadyetākṣitam asy acyutam asi prāṇasaṃśitam asīti | ...[9]

Two *ṛc* are quoted on this point: SS 1.1.2.10 (ṚS 8.6.30) and VS 20.21 (ṚS 1.50.10) expressing the worship of the light and of the Sun – Sūrya, the highest light far beyond the surrounding darkness, the god among the gods, to whom the worshippers attain.

In spite of differences between ChU 3.17 and the BhG, it is hard to reject or neglect the precious testimony of the ChU as a historic parallel in reconstructing the genesis of the character of Kṛṣṇa as teacher in the BhG. The burden of proof lies with those who reject the identity of the "two Kṛṣṇas".

Of course, the identity for a philologist does not mean that Kṛṣṇa is equally conceived in the two texts, but that the Gītā (the first Yoga layer) and the Mbh do refer, directly or indirectly – through the intermediary of tradition – to that Kṛṣṇa who appears in the ChU, and (in various ways) reinterpret his character.[10]

---

[9] Edition: Limaye & Vadekar 1958. In Hume's translation (1931): "When Ghora Āngirasa explained this to Kṛṣṇa, the son of Devakī, he also explained – for he had become free from desire – 'In the final hour one should take refuge in these three thoughts: "You are the Indestructible; you are the Unshaken; you are the very essence of life (*prāṇa*)".'"

It may be philologically worth noticing that the expression *prāṇasaṃśita* (in Hume's translation: the very essence of life; literally: that which is sharpened by breath/~~life)~~ does not occur in other Upaniṣads nor in the BhG, but that BhG 4.28 (in the second *yajña* interpolation) ends by mentioning *yatayaḥ saṃśitavratāḥ*, (ascetics of severe/"sharpened" vows, who sacrifice material possessions. austerities, yoga, or learning and knowledge) while stanza 27 mentions *prāṇa-karmāṇi* ("activities of breath") along with the "oblation" of the *indriyakarmāṇi* (activities of the senses) into the fire of yoga kindled by knowledge) and stanza 29 those who are devoted to breath control (*prāṇāyāmaparāyaṇāḥ*). The ChU passage could already point to the tradition of ascetics practicing sharp breathing exercises (or even vows), something like *yati *prāṇakarma-saṃśitavrata* (or *prāṇasaṃśita*?). It could have been based on the Upaniṣadic concept of *prāṇa* (like e.g. in the AiĀ 2.1, BĀU 1.3 and 6.1, KU 2.13 and 3.2-3) close to the later concept of *jīvātman*, and considered as the faculty (*prāṇa*, *indriya*) in which all other faculties merge in death.

DOCTRINAL PARALLELS

The survey of explicit doctrinal parallels of the BhG with the Upaniṣads could be introduced with an inexplicit parallel, that was never explicitly developed in the Gītā. However, it may illustrate some of the symbolic potential of the Gītā episode.

The chariot

In the description of the heroes on both sides, Duryodhana presents to his teacher Droṇa the warriors[11] who are *sarva eva mahārathāḥ* "all of them having mighty chariots" (1.6). In 1.14 Kṛṣṇa and Arjuna are thus introduced:

> BhG 1.14 / Mbh 6.23.14
> *tataḥ śvetair hayair yukte mahati syandane sthitau* |
> *mādhavaḥ pāṇḍavas caiva divyau śaṅkhau pradadhmatuḥ* || 14 ||[12]

In 1.21 Arjuna asks his charioteer Kṛṣṇa to bring his chariot (*ratha*) into the space between the two armies. Kṛṣṇa does it in 1.24. And in 1.47, the last stanza of the chapter, Arjuna sinks down in the chariot pit after having seen from vicinity his kin and teachers in the rows of the opposite army. The stress on the chariots in the literal sense is only natural in the context of a battle of warriors on chariots. However, can it awaken some symbolic associations in the minds of Indian listeners, especially in the light of the fact that in later portions of the Gītā it is various yoga teachings that are dwelt upon so extensively?

---

[10] Would we say that Vasiṣṭha and Viśvāmitra in the Rāmāyaṇa have no connection with the Vedic seers, or rather that their characters underwent reinterpretation and even shift to another place and time in the tradition?

[11] G. von Simson (1969: 168 ff.) has demonstrated that BhG 1.2-19 is largely adapted from Mbh 6.47.2-29. Cf. also Szczurek 2002: 61 ff.

[12] Editions: Belvalkar 1947; van Buitenen 1981. In van Buitenen's translation (1981): "The Mādhava and Pāṇḍava, standing on their chariot yoked with the [four] white horses, both blew their [divine] conches."

One of the two Upaniṣads that come closest to the Gītā, the *Kaṭha-upaniṣad* 3 dwells upon analogies between a chariot with a warrior and a charioteer, and the self with the psychic faculties:

KaU (1) 3.3-9
ātmānaṃ rathinaṃ viddhi śarīraṃ ratham eva tu ।
buddhiṃ tu sārathiṃ viddhi manaḥ pragraham eva ca ॥ 3 ॥
indriyāṇi hayān āhur viṣayāṃs teṣu gocarān ।
ātmendriya-mano-yuktam bhoktety āhur manīṣiṇaḥ ॥ 4 ॥
yas tv avijñānavān bhavaty ayuktena manasā sadā ।
tasyendriyāṇy avaśyāni duṣṭāśvā iva sāratheḥ ॥ 5 ॥
yas tu vijñānavān bhavati yuktena manasā sadā
tasyendriyāṇi vaśyāni sadaśvā iva sāratheḥ ॥ 6 ॥
yas tv avijñānavān bhavaty amanaskaḥ sadā 'śuciḥ ।
na sa tat padam āpnoti saṃsāraṃ cādhigacchati ॥ 7 ॥
yas tu vijñānavān bhavati samanaskaḥ sadā śuciḥ ।
sa tu tat padam āpnoti yasmād bhūyo na jāyate ॥ 8 ॥
vijñānasārathir yas tu manaḥpragrahavān naraḥ ।
so 'dhvanaḥ pāram āpnoti tad viṣṇoḥ paramaṃ padam ॥ 9 ॥[13]

The comparison is used by the other, the ŚvU, as well:

ŚvU 2.9
prāṇān prapīḍya iha sa yuktaceṣṭaḥ
kṣiṇe prāṇe nāsikayoccvasīta ।
duṣṭāsvayuktam iva vāham enam
vidvān mano dhārayetāpramattaḥ ॥ 9 ॥[14]

[13] Edition: Limaye & Vadekar 1958. In Olivelle's translation (1998): "3. Know the self as a rider in the chariot, and the body, as simply the chariot. Know the intellect as the charioteer, and the mind, as simply the reins. 4. The senses, they say, are the horses, and sense objects are the paths around them; He who is linked to the body (*ātman*), senses, and mind, the wise proclaim as the one who enjoys. 5. When a man lacks understanding, and his mind is never controlled; His senses do not obey him, as bad horses, a charioteer. 6. But when a man has understanding, and his mind is ever controlled; His senses do obey him, as good horses, a charioteer. 7. When a man lacks understanding, is unmindful and always impure; He does not reach that final step, but gets on the round of rebirth. 8. But when a man has understanding, is mindful and always pure; He does reach that final step, from which he is not reborn again. 9. When a man's mind is his reins, intellect, his charioteer; He reaches the end of the road, that highest step of Viṣṇu."

The comparison of the mind with the chariot is older than the Vedas themselves, and can be traced in other Indo-European traditions, e.g. in Greek and Latin literature (Ježić 1989: 193-202). We cannot regard this Indo-European formulaic comparison as an expression of yoga practices, but, on the contrary, we can suppose that the *dhyāna*, meditation, received the name of *yoga* in Indian tradition by applying that comparison to its spiritual exercises. And that comparison, even if not deliberately alluded to by author(s) of the Gītā, obviously originated from warrior circles or from sacerdotal circles who wanted to compare their spiritual occupations with the occupations of warriors.[15] This cannot be taken as a literal parallel of the Gītā with those Upaniṣads, but as an element of the spiritual universe which makes up the backgroud of those Upaniṣads as well as of the Gītā – in harmony with the epic setting of the Gītā.

Let us now turn to literal parallels. They cover the following topics: a) Sāṃkhya and Yoga, b) the *indriyas* – faculties, c) *puruṣa/ dehin* – person/soul, d) *navadvāre pure dehin* – soul in the citadel of nine doors, e) *aṇor aṇīyān* – smaller than the smallest, f) *tat padam* – that word/step, g) *paraṃ brahma* – the supreme *brahman*, h) *aśvattha* – the cosmic fig tree.

---

[14] Edition: Oberlies 1996. In Olivelle's translation: "Compressing his breaths in here and curbing his movements, a man should exhale through one nostril when his breath is exhausted. A wise man should keep his mind vigilantly under control, just as he would that wagon yoked to unruly horses."

[15] The beginning of chapter 2 of the ŚvU can be adduced here as a very eloquent example. ŚvU 2. 1-5 cites the TS 4.1.1.1-5, KS 15.33-37 (anu. 11), MS 2.7.1.1-5 and VS 11.1-5, which in its turn (stanzas 4-5) cite the ṚS 5.81.1 and 10.13.1. Oberlies (1998: 126-128) does not translate those stanzas because they are cited simply because of different forms of the verb √*yuj*. However, the point is that the verb √*yuj* "to harness, yoke (horses to a chariot)" in these citations occurs always in the transposed meaning in the phrase *manas yuj-* "to harness the mind", and in connection with *dhī-*, and bears witness to the application of the comparison with the chariot to the "harnessed" mind able to produce *dhī-* (poetical) "insight" (later *dhyāna-* "meditation").

a) *sāṃkhyayoga*

BhG 2.39 / Mbh 6.24.39	ŚvU. 6.13(-14)
eṣā te 'bhihitā ***sāṃkhye*** *buddhir* **yoge** *tv imāṃ śṛṇu* | *buddhyā yukto yayā Pārtha* *karmabandhaṃ prahāsyasi* || 39 ||[18]	*nityo nityānāṃ cetanaś cetanānām* *eko bahūnāṃ yo vidadhāti kāmān* | *tatkāraṇaṃ*[16] ***sāṃkhyayogā****dhigamyaṃ*[17] *jñātvā devaṃ mucyate sarvapāśaiḥ* || 13 ||[19] *na tatra sūryo bhāti na candratārakaṃ* (= KaU 5.15 [2.2.15]) <u>KaU 5.13(-14, 15ab) (2.2.13[-14, 15ab])</u> *nityo 'nityānāṃ cetanaś cetanānām* *eko bahūnāṃ yo vidadhāti kāmān* | (= ŚvU 6.13ab) *tam ātmasthaṃ ye 'nupaśyanti dhīrās* *teṣāṃ śāntiḥ śāśvatī netareṣām* || 13 || *tad etad iti manyante* *'nirdeśyam paramaṃ sukham* | *kathaṃ nu tat vijānīyāṃ* *kim u bhāti vibhāti vā* || 14 || *na tatra sūryo bhāti na candratārakaṃ* *nemā vidyuto bhānti kuto 'yam agniḥ* | *tam eva bhāntam anubhāti sarvaṃ* *tasya bhāsā sarvam idaṃ vibhāti* || 15 || (= ŚvU 6.14)[20]

[16] Schrader (1910): v.l. *taṃ* for *tat*.

[17] V.l. *abhipannaṃ* for *adhigamyaṃ*.

[18] Van Buitenen 1981: "This is the spirit [*buddhi*] according to theory [*sāṃkhya*]; now hear how this spirit applies in practice [*yoga*], yoked with which you will cut away the bondage of the act."

[19] Olivelle 1998: "13. The changeless among the changing [*anityānāṃ*; v.l. *nityānāṃ* – Oberlies: unter den Ewigen; see Rau 1964; already Indian commentators], the intelligent among the intelligent beings, the one, who dispenses desires among the many – when a man knows that cause, which is to be comprehended through the application of Sāṃkhya [or: through Sāṃkhya and Yoga], as God, he is freed from all fetters. 14. There the sun does not shine, nor the moon and stars: ..."

[20] Olivelle 1998: "13. The changeless among the changing [v.l. *anityānāṃ*; *nityānāṃ*, like ŚvU in Oberlies: unter den Ewigen], the intelligent among the intelligent beings, the one, who dispenses desires among the many; The wise who perceive him within themselves; they alone, not others, enjoy unending bliss. 14. "This is that" – so they think, although the highest bliss can't be described. But how should I perceive it? Does it shine? Or does it radiate? 15.

The *Kaṭha* passage, like ŚvU 6.13, speaks of the cognition of God as the way to salvation, but does not mention Sāṃkhya nor Yoga as means for it, but only the perception of God in one's self. The ŚvU introduces the expression *sāṃkhya-yoga-adhigamya-* "which is to be apprehended through the application of Sāṃkhya" (Olivelle), or, more probably, "erreichbar durch (die Pfade des) Sāṃkhya und Yoga" (Oberlies)[21], where Sāṃkhya and Yoga need not be, but more probably are – separate concepts of equal status. BhG 2.39 clearly differentiates and opposes Sāṃkhya and Yoga, more or less as complementary concepts, certainly not yet denoting the classical *darśanas*, but also not so far from them as van Buitenen's generalized translation "theory" and "practice" could suggest. The contrast between the *dehin* "dweller of the body, soul" and *deha* "body" in the Gītā 2 is not the same, but is analogous to that between the *puruṣa* and *prakṛti* in Sāṃkhya, while the *buddhiyoga* "the control (harnessing) of the intellect" defined as *samatva* "equanimity" is close to the practices of classical Yoga. One could guess that the ŚvU introduces the concepts of Sāṃkhya and Yoga into a context which, according to KaU 5.13 did not contain them, and thus comes close to the Gītā in which the doctrinal parts start with teachings under these names.

However, the relationship between the texts is even more complex: KaU 5.13ab corresponds to ŚvU 6.13ab, but KaU 5.13cd repeats the second part of the previous stanza KaU 5.12cd. Its first part KaU 5.12ab does not speak unequivocally of the cognizance of God, but could be taken as speaking of the universally immanent Self; it can be but need not be God. If KaU 5.12 and 13 have originally been connected in a fugue-like composition, and if we can infer from 13 that the *eko vaśī sarva-bhūta-antarātmā* in 12 is also God, maybe in the sense of the inner-controller *antaryāmin*, then

---

There the sun does not shine, nor the moon and stars; There lightning does not shine, of this common fire need we speak! Him alone, as he shines, do all things reflect; this whole world radiates with his light."

[21] In spite of Böhtlingk (1897: 131) who argues against taking *sāṃkhyayoga* as a *dvandva* compound; see Olivelle 1998: 628.

our supposition that ŚvU 6.13 cites and reinterprets KaU 5.13 fits in well. But if KaU 5.13 was so formulated in order to combine ŚvU 6.13ab with KaU 5.12cd, and to reinterpret the latter in accordance with the former, then KaU 5.13 has been influenced by ŚvU 6.13, and is younger.

Maybe, in resolving this playful relationship of formulaic texts of oral origin, where so many different reconstructions of their genesis can look alluring, an observation of Deussen and Hauschild can help us. They assume that the ŚvU misses a stanza between ŚvU 6.13 and 14, and that it appears in proper order in KaU 5.14 between stanzas 13 and 15 (= ŚvU 6.14, q.v.). It can help us in concluding, just as they do, that the ŚvU is the borrowing text: "man sieht die Entlehnung von seiten der Śvet.-Up." (Hauschild 1927: 78).[22]

If this is true, than both ŚvU 6.13, and BhG 2.39 explicitly mention teachings they call Sāṃkhya and Yoga, which are missing in the KaU passage parallel to ŚvU 6.13. It could imply that the KaU passage is most probably older than the other two, but it would be hard to propose any chronological relationship between the BhG and the ŚvU passages if we regard them in isolation from their context. They have in common only that which differentiates the ŚvU from the KaU passage – the terms Sāṃkhya and Yoga, without any larger corresponding context. However, the use of these two terms is no negligible correspondence because it is only the ŚvU among the middle, metrical Upaniṣads (according to Deussen's classification) that mentions Sāṃkhya, and only KaU 6.11, along with the ŚvU, that uses the term *yoga*. All occurrences in other texts (like *Maitrāyaṇīya*, *Mahānārāyaṇa*, etc.) can with reasonable probability be considered later. Together with other elements of Yoga and of Sāṃkhya to be found in these three texts,

[22] It is corroborated by the fact that two commentators of the ŚvU Śaṅkarānanda and Nārāyaṇa inserted KaU 5.14 after ŚvU 6.13, a long time before Deussen and Hauschild. Cf. Oberlies 1998: 118-119. However, even that observation is not unassailable: KaU 5.14 is the only *śloka* in the *triṣṭubh* (+ *jagatī*) sequence KaU 5.9-15.

the use of these two terms (or one of them) marks them off among all texts which are not posterior to them.[23]

That poses again the question of their relative chronology. The relationship between the ŚvU and the Gītā passages has remained undecided. However, if we suppose that the ŚvU introduced the concepts of Sāṃkhya and Yoga into a context which, according to KaU 5.13, did not contain them, the Gītā passage could be assumed to be older for two reasons. First, this is the only passage in the ŚvU where the term Sāṃkhya is used, while it appears in the Gītā seven times: two times for the followers of Sāṃkhya (pl.), and five times for the Sāṃkhya teaching (sg.); and what is even more, six times – four times for the teaching[24] and two times for its followers[25] – it is used in connection with the term *yoga* denoting the "practical" teaching (sg.) or its followers (pl.)[26]. This means that the collocation of Sāṃkhya and Yoga became formulaic in the Gītā and thus could have served as the model for the ŚvU passage. And second, the term Sāṃkhya in the BhG does not refer to the classical *Sāṃkhyadarśana* up to the *adhyāya* 13, but to a comparable but simpler and presumably older epic Sāṃkhya doctrine. On the other hand, in the ŚvU some passages, like – at the very beginning – ŚvU 1.4-5, presuppose a much more developed Sāṃkhya system and seem to give it a bold theistic reinterpretation[27]. All that points to a later stage of development of the Sāṃkhya system as reflected in the ŚvU in comparison with that in the BhG (especially BhG 2-6),

---

[23] In any case, with all literal correspondences between them, KaU, ŚvU and BhG would be marked off even if some other text mentioning yoga proved to be (partially) older than any of them.

[24] BhG 2.39; 5.4, 5c; 13.24.

[25] BhG 3.3; 5.5ab.

[26] Only in BhG 18.13 *sāṃkhya kṛtānta* appears alone, but in a misleading sense, so that Śaṅkara and Madhusūdana suppose that it refers here to the Vedānta.

[27] See the short interpretation in Hauschild 1927: 4-5. Johnston (1937) also enumerates a number of developed Sāṃkhya concepts in the ŚvU (8 *prakṛtis*, 16 *vikṛtis*, *ahaṃkāra*, *kṣetrajña*, etc.), and states that the ŚvU "adapts them to fit into its theistic scheme" (p. 84).

and further corroborates the presupposition of a later date of the ŚvU passage.

b) *indriyāni, manas, buddhi, ātman*

KaU (1) 3.10-11

indriyebhyaḥ parā hy arthā
arthebhyas ca paraṃ manaḥ |
manasas tu parā buddhir
buddher ātmā mahān paraḥ || 10 ||
mahataḥ param avyaktam
avyaktāt puruṣaḥ paraḥ |
puruṣān na paraṃ kiṃcit
sā kāṣṭhā sā parā gatiḥ || 11 ||[28]

BhG 3.34, 36-37, 40-43 /
Mbh 6.25.36-37, 40-43

indriyasyendriyasyārthe
rāgadveṣau vyavasthitau |
tayor na vaśam āgacchet
tau hy asya paripanthinau || 34 ||
atha kena prayukto'yam
pāpaṃ carati puruṣaḥ |
anicchann api vārṣṇeya
balād iva niyojitaḥ || 36 ||
kāma eṣa krodha eṣa
rajoguṇasamudbhavaḥ |
mahāśano mahāpāpmā
viddhy enam iha vairiṇam || 37 ||
indriyāṇi mano buddhir
asyādhiṣṭhānam ucyate |
etair vimohayaty eṣa
jñānam āvṛtya dehinam || 40 ||
tasmāt tvam indriyāṇy ādau
niyamya bharatarṣabha |

---

[28] Olivelle 1998: "10. Higher than the senses are their objects; Higher than sense objects is the mind; Higher than the mind is the intellect; Higher than the intellect is the immense self; 11. Higher than the immense self is the unmanifest; Higher than the unmanifest is the person; Higher than the person there's nothing at all. That is the goal, that's the highest state."

pāpmānaṃ prajahi hy enaṃ
jñānavijñānanāśanam ǁ 41 ǁ
indriyāṇi parāṇy āhur
indriyebhyaḥ paraṃ manaḥ ǀ
manasas tu parā buddhir
yo buddheḥ paratas tu saḥ ǁ 42 ǁ
evaṃ buddheḥ paraṃ buddhvā
saṃstabhyātmānam ātmanā ǀ
jahi śatruṃ mahābāho
kāmarūpaṃ durāsadam ǁ 43 ǁ[29]

KaU 6.6-8 (2.3.6-8)
indriyānāṃ pṛthagbhāvam
udayāstamayau ca yat ǀ
pṛthag utpadyamānānāṃ
matvā dhīro na śocati ǁ 6 ǁ
indriyebhyaḥ param mano
manasaḥ sattvam uttamam ǀ
sattvād adhi mahān ātmā
mahato 'vyaktam uttamam ǁ 7 ǁ
avyaktāt tu paraḥ puruṣo
vyāpako 'linga eva ca ǀ
yaṃ jñātvā mucyate jantur
amṛtatvaṃ ca gacchati ǁ 8 ǁ[30]

---

[29] Van Buitenen 1981: "34. Love and hatred lie waiting in the sense and its object [in the object of every single sense]: one should not fall into their power, for they ambush one ... *Arjuna said*: 36. What is it that drives a man to commit evil, Vārṣṇeya, however reluctantly, as though propelled by force? *The Lord said*: 37. It is desire, it is anger, which springs from the force of rajas, the great devourer, the great evil: know that that is the enemy here. 40. The senses, the mind, and the spirit are said to be its lair: by means of them it clouds knowledge and leads into delusion the one within the body. 41. Therefore, bull of the Bharatas, first control your senses, then kill off that evil which destroys insight and knowledge. 42. The senses, they say, are superior to their objects; the mind is higher than the senses; the spirit [*buddhi*] is higher than the mind; and beyond the spirit is he. 43. Thus knowing the one beyond the spirit, pull yourself together [*saṃstabhya ātmānam ātmanā*] and kill desire, your indomitable enemy [*śatruṃ ... kāmarūpaṃ durāsadam*], strong-armed prince!"

[30] Olivelle 1998: "6. The separate nature of the senses; Their rise and fall as they come separately into being – when a wise man knows this, he does not grieve. 7. Higher than the senses is the mind; Higher than the mind is the essenoe [*sattva*]; Higher than the essence is the immense self [*mahān ātmā*]; Higher than the immense is the unmanifest. 8. Higher then the unmanifest is the person

In his study on the *Kaṭha-upaniṣad* Friedrich Weller (1953) has in his analytic approach supposed that *vallī* 3 had approximately 8 authors. He argues that KaU 3.3-4 (and 5-9, all cited above, in paragraph 5) and KaU 3.10-11 (cited here) have different authors (Weller 1953: 68), and, moreover, probably even stanzas 10 and 11 do not come from the same person. Weller says that in stanzas 3.3-4 the self is compared to the owner of the chariot, the body to the chariot, the intellect to the charioteer, the inner organ (*manas*) to the reins, the faculties of perception to the horses, and their respective objects to the race-tracks (Weller 1953: 48). In accordance with that order, the objects are lower, not higher, than the senses. None will doubt, he says, that *artha* (things, objects) in stanza 4 and *viṣaya* (domains, objects) in stanza 10 are the same thing. How can we then explain that in stanza 10 the objects are higher than the senses – contrary to stanzas 3-4? Weller thinks that both statements have not been made by the same author.[31]

He also notices that *ātman* mentioned in KaU 3. 3 is taken up in stanza 10 with the epithet *mahant*, but that this *mahant* is in stanza 11 at once subordinated to two new concepts *avyakta* and *puruṣa*, which occur nowhere until this stanza. Weller concludes that stanza 11 cannot convincingly be brought into accord with stanza 3 nor stanza 10, where *ātman*, and not *puruṣa*, is conceived as the highest principle (Weller 1953: 49). I fully agree with him and think that the comparison with the Gītā 3.42 strongly corroborates his case.

BhG 3.42 has a relatively rich context: the passions, *kāma* "desire" and *krodha* "anger", lead us into sin or evil; their bases are the senses, mind and intellect (*buddhi*); therefore they should be restrained and controlled. Stanza 42 introduces a principle higher than *buddhi*, and in stanza 43 we learn that it is *ātman*. KaU 3.10 largely corresponds to BhG 3.42, and explicitly states, like BhG

[*puruṣa*], pervading all and without any marks. Knowing him, a man is freed, and attains immortality."

[31] Weller 1953: 48: "Beide Ordnungen schliessen sich aus. Sie können also nicht in einem Kopfe entstanden sein."

3.43, that the principle higher than *buddhi* is *ātman*. This correspondence with the Gītā explains why stanza 3.11 could be omitted from the KaU without leaving any gap in the text. Even the following stanzas 12 and 13 (whatever difficulties for interpretation they may pose) speak only of *ātman*, and do not mention *puruṣa* at all. Thus it seems that KaU 3.11 must be an interpolation younger than the surrounding stanzas, and could have served to reinterpret the previous stanza or stanzas in the spirit of Sāṃkhya[32]. It means that its content, and presumably also the text, are equally younger than BhG 3.42-43. In KaU 6, stanzas 7-8 take up the same Sāṃkhya theme and develop it as an already well known subject in their times. The interpolation of the stanza KaU 3.11 might be close not only in content, but also in time to KaU 6.7-8.

However, even in KaU 6.7-8 the strange statement that sense-objects are higher than senses does not occur. The comparison of KaU 3.10, where it occurs, and BhG 3.42 shows that they have an equal *pāda* c, different *pāda*s d but of equal meaning, and similar *pāda*s a and b, but of contrary meaning. The gradation of BhG 3.42 is in full accordance with KaU 3.3-4: *ātman*, *buddhi*, *manas*, *indriyāṇi*, *viṣayāḥ*, only the order of faculties enumerated is inverse. From KaU 3.4 we can clearly deduce why *indriyāṇi* are called *parāṇi* "high, higher" in BhG 3.42: because they are higher than the sense objects. KaU 3.10 partly takes up stanzas 3-4, but seems to change the order: *indriyaṇi*, *arthāḥ*, *manas* ... Could not one correct KaU 10 with the help of BhG 3.42, and substitute BhG 3.42b *indriyebhyaḥ paraṃ manaḥ* for KaU 3.10b *arthebhyaś ca paraṃ manaḥ*? In that case, obviously KaU 3.10a should also be changed accordingly. If *indriyebhaḥ parā hy arthāḥ* can be taken as a corruption of **indriyebhyo 'parā hy arthā(ḥ)*, a very simple emendation can make *pāda*s a and b appropriate and their meaning coherent:

[32] It reflects a later, more classical (and less Vedāntic) stage of the Sāṃkhya than that of BhG 3 (presented as a yoga teaching).

* *indriyebhyo 'parā hy arthā indriyebhyaḥ paraṃ manaḥ* I
manasas tu parā buddhir buddher ātmā mahān paraḥ II 10 II

Lower than the senses are their objects. Higher than the senses is the mind. Higher than the mind is the intellect; Higher than the intellect is the immense self.[33]

We cannot say for sure if this was the original reading of KaU 3.10 or of a stanza, maybe a floating verse, that could have served as its model. and can be tentatively reconstructed from KaU 3.10 and BhG 3.42.

The actual wording of KaU 3.10 is obviously suspect, and looks inferior to the wording of BhG 3.42, especially *pāda* b, which could have been modified in the KaU after the probable corruption of the *pāda* a. Does the supposed corruption of the text in KaU 3.10 imply that the reading of the stanza should be considered younger than BhG 3.42? This is more than probable: even KaU 6.7-8 does not reflect the assumed corruption in KaU 3.10a[34]. The actual text of KaU 3.10 cannot be the source of BhG 3.42 because the BhG has a superior reading, and it is not appropriate to say that the Gītā cites it.[35] It is not excluded, if the above reconstructed reading was the original reading of KaU 3.10 itself, that the Gītā stanza could have been modelled upon that original reading. However, even in such a case, KaU 3.11 must be younger than the Gītā passage.

---

[33] Thus emended KaU 3.10 could have read:
* *indriyebhyo 'parā hy arthā indriyebhyaḥ paraṃ manaḥ* I
manasas tu parā buddhir buddher ātmā mahān paraḥ II 10 II

[34] It is worth noticing that KaU 6.7 introduces the term *sattva* in the place of *buddhi*, in accordance with the later Yoga terminology (e.g. YS 3.48).

[35] As an interesting fact, we may add that the Mbh does cite the Kaṭha passage: in the dialogue between Vyāsa and Śuka, in Mbh 12.238, stanzas 3-5 do not cite the Gītā passage, but KaU 3.10-12!. That passage is certainly younger than the KaU, and it is obviously much younger than BhG 3.42. But Mbh 12.238.4 surprises us again by putting both times the concept of *amṛta*(*m*) "the immortality" in place of *puruṣa*(*ḥ*) "person" from KaU 3.11.

c) *puruṣa/dehin*

KaU 6.9 (2.3.9)
na saṃdṛśe tiṣṭhati rūpam asya
na cakṣuṣā ***paśyati kaścanainam*** I
hṛdā manīṣā manasābhikḷpto
ya etad vidur amṛtās te bhavanti II 9 II[36]
(= TĀ 10.1.3 = MNU 21)

ŚvU 4.20
na saṃdṛśe tiṣṭhati rūpam asya
na cakṣuṣā ***paśyati kaścanainam*** I
hṛdā hṛdistham manasā ya enam
evaṃ vidur amṛtās te bhavanti II 20 II[37]

BhG 2.29 / Mbh 6.24.29
āścaryavat ***paśyati kaścid enam***
āścaryavad *vadati tathaiva cānyaḥ* I
āścaryavac *cainam anyaḥ śṛṇoti*
śrutvāpy enaṃ veda na caiva kaścit II 29 II[38]

KaU (1) 2.7
śravaṇāyāpi bahubhir yo na labhyaḥ[39]
śṛṇvanto 'pi bahavo yaṃ na vidyuḥ I
āścaryo *vaktā kuśalo 'sya labdhā*
āścaryo *jñātā kuśalānuśiṣṭaḥ* II 7 II[40]

---

[36] Olivelle 1998: "9. His appearance is beyond the range of sight; No one can see him with his sight; With the heart, with insight, with thought, has he been contemplated – Those who know this become immortal."

[37] Olivelle 1998: "His appearance is beyond the range of sight; no one can see him with his sight. Those who know him thus with their hearts – him, who abides in their hearts – and with insight become immortal."

[38] Van Buitenen 1981: "It is a rare chance that a man does see him, It's a rarity too if another proclaims him, A rare chance that someone else will hear him, And even if hearing him no one knows him."

[39] Alsdorf (1950: 632) proposes a metrical emendation of 7a: *śravaṇāya bahubhir yo na labhyaḥ.*

[40] Olivelle 1998.: "7. Many do not get to hear of that transit; and even when they hear, many don't comprehend it. Rare is the man who teaches it, lucky is the man who grasps it; Rare is the man who knows it, lucky is the man who's taught it." Olivelle connects *yo na labhyaḥ* with *sāṃparāyaḥ* "transit" from the stanza 6: "This transit lies hidden from a careless fool ..."; Hume 1931: 322: "6. The passing-on is not clear to him who is childish ..." However, Hume leaves that context in his translation of stanza 7, supposing that *yo na labhyaḥ* refers to

These passages bear witness to the close relationship between these three texts, even closer between the KaU and the ŚvU, but still very close with the BhG. The formulae recurring in them cannot easily be adduced as a criterion to judge which text is the providing and which the receiving part. They express in very similar wording the difficulty of perceiving and of knowing the ultimate entity, but in the case of the Gītā 2 it is *dehin* "the incarnated soul" who is hard to know, in KaU 6.9 the difficulty should refer to *puruṣa* "person, subject of cognition" who is higher than the *avyakta*, and in ŚvU 4.20 it should refer to Rudra – Śiva, while in KaU 2.7 it is not clear to what it refers.

Olivelle (1998) thinks that it refers in KaU 2.7 to *sāṃparāya(ḥ)* "transit" (?) (of soul to the other world) from stanza 6. Here he follows Rudolf Otto who takes *sāṃparāya* "Hinübergang" und *para loka* "die höhere Welt" from stanza 6 as subjects referred to in stanza 7. However, Weller (1953) sharply criticizes Otto's interpretation; his strongest argument is that *aṇīyān aṇupramāṇāt* "(one) smaller than the size of an atom", which is *atarkya(m)* "difficult to grasp", in stanza 8 cannot refer to *sāṃparāya* but only to *ātman*, as *aṇor aṇīyān* "smaller than an atom" explicitly does in KaU 2.20.[41]

Oberlies (1998: 90) states that ŚvU 4.20 is "eine Umbildung von KU VI 9" [KaU 6.9]. The BhG 2.29 has the formula expressing the difficulty of seeing the immortal entity in common with KaU 6.9 and ŚvU 4.20, while it has the formula referring to hearing, and the forms of the stem *āścarya-* "rare(ly), wonderful(ly)", in common with KaU 2.7. The context in BhG 2 is probably more archaic (*dehin*): it does not presuppose the developed Sāṃkhya

ātman (p. 347, fn 1) and translates it: "7. He who by many is not obtainable even to hear of ... "; in it he may follow Śaṅkara who also understands it as referring to *ātman*; Hume mentions the parallel in MuU 3.2.4.

[41] Cf. Weller 1953: 85-88. Weller takes stanzas 7 and 8 as connected, but separates them very clearly from KaU 2.1-6, and considers that with stanza 6 the first part ends, and that with stanzas 7 and 8 the second part of chapter 2 of the KaU begins; cf. pp. 107-109. The first part speaks of two kinds of people: those who care of worldly goods only and fall as pray to repeated death, and those who seek salvation. The second part teaches about *ātman*.

system like KaU 6.7-9 (*puruṣa, avyakta)*, or even its application to the theology of Rudra – Śiva like ŚvU 4.20-21. In all three texts the composition of stanzas is basically harmonious, in the BhG with a nice gradation in meaning. Both in BhG 2 and KaU 6 the *triṣṭubh* in question is, however, surrounded by *anuṣṭubh*s or *śloka*s, and looks as it were inserted into the text from some repertory of proverbial formulae. Apart from the (presumably younger) ŚvU 4 passage, only KaU 2.7 is surrounded by other *triṣṭubh*s[42], but their semantic connection is rather puzzling or elliptical; in Weller's opinion. With KaU 2.7 begins the second part of the chapter referring to *ātman.*

BhG 2.(18)19-20 / Mbh 6.24.(18)19-20	KaU (1) 2.18-19
	na jāyate mriyate vā vipaścin
	nāyaṃ kutaścin na babhūva kaścit I
(*antavanta ime dehā*	*ajo nityaḥ śāśvato 'yaṃ purāṇo*
nityasyoktāḥ śarīriṇaḥ I	*na hanyate hanyamāne śarīre* II 18 II
anāśino 'prameyasya	
tasmād yudhyasva bhārata II 18 II)	
ya enaṃ vetti hantāraṃ	*hantā cen manyate hantuṃ*
yas cainam manyate hatam I	*hataś cen manyate hatam* I
ubhau tau na vijānīto	*ubhau tau na vijānīto*
nāyaṃ hanti na hanyate II 19 II	*nāyaṃ hanti na hanyate* II 19 II[43]
na jāyate mriyate vā kadācin	
nāyaṃ bhūtvā bhavitā vā na bhūyaḥ I	
ajo nityaḥ śāśvato 'yaṃ purāṇo	
na hanyate hanyamāne sarīre II 20 II[44]	

[42] The great prevalence of hendecasyllabic (dodecasyllabic) verses in the first two *vallī*s (chapters, of the KaU) is one of Weller's main arguments to consider them as the original core of the KaU, and *vallī*s 3-6, where octosyllables largely prevail, as later additions. See Weller 1953: 202.

[43] Olivelle 1998: "18. The wise one – he is not born, he does not die; he has not come from anywhere; he has not become anyone. He is unborn and eternal, primeval and everlasting. And he is not killed, when the body is killed. 19. If the killer thinks that he kills; if the killed thinks that he is killed; both of them fail to understand. He neither kills, nor is killed."

[44] Van Buitenen 1981: "18. What ends of this unending embodied, indestructible and immeasurable being is just its bodies – therefore fight, Bhārata! 19. He who thinks that this being is a killer and he who imagines that that it is killed do neither of them know. It is not killed nor does it kill. 20. It is never born nor does

ChU 8.1.5
na asya jarayainaj jīryati
na vadhenāsya hanyate |
etat satyaṃ brahmapuram ...[45]

Friedrich Weller (1953) pays due attention to these parallels and claims that both stanzas could neither have been directly transferred from the BhG to the KaU, nor from the KaU to the BhG. They follow in a different order in each text, and both differ in some *pāda*s from each other. Therefore Weller supposes that they can be only indirectly connected. From their different order in both texts he concludes that one of the two corresponding stanzas must be a younger addition, and therefore was inserted at a (adjacent but) different place. Moreover, in his opinion the form of both stanzas is from the viewpoint of the text history more original in the KaU because both have *lectiones difficiliores* in the KaU. Further, Weller thinks that KaU 2.19 speaks of a mortal, human killer and a killed person (he suggests that it does not mean "killed" but "mortally wounded"), while 2.18 and 2.20 speak of *ātman*, and therefore 2.19 interrupts the continuity of the text and must have been later inserted in that place (Weller 1953: 100-103).

---

it die; Nor once that it is will it ever not be; Unborn, unending, eternal, and ancient It is not killed when the body is killed." L. Rocher (1963) assumes that *bhūtvā* could at the time of the composition of BhG 2.20 have been understood as Nom. of *bhūtvan-*, and have been parallel to *bhavitā*, as *vā* suggests, and could thus have expressed the meaning that "this one" neither undergoes "the past" nor (*vā na*) the "future", i.e. does not undergo the *dhvaṃsābhāva* nor *prāgabhāva*. Rocher's opinion is that KaU 2.18 has the same meaning expressed in different wording. Unfortunately, he does not offer a translation of BhG 2.20. I still prefer to understand *vā* as connecting the two *pāda*s, the first *na* as referring to the whole sentence, and the second *na* as referring to *bhavitā*: "or, it is not (so) that this one, having become, is not going to be (will stop being) in future". I do not agree with Rocher nor Edgerton (1944) that this interpretation implies the "inconsistency" that the *dehin* has, however, come to being; it denies that he will (like transitory beings), cease to be after having come to being (i.e. it denies both).

[45] Olivelle 1998; "That does not age, as this body grows old; That is not killed, when this (body) is slain – That is the real fort of brahman ..."

In chapter 2 of the BhG there are 8 *triṣṭubh*s among 64 *śloka*s: 5-8, 20, 22, 29, and 70. The first four, stanzas 5-8, are inserted into the surrounding *śloka*s and belong to the hymn of which the core appears in BhG 11.15-50.[46] Of the rest, two have parallels in the KaU, stanzas 20 and 29. The last two, stanzas 22 and 70, look like proverbial formulae. All of them are in some sense inserted, and if they are skipped over, it cannot be noticed that something is missing in the text: on the contrary, the text flows more smoothly. However, they do embellish it, or make it more dignified, and are not inserted inappropriately. BhG 2.20 fits especially well in its context. Even if inserted, it fits on the whole better in the BhG context than its parallel version to the KaU context, because in a discussion about killing in the battle, which is the theme in the BhG, and in an argumentation that none is killed because the incarnated soul is immortal, stanza 20 is put in a proper place. The theme is essential for the BhG, while it is quite secondary for the KaU. It is therefore understandable that Hillebrandt (1921: 122) argued that the two stanzas must have belonged to the BhG first, and were transferred to the KaU afterwards.

In KaU 2 the proportion of metres is almost opposite: there are 17 hendecasyllables (or dodecasyllables) vs. only 8 octosyllables. Here it is – as Weller systematically shows – the *śloka*s that are suspect of being later inserted. In this case too, Weller considers stanza 19 as a later insertion.

It is hard to exclude the possibility that both KaU 18 and 19, as well as BhG 19 and 20, are taken, as Weller suggests, from some third source or from a repertory of floating formulae. However, it seems that in BhG 2 stanzas 19, 21 and 23-24 continue after each other rather smoothly. Just as Weller remarks that in the KaU stanza 20 continues the teaching about *ātman* from stanza 18, while stanza 19 interrupts the subject. It is imaginable that the *śloka* KaU 2.19 was modelled upon the BhG 2.19, and the *triṣṭubh* BhG 2.20 upon the KaU 2.18.

---

[46] See Ježić 1986.

BhG 2.19 looks not only like a *lectio facilior*, as Weller says, but also as a syntactically more harmonious text. While in it the constructions *vetti enam hantāram* and *enam manyate hatam* are simple and blameless, in KaU 2.19 the construction *hataś cen manyate hatam* needs both semantic interpretation in the sense that *hataḥ* here does not mean *getötet* but *tödlich getroffen*, as Weller claims, and syntactic interpretation: one would expect N. *hataḥ*, not Acc. *hatam*. Or, if we do not take it as a *corruptio*, we must understand it as an ellipsis, and ask ourselves who is the logical subject of *hatam*. Is it *enam* "him", as in the BhG, or *ātmānam* "himself"? That troubled syntax can be called either *lectio difficilior* or *corruptio*, according to the approach of each philologist. Or, can we see it as a discrete adaptation to the context in the KaU: if we must fill in *ātmānam* before *hatam*, does it create a hidden formal connection with the surrounding stanzas speaking of *ātman*? However, even in that case, the word *ātman* has a different meaning in stanza 19 ("himself") on the one side and in stanzas 18 and 20 ("the Self") on the other. Moreover, *hantā* and *hataḥ* remain two persons, *ubhau.* On the contrary, in BhG 2.19 *enam* occuring twice does not refer to two "mortal men", but to one *dehin.* All these considerations point to the probability that the source of that *śloka* could be the Gītā, and its form in the KaU its modification.[47]

The *triṣṭubh* KaU 2.18 can on the whole look like *lectio difficilior* in comparison with BhG 2.20. However, *pāda* 2.20b may equally look like the more difficult reading of the two because of its difficult word order: *nāyaṃ bhūtvā bhavitā vā na bhūyaḥ* is a metri causa permutation of something like: *na vāyaṃ bhūtvā na bhavitā bhūyaḥ.* One *yamaka* (*paronomasia*) plus *figura etymologica* appears in the KaU (... *vipaścin nāyaṃ kutaścin na babhūva kaścit*), another in the BhG (... *kadācin nāyaṃ bhūtvā bhavitā vā na*

[47] An example how it can be further modified gives Mbh 12.217.14:
hataṃ hanti hato hyeva yo naro hanti kaṃcana |
ubhau tau na vijanīto yaś ca hanti hataś ca yaḥ || 14 ||
Cf. Malinar 1996: 304.

bhūyaḥ); both are coherent, but the latter could more easily be derived from the former (*kadācit* from *kutaścit* and *kaścit*, and possibly – but not so evidently – *bhūtvā bhavitā vā na bhūyaḥ* from *babhūva)* than vice versa. The BhG could have avoided the term *vipaścit* because the intention of its redactor could have been to connect the stanza with the concept of *dehin* without distracting in-between concepts (the idea of a *brahman-vipra*, or a deity comparable to him as a knower of insights). What is more important, the BhG could have avoided the expression *na babhūva kaścid* "he has not become anyone", because *dehin* is individual, while *ātman* in the KaU is not. On the other hand, the redactor of the BhG 2 could have wanted to introduce the negation of temporality in order to stress the immortality of *dehin*, which is his topic. I would not be able to adduce comparable reasons for the transformation of the BhG version into KaU 2.18, because the BhG version could fit the KaU context without modifications, as far as I can see.

Therefore it seems rather probable that KaU 2.18 was the model for BhG 2.20 and was put after the akin stanza 19. Probably after that, the BhG 2.19, so closely connected with the inserted stanza 20, could have been transferred with modifications to KaU 2 after the corresponding stanza 18. It would most easily explain the reversal of order of the two connected stanzas in our texts: each text has inserted the borrowed stanza after its own.

If each text borrowed something from the other, then this stratum of the KaU and that of the BhG most probably came into being in the approximately same period.[48] At least the lines of tradition of both texts have been somehow interconnected.

[48] And even if the KaU and the BhG modelled their parallel stanzas upon a third source, these strata in them could be considered very close in time.

d) *navadvāre pure dehī*

<u>BhG 5.13 / Mbh 6.27.13</u>

sarvakarmāṇi manasā saṃ
nyasyāste sukhaṃ vaśī I
navadvāre pure dehī
naiva kurvan na kārayan II 13 II[49]

<u>ŚvU 3.18</u>

navadvāre pure dehī
haṃso lelāyate bahiḥ I
vaśī sarvasya lokasya
sthāvarasya carasya ca II 18 II[50]

<u>KaU 5.1-2 (2.2.1-2)</u>

puram ekādaśadvāram
ajasyāvakracetasaḥ I
anuṣṭhāya na śocati
vimuktaś ca vimucyate II 1 II
etad vai tat I
haṃsaḥ śucisad vasur
antarikṣasad dhotā vediṣad ...[51]
(cf. ṚS 4.40.5, Dadhikrā, Sūrya;
kavi Vāmadeva)

The formula describing the *dehin* as *navadvāre pure dehī* "the soul ... in its nine-gated fortress" (van Buitenen) / "the embodied one ... within the fort of nine gates" (Olivelle) appears both in the BhG and he ŚvU. It describes the embodied one in its body which has nine gates, and fits well with the meaning of the term *dehin.* In the KaU the concept is modified as *puram ekādaśadvāram ajasya* "the fort with eleven gates of the unborn one"[52]; the continuation in KaU

[49] Van Buitenen 1981: "Having renounced all *karman* with the mind, the soul dwells, happy and masterful, in its nine-gated fortress, neither doing nor causing acts."

[50] Olivelle 1998: "Within the fort of nine gates, the embodied one flutters to the outside like a goose; it is the master of the whole world, of both the immobile and the mobile."

[51] Olivelle 1998: "1. The unborn one, free of crooked thoughts, has a fort with eleven gates; One who attends to it will not grieve, but, freed from it, he will be set free. So, indeed, is that! 2. The goose seated in the light, the Vasu seated in the sky; The Hotṛ seated at the altar ..."

[52] Nine gates are two eyes, two ears, two nostrils, mouth, anus and urinal opening. It is mentioned first in the AS(Ś) 10.2.31, 8.43. Cf. Oberlies 1996: 150. In the number eleven the two added gates are the navel and the cranial opening. Cf. Olivelle 1998: 609.

5.2 with the citation of ṚS 4.40.5 may partially explain the rest of the wording in ŚvU 3.18.

The context in the BhG 5 is relatively the most coherent one, and describes the embodied soul in the context of yoga. The KaU 5 collection of stanzas is very syncretistic, as Weller shows. And the ŚvU 3 combines the stanzas praising Rudra/Śiva (like 3.2, 4, 5, 6) as the highest divinity, those inspired by or borrowed from the *Puruṣasūkta* ṚS 10.90, and its later variants (like 3.3, 14, 15, 16) speaking of the universal *Puruṣa*, and those speaking of the inner *puruṣa* (like 3.13, 18) that can perhaps be understood as the immanent god.

The relationship between the cited passages looks at first rather like the relationship between older and younger oral compositions, where formulae are freely used in appropriate contexts, than as one between texts where the whole units (stanzas or larger passages) were borrowed from one text to another.

Generally speaking, ŚvU 3.18 could probably presuppose BhG 5.13, and necessarily ṚS 4.40.5. KaU 5.1-2 could presuppose the same passages. In this case it is less obvious whether ŚvU 3.18 presupposes KaU 5.1-2, or is itself presupposed by it. What can be noticed is that KaU 5.1-2 could have changed the formula concerning the number of gates, and cites much more directly ṚS 4.40.5, as if disclosing in a learned way the Vedic source of ŚvU 3.18.

e) *aṇor aṇīyāṃ*

BhG 8.9-10ad / Mbh 6.30.9-10ad	ŚvU 3.8, 20-21
kaviṃ purāṇam anuśāsitāram	*vedāham etaṃ puruṣam mahāntam*
aṇor aṇīyāṃsam *anusmared yaḥ* ǀ	***ādityavarṇam tamasaḥ parastāt*** ǀ
sarvasya dhātāram acintyarūpam	*tam eva viditvāti mṛtyum eti*
ādityavarṇam tamasaḥ parastāt ǁ 9 ǁ	*na anyaḥ panthā vidyate 'yanāya* ǁ 20 ǁ[53]
	(= TĀ 3.12.16ab, 17cd; 3.13.2;
	VS 31.18; MNU 25-26)

[53] Olivelle 1998: "I know that immense Person, having the color of the sun and beyond darkness. Only when a man knows him does he pass beyond death; there is no other path for getting there."

prayāṇakāle manasācalena ...
... sa
taṃ paraṃ puruṣam upaiti divyam || 10 ||[54]

KaU (1) 2.20

aṇor aṇīyān mahato mahīyān
ātmāsya jantor nihito guhāyām |
tam akratuḥ paśyati vītaśoko
dhātuprasādān mahimānam ātmanaḥ ||[55]

aṇor aṇīyān mahato mahīyān
ātmā guhāyāṃ nihito 'sya jantoḥ |
tam akratuṃ paśyati vītaśoko
dhātuḥ prasādān mahimānam īśam ||

(TĀ 10 = MNU 201-202)
vedāham etam ajaraṃ purāṇam |
sarvātmānaṃ sarvagataṃ vibhutvāt |
janmanirodhaṃ pravadanti yasya
brahmavādino hi pravadanti nityam ||[56]

In the cited passages the formula *aṇor aṇīyān (mahato mahīyān)* "smaller than the smallest (larger than the largest)" appears in BhG 8, KaU 2 and ŚvU 3. In BhG 8.9 we come across another formula which occurs equally in ŚvU 3.8: *ādityavarṇaṃ tamasaḥ parastāt* "having the colour of the sun and beyond darkness".

In BhG 8.9 both formulae refer to the *kaviḥ purāṇaḥ* "the primordial sage/poet" who is explained in BhG 8.10 (also *triṣṭubh*) as *paraḥ puruṣo divyaḥ* "the Person supreme and divine" (van Buitenen); the context in the *triṣṭubh*s says that a person who with an unshaken mind, armed with devotion (*bhaktyā yuktaḥ*) and with the power of yoga (*yogabalena ca*), thinks of him in his final hour, attains to that Supreme Person (BhG 8.10).

---

[54] Van Buitenen 1981: "9. The sage and Preceptor primordial, More minute than an atom, creator of all, Of form unimaginable, hued like the sun At the back of the night – who thus thinks of him 10. in his final hour ... Attains to the Person Supreme and Divine."

[55] Olivelle 1998: "Finer than the finest, larger than the largest, is the self (*ātman*) that lies here hidden in the heart of a living being. Without desires and free from sorrow a man perceives by the creator's grace the grandeur of the self."

[56] Olivelle 1998: "20. Finer than the finest, larger than the largest, is the self that lies here hidden in the heart of a living being. A man who, by the creator's grace, sees that desireless one as the majesty and as the Lord will be free from sorrow. 21. I know that unaging and ancient one as the self in all beings, as present in all because of his pervasiveness; the one, about whom those who inquire after *brahman* proclaim – he always brings about the cessation of birth."

KaU 2.20 and ŚvU 3.20 are originally the same stanza: first, with slight variations in the word order in *pāda* b; second, with a syntactic difference in *pāda* c, where *akratu* is in N. in KaU and in Acc. in ŚvU; and third, with a significant difference in meaning in the last word of *pāda* d: in KaU the person free from sorrow sees Him (*ātman*) as *mahimānam ātmanaḥ* "the grandeur of the self", and in the ŚvU as *mahimānam īśam* "the majesty and the Lord". In ŚvU 3.21 He is moreover called *purāṇa* "primordial, ancient", as in BhG 8.9.

All three texts – BhG, ŚvU and a variant of KaU – call Him also *dhātar* "creator". However, probably the *varia lectio dhātu-prasādāt* is to be preferred to the reading *dhātuḥ prasādāt* in the KaU, as Weller (1953) suggests and translates (following Böhtlingk) "dadurch, dass die Elemente zur Ruhe gelangen". This reading is found in Śaṅkaras commentary[57] and accepted, for example, by Böhtlingk and Deussen. For Weller, this reading is crucial in deciding whether stanza 20 belongs to the core of the KaU 2 (1-8, 13, 18) – if we suppose that the reading *dhātu-* is original, or to later additions to it (if the reading *dhātuḥ* is correct).[58]

A triple correspondence is thus documented by parallels between KaU 2.20, BhG 8.9 and ŚvU 3.8 and 20-21 (see above). Here KaU 2.20 and ŚvU 3.20 are obviously, as mentioned, variants of one and the same stanza. Both stanzas in *pāda* b obviously speak of *ātman*, while in *pāda* d KaU 2.20 speaks of *mahiman ātmanaḥ* and ŚvU 3.20 of *mahiman īśa*: the former is hypermetrical, dodecasyllabic, the letter metrically regular, but the former seems to keep the subject *ātman* "Self" unchanged, while the latter seems to change the subject to *īśa* "Lord". Therefore, in the opinion of Belvalkar and Ranade (1927: 93), the reading in KaU 2.20 should be considered earlier than the theological reading of ŚvU 3.20. Weller

[57] Śaṅkara: *eṣāṃ dhātūnāṃ prasādād ātmano mahimānam karmanimitta-vṛddhikṣayarahitaṃ paśyati.*

[58] Weller 1953: 106. The stanza occurs with the reading *dhātuḥ prasādāt* in TĀ 10.10.1, in full correspondence with the ŚvU 3.20. TĀ 10 = MNU.

(1953: 107, especially fn. 3) thinks that KaU 2.20 either does not belong to the old stock of KaU 2 (to the second oldest group of stanzas), but represents a remade reading, younger than the metrically correct one in ŚvU 3.20, or we must find a satisfactory explanation of the way how its *pāda* d became hypermetrical. Oberlies (1996: 151, fn 153) says that ŚvU 3.20 is probably a modification of KaU 2.20.[59] Anyway, BhG 8.9 also shares crucial formulae with the two Upaniṣads (*aṇor aṇīyān*, possibly *dhātar* – at least with ŚvU 3.20, *purāṇa* – only with ŚvU 3.21, and *āditya-varṇaṃ tamasaḥ parastāt* – with ŚvU 3.8), and proves to have a share in the same heritage.

f) *tat te padaṃ saṃgraheṇa ...*

BhG 8.11, 13 / Mbh 6.30.11, 13

yad akṣaraṃ vedavido vadanti
viśanti yad yatayo vītarāgāḥ I
yad icchanto brahmacaryaṃ caranti
tat te padaṃ saṃgraheṇa *pravakṣye* II 11 II

om ity ekākṣaraṃ brahma
vyāharan mām anusmaran I
yaḥ prayāti tyajan dehaṃ
sa yāti paramaṃ gatim II 13 II[60]

KaU (1) 2.15-17

sarve vedā yat padam āmananti
tapāṃsi sarvāṇi ca yad vadanti I
yad icchanto brahmacaryam caranti
tat te padaṃ saṃgraheṇa *bravīmi* II 15 II
om ity etat I

[59] Oberlies 1996: 151, fn 153, enumerates other texts that repeat or modify this stanza, especially the expression *aṇor aṇīyān*: MNU 201-202 agrees with the ŚvU (*pāda* a = *Īśvaragītā* 5.23c, 8.17c); other parallels: Mbh 12.231.30ab; 232.33a; 294.22ab, the BhG passage and Mbh 5.45.28ab.

[60] Van Buitenen 1981: "11. The abode [word, *pada*] that the Veda-wise call the eternal [syllable, *akṣara*], And the aspirants enter with passions shed, And in search of which they practice the *brahman*, I shall now propound to you summarily. 13. He reaches the highest goal who relinquishes the body and departs life while uttering the one-syllabed *brahman* that is OṂ and thinking of me."

etaddhy evākṣaraṃ brahma
etaddhy evākṣaram param ।
etaddhy evākṣaraṃ jñātvā
yo yad icchati tasya tat ॥ 16 ॥
etad ālambanam śreṣṭham
etad ālambanam param ।
etad ālambanaṃ jñātvā
brahmaloke mahīyate ॥ 17 ॥[61]

In the Gītā two stanzas after the passage discussed in the previous paragraph, and in the KaU five stanzas before the discussed passage, there occur again parallel *pāda*s announcing the concise word (*pada*) expressing what people seek when they follow students' discipline: *yad icchanto brahmacaryaṃ caranti tat te padaṃ saṃgraheṇa pravakṣye/bravīmi.* In both texts, as they are transmitted, that *pada* is explained as the syllable ("imperishable", "eternal", "indivisible" sound unit) *akṣara* OṂ which is *brahman*: the BhG introduces it as the syllable on which one should concentrate in yoga in the hour of death: *om ity ekākṣaraṃ brahma* ..., in the KaU it is inserted between the stanzas: *om ity etat*, and the next stanza continues *etaddhy evākṣaraṃ brahma* ... In both texts the continuation after the introductory *triṣṭubh* follows in octosyllabic *śloka*s.

The next *triṣṭubh* BhG 8.28 could be connected with BhG 8.11. The intervening *śloka*s continue the topic of BhG 8.11 and elaborate it, although they could belong to younger text layers. Weller does not connect stanzas 16 and 17 in KaU 2 closely with 15, which seems to him rather isolated. However, these stanzas are a continuation of KaU 2.15, regardless of how much younger they may be, just as BhG 8.13, which runs even more smoothly, is a

[61] Olivelle 1998: "15. The word [*pada*] that all the Vedas disclose; The word that all austerities proclaim; Seeking which people live student lives; That word now I will tell you in brief – It is OṂ! 16. For this alone is the syllable [*akṣara*] that's *brahman*! For this alone is the syllable that's supreme!" When, indeed, one knows this syllable, he obtains his every wish. 17. This is the support that's best! This is the support supreme! And when one knows this support, he rejoices in *brahman*'s world."

continuation of 8.11, and there is no need in the Gītā for a prose addition *oṃ ity etad* to connect them with the announcement of the *tat padam.*

In chapter 8 of the BhG there are 4 *triṣṭubh*s: 9-11 and 28 among 24 *śloka*s. Two of them show parallels with the KaU (the first one with the ŚvU too): 9 and 11. It is noteworthy that KaU 2 has four *triṣṭubh*s that have parallels in the BhG: 7, 15, 18 and 20, and two *śloka*s: 16 and 19.

This means that KaU 2.7 and the whole sequence KaU 2.15-20 has parallels in the BhG (The *anuṣṭubh*s/*śloka*s are printed in italic.):

KaU	**BhG**	**ŚvU**
2.7 (6.9)	2.29	4.20
2.15-*16 (17)*	8.11, *13*	
2.18-*19*	2.*19*-20	
2.20	8.9	3.8, 20-21

It shows that the core of correspondances between the BhG and the KaU is concentrated in KaU 2, and is distributed in BhG 2 and 8.

It also shows, as mentioned, that the four corresponding passages are in *triṣṭubh*s, and two are in *śloka*s connected with them.

The *triṣṭubh* formulae could be (partly) borrowed by the Gītā from the KaU, or from a third text, or from a floating repertory of formulae. Weller (1953) considers KaU 2.7, 18 and possibly 20 (with the reading *dhātu-*; and with the open problem of its hypermetrical *pāda* d) as original parts of KaU 2 (although as the second oldest group of stanzas in it). On the other hand, he takes 15 as a relatively isolated *triṣṭubh*, younger even than *śloka*s 14 and 16-17.

The *śloka* formulae, as Weller (1953) argues, do not belong to the older strata of KaU 2. They are relatively later additions. It means that they could be (partly) taken from the BhG or from a third source. For KaU 2.19, I tried to argue (see above) that it could have been borrowed from the BhG and then modified. For

KaU 2.16 (17), it is not easy to say the same because BhG 8.13 obviously belongs to the Bhakti layer of the Gitā, which is the youngest one in the poem, and KaU 16-17 do not show any traces of *bhakti*. On the other hand, even the *triṣṭubh* BhG 8.10 speaks of *bhakti*.

g) *paraṃ brahma*

Another striking example of parallelism appears at BhG 13.13-14ab and ŚvU 3.16-17ab. In the ŚvU the passage occurs in the context of many quotations from Vedic texts in chapter 3.

BhG 13.(12,)13-16 / Mbh 6.35.(12,)13-16	ŚvU 3.3, (14-15,) 16-17
	viśvataścakṣur uta viśvatomukhaḥ *viśvatobāhur uta viśvataspāt* ׀ *saṃ bāhubhyāṃ dhamati saṃ patatrair* *dyāvābhūmī janayan deva ekaḥ* ॥ 3 ॥ (= ṚS 10.81.3; TS 4.6.2.10; MS 2.10.2: 133.8 f.; VS 17.19; cited also in MNU 53-54)
	sahasraśīrṣā puruṣaḥ *sahasrākṣaḥ sahasrapāt* ׀ *sa bhūmiṃ viśvato vṛtvā* *atyatiṣṭhad daśāngulaṃ* ॥ 14 ॥ (= ṚS 10.90.1; VS 31.1; TĀ 3.12.1)
jñeyaṃ yat tat pravakṣyāmi *yajjñātvāmṛtam aśnute* ׀ *anādimat paraṃ brahma* *na sat tan nāsad ucyate* ॥ 12 ॥	*puruṣa evedam sarvaṃ* *yad bhūtaṃ yac ca bhavyaṃ* ׀ *utāmṛtatvasyeśāno* *yad annenātirohati* ॥ 15 ॥ (= ṚS 10.90.2; VS 31.2; TĀ 3.12.2)[62]
sarvataḥ pāṇipādaṃ tat ***sarvato 'kṣiśiromukham*** ׀ ***sarvataḥ śrutimal loke*** ***sarvam āvṛtya tiṣṭhati*** ॥ 13 ॥	***idem*** ॥ 16 ॥ (cf. ṚS 10.81.3; Viśvakarman, *kavi* Viśvakarman Bhauvana)
sarvendriyaguṇābhāsaṃ ***sarvendiyavivarjitam*** ׀	***sarvendriyaguṇābhāsaṃ*** ***sarvendriyavivarjitam*** ׀

[62] See Oberlies 1988: 56.

asaktaṃ sarvabhṛc caiva
nirguṇaṃ guṇabhoktṛ ca ‖ 14 ‖
(cf. BhG 11.16, 23 = Mbh 6.33.16, 23)

sarvasya prabhum īśānaṃ
sarvasya śaraṇaṃ suhṛt ‖ 17 ‖[63]

Īśa 5

bahir antaś ca bhūtānām
acaraṃ caram eva ca ǀ
sūkṣmatvāt tad avijñeyaṃ
dūrasthaṃ cāntike ca tat ‖ 15 ‖
avibhaktam ca bhūteṣu
vibhaktam iva ca sthitam ǀ
bhūtabhartṛ ca taj jñeyaṃ
grasiṣṇu prabhaviṣṇu ca ‖ 16 ‖[65]

tad ejati taṇ naijati
tad dūre tadvad antike ǀ
tad antar asya sarvasya
tad u sarvasyāsya bāhyataḥ ‖ 3 ‖[64]

We may cite the opinion of Belvalkar and Ranade concerning the structure of ŚvU 3 and 4:

[63] Olivelle 1998: "3. Eyes everywhere and face everywhere, arms everywhere and feet everywhere, he forges with his two hands, he forges with the wings, producing the heaven and earth, the one God. 14. The Person had a thousand heads, a thousand eyes, and a thousand feet. Having encompassed the earth on all sides, he extended ten fingers' beyond it. 15. This whole world is just the Person, whatever there was and whatever there will be. Even over immortality he rules, when he rises above (the world) through food. 16. With hands and feet everywhere, with eyes, heads, and faces everywhere, and with ears everywhere, that remains encompassing everything in the world – 17. That, which appears to possess the powers of all the senses but is devoid of every sense, which is the lord, the ruler of whole world, the vast refuge of the whole world."

[64] Olivelle 1998: "5. It moves – yet it does not move! It's far away – yet it is near at hand! It is within this whole world – yet it's also outside this whole world."

[65] Van Buitenen 1981: "12. I shall set forth to you that object of knowledge by knowing which one attains to the beginningless *brahman*, which is called neither existent nor nonexistent. 13. Its hands and feet stretching everywhere, its head and face looking in every direction, its ears reaching out every way, it covers all in the universe. 14. While devoid of all the senses, it appears to have the qualities of all of them; while disinterested, it sustains all; while beyond the guṇas, it experiences the guṇas. 15. While within and outside the creatures, it is both that which moves and that which stands; it is hard to know because of its subtleness; and it is both far away and nearby. 16. Although undistributed, it appears distributed among the creatures. It should be conceived of as at once sustaining, bringing forth, and devouring the creatures."

> The description of Śiva given in the third and the fourth chapters is so much suffused by quotations from the Saṃhitās and other Upanishads that it is almost impossible to decide what is original and what is borrowed in these two chapters, excepting the doctrine of Śiva himself, which is the peculiar contribution of these chapters. (Belvalkar & Ranade 1927: 306.)

In that sense, we can see that ŚvU 3.3 cites a stanza that appears in Yajurvedic *saṃhitā*s but originates from ṚS 10.81.3, while ŚvU 3.14-15 cite the *Puruṣasūkta* from ṚS 10.90.1-2, which equally occurs in Yajurvedic *saṃhitā*s. The immediately following stanzas ŚvU 3.16-17ab are identical to BhG 13.13-14ab, and could have been modelled upon the cited Ṛgvedic, respectively Yajurvedic, stanzas: *sarvataḥpāṇipādaṃ tat sarvato'kṣiśiromukham ... sarvam āvṛtya tiṣṭhati* is obviously modelled on passages like ṚS 10.81.3 *viśvataścakṣur uta viśvatomukhaḥ viśvatobāhur uta viśvataspāt* or ṚS 10.90.1 *sahasraśīrṣā puruṣaḥ sahasrākṣaḥ sahasrapāt* | *sa bhūmiṃ viśvato vṛtvā atyatiṣṭhad daśāṅgulaṃ* (√*vṛ*, *tiṣṭhati*).

Now, considering the parallelism between ŚvU 3.16-17ab and BhG 13.13-14ab, Oberlies has already decisively stated that the corresponding stanzas are syntactically incongruent with the preceding text in the ŚvU, while in the BhG they normally syntactically fit into the context:

> Stellt man jedoch die beiden in ŚU [= ŚvU] (3.16/17ab) und BhG (13.13/14ab) jeweils aufeinander folgenden Verse einander gegenüber, so stellt man fest, dass in der ŚU von 3.15 [= RV 10.90.2] auf 3.16 zwar kein unerklärbarer, so doch merkwürdiger Geschlechtswechsel des Subjekts erfolgt (*puruṣaḥ* → *sarvataḥpāṇipādaṃ tat*) wärend in der BhG diese Bahuvrīhis auf *brahman* (BhG 13.12) zu beziehen sind ... Doch, scheint es so, als hätten die Verfasser der ŚU im Anschluss and das RV-Zitat die Verse BhG 13.13/14ab übernommen, ohne die Bahuvrīhis dem neuen Subjekt *puruṣaḥ* anzupassen. Die vermeintlichen Akkusative *sarvendriyaguṇabhāsam* und -*vivarjitam* zogen dann in 3.17c (d), das kein Zitat ist, die "wirklichen Akkusative *prabhum* und *īśānam* nach sich, die nun aber unkonstruierbar in der Luft hängen. (Oberlies 1988: 58.)

Oberlies tentatively concludes that the BhG has to be regarded as prior to the ŚvU (Oberlies 1988: 60).

On the other hand, it is worth mentioning that the redactors of the ŚvU 3 were learned Brahmans who were able not only to cite the BhG, but also to cite its Vedic sources or models. However strange it may seem, at the same time they could overlook the syntactic incongruence between the cited stanzas and the syntactic construction in what was their peculiar contribution, the application of those quotations to the doctrine of Śiva/Rudra. The example confirms that the citations tended to be literal, without modifications, and that the memorizing of texts was cultivated, but the additions do not confirm the equal level of active mastery of Sanskrit.

In the ŚvU it is again significant that the parallels with the BhG are concentrated in chapter 3, especially in the sequence ŚvU 3.15-21 (the *anuṣṭubh*s/*śloka*s are printed in italics):

ŚvU	**BhG**	
3.8	8.9	TĀ 3.12.16ab, 17cd; 3.13.2 VS 31.18
3.*(15) 16-17*	13.*(12) 13-14*	ṚS 10.81.*3*
3.*18*	5.*13*	cf. KaU 5.*1*-2
3.20-21	8.9	KaU 2.20

In this case, the fact that the parallels are so widely scattered in the BhG (chapters 5, 8, 13), and so concentrated in the ŚvU (chapter 3) seems to confirm the assumption that ŚvU 3 is a collection of citations of stanzas and formulae, and is later than BhG 13, as well as all the layers of the BhG older than chapter 13.

In ŚvU 3.18, we can notice a kind of combination of Vedic and BhG citations similar to the combination in the series of stanzas ŚvU 3.3, 14-17 that we have just observed: *navadvāre pure dehī* in ŚvU 3.18 can be a cited formula from BhG 5.13, while the continuation *haṃso līlāyate bahiḥ* | *vaśī sarvasya lokasya sthāvarasya carasya ca* may be analysed in two parts. It has the expression *vaśī* in common with BhG 5.13, nicely interpreted by the expanded formula. The rest *haṃso līlāyate bahiḥ* is modelled upon passages like ṚS 4.40.5. This is shown by KaU 5.1 which cites the ṚS stanza *in extenso* after the expression *puram ekādaśadvāram* (see above). Here again, we meet with the correspondences between all the three texts: the KaU, the ŚvU and the BhG.

BhG and Īśā 5

The parallels between BhG 13.15 and Īśā 5, which are not citations, but are expression of the same content with the help of common formulaic repertory in the same metre, could imply that BhG 13 and Īśā, i.e. VS 40, could be close in time. That could be another valuable chronological reference point.

h) The tree

BhG 15.1-4, 6 / Mbh 6, 37.1-4, 6	KaU 5.15; 6.1 (2.2.15; 2.3.1)
	na tatra sūryo bhāti na candratārakam *nemā vidyuto bhānti kuto 'yam agniḥ* I *tam eva bhāntam anubhāti sarvaṃ* *tasya bhāsā sarvam idaṃ vibhāti* II 15 II (= ŚvU 6.14)
***ūrdhvamūlam** adhaḥśakham* ***aśvatthaṃ** prāhur avyayam* I *chandūṃsi yasya parṇāni* *yas tam veda sa vedavit* II 1 II	***ūrdhvamūlo** 'vākśākha* *eṣo **'śvatthaḥ** sanātanaḥ* I *tad eva śukraṃ tad brahma* *tad evāmṛtam ucyate* II 1 II *tasmiṃl lokāḥ śritāḥ sarve* *tad u nātyeti kaścana* I *etad vai tat* I[66]
adhaś cordhvaṃ prasṛtās tasya śakhā *guṇapravṛddhā viṣayapravālāḥ* I *adhaś ca mūlāny anusaṃtatāni* *karmānubandīni manuṣyaloke* II 2 II	

[66] Olivelle 1998: "5.15 There the sun does not shine, nor the moon and stars; There lightning does not shine, of this common fire need we speak! Him alone, as he shines, do all things reflect; this whole world radiates with his light. 6.1. Its roots above, its branches below, this is the eternal banyan tree. That alone is the Bright! That is brahman! That alone is called the Immortal! On it all the worlds rest; beyond it no one can ever pass. So, indeed is that!"

na rūpam asyeha tathopalabhyate
nānto na cādir na ca saṃpratiṣṭhā |
aśvattham enaṃ suvirūḍhamūlam
asaṅgaśastreṇa dṛḍhena chittvā || 3 ||

tataḥ padaṃ tat parimārgitavyaṃ
yasmin gatā na nivartanti bhūyaḥ |
tam eva cādyaṃ puruṣaṃ prapadye
yataḥ pravṛttiḥ prasṛtā purāṇī || 4 ||

na tad bhāsayate sūryo
na śaśānko na pāvakaḥ |
yad gatvā na nivartante
tad dhāma paramaṃ mama || 6 ||[68]

ChU 6.11.1

asya somya mahato vṛkṣasya yo
mule 'bhihanyāj jīvan sravet ...[67]

Śvetup. 3.9
yasmāt paraṃ nāparam asti kiṃcid
yasmān nāṇīyo na jyāyo 'sti kiṃcit |
vṛkṣeva stabdho divi tiṣṭhaty ekas
tenedaṃ pūrṇaṃ puruṣeṇa sarvam || 9 ||[69]
(cf. 6.6: *sa vṛkṣakālākṛtibhiḥ paro 'nyo*
yasmāt prapañcaḥ parivartate 'yam |[70])

[67] Olivelle 1998: "Now, take this huge tree here, son. If someone were to hack it at the bottom, its living sap would flow ..."

[68] Van Buitenen 1981: "1. They speak of the eternal Aśvattha tree whose roots are above, whose branches below, and whose leaves are the hymns: he who understands it understands the Veda. 2. Its branches are stretching downward and up; They thrive on the *guṇas* with buds that are objects; The roots reach gradually down to the ground In the world of men, connecting with *karman.* 3. No form can there be perceived of it. Neither end nor beginning nor final foundation – Cut down this Aśvattha so thoroughly rooted With the hardened axe of disinterest. 4. Then try to seek out that singular spot Whence one does not return once he has found it: "I draw near to that primordial Person From whom has derived this ancient impulse" ...." 6. Neither sun nor moon nor fire illumine it, that supreme domain of mine, on reaching which they do not return."

[69] Olivelle 1998: "9. This whole world is filled by that Person, beyond whom there is nothing; beneath whom there is nothing; smaller than whom there is nothing; larger than whom there is nothing; and who stands like a tree planted firmly in heaven."

[70] Olivelle 1998: "6. He, from whom the unfolding of the world has come forth, is higher than and different from the time-confined forms of the tree."

The metaphor of the tree, even of the inverted tree, is very old. In Indian tradition, we can pursue it to the Vedas. Thus, the *sūkta* ṚS 1.24.7-8, attributed to Śunaḥśepa, full of riddles, reads:

abudhné rā́jā váruṇo vánasya
ūrdhvám stū́paṃ dadate pūtádakṣaḥ ।
nīcīnā́ sthur upári budhná eṣām
asmé antár níhitā́ḥ ketávaḥ syuḥ ॥ 7 ॥

urúṃ hí rā́jā váruṇaś cakā́ra
sū́ryasya pánthām ánuetavā́ u ।
apáde pā́dā prátidhātave 'kar
utā́pavaktā́ hṛdayavídhaś cit ॥ 8 ॥[71]

This passage describes an inverted tree in free space, with the bottom above and (the branches) turned down. Its branches are rays of light. The next stanza seems to offer an apparent solution of the riddle: it is the Sun, which follows its path in the sky and runs along it.[72]

In KaU 6.1, the metaphor of the inverted tree is explained as *brahman*, the Bright, the Immortal; and later on (6.7, 8-17), as *puruṣa.* However, the *pāda*s c-f explaining the metaphor occur equally in KaU 5.8 where they are applied to *puruṣa* who is awake and creates desires within those who sleep. Therefore the context is uncertain. Weller takes this identical wording of KaU 5.8c-f as an important argument for the inauthenticity of KaU 6.1c-f:

tad eva śukram tad brahma tad evāmṛtam ucyate ।
tasmiṃ lokāḥ śritāḥ sarve tad u nātyeti kaścana ॥ 1 ॥

Moreover, even in KaU 5.8 *tad* should refer to *puruṣa* from the *pāda*s ab, as it should refer to *aśvattha* in KaU 6.1, which are both

[71] Translation: "7. King Varuṇa, whose skill is purified/refined, gives/holds the raised top of the tree in the bottomless (space), (the branches/rays) are turned down, the foot (bottom) is above. Let its rays of light be stored in us. 8. King Varuṇa has made a broad path for the Sun to follow it. He made feet to the footless (Sun) for running. He is proclaimer of what has penetrated hearts."

[72] See for discussion Falk 1994: 10 ff.; Bosch 1960: 65 ff.; Kuiper 1983: 23 ff.

incongruent, and the *pāda* c can be found in ŚvU 4.2 (Weller 1953: 176):

> *tad evāgnis tad ādityas tad vāyus tad u candramāḥ* ।
> *tad eva śukraṃ tad brahma tad āpas tat prajāpatiḥ* ॥ 2 ॥

In ŚvU 3.9, the metaphor of the tree is applied to the Person who fills the whole world. Later on (6.6), it is said that He is higher and different from the tree.

In BhG 15.1, the metaphor is first applied to the Vedas/ *chandāṃsi* in the opening *śloka* of the chapter, but in the following *triṣṭubh*s 2-4 it is applied to *karman* or *saṃsāra* (stanzas 2-3), and, when it is cut off, the wise will reach the eternal abode (stanzas 4-5).

BhG 15.6, a *śloka* again, states that the supreme abode of God (in the 1st person sg.), which the wise attain after they have cut off the *aśvattha* tree, is not illumined by the Sun nor the Moon. That connects it in some way with the cited Vedic mantras ṚS 1.24.7-8, where the metaphor of the tree is used for the Sun. It is worth noticing that, in the KaU, the stanza which precedes the metaphor of the *aśvattha* tree, at the end of chapter 5 (it ends the series of stanzas KaU 5.12-15), says that "there the Sun does not shine, nor the Moon and stars ...", and is parallel to the stanzas ŚvU 6.12-14, which lack a connection with the metaphor of the tree. The stanza KaU 5.15 = ŚvU 6.14 alone occurs also in the MU as 2.2.10. In spite of all the shifts, the interconnection of the tradition of the three texts (and occasionally even some other like MU) is confirmed once again.

After a long discussion of parallels between the KaU and the ŚvU, Weller concludes that the three stanzas must have come into these two texts from a third source, which is older than the KaU and the ŚvU in their present shape. The variants exclude, in his opinion, the possibility that one Upaniṣad was directly the source for the other (Weller 1953: 155). He is quite right from the standpoint of the philology of written texts. However, if the stanzas were inserted in the process of oral transmission of texts, the variants, which obviously do not show the characteristics of scribal errors, need not be the result of intervention of a redactor of a written text, but can also be the result of oral performance using different formulae at different occasions. This does not preclude the intentional "oral redaction" of the transmitted and incorporated material, but this cannot be discussed here. The proportion of *śloka*s and *triṣṭubh*s in KaU 5 (7 5/6 : 7 1/6) shows the probable composite nature of that *vallī*, partly comparable to that of the 8th *adhyāya* of the BhG.

Now, even if the metaphor of the cosmic tree can refer to the cosmic axis elsewhere, in ṚS 1.24 it seems to refer to the Sun, whose rays, which can reach us on earth, are compared to branches, and whose roots are in the sky, and whose crown is up high, but still turned down, while the roots are turned upwards. In the next stanza, the Sun is metaphorically given even legs to run along its path. All these wonders are created by the god Varuṇa who remains aloof, and is not identified with the tree. Now, this sphere under the Sun can be imagined as the realm of *saṃsāra*, while the *ādyaḥ puruṣaḥ* introduced in BhG 15.4 (and reminiscent of *paraḥ puruṣo divyaḥ* from BhG 8.10, or of *ādidevaḥ puruṣaḥ purāṇaḥ* from 18.38) transcends it.

Therefore, although BhG 15.1 and 15.6 ff. can be a younger frame in *śloka*s for the cited *triṣṭubh*s 15.2-5, it does not seem inappropriate when 15.6 mentions that "Neither sun nor moon nor fire illumine it, that supreme domain of mine, on reaching which they do not return." That *śloka* does remind one of the *triṣṭubh* KaU 5.15 and ŚvU 6.14, expressing the transcendence of *ātman* in the KaU and that of God in the ŚvU (this is the reason why the previous stanzas in them differ as they do; see above 6.a). The contiguity of KaU 5.15 and 6.1 with the metaphor of the tree reveals that BhG 15.6 is closer to the *Kaṭha* text.

The cited parallels can also be shown in a table (the *anuṣṭubh*s/*śloka*s are printed in italics):

BhG 15.*1*, 2-5, (*6*)	KaU (5.15) – 6.*1*	ŚvU 3.9, (6.14 = KaU 5.15)

The difference between the application of the metaphor of the tree on *saṃsāra*, on *brahman* and on *puruṣa*, implies that the first application, although it is a reinterpretation in the sense of renunciation of the world, remains faithful to the Ṛgvedic use of the metaphor, preserving the cosmic meaning of the metaphor and differentiating the transcendent divine person (Varuṇa; *ādyaḥ puruṣaḥ*) from it. On the other hand, the applications of the metaphor in KaU 6.1 and in ŚvU 3.9 are secondary confusion of the cosmic metaphor and the concept of the transcendent principle (*brahman*; *Puruṣa*). Maybe that can be explained by the confusion of the Vedic cosmic being *Puruṣa* with the individual person, *puruṣa* of Sāṃkhya, or by the identification of *brahman* with *prakṛti* in some theistic preclassical Sāṃkhya texts (reflected indirectly in BhG 14.3-4). It is interesting to note that the BhG 15 preserves, in the inserted *triṣṭubh* series, a conception of the metaphor closer to the original one.

It remains an open question wherefrom the BhG has taken these *triṣṭubh*s. It seems that the possibility that they were taken from the didactic parts of the *triṣṭubh* hymn, from which also BhG 8.9-11 may have originated, cannot be excluded.

CONCLUSIONS

Interconnected text tradition of the BhG, KaU and ŚvU

On the whole, the close intertextual interrelationship among the KaU, the BhG and the ŚvU proves that these three texts (as they have come to us) form a closely related group of Upaniṣadic texts that should be investigated together. They must have been transmitted in some common way – either performed on the same occasions, at the same places during the same historical period, or transmitted in the same or in related circles.

Already in descriptions of Vedic rituals we meet performances of various literary genres on the same occasions, such as the recitations of the *pāriplava-ākhyānas* in the cycles of 10 days during the *aśvamedha.* During these cycles the mantras from the *Ṛgveda, Yajurveda, Atharvaveda, Āngirasaveda and Sāmaveda,* different *vidyās* (about dangerous creatures: *sarpas, piśācas* or *asuras*), as well as *purāṇaveda* and *itihāsaveda,* were recited or sung. In such occasions a Brahman with a *vīṇā* sang *gāthās* praising the king's munificience (*ayajata, adadāt*) while a Kṣatriya with a *vīṇā* sang *gāthā nārāśaṃsīs* (*ayudhyata, ajayat*) (ŚB 13.4.3.2-12). In the Upaniṣads we have frame stories depicting how the Brahmans exerted themselves or even competed to show their knowledge at sacrificial gatherings, the most famous case probably being the great debate between Yājñavalkya and his brahmanical contestants in BĀU 3. The Mbh frame stories or frame stories of the *Harivaṃśa* and of the Purāṇas confirm that the long epic or Purāṇic recitations took place at long sacrificial rituals.[73] In Mbh 1.1.8 we

---

[73] Witzel speaks of the Vedic ritual technique which developed "in (or rather before) the period of the YV Saṃhitās when the existing pre-classical (Ṛgvedic, and various unknown or more popular) rites were assembled and put into a complicated, interdependent, and mutually interactive framework of their own by merging larger or smaller units of various rites in an additive fashion characterized by framework-like insertions ... This must have been the background of what became a technique of literary composition" (Witzel 1987: 413). He takes the story of Cyavana as "perhaps the most instructive example of complicated early Sanskrit narrative prose", which served in the JB as the frame story for the aetiological myth explaining how the Aśvins gained their share of the Soma drink at sacrifice after they received from Dadhyañc the instruction on the *pravargya* rite, and taught the gods how to embed it into the Soma sacrifice.

Minkowski starts from the frame stories in the Mbh, depicting Janamejaya's *sarpasattra* and Śaunaka's twelve-year *sattra* as occasions for recitation of the Mbh, and shows from the epic perspective how probable it is "that the Mahābhārata drew its inspiration for using a sustained frame story from the embedding structure of the Vedic ritual"(Minkowski 1989: 420).

We cannot dwell here upon questions about the status of king Janamejaya as a *yajamāna* at a *sattra* (Horsch [1966: 426-441] enumerates examples of Kṣatriyas in Vedic literature who seem to have been priests at the same time, and assumes that the term *rājarṣi* denotes exactly such Kṣatriyas), nor about the possible range of audiences at such occasions. The Vedic practice appears to have long been more conservative than in later more brahmanized times (e.g. concerning the *rājarṣis*), and more flexible than brahmanic regulations in normative texts claim.

Witzel is, however, well aware of the fact that "The evidence from Indo-Iranian, as well as the parallels from Greek literature indicate that the use of

hear that Vaiśampāyana narrated the auspicious stories – that were proclaimed first by Vyāsa – "at the snake session of the sage-king Janamejaya" *janamejayasya rājarṣeḥ sarpasatre.* Mbh 1.1.57-58 explains that the Mbh was recited in the intervals between the ritual actions at the sacrifice:

janamejayena pṛṣṭaḥ san brāhmaṇaiś ca sahasraśaḥ |
śaśāsa śiśyam āsīnaṃ vaiśampāyanam antike || 57 ||
sa sadasyaiḥ sahāsīnaḥ śravayāmāsa bhāratam |
karmāntareṣu yajñasya codyamānaḥ punaḥ punaḥ|| 58 ||[74]

In later times, as Yaroslav Vassilkov (2002) expounds,

> the full-fledged epic tradition cannot limit itself to performances at royal courts or at archaic tribal sacrifices ... In societies where the life of the majority of the population follows the rules established by the institutions of an organized soteriological religion, the only places where masses of people gather and (due to climatic conditions) often have a lot of forced leisure are naturally centres of pilgrimage. Therefore, epic singers badly needed permission from the local priests and monks to perform at holy places." (Vassilkov 2002: 139.)

---

frame structures, at least in poems, can be traced back far into prehistory" (Witzel 1987: 411-412), and cites e.g. Willamowitz-Möllendorf, *Aischylos-Interpretationen* (1914), for "ring compositions" or frame stories in Homer, Hesiod, Herodotus and Aeschylus. Therefore the frames in Vedic rituals and in Sanskrit literature can be seen only as a parallelism, maybe stimulating the creation of frame stories, not as the explanation of the origin of ring compositions or frame stories.

For our topic, therefore, the essential point is that narrative and epic performances are depicted in Sanskrit tradition as taking place in the intervals of long Vedic rituals.

Concerning the form, we can recall that even in the BhG – as in the case of the story of Cyavana – the *śrīkṛṣṇārjunasaṃvādaḥ* represents its epic "frame-story" by means of which all its *upaniṣadaḥ* were gradually embedded into the Mbh. See above.

[74] Translation (Minkowski 1989: 403): "(Vyāsa) being asked (to tell the story of the Bhāratas) by Janamejaya and by thousands of Brahmins, instructed his student Vaiśampāyana, who was sitting nearby. Sitting with the *sadasyas*, urged repeatedly, he recited the Bhārata in the intervals between the actions of the rite."

At the *tīrtha*s people could listen not only to the epic singers and Brahmans but most probably to other religious teachers or preachers as well, such as the teachers of Sāṃkhya and Yoga.

The fact that the Gītā, the *Kaṭha* and the *Śvetāśvatara* have corresponding metres (*śloka*s and *triṣṭubh*s, sometimes *jagatī*s), just as they have some significant common contents, e.g. instructions on *ātman*, on *puruṣa*, Yoga and Sāṃkhya teachings, and that they share some common linguistic traits, implies the conclusion, strongly corroborated by the fact that they show remarkable literal parallels, that they must have been composed and transmitted on occasions when and where they could mutually have influenced each other directly or indirectly.

The Epic layer, the first Sāṃkhya layer and the *triṣṭubh* hymn in the BhG vs. the frame story and the doctrinal part in the KaU

The Epic layer of the BhG had served as the model for the *triṣṭubh* hymn.[75] If the hymn contained didactic parts as well, as will be shown below, then even the first Sāṃkhya layer must have preceded it, or it must have been contemporaneous with it.

The correpondences between the KaU and the BhG occur in the *triṣṭubh* parts teaching the doctrine of *ātman*, not in those which give the frame-story about Naciketas and Yama, which the KaU has in common with the TB 3.11.8 (in the context of the *nāciketacayana*, the Nāciketa altar).

Parallels in BhG 2 and KaU 2

This is a striking case of intertextuality. The concentration of correspondences in the KaU (in chapter 2) and to some extent in the BhG (in only 2 chapters) shows a greater interconnection of these two texts than isolated instances would demonstrate.

---

[75] See Ježić 1986.

The presented evidence suggests that the *triṣṭubh* insertions (BhG 2.20, 29) in the first Sāṃkhya layer of the BhG (BhG 2.11-30) could chronologically be younger than approximately what appears to Weller as the two oldest groups of stanzas in KaU 2 [a) 1-6; b) 7-8, 13, 18, (20)], but that the *śloka* BhG 2.19 could be the source of KaU 2.19. That could imply that the first Sāṃkhya layer of the BhG is probably older than the *śloka* passages of KaU 2 (although it cannot be demonstrated for the *śloka*s which have no parallels). It would suggest that the first Sāṃkhya layer and KaU 2 were in part simultaneously being composed: in the same shorter period, or during a longer period, but in the framework of an interconnected tradition. It is even more important as Weller has reasonably claimed that the original KaU once ended with chapter 2 (although not necessarily in its full extent).

Parallels in BhG 8 and KaU 2

Chapter 8 of the BhG is quite a complex case. The first six chapters of the Gītā, as well as the last six, can be proved[76] – and in fact it has quite recently been exhaustively proved by Przemysław Szczurek (2005)[77] – to precede the *bhakti* redaction of the text which reinterpreted the didactic poem in the light of *bhakti* by giving it a new synthesis through the last textual layer, the Bhakti layer. All *bhakti* passages in these chapters can be isolated – although they were interpolated with great ingenuity – and, if excised, the text

[76] See Ježić 1979; 1986.

[77] For my part I can confirm that I was struck by the fact that Dr. Szczurek identified exactly the same 22 *bhakti* interpolations throughout the text, as I did in my first attempt to survey them 20 years ago, with three minor modifications, although I have never published that part of my research (except for the first four cantos, and for the general survey of all the layers without specifying the *bhakti* interpolations), and had not the slightest influence on the precise identification of them by Dr. Szczurek. In my opinion it is a strong indication of the great degree of certainty with which such interpolations can be discovered with our methodology, and at the same time a proof of the possible strictness and precision of application of that methodology if two persons independenty come to the same results. Dr. Szczurek's published results seem therefore to me to be conclusive.

will show no interruption. Chapters 7 and 9-12 are the core of the Bhakti layer. Of course, in chapter 11, as mentioned above, the *triṣṭubh* stanzas 15-50 form a special unit and represent an originally independent hymn to Vāsudeva in his all-encompassing Viśvarūpa and Kāla aspects, modelled upon the Epic layer of the Gītā, but opening up quite different, religious dimensions of events. The hymn was created outside the Mbh frame, and only later inserted in it through the *bhakti* redaction of the text.[78] Chapter 8 belongs in part to the Upaniṣadic layers and in part to the Bhakti layer. Gajanan Shripat Khair (1969: 58 ff.) claimed that the major part of chapter 8 belongs to the third sextet of chapters along with chapters 13-15 and 17-18, which he rightly considered older than the *bhakti* chapters 7 and 9-12, to which group he ascribed chapter 16 too. However, the *bhakti* portion, or that part in which Kṛṣṇa speaks of himself as the highest being, amounts to 14 stanzas, i.e. half of the chapter – if we completely exclude the 4 *triṣṭubh*s from it. Moreover, *triṣṭubh* 11 speaks of *bhakti* for the *puruṣa purāṇa divya* in the hour of death, so it is not that far from the *bhakti* portion in which Kṛṣṇa is extolled in the first person. Even more so, if we compare BhG 8.9-11 to 11.18, 37-38, or 8.28 to 11.48:

BhG 8.9-11 / Mbh 6.30.9-11	BhG 11.18, 37-38 / Mbh 6.33.18, 37-38
kaviṃ purāṇam anuśāsitāram	*tvaṃ* ***akṣaraṃ*** *paramaṃ veditavyaṃ*
aṇor aṇīyāṃsam anusmared yaḥ |	tvam asya viśvasya paraṃ nidhānam |
sarvasya dhātāram acintyarūpam	*tvam avyayaḥ śāśvatadharmagoptā*
ādityavarṇaṃ tamasaḥ parastāt || 9 ||	*sanātanas tvaṃ* ***puruṣo*** *mato me* || 18 ||
prayāṇakāle manasācalena	*kasmāc ca te na nameran mahātman*
bhaktyā yukto yogabalena caiva |	*garīyase brahmaṇo 'py ādikartre* |
bhruvor madhye prāṇam āveśya saṃyak	*ananta deveśa jagannivāsa*
sa taṃ **paraṃ puruṣam** upaiti *divyam* || 10 ||	*tvam* ***akṣaraṃ*** *sad asat tatparaṃ yat* || 37 ||
yad ***akṣaraṃ*** *vedavido vadanti*	*tvam ādidevaḥ* ***puruṣaḥ*** *purāṇas*
viśanti yad yatayo vītarāgāḥ |	tvam asya viśvasya **paraṃ** nidhānam |
yad icchanto brahmacayaṃ caranti	*vettāsi vedyaṃ ca* ***paraṃ*** *ca dhāma*
tat te padaṃ saṃgraheṇa pravakṣye || 11 ||[79]	*tvayā tataṃ viśvam anantarūpa* || 38 ||[80]

[78] See Ježić 1986.

[79] Van Buitenen 1981: "9. The Sage and Preceptor primordial, More minute than an atom, creator of all, Of form unimaginable, hued like the sun At the back

BhG 8.28 /Mbh 6.30.28

vedeṣu yajñeṣu ***tapaḥṣu*** *caiva*
dāneṣu yat puṇyaphalaṃ pradiṣṭam |[81]
atyeti tat sarvam idaṃ viditvā
yogī ***paraṃ*** *sthānam* upaiti *cādyaṃ* || 28 ||[82]

BhG 11.48 / Mbh 6.33.48

na ***vedayajñā****dhyayanair na* ***dānair***
na ca kriyābhir na ***tapobhir*** *ugraiḥ* |
evaṃrūpaḥ śakya ahaṃ nṛloke
draṣṭuṃ tvadanyena kurupravīra || 48 ||[83]

The net of corresponding terms between the cited *triṣṭubhs* from chapter 8 and those from chapter 11 shows obvious repetitions (those between 8.9-11 and 28 with 11.18, 37-38 and 48 look similar to those between 11.18 and 11.38). Do these repetitions prove con-

---

of the night – who thus thinks of him 10. Armed with his devotion and power of yoga, With his breath ensconced between his eyebrows, Attains to the Person Supreme and Divine. 11. The abode that the Veda-wise call the eternal [*akṣara*], And the aspirants enter with passions shed, And in search of which they practice the *brahman*, I shall now propound to you summarily."

[80] Van Buitenen 1981: "18. You are Akṣara, highest of truths to be known, the highest foundation of all this world, Undying protector of Law sempiternal, The Person Eternal I hold you to be. 37. And why should they fail to bow down, great-souled One, Creator more worthy of honor than Brahmā? Unending Lord God, repose of the world, You're what is and is not and what is beyond it. 38. The Original God, the Person Eternal, You are of this world the ultimate support, The knower, the known, the final abode – All is strung upon you, of infinite form."

[81] Maybe the *puṇyaphala* topic connects this *triṣṭubh* with BhG 9.20-21:

traividyā māṃ somapāḥ pūtapāpā yajñair iṣṭvā svargatiṃ prārthayante |
te puṇyam āsādya surendralokam aśnanti divyān divi devabhogān || 20 ||
te taṃ bhuktvā svargalokaṃ viśālaṃ kṣīṇe puṇye martyalokaṃ viśanti |
evaṃ trayidharmam anuprapannā gatāgataṃ kāmakāmā labhante || 21 ||

Van Buitenen 1981: "20. The purified Vedic drinkers of Soma Seek me with oblations to win their heaven; And on reaching the blessed domain of Indra Enjoy the celestial joys of the Gods. 21. But upon enjoying the vast world of heaven, Their merit exhausted, they rejoin the mortals; Thus following devoutly the Law of the Vedas And craving desires they come and they go." If these *triṣṭubhs* are really connected, they could also belong to the stock of *triṣṭubhs* from the BhG hymn. In that case a god portion of the hymn could have been preserved thanks to the insertion throughout the BhG in the scheme of the *bhakti* redaction.

[82] Van Buitenen 1981: "28. What reward of merit has been assigned To rituals, Vedas, austerities, gifts, All that merit the yogin who knows transcends To attain the supreme, primordial place."

[83] Van Buitenen 1981: "Not with Veda or rites, not with study or gifts, Not with sacrifice or with awesome *tapas* Can I in this world be beheld in this form By any but you, great hero of Kuru."

tinuity between them or do they show reinterpretation that would lead us to assign them to different layers of text? The difference between the *triṣṭubh*s in BhG 8 and those in BhG 11 lies in the fact that in BhG 8 *kaviḥ purāṇo 'nuśāsitā ... sarvasya dhātā* or *paraḥ puruṣo divyaḥ* or *akṣaraṃ* is not explicitly identified with the speaker, Kṛṣṇa, while in BhG 11 it is Vāsudeva (*tvam*) who is explicitly called *akṣaram* and *puruṣaḥ purāṇaḥ* or *sanātanaḥ puruṣaḥ.* This could be a reinterpretation. However, if we suppose that the hymn in *triṣṭubh*s already knew the gradation between Kṛṣṇa the friend, Kṛṣṇa the teacher instructing about the *puruṣa purāṇa, akṣara, paraṃ sthānam ādyam* etc., and Kṛṣṇa in whom the *ādideva* "the Primordial God" reveals himself, then the said difference does not mean a reinterpretation of the previous text, but a gradation of one and the same text. And indeed, the hymnic stanzas BhG 11.41-42 (43) express clearly and beautifully Arjuna's shock and astonishment at the revelation that his interlocutor and companion is not simply his friend Kṛṣṇa Yādava, but God, "Father of the world with everything that is moving or stable in it". It shows that the hymn knew of the gradation from Kṛṣṇa the friend to the *ādideva.* What we still miss in BhG 11, is Kṛṣṇa the teacher, but he is somehow presupposed in the prehistory of the hymn from the ChU onwards, and if we find convincing traces of Kṛṣṇa's instruction in other chapters of the BhG with possible continuity repetitions with BhG 11.15-50, then the most probable implication is that the hymn contained also didactic portions with Kṛṣṇa as the teacher. It is additionally corroborated by BhG 2.7 where Arjuna states *śiṣyas te 'ham* "I am your pupil", and begs *śādhi māṃ tvāṃ prapannam* "teach me, who am resorting to you". In that case here we are not dealing with simple *triṣṭubh* interpolations in chapter 8, but have found additional stanzas of the *triṣṭubh* hymn, the key parts of which I identified earlier in chapters 2 and 11![84]

In that case I must correct myself on one point. In Ježić 1986 I have taken the *bhakti* stated in BhG 11.54 to be the only means to

---

[84] See Ježić 1986.

see God, as Arjuna has seen him in his vision, shows how the *śloka*s (from the Bhakti layer) reinterpreted the *triṣṭubh* hymn, in which Kṛṣṇa simply said, in BhG 11.48 (cited above), that no one in the world of men but Arjuna (in the 2nd person: *you*) can behold God (expressed in the 1st person: *me*) in this (all-embracing) form.

Now, I am inclined to understand it slightly differently. BhG 11.48 states that no one in the world of men, except Arjuna, can see God (*me*) in this form "with Veda, or sacrifices, or study, or gifts, or rites, or with awesome austerities". This limitation of the enumerated means, leaves room for the possibility for someone else apart from Arjuna to see God by *bhakti* as well. And that is what the relationship between the cited *triṣṭubh*s BhG 8.10 respectively BhG 11.48 and the corresponding *śloka*s BhG 8.22 and BhG 11.53-54 from the Bhakti layer additionally confirms:

BhG 8.22 (Mbh 6.30.22)	BhG 11.53-54 (Mbh 6.33.53-54)
	nāhaṃ vedair na tapasā
	na dānena na cejyayā I
	śakya evaṃ*vidho* draṣṭuṃ
	dṛṣṭavān asi mām yathā II 53 II
puruṣaḥ sa paraḥ *pārtha*	***bhaktyā tv ananyayā*** *śakya*
bhaktyā *labhyas* ***tv ananyayā*** I	*aham* evaṃ*vidho 'rjuna* I
yasyāntaḥsthāni bhūtāni	*jñātuṃ* draṣṭuṃ *ca tattvena*
yena sarvam idaṃ tatam II 22 II[85]	*praveṣṭuṃ ca paraṃtapa* II 54 II[86]

We can also notice that BhG 8.13, on the one hand, shows the link with 8.10 by alluding to the expression *prayāṇakāle* with the phrase *yaḥ prayāti tyajan deham*, but seems, on the other, to reinterpret *paraṃ puruṣaṃ (upaiti) divyam* "the Person supreme and divine" with "me" *mām (anusmaran)*, and therefore looks as a duplication

[85] Van Buitenen 1981: "22. It is the Supreme Person, attainable only through exclusive devotion, Pārtha, in whom the creatures inhere, the one on whom all this is strung."

[86] Van Buitenen 1981: "53. Thus, as I am and as you have seen me, I cannot be seen with the aid of the Vedas, austerities, gifts, and sacrifices. 54. Only through exclusive *bhakti* can I be seen thus, Arjuna, and known as I really am, and entered into, enemy-tamer."

repetition belonging to a more recent redaction of the text in which Kṛṣṇa is explicitly deified, while in the *triṣṭubh*s in BhG 8 this is not yet the case.

A special problem lies in the fact that *triṣṭubh* 8.10 already describes the devotee as *bhaktyā yuktaḥ* "armed with his devotion", which is picked up by *śloka* 8.22 where *puruṣaḥ paraḥ* "the Supreme Person" is described as *bhaktyā labhyas tv ananyayā* "attainable only though exclusive devotion". It shows that here the *triṣṭubh* presupposes already a *bhakti* background, participation in or maybe devotion to the Supreme Person, although only the *śloka*s explicitly connect that *bhakti* with the person of Vāsudeva or Kṛṣṇa (*aham, mām*).

The term *bhaktyā* in BhG 8.10 governed by *yuktaḥ* and juxtaposed with *yogabalena caiva* could have a different shade of meaning than the later concept of *bhakti* "devotion". On the one hand, we could think of the concept of *īśvarapraṇidhāna* "the submission to the Lord" (YS 1.23; 2.1, 32, 45), and on the other of something not excluding *pravṛtti*, because the text of the hymn in BhG 11 urges Arjuna to act and to fight. In any case, *bhakti* is already present as a term in the *triṣṭubh* text. It means that the supposed "reinterpretation" in BhG 11.54 where Arjuna's vision is explained by "exclusive devotion" to God can be justified not only by BhG 8.22, with which it shares the whole formula *bhaktyā tv ananyayā*, but also by referring to the *triṣṭubh* BhG 8.10, and therefore can be defended as a legitimate "interpretation" of the *triṣṭubh* BhG 11.48. A degree of reinterpretation can, however, be seen in the probable difference between *bhakti* plus *yoga* (the *triṣṭubh* version) and *bhakti* alone (*ananyā*; the Bhakti layer in *śloka*s). Since in BhG 11.15-50 the activities of the Lord are also called *yogaḥ aiśvaryaḥ*, the underlying idea of the teaching in the *triṣṭubh* version could be *bhakti* "the participation" through the *yoga* in the "yoga of the Lord".[87]

---

[87] And *yoga* here seems to combine both meanings of "activity, exertion" (opposite: *kṣema*) and "self-control" (opposites: *saṅga, kāma, krodha*, etc.). It is

The reinterpretation of *paraḥ puruṣaḥ divyaḥ* as referring to the interlocutor, the teacher, through the 1st person pronoun *aham* is in that case not an inappropriate reinterpretation of the preceding *triṣṭubh*s, but it is still a "reinterpretative anticipation" of what most probably was only later revealed in the *triṣṭubh* hymn[88]. Yet, in the *bhakti* redaction of the Gītā, which started with chapter 7 (apart from *bhakti* interpolations in earlier chapters), that divine nature of the interlocutor has already been stated, and was then applied in the interpretation (in *śloka*s) of those *triṣṭubh*s in chapter 8, which we now assumed to be incorporated citations from the hymn in that chapter. That is one of many indications of the unity of the extensive Bhakti layer.

If we deal in chapter 8 with *triṣṭubh*s from the hymn (2a), then the question of textual relationship with the KaU has a very different meaning than it would have if we dealt here simply with some isolated *triṣṭubh*s from chapter 8 of the Gītā. It is no more a question of the chronological relationship between BhG 8 and KaU 2, but between the originally independent *triṣṭubh* hymn and KaU 2!

The BhG *triṣṭubh* hymn and the KaU 2 *triṣṭubh*s

BhG 8.9b obviously presupposes the full-fledged formula which we find in KaU 2.20a *aṇor aṇīyān mahato mahīyān* (and ŚvU 3.20), and most scholars find it probable that it was applied to *ātman*, as is the case in the KaU, before it was used for *kaviṃ purāṇam anuśāsitāram* in the BhG or *mahimānam īśam* in the ŚvU (although it cannot so far be philologically demonstrated). KaU 2.20 would need a metrical emendation in *pāda* d, but it could be close to the model from which the corresponding formula in BhG 8.9b could have been taken; of course, the formula could also have been simply a part of the floating repertory of formulae.

---

a reinterpretation of the traditional concept *yoga*, which in the BhG takes an active sense, and in the compound *karmayoga* stands moreover for *ethics (of activity)* in the proper sense!

[88] An anticipative allusion to the identity of the teacher and God in the *triṣṭubh* text could, however, be the expression *kavim purāṇam anuśāsitāram.*

BhG 8.11 has *pāda*s c and d corresponding to KaU 2.15c and d. From the parallel passages in the Gītā it can be considered as relatively well fitted into the content and terminology of the hymn in *triṣṭubh*s.

The *communis opinio* is that the *triṣṭubh* parts of KaU 2 (15, 20) have lent some formulae to the BhG (8.11; 8.9). It is also not excluded that they belonged to the floating repertory of formulae, but their concentration in KaU 2 and the BhG hymn enhance the probability of influence. If Weller is right in considering KaU 2.15 and 2.20 (as well as 2.23) as considerably younger than KaU 2.1-6 and 7-8, 13 and 18 (the oldest and the second oldest group in his opinion), the former two stanzas (15, 20) could have been influenced by the BhG hymn.

However, KaU 2.20 (*aṇor aṇīyān*) seems to be a continuation of 2.8 (*aṇīyān ... aṇupramāṇāt*), and 2.23 (*nāyam ātmā pravacanena labhyaḥ ...*) to be a continuation of 2.7 (*śravaṇāyāpi* (?) *bahubhir yo na labhyaḥ ...*).[89] KaU 2.15 (*sarve vedā yat padam āmananti ... tat te padaṃ saṃgraheṇa bravīmi*) could be connected with 2.8 (*na nareṇāvareṇa prokta eṣa suvijñeyo ... ananyaprokte gatir atra nāsti ...*), possibly also with 2.9 (*... eṣā matir ... proktānyenaiva suvijñānāya ...*), and (paradoxically) with 2.23 (where the expression *tasyaiṣa ātmā vivṛnute tanūṃ svām* could be an allusion to the Vedic Vāc, cf. ṚS 10.71.4, and thus allude to *brahman* which is *padam* "the word that all the Vedas disclose..."). If this is true (if these are continuity repetitions, and not duplication repetitions), then all the *triṣṭubh*s in KaU 2 are older than the *śloka*s[90]. In that case their influence on the BhG hymn could be, in general, estimated to be more probable than the influence in the opposite direction.

[89] We can also ask: Do they reinterpret 2.7-8? In that case they would not be a continuation, but later additions. Weller's arguments would support such a doubt, but they are not formal, but rely solely on interpretation.

[90] If they therefore can be moved in Weller's table (1953: 109) to the left of all the groups of *śloka*s, that would considerably simplify his scheme.

The continuation in *śloka*s in both texts shows equally noticeable correspondences. The fact that the KaU *śloka*s do not show traces of *bhakti* and the chronological considerations are in favour of the assumption that KaU 2 was expanded by *śloka*s before the *bhakti* redaction of the BhG. In this case BhG 2.19 (part of the first Sāṃkhya layer) most probably influenced KaU 2.19, but BhG 8.13 (part of the Bhakti layer) is not likely to have influenced KaU 2.16-17.

The parallel between BhG 3 and KaU 3

BhG 3.42, as it was demonstrated, is not based on KaU 3.10-11, as was often assumed, because it has a superior reading which can help us to tentatively emend KaU 3.10; and KaU 3.11 is, as Weller argued, anyway a younger addition. If the above reconstructed reading, presupposed by KaU 3.10 and BhG 3.42, was in fact the original reading of KaU 3.10 itself, it is not excluded that the Gītā stanza could have been modelled upon that original reading. And if this is not the case, KaU 3.10 as it reads has a corrupted reading, and is most probably later than BhG 3.42, which belongs to the first Yoga layer of the BhG.

Parallels between BhG and ŚvU 3

The fact that the parallels are widely scattered in the BhG in chapters 5, 8, 13, and very concentrated in the ŚvU in chapter 3 seems to corroborate the assumption that ŚvU 3 is a collection of citations of older stanzas and formulae.

In ŚvU 3.18 we can notice a kind of combination of Vedic and BhG citations similar to the combination we have observed in the series of stanzas ŚvU 3.3, 14-17: the Vedic material and parallels with the BhG are combined in the stanzas of ŚvU 3. The case of variant stanzas KaU 2.20 and ŚvU 3.20 and the formulaic correspondence with BhG 8.9 has been amply discussed above.

The example of ŚvU 3.(15) 16-17 convincingly shows, not simply that the ŚvU is later than the BhG, but, much more precisely, that ŚvU 3 is later than BhG 13.[91] And BhG 13 is, generally speaking, younger than the core parts of BhG 1-6, and older than the core parts of BhG 14-18, while the *bhakti* redaction is the latest of all the layers. That chronological relationship between ŚvU 3 and BhG 13 could be corroborated by the fact that already the first two *adhyāya*s of the ŚvU presuppose the full-fledged Sāṃkhya and Yoga systems, while in the BhG nothing up to chapter 13 confirms the acquaintance with the more or less classical Sāṃkhya.

BhG 15.(1)2-5(6) and KaU 6.1

This is a peculiar case of correspondence, where only the BhG has a coherent passage on the cosmic tree – in *triṣṭubh*s, while KaU 6.1 has a troubled octosyllabic stanza of 6 *pāda*s combining some expressions parallel but not identical with the BhG passage in *pāda*s a-b with a formula in *pāda*s c-f, which is widely used to define the *aśvattha* here, the *puruṣa* in KaU 5.8 and the omnipresent God in KaU 4.2. The metaphor of the tree occurs in ŚvU 3.9, but without literal correspondences, and with a different meaning.

If BhG 15.2-5 possibly belonged to the didactic part of the *triṣṭubh* hymn, then it may have been placed in the hymn before the description of Arjuna's vision of God, which the *bhakti* redactor placed in what is now chapter 11, while he used the *aśvattha* passage in what is now chapter 15.

In that case, the BhG hymn almost certainly preceded KaU 6.1. It could have served as a model for KaU 6.1, and the juxtaposition of KaU 5.15 and 6.1 could have influenced BhG 15.1 and 6.

---

[91] At least ŚvU 3.16-17ab is later than BhG 13.13-14ab, but most probably it implies the general chronological relationship between the chapters, with possible further differentiation of chronology for some single stanzas or passages.

A TENTATIVE SCHEME OF THE PARALLEL GENESIS OF THE KaU, BhG AND ŚvU

Maybe the most far-reaching philological implication of the analyses in this paper is that we must learn to deal philologically not only with texts but also with text traditions. In the tradition of written texts, philology has mastered its task by developing the methodology of the elaboration of *stemmata codicum*. The elaboration of a methodology of dealing with oral or partly oral text traditions remains an important task and a challenge for philology. The first great difference is that the concept of a text as a unit with recognizable identity is in the oral tradition defined not by its surface structure, but by a kind of deep structure. And the second, that all texts in the oral tradition can be "contaminated"[92], and that their interdependence must be checked throughout the text in order to find the relationships of dependence or influence not between the whole texts, but between all sections of different texts (or text variants) which we can identify as their layers or strata.

We can now make a common survey of the observed parallels:

[92] The term *contaminated* is not used in its technical sense in philology: it does not refer to a manuscript containing scribal errors from different branches of the stemma, because it was copied from other (older) manuscripts that belong to different branches of the stemma, and because it has contaminated their readings,. The term is here used in a transposed meaning for texts that have included passages or formulas from other texts which have their different identity and tradition. It would be wrong to evaluate such cases of intertextuality as *contamination* in order to discredit the texts which betray it, because that kind of intertextual relationship or mutual influence is the very life of their living oral traditions.

Vedic texts	**KaU**	**BhG**	**ŚvU (IU, MU)**
	2.7 → ↓ 6.9 (?)←	2.29 → (?) (?)←	4.20
	2.18 →	2.20	
	2.*19* ←	2.*19*	
	2.15-*16* (*17*) →	8.11 (13)	
TĀ 3.12.16ab, 17cd; 3.13.2; VS 31.18	2.20 → →(?)	8.9 (→ ?) → (?)	3.8; 3.20-21 (3.20 = KaU 2.20)
	(5.13ab = ŚvU 6.13ab)	2.39 →	6.13c
	3.10 (-11) (?) ←	3.42(-43)	
	(5.*1*-2)	5.*13* → (?) (?) ←	3.*18* (?) ←
ṚS 10.81.*3*		13 *(12) 13-14* → 13.15	3.*(15) 16-17* (?) ← (IU 5)
	6.*1* (?) ← → (?) 5.15 →	15. 2-5 15.*1* 15.*6*	3.9 (6.6) (6.14 = KaU 5.15 = MU 2.2.2)

The cited parallels can be interpreted in terms of layers in the following way:

KaU: the story of Naciketas given to Death	BhG: the despondency of Arjuna on the battlefield – the Epic layer	
The oldest group of stanzas in KaU 2: 1-6 (Yama's answer to Naciketas: *preyas* and *śreyas*, *avidyā* and *vidyā*, the other world)	The oldest version of Kṛṣṇa's answer on the duties of a Kṣatriya in chapter 2 (in *śloka*s) – the Epic layer	
The second oldest group of stanzas in KaU 2: 7-8, 13, 18. (20) (the instruction on *ātman*)	The first Sāṃkhya-Upaniṣadic layer (the instruction on *dehin*): BhG 2.11-30	

KaU 2.20	The *triṣṭubh* hymn (2.5-8, 87*; 8.9-11; 11.15-50; 15.2-5 [?])	ŚvU 3.8, 20-21
KaU 3 (*indriyas*)	The first Yoga-Upaniṣadic layer: BhG 2.39 – 4.42 (*karmayoga*)	
KaU 5.*1*-2	BhG 5.13 (The second Yoga-Upaniṣadic layer)	ŚvU 3.18
	BhG 13 (The second Sāṃkhya-Upaniṣadic layer?)	ŚvU 3.(15) 16-17, IU
KaU 5.15 – 6.*1*	BhG 15.(*1*) 2-5(*6*) (15.2-5: The hymn? Or a subsequent Yoga-Upaniṣadic layer?)	ŚvU (3.9) 6.14, MU
	The Bhakti layer: BhG 7-12 and 22 *bhakti* interpolations in other chapters	

From the survey of layers it is apparent that:

- KaU 2 has parallels with the first Sāṃkhya layer of the BhG 2,
- KaU 2 has parallels with the *triṣṭubh* hymn in the BhG 2 and 8 (and probably the KaU 2 *triṣṭubh* parts precede the BhG hymn),
- KaU 3 has parallels with BhG 3-4 – the first Yoga layer (BhG 3.42 possibly precedes KaU 3.10, or the original reading of KaU 3.10 must be reconstructed by emendation),
- BhG 13 has parallels with ŚvU 3 (and seems to precede it); the IU shows a parallel passage to BhG 13.15,
- BhG 15.2-5 (possibly a hymn passage) is most probably more original than KaU 6.1 or ŚvU 3.9; the BhG 15.6 (the Bhakti layer) is younger than KaU 5.15 (= ŚvU 6.14); the MU 2.2.10 is parallel to KaU 5.15, ŚvU 6.14 and partly to BhG 15.6.

The results confirm that we are dealing here with interconnected text traditions. It must have an impact on our future understanding of the history of texts, especially of oral or partly oral texts, and on our understanding of the history of Old Indian literature (and literatures comparable to it in that respect).

This tentative reconstruction of the interrelated textual history of the *Bhagavadgītā*, the *Kaṭha-upaniṣad* and the *Śvetāśvatara-upaniṣad*, involving sometimes elements from other Upaniṣads, discloses some text-historical reasons why the BhG, although it is a part of the great epic, and therefore technically a *smṛti* text, was regarded as an authoritative text on an equal footing with the Upaniṣads, and as one of the *prasthāna*s of the Vedānta.

I hope that this is also a contribution to the old discussion about the role of the Kṣatriyas in the creation of the Upaniṣads and Upaniṣadic thought. They cannot be credited to have been more important thinkers in the Upaniṣadic texts than the Brahmans although they play no negligible role in them, and it seems that the Vedic texts record some kings-priests as *rājarṣi*s. However, if there is a clear example of a text of Upaniṣadic character, but belonging to the Kṣatriya tradition, to which epics basically belong, it is the BhG, i.e. its Upaniṣadic layers. It is no accident that these Upaniṣads which show most parallels with the BhG, moreover the only ones which show literal parallels with the Gītā, are the metrical Upaniṣads, the KaU and the ŚvU. They are composed in basically the same metres as the epics.

The intellectual meeting ground of the Brahmans and Kṣatriyas in ancient Indian society, in the times of the Brāhmaṇas and Upaniṣads, as already mentioned, were ritual and religious festivities, especially royal rites and long sacrificial rituals. The discussions held at such occasions are partially documented in the Brāhmaṇas and old Vedic Upaniṣads, like the *Śatapathabrāhmaṇa*, *Bṛhadāraṇyaka-upaniṣad*, *Chāndogya-upaniṣad*, *Kauṣītaki-upaniṣad*, etc., and represent the brahmanic records of those events. The recitations of epic texts, according to the Sanskrit epics themselves, took place at the same kind of long rituals. In later times occasions for the exchange of ideas and instruction must have been festivals at centres of pilgrimage, *tīrtha*s.

The Vedic Gāthā and Śloka literature inserted in those old brahmanical texts was, in the opinion of Paul Horsch, largely not the brahmanic but the *śramaṇa* lore. Horsch says:

> Exactly at that most important turning point of the Indian cultural history, when the oldest Upaniṣads and the heterodox religions of Buddhism, Jinism and the Śramaṇa sects took shape, in the solution of so far unelaborated questions – reincarnation, retribution of acts, essence of soul, pessimistic attitude towards the world, final liberation – the Kṣatriya caste clearly occupies the foreground (Horsch 1966: 2-3).

In that sense the metrical Upaniṣads are, at least in part, the most extensive specimens of that literature, which Horsch studied on smaller specimens of *gāthā*s and *śloka*s in earlier Vedic texts. Richard Salomon (1995) recognizes the characteristics of a Kṣatriya Sanskrit, as documented in the epics, in the middle Upaniṣads in verses, and in the younger ones in prose: to some extent in the *Śvetāśvatara-* and *Maitrī-upaniṣad*, and in a very pronounced manner in the *Muṇḍaka-* and *Praśna-upaniṣad.*

The correspondences between the KaU, the ŚvU and the BhG, especially its Upaniṣadic passages (preceding the *bhakti* redaction), bear clear witness to their interrelationship during their interconnected textual tradition. In that interrelationship the BhG was by no means only the receiving part. Its role (as well as that of other epic didactic passages to some degree) in the exchange of ideas and formulaic expressions with the metrical Upaniṣads and later texts reflects in part the role of the Kṣatriyas and their singers of epic poetry as authors and as recipients of ideas and cultural patterns in the intellectual life of ancient India during the tumultuous period of changes in the middle-Upaniṣadic and early post-Vedic period.

If people from various strata of society were permitted to listen to epic texts, the BhG could have influenced anybody, including the Brahmans. And if the Upaniṣadic teachings remained limited only to the restricted circles of the Brahmans and *brahmacārin*s even in the period of the KaU, or even that of the ŚvU[93], then the influence of the KaU on the BhG, just as that of the BhG on the Upaniṣadic texts, could have been effected only through brahmanic redactors, or at least such that have passed the brahmanic education. In any case, according to philological evidence, the transmission of these three texts was in some way, directly or indirectly, interconnected. That interconnected tradition shows that the BhG was already during its redaction treated partly as Upaniṣadic text.[94] This helps us to understand why, in the later period, the BhG was in a position to play the role of a *prasthāna* in the philosophy of Vedānta, or how it was possible that, being as sacred as the Vedic texts and as popular as epic poems, it had such a great impact on the later development of Hinduism.

ABBREVIATIONS

AiĀ = *Aitareya-āraṇyaka*
AS(Ś) = *Atharvasaṃhitā* (Śaunaka)
BĀU = *Bṛhadāraṇyaka-upaniṣad*
ChU = *Chāndogya-upaniṣad*
JB = *Jaiminīyabrāhmaṇa*

---

[93] Devasthali (1953: 141) stresses that BhG 18.67 states that its teaching "is not to be taught or imparted to one who is not leading a life of austerity, who is not a devotee, who is not eager to listen, or one who traduces the Lord". He compares it to the restrictions on the imparting of knowledge in ŚvU 6.22, MU 3.2.10, and ChU 3.11.5-6. However, the restrictions in the ChU are traditional: the knowledge can be imparted only to the eldest son or to a worthy pupil (a Brahman by birth, or a *brahmacārin*), and to no one else. In the ŚvU the secret knowledge similarly can be transmitted only to a son or a pupil, but, in the next and last stanza (6.23), devotion to God and to one's teacher are added as qualities of one to whom these things can be told. In the MU the knowledge of *brahman* can be given only to those who are versed in the Vedas, who perform rites, who are grounded in *brahman*, who offer for themselves – all the qualities pointing to Brahmans (or possibly *brahmacārins*). While in the BhG, on the other hand, the restrictions remind of those in the Vedic Upaniṣads, but refer only to the spiritual and religious qualities of the listener or pupil, and not to his origin or social rank. When extolling a devotee, the BhG, however, may imply the existence of a community of *bhaktas*.

[94] That was reflected in the colophons of the *adhyāyas* of the Gītā: *iti śrīmad-bhagavadgītāsu upaniṣatsu ... adhyāyaḥ*.

KaU = *Kaṭha-upaniṣad*
KS = *Kāṭhakasaṃhitā*
MNU = *Mahānārāyaṇa-upaniṣad*
MS = *Maitrāyaṇīsaṃhitā*
ṚS = *Ṛksaṃhitā*
SS = *Sāmasaṃhitā*
ŚB = *Śatapathabrāhmaṇa*
ŚvU = *Śvetāśvatara-upaniṣad*
TĀ = *Taittirīya-āraṇyaka*
TS = *Taittirīyasaṃhitā*
VS = *Vājasaneyisaṃhitā*
YS = *Yogasūtra*

REFERENCES

Editions and Translations

AUFRECHT, Theodor (ed.) 1955. *Die Hymnen des Ṛgveda*, I-II. 3rd edition. Wiesbaden: Otto Harrassowitz – Berlin: Akademie Verlag. (1st edition: Berlin: Ferd. Dümmler's Verlagsbuchhandlung, 1861-63.)

BELVALKAR, Shripad Krishna (ed.) 1947. *The Bhīṣmaparvan. Being the Sixth Book of the Mahābhārata the Great Epic of India.* (*Mahābhārata. Critical Edition*, 7.) Poona: BORI.

—— (ed.) 1968. *The Bhagavadgītā. Being a Reprint of Relevant Parts of Bhīṣmaparvan from B. O. R. Institute's Edition of the Mahābhārata.* Poona: BORI.

BUITENEN, J. A. B. van (ed. & trans.) 1981. *The Bhagavadgītā in the Mahābhārata. A Bilingual Edition.* Chicago: Chicago University Press.

EDGERTON, Franklin 1944. *The Bhagavad Gītā.* (Harvard Oriental Series, 38-39.) Cambridge, Mass: Harvard University Press.

HAUSCHILD, Richard 1927. *Die Śvetāśvatara-Upaniṣad. eine kritische Ausgabe mit einer Übersetzung und einer Übersicht über ihre Lehren*, (Abhandlungen für die Kunde des Morgenlandes 17.3.) Leipzig, Deutsche Morgenländische Gesellschaft.

HILL, W. Douglas P. 1928. *The Bhagavadgītā*. Oxford: OUP.

HILLEBRANDT, Alfred 1921. *Aus Brāhmaṇas und Upanishaden: Gedanken altindischer Philosophen.* Jena: Eugen Diederich.

HUME, Robert Ernest 1931. *The Principal Upanishads*. 2nd edition. London: OUP. (Reprint: Delhi: OUP, 1984; 1st edition 1877.)

LIMAYE, V. P. & R. D. VADEKAR (eds.) 1958. *Eighteen Principal Upaniṣads*, I. Poona: Vaidika Saṃśodhana Maṇḍala.

NOOTEN, Barend A. van & Gary B. HOLLAND (eds.) 1994. *Rig Veda. A Metrically Restored Text with an Introduction and Notes.* (Harvard Oriental Series, 50.) Cambridge, Mass: Harvard University Press.

OBERLIES, Thomas 1995. Die Śvetāśvatara-Upaniṣad: Einleitung, Edition und Übersetzung von Adhyāya I. *WZKSA* 39: 61-102.

—— 1996. Die Śvetāśvatara-Upaniṣad: Edition und Übersetzung von Adhyāya II-III. *WZKSA* 40: 123-160.

—— 1998. Die Śvetāśvatara-Upaniṣad: Edition und Übersetzung von Adhyāya IV-VI. *WZKSA* 42: 77-138.

OLIVELLE, Patrick 1998, *The Early Upaniṣads. Annotated Text and Translation.* New York: OUP.

RAU, Wilhelm 1964. Versuch einer deutschen Übersetzung der Śvetāśvatara-Upaniṣad. *AS/ÉA* 17: 25-46.

SASTRI, Mahadeva & K. RANGACARYA (eds.) 1900-02. *Taittirīya Āraṇyaka. With the Commentary of Bhaṭṭa Bhāskara Miśra*, I-III. (Bibliotheca Sanskrita, 26-28.) Mysore: Government Branch Press. (Reprint in one volume: Delhi: MLBD, 1985.)

SCHREINER, Peter 1991. *Bhagavad-Gita. Wege und Weisungen.* Zürich: Benziger.

VARENNE, Jean 1960. *La Mahānārāyaṇa Upaniṣad. Édition critique, avec une traduction française, une étude, des notes, et, en annexe, La Prāṇāgnihotra Upaniṣad*, I-II. Paris: Éditions de Boccard.

ZAEHNER, Robert C. 1966. *Hindu Scriptures.* London: J. M. Dent & Sons.

Secondary Literature

ALSDORF, Ludwig 1950. Contributions to the textual criticism of the Kaṭhopaniṣad. *ZDMG* 100 (Neue Folge Bd. 25): 621-637.

BASHAM, Arthur Llewellyn 1989. *The Origins and Development of Classical Hinduism.* Ed. by K. G. Zysk. New York: OUP.

BELVALKAR, Shripad Krishna & Ramchandra Dattatraya RANADE 1927. *History of Indian Philosophy.* Poona: Bilvakuñja Pub. House. (Reprint: New Delhi: Oriental Books Reprint Corporation, 1974.)

BOSCH, F. D. K. 1960. *The Golden Germ. An Introduction to Indian Symbolism.* 's-Gravenhage: Mouton & Co.

BROCKINGTON, John 1997. The Bhagavadgītā: text and context. In: Julius Lipner (ed.)., *The Fruits of Our Desiring*: 28-47. Calgary: Bayeux Arts, Inc.

—— 1998, *The Sanskrit Epics.* (Handbuch der Orientalistik, 2.12.) Leiden: E.J. Brill.

BÖHTLINGK, Otto von 1897. Kritische Beiträge. *Berichte über die Verhandlungen der Königlich-Sächsischen Gesellschaft der Wissenschaften, Philologisch-Historische Klasse* 4: 127-138.

CHARPENTIER, Jarl 1930. Some remarks on the Bhagavadgītā. *Indian Antiquary* 59: 46-50, 77-80, 101-105, 121-126.

DEUSSEN, Paul 1906. *The Philosophy of the Upaniṣads*. Engl. trans. by A. S. Geden. T. & T. Clark, 1906. (Reprint: New York: Dover Edition, 1966; First German edition: *Die Philosophie der Upanishads*. [Allgemeine Geschichte der Philosophie, 1.2.] Leipzig: Brockhaus, 1907.)

DEVASTHALI, G. V. 1953. Bhagavadgītā and Upaniṣads. In: J. N. Agrawal & B. D. Shastri (eds.), *Sārupa-Bhāratī or the Homage of Indology Being the L. Sarup Memorial Volume*: 132-142. Hoshiarpur: Vishveshvaranand Institute Publications.

FALK, Harry 1994. Die Kosmogonie von RV X 72. *WZKSA* 38: 3-22

GARBE, Richard 1921. *Die Bhagavadgītā*. 2nd rev. edition. Leipzig: H. Haessel. (Reprint: Darmstadt: Wissenschaftliche Buchgesellschaft, 1978.)

HAAS, George C. O. 1922. Recurrent and parallel passages in the principal Upanishads and the Bhagavadgītā with references to other Sanskrit texts. *JAQS* 42: 1-43.

HORSCH, Paul 1966. *Die vedische Gāthā und Śloka Literatur*. Bern: A. Francke Verlag.

HUMBOLDT, Wilhelm von 1826. *Über die unter dem Namen Bhagavadgītā bekannte Episode des Mahābhārata*. Berlin: Königliche Akademie der Wissenschaften.

JACOB, George A. 1891. *Upaniṣadvākyakośaḥ. A Concordance to the Principal Upanishads and Bhagavadgītā*. (Bombay Sanskrit Series, 39.) Bombay. (Reprint: Delhi, MLBD, 1963.)

JACOBI, Hermann 1918. Über die Einfügung der Bhagavadgītā im Mahābhārata. *ZDMG* 72: 323-327.

—— 1924. Über Viṣṇu – Nārāyaṇa – Vāsudeva. In: *Streitberg-Festgabe*: 159-168. Leipzig. (Reprint in: Bernhard Kölver (ed.), *Kleine Schriften*, II: 872-881. Wiesbaden: Franz Steiner, 1970.)

JEŽIĆ, Mislav 1979. The first Yoga layer in the Bhagavadgītā In: *Ludwik Sternbach Felicitation Volume*, I: 545-557. Lucknow: Akhila Bharatiya Sanskrit Parishad.

—— 1986. Textual layers of the Bhagavadgītā as traces of Indian cultural history. In: *Sanskrit and World Culture: Proceedings of the Fourth World Sanskrit Conference*: 628-638. Berlin: Akademie Verlag.

—— 1989. *Mișljenje i riječ o bitku u svijetu. Filozofsko-filoloșki ogledi.* (Biblioteka Filozofska istraživanja, 20.) Zagreb: Hrvatsko filozofsko druștvo.

JEŽIĆ, Mislav 2002. The Bāṣkalamantra-Upaniṣad and the Bhagavadgītā. In Mary Brockington (ed.), *Stages and Transitions: Temporal and Historical Frameworks in Epic and Purāṇic Literature. Proceedings of the Second DICSEP, August 1999*: 35-54. Zagreb: Croatian Academy of Sciences and Arts.

JOHNSTON, E. H. 1937. *Early Sāṃkhya*. London: The Royal Asiatic Society. (Reprint: Delhi: MLBD, 1974.)

KHAIR, Gajanan Shripat 1969. *Quest for the Original Gītā*. Bombay: Somaiya Publications.

KUIPER, F. B. J. 1983. *Ancient Indian Cosmogony*. Essays selected and introduced by John Irwin. New Delhi: Vikas Publishing Hiouse.

LAMOTTE, Etienne 1929. *Notes sur la Gītā*. Paris: Geuthner.

MALINAR, Angelika 1996. *Rājavidyā: das königliche Wissen um Herrschaft und Verzicht. Studien zur Bhagavadgītā*. (Purāṇa Research Publications, Tübingen, 5.) Wiesbaden, Otto Harrassowitz.

MINKOWSKI, Christopher Z. 1989. Janamejaya's sattra and ritual structure. *JAOS* 109.3: 401-420.

OBERLIES, Thomas 1988. Die Śvetāśvatara-Upaniṣad: Eine Studie ihrer Gotteslehre. *WZKSA* 32: 35-62.

—— 1995, 1996, 1998. See above Editions and Translations.

OLDENBERG, Hermann 1919. Bemerkungen zur Bhagavadgītā. *Nachrichten von der Königlichen Gesellschaft der Wissenschaften zu Göttingen, Philologisch-historische Klasse* 3: 321- 338. (Reprint in: K. L. Janert (ed.), *Kleine Schriften*, II: 1459-1476. Wiesbaden: Franz Steiner, 1967.)

OTTO, Rudolf 1934. *Die Urgestalt der Bhagavad-Gītā*. Thübingen: J. C. B. Mohr.

—— 1935, *Die Lehrtraktate der Bhagavad-Gītā*. Thübingen: J. C. B. Mohr.

PODZEIT, Utz 1994. Bemerkungen zum "Sinn" des Namens Vāsudeva. *WZKSA* 38 (Orbis Indicus, Festschrift G. Oberhammer): 191-200.

—— 1995. Devakī, die Mutter Kṛṣṇas. *WZKSA* 39: 25-43.

ROCHER, Ludo 1963. Bhagavadgītā 2.20 and Kaṭhopaniṣad 2.18: A new interpretation. *Adyar Library Bulletin* 27: 45-58.

SALOMON, Richard 1995, On Drawing Socio-linguistic Distinctions in Old Indo-Aryan: The question of Kṣatriya Sanskrit and related problems. In: Georg Erdosy (ed.), *The Indo-Aryans of Ancient South Asia. Language, Material Culture and Ethnicity*: 293-306. Berlin: Walter de Gruyter.

SCHRADER, Friedrich Otto 1910. Über Bhagavadgītā II 46. *ZDMG* 64: 336-340. (Reprint in: J. F. Sprockhoff (ed.), *Kleine Schriften*: 227-231. Wiesbaden: Franz Steiner, 1983.)

SIMSON, Georg von 1969. Die Einschaltung der Bhagavadgītā im Bhīṣmaparvan des Mahābhārata. *IIJ* 11.3: 159-174.

SZCZUREK, Przemysław 2002. Some remarks on the so-called Epic layer of the Bhagavadgītā. In: Mary Brockington (ed.), *Stages and Transitions: Temporal and Historical Frameworks in Epic and Purāṇic Literature. Proceedings of the Second DICSEP, August 1999*: 55-72. Zagreb: Croatian Academy of Sciences and Arts.

—— 2005. Bhakti interpolations and additions to the Bhagavadgītā. In: P. Koskikallio (ed.), *Epics, Khilas and Purāṇas: Continuities and Ruptures. Proceedings of the Third DICSEP, September 2002*: 183-220. Zagreb: Croatian Academy of Sciences and Arts.

THIEME, Paul 1985. Nennformen aus Anrede und Anruf im Sanskrit. *Münchener Studien zur Sprachwissenschaft* 44 (Festgabe für Karl Hoffmann, I): 239-258.

VASSILKOV, Yaroslav 2002. Indian practice of pilgrimage and the growth of the Mahābhārata. In: Mary Brockington (ed.), *Stages and Transitions: Temporal and Historical Frameworks in Epic and Purāṇic Literature. Proceedings of the Second DICSEP, August 1999*: 133-156. Zagreb: Croatian Academy of Sciences and Arts..

WELLER, Friedrich 1953. *Versuch einer Kritik der Kaṭhopaniṣad.* Veröffentlichungen des Instituts für Orientforschung der deutschen Akademie der Wissenschaften zu Berlin, 12.) Berlin: Akademie-Verlag.

WITZEL, Michael 1987. On the origin of the literary device of the "Frame Story" in Old Indian literature. In: Harry Falk (ed.), *Hinduismus und Buddhismus: Festschrift für Ulrich Schneider*: 380-414. Freiburg: Hedvig Falk.

Patterns of *tejas* (and *kṣamā*) in the Epics

PAOLO MAGNONE

INTRODUCTION

Among the manifold *Daseinsmächte*[1] or "substance-powers" which are rife in Indian thought from the Vedic times onwards, *tejas* can be singled out as the one which attained greatest prominence in the epics and Purāṇas, where, besides lying at the core of sundry narrative motives, it plays a central role in some of the most characteristic mythical themes of each of the great Hindu gods. In spite of its all-importance in the epico-puranic world view, after Vogel's seminal article back in 1930 *tejas* did not elicit consistent attention from scholars – with some notable exceptions,[2] including my own paper delivered at the 8th WSC, wherein I briefly sketched the development of the notion of *tejas* from the Vedic to the puranic literature – how the word, originally connected with the root √*tij* 'be sharp', hence meaning 'sharpness' in its pristine occurrences, through the metaphor of the 'sharpness' of the blade-like or horn-like flames of fire came to convey the notion of a

> peculiar kind of "substance" or "energy" with distinctive fiery connotations. manifest as "glow" on the physical and as "ardour" or "fierceness" on the psychical level (Magnone 1992: 137).

---

[1] As Glasenapp (1940: 281 ff) first called them.

[2] The two most useful studies dealing with *tejas*, albeit as a subordinate topic, being Gonda 1952 and 1957.

The present contribution is meant to resume that thread, which against my original intentions has been lying idle[3] for more than a decade now.[4] As an introduction, it may be worthwhile to briefly retrace the most important stages in the evolution of *tejas* as identified there.

Whereas the few occurrences of the word in the *Ṛgveda* are still closely associated with (metaphoric extensions of) the root meaning of 'sharpness', by the time of the *Atharvaveda* the picture has changed considerably. Now *tejas* is found in association with a host of other *Daseinsmächte* expressing notions of different kinds of "splendid" energies, and inaugurates its soon to become regular relationship with Viṣṇu. The Brāhmaṇa contribution consists in an attempt at systematizing the symbolic pertinences of the different energies by their regular association to different domains of a multi-layered cosmos. While cautioning against over-simplification of the highly structured brahmanical discourse, I believed that it is 'safe to assume the alliance (if not equivalence) of *brahman/tejas/brahmavarcasa* on the one hand versus *kṣatra/ojas/indriyavīrya* on the other hand" (Magnone 1992: 141). A definite step towards the future pre-eminence of *tejas* is taken in the Upaniṣads, where *tejas* severally appears, in a monistic context, as "the most intimate body of *ātman*", its "subtle centrifugal energy presiding over manifestation", or the "ever-changing energy which is passed on along the downward current of evolution and taken back in involution" (Magnone 1992: 142). On the other hand, in a theistic context, the *Atharvaveda* hint is furthered by the late *Maitrāyaṇi-upaniṣad*'s identification of the *puruṣa* Viṣṇu as the original source of *tejas*.

As a result of these developments, we are thus confronted with two potentially conflicting dimensions of *tejas*: a regional one,

[3] Except for a paper delivered at the 11th WSC exploring the relationship of *tejas* to *avatāra*-hood (see below footnote 5).

[4] Meanwhile, other scholars have contributed on single aspects of the polyvalent notion of *tejas*, such as Smith 1994 (on the *varṇa* affiliation of *tejas* and kindred power-substances in the Vedic world view) and most recentiy Whitaker 2000 and 2002 (on *tejas* of divine weapons).

deeply engrained in the socio-cosmic foundations of the *varṇa* system as enunciated in the Brāhmaṇas, on the one hand; and an all-embracing one, as the selfsame creating and sustaining power of the supreme Godhead permeating the universe, on the other.

We shall presently turn to the epics, to observe these conflicting ways at play in diverse strands of the prodigiously complex epic tapestry.[5]

THE MONADIC SCHEME OF *TEJAS* AS SUPREME ENERGY

The dimension of *tejas* as the Lord's supreme energy, which sets it apart as paramount among all other substance-energies, is proclaimed in the most unambiguous terms in the well known *Bhagavadgītā* strophe, where Kṛṣṇa concludes the enumeration of his *vibhūti*s or 'manifestations of excellence' by saying:

> know that whatever being is excellent, splendid or powerful is born from a particle of my *tejas*.[6]

Such a notion of *tejas* as the hallmark of excellence is so widespread in the epics that it is unnecessary to quote specific instances; time and again, the best of kings, sages, heroes, virtuous women etc. are routinely described as plentifully endowed with *tejas*. In this connection, the formulaic expression *amitatejas* 'possessing

---

[5] More semantic traits associated with the epico-puranic notion of *tejas* may be recalled here, even though they will be but cursorily touched upon in this paper, to wit: connotations of abruptness, keenness and excess; destructive associations and dangerous potential; congeniality to certain classes of beings; liability to transfer (perhaps the most typical feature; for a case study see Magnone 2002, analyzing an early puranic version of the Paraśurāma myth where *tejas* supplies an alternate way of structuring the exclusive *vaiṣṇava* theme of *avatāra*s)

[6] BhG 10.41:
yad yad vibhūtimat sattvaṃ śrīmad ūrjitam eva vā |
tat tad evāvagaccha tvaṃ mama tejo'ṃśasaṃbhavam || 41 ||

boundless *tejas*' is specially frequent, occurring about a hundred times in the *Mahābhārata*, regularly at the end of a verse.[7]

All these illustrious personages, according to the quoted BhG strophe, owe their outstanding rank to a lavish infusion of Viṣṇu's *tejas*. The Vaiṣṇava specificity of *tejas* is brought out by its co-occurrence in significant contexts with the appellative *vaiṣṇava* or *nārāyaṇa* or in compounds with Vaiṣṇava names, as contrasted with its virtual non co-occurrence in the corresponding Śaiva combinations.[8]

To mention but a couple of examples, in the *Nārāyaṇīyaparvan* all beings from Brahmā down to inanimate objects are said to merge into *nārāyaṇatejas* at the end of the *kalpa*.[9] In the *Anuśāsanaparvan* there is a marvellous story of a party of *ṛṣi*s who once visited Kṛṣṇa while he was engaged in the performance of a vow for obtaining a son. They were filled with wonder seeing *nārāyaṇatejas* issuing from the mouth of Kṛṣṇa in the form of fire and consuming the surrounding mountain forests,[10] which were later restored by his *saumya* look. The fire eventually returned to Viṣṇu-Kṛṣṇa, paying homage at his feet. Questioned by the *ṛṣi*s, the god explained that the uncanny apparition was nothing else than *vaiṣṇavatejas* sent by him as a messenger to the boon-giver Brahmā to plead for the boon of a son.[11]

---

[7] It may be worth noticing that, with respect to the epic characters, the expression occurs most of all in connection with Vyāsa (12 times), followed by Arjuna (11 times), Viṣṇu/Kṛṣṇa (7 times), Śiva/Rudra/Bhava/Hara/Śarva as well as Bhīṣma (6 times), Rāma and Droṇa (3 times).

[8] The scanty occurrences are either stereotyped expressions involving *amitatejas*, *tejasvin* etc., or they are in connection with Skanda's birth, in which context *tejas* means more specifically Śiva's "fiery seed".

[9] Mbh 12.331.5cd-6:
aho nārāyaṇaṃ tejo durdarśaṃ dvijasattama ‖ 5 ‖
yatrāviśanti kalpānte sarve brahmādayaḥ surāḥ |
ṛṣayaś ca sagandharvā yac ca kiṃ cic carācaram ‖ 6 ‖

[10] Mbh 13.126.16-17ab:
tato nārāyaṇaṃ tejo vratacaryendhanotthitam |
vaktrān niḥsṛtya kṛṣṇasya vahnir adbhutakarmaṇaḥ ‖ 16 ‖
so 'gnir dadāha taṃ śailaṃ sadrumaṃ salatākṣupam |

Even more significant is the episode of Arjuna's fight with Śiva disguised as a hunter, where the latter, after initially declaring Arjuna to be his equal in *vīrya* and *tejas*, subsequently qualifies the assertion by professing that Arjuna and Kṛṣṇa are in reality Nara and Nārāyaṇa; accordingly, supreme *tejas* belongs to Arjuna as well as to the *puruṣottama* Viṣṇu-Kṛṣṇa, both of them being the foremost *puruṣa*s who support the world by their *tejas.*[12]

But the most substantive instance is no doubt found in the final apotheosis of Rāma in the Rāmāyaṇa, when Brahmā's disembodied voice summons the hero to merge back into his own *vaiṣṇava* body of ethereal everlasting *tejas*, and to rejoin his own cherished form, the inconceivable great being which is imperishable, all-embracing great *tejas*. Responding to the Grandfather's call, Rāma together with his brothers bodily enters *vaiṣṇava tejas*, and the heavenly hosts welcome back the god who had merged again into Viṣṇu.[13]

In all these instances *tejas* appears unequivocally as the supreme energy which is distinctively Viṣṇu's own, insofar as Viṣṇu (-Nārāyaṇa-Vāsudeva-Kṛṣṇa) is the supreme Person. Besides, in conformity with the doctrine of the BhG passage mentioned before, such energy may secondarily reside in subordinate receptacles,

---

[11] Mbh 13.126.30 ff.:
etat tad vaiṣṇavaṃ tejo mama vaktrād viniḥsṛtam I
kṛṣṇavartmā yugāntābho yenāyaṃ mathito giriḥ II 30 II ...

[12] Mbh 3.41.1-2:
naras tvaṃ pūrvadehe vai nārāyaṇasahāyavān I
badaryāṃ taptavān ugraṃ tapo varṣāyutān bahūn II 1 II
tvayi vā paramaṃ tejo viṣṇau vā puruṣottame I
yuvābhyāṃ puruṣāgryābhyāṃ tejasā dhāryate jagat II 2 II

[13] Ram 7.100.6-7, 9-11ab:
tataḥ pitāmaho vāṇīm antarikṣād abhāṣata I
āgaccha viṣṇo bhadraṃ te diṣṭyā prāpto 'si rāghava II 6 II
bhrātṛbhiḥ saha devābhaiḥ praviśasva svakāṃ tanum I
vaiṣṇavīṃ tāṃ mahātejas tadākāśaṃ sanātanam II 7 II ... II
tvam acintyaṃ mahad bhūtam akṣayaṃ sarvasaṃgraham I
yām icchasi mahātejas tāṃ tanuṃ praviśa svayam II 9 II
pitāmahavacaḥ śrutvā viniścitya mahāmatiḥ I
viveśa vaiṣṇavaṃ tejaḥ saśarīraḥ sahānujaḥ II 10 II
tato viṣṇugataṃ devaṃ pūjayanti sma devatāḥ I

whence it can be withdrawn according to Viṣṇu's will. The most striking illustration can be found in the well known episode of the killing of Śiśupāla, where Bhīṣma, censuring the king of Cedi's inordinate railings against Kṛṣṇa, offers the following explanation: Kṛṣṇa desires to take back the portion of his own *tejas* which resides in Śiśupāla, and for this reason he has perverted his mind to drive him to ruin, as he is wont to do whenever he wants to take back his *tejas* from somebody.[14] When at last Śisupāla is beheaded by Kṛṣṇa's discus, the assembled kings can see a blaze issuing from the fallen body, making obeisance to the *puruṣottama* and finally merging into him.[15]

In this circumstance the withdrawal of *tejas* has the effect of terminating forthwith the subsistence of the receptacle, but this is not always the case. Often, *tejas* is infused *pro tempore* to boost the energy of the recipient so as to make him equal to some demanding task. For example, when Indra was to encounter Vṛtra, Viṣṇu increased his strength by his own *tejas*, and all the other gods followed suit.[16] Similarly, in the episode of the killing of demon Dhundhu, *ṛṣi* Uttaṅka enlists the help of king Bṛhadaśva promising to enhance his *tejas* by that of Viṣṇu, and announcing that Viṣṇu had vowed to imbue with *vaiṣṇavatejas* the king who would take it upon himself to kill the demon: for Dhundhu, being endowed with great *tejas*, could not be subdued by anyone possessing *tejas* in a scanty degree. Pledging his help, the king's son Kuvalāśva is per-

---

[14] Mbh 2.37.11-14, 2.41.3.

[15] Mbh 2.42.22-23:

tataś cedipater dehāt tejo 'gryaṃ dadṛśur nṛpāḥ ǀ
utpatantaṃ mahārāja gaganād iva bhāskaram ǁ 22 ǁ
tataḥ kamalapatrākṣaṃ kṛṣṇaṃ lokanamaskṛtam ǀ
vavande tat tadā tejo viveśa ca narādhipa ǁ 23 ǁ

[16] Mbh 3.99.9-10:

taṃ śakraṃ kaśmalāviṣṭaṃ dṛṣṭvā viṣṇuḥ sanātanaḥ ǀ
svatejo vyadadhāc chakre balam asya vivardhayan ǁ 9 ǁ
viṣṇunāpyāyitaṃ śakraṃ dṛṣṭvā devagaṇās tataḥ ǀ
svaṃ svaṃ tejaḥ samādadhyus tathā brahmarṣayo 'malāḥ ǁ 10 ǁ

meated by Viṣṇu's energy and thus filled up with *nārāyaṇatejas* goes forth to his task.[17]

In all the passages so far considered, the notion of *tejas* is cast in a monadic scheme which recognizes *tejas* as the universal underlying energy, and the common source of whatever truly is, hence making its presence more characteristically conspicuous in such beings as are eminent in their respective domains. In such capacity, *tejas* rules supreme and suffers no antagonist on its own plane. Besides this notion, however, we do come across – especially in the

---

[17] Mbh 3.193 ff. *passim*; e.g. 3.193.24-25, 195.12, 18, etc.:
tvaṃ hi tasya vināśāya paryāpta iti me matiḥ |
tejasā tava tejaś ca viṣṇur āpyāyayiṣyati || 24 ||
viṣṇunā ca varo datto mama pūrvaṃ tato vadhe |
yas taṃ mahāsuraṃ raudraṃ vadhiṣyati mahīpatiḥ |
tejas taṃ vaiṣṇavam iti pravekṣyati durāsadam || 25 ||
tam āviśat tato viṣṇur bhagavāṃs tejasā prabhuḥ |
uttaṅkasya niyogena lokānāṃ hitakāmyayā || 12 ||
nārāyaṇena kauravya tejasāpyāyitas tadā |
sa gato nṛpatiḥ kṣipraṃ putrais taiḥ sarvatodiśam || 18 ||

Although this is not the place for a thorough discussion, some brief remarks on the rather tricky finale of this story may be permitted. After Kuvalāśva's sons have been consumed by fire vomited forth from Dhundhu's mouth, the king himself approaches him for the final combat (Mbh 3.195.27):
tasya vāri mahārāja susrāva bahu dehataḥ |
tad āpīyata tat tejo rājā vārimayaṃ nṛpa |
yogī yogena vahniṃ ca śamayāmāsa vāriṇā || 27 ||

This passage is interpreted by Whitaker (2002: 410, n. 36) to the effect that the king quenches the monster's fire by copious sweat generated by *tapas*: "much water flowed from [Kuvalāśva's] body, O great king; thus that *tejas* [the fiery breath of Dhundhu] was absorbed by the king as watery [*tejas*], O king, and as a yogin does with his yoga, he [Kuvalāśva] neutralized the fire with water" (square brackets in the original). The Mbh passage is admittedly somewhat obscure (probably corrupt); however, the uncanny visions of *pañcāgnisādhana* and sauna can luckily be dispensed with, by taking advantage of parallel puranic passages making it clear that not the king, but Dhundhu (*tasya* refers to him) sends forth *both* fire *and* water (e.g. *Śivapurāṇa*, *Umāsaṃhitā* 37.32:
mukhajenāgninā krodhāl lokān saṃvartayann iva |
vāri susrāva vegena vidhoḥ kadhir ivodaye || 32 ||
cf. also *Vāyupurāṇa*, *Uttarārdha* 26.54cd-55)

– which is not surprising, for he behaves like a volcano of sorts – and Kuvalāśva has to cope with *both*: he drinks up the water (by a fiery arrow, according to ŚiP; or just by *yoga*, according to VāP) and drowns the fire in water.

Mbh – a different one, envisaging *tejas* as a more restricted kind of energy, defined by its polar relationship to a complementary energy in a dyadic scheme, with which *tejas* has now to come to terms on a footing of equality.

THE DYADIC SCHEME OF *TEJAS* - *KṢAMĀ*

A bare statement of this dyadic scheme in its simplest form is found in a Mbh passage styling the virtuous and deathless inhabitants of the fabulous Śakadvīpa as "endowed with both *tejas* and *kṣamā*" (Mbh 6.12.10). Whenever they are juxtaposed in a significant context like this, *tejas* and *kṣamā* mean something like the opposite attitudes for action and patience, dynamic conquering force and static sustaining power. But their joint occurrence in one and the same subject is exceptional, by the very reason of their opposition. Here, they are in fact jointly predicated of exceptional beings such as the inhabitants of Śakadvīpa, who in every respect appear to be immune from the common deficiencies of mankind.

The Ram attributes the unlikely combination to another truly wondrous creature, the golden antelope later to become responsible for Sītā's abduction, whose appearance first strikes the princess's mind as being beyond compare for *tejas* and *kṣamā*: and words like *adbhuta*, *āścarya* and *vismaya*, underscoring the wonderful nature of the apparition, will turn up more than once in the subsequent handful of verses.[18]

More importantly, an exceptional figure being sometimes credited with both energies at once is that of the (ideal) king: thus, for instance, while enumerating king Bṛhadratha's many virtues, he is said to resemble the sun in *tejas* and the earth in *kṣamā*. The twin

---

[18] Ram 3.41.12:
na cāsya sadṛśo rājan dṛṣṭapūrvo mṛgaḥ purā |
tejasā kṣamayā dīptyā yathāyaṃ mṛgasattamaḥ || 12 ||
And further on (Ram 3.41.14cd, 15cd):
mṛgo 'dbhuto vicitro 'sau hṛdayaṃ haratīva me || 14 || … |
āścaryabhūtaṃ bhavati vismayaṃ janayiṣyati || 15 || …

similes here occur juxtaposed in a single half *śloka*: *tejasā sūrya-sadṛśaḥ kṣamayā pṛthivīsamaḥ.*[19] We shall revert to the peculiar status of the king later with more examples. For the time being, we may retain the symbolic equation of *tejas* with the sun and *kṣamā* with the earth which is a recurrent one in the dyadic pattern under consideration.

Barring exceptions like the above, *tejas* and *kṣamā* are not normally inherent in one and the same subject, being quite literally "poles apart", as the distinctive energies pertaining to the opposite symbolic provinces of sun and earth, impulse and forbearance, impetus and inertia, or, we could even say, in the familiar terms of a pervasive structuring opposition, *pravṛtti* and *nivṛtti.* Such originally conflicting appurtenances of *tejas* and *kṣamā* are clearly at issue in the story of the infancy of Satyavant, who was brought up in a hermitage where his father chose to repair when his kingdom was usurped. Nārada's account of the prince's unbefitting childhood elicits the doubt whether he be endowed with *tejas* or discernment, whether with *kṣamā* or prowess: the idea of these couples of intendedly exclusive alternatives in chiasmatic arrangement being evidently that the prince might either derive *tejas* and prowess from his royal descent, or *kṣamā* and discernment from his ascetic way of life. Nārada's reply, much in the same vein as the passages mentioned before, purports that such is Satyavant's excellence that he unites the best of both worlds: he equals the sun in *tejas*, Bṛhaspati in discernment, Indra in prowess and the earth in *kṣamā.*[20]

[19] Mbh 2.16.14:
tejasā sūryasadṛśaḥ kṣamayā pṛthivīsamaḥ ǀ
yamāntakasamaḥ kope śriyā vaiśravaṇopamaḥ ǁ 14 ǁ

[20] Mbh 3.278.14-15:
[King:] *apīdānīṃ sa tejasvī buddhimān vā nṛpātmajaḥ* ǀ
kṣamāvān api vā śūraḥ satyavān pitṛnandanaḥ ǁ 14 ǁ
[Nārada:] *vivasvān iva tejasvī bṛhaspatisamo matau* ǀ
mahendra iva śūraś ca vasudheva kṣamānvitaḥ ǁ 15 ǁ

TEJAS/KṢAMĀ AND *VARṆA*

By this newly gained dimension of *pravṛtti* and *nivṛtti* integrating the symbolic nexus of *tejas* and the sun, respectively, *kṣamā* and the earth, we are introduced to the core aspect of the opposition between the two energies in the dyadic scheme: namely, their implication in the axiological dialectics of the two upper *varṇas*. *Tejas* and *kṣamā* are juxtaposed in an enumeration of divine (as opposed to asuric) virtues in the BhG (16.3); but, as specified further on, *tejas* (together with kindred virtues like prowess, firmness etc.) is the inborn apanage of *kṣatra*, whereas *kṣamā*, or more exactly *kṣānti* (with such attendant virtues as calmness, restraint etc.) is the apanage of *brahman*.[21]

Elsewhere, *dama* occurs as a substitute for *kṣamā* in the same capacity. Aśvatthāman declares that Dharma has ordained for each caste its own duty: *dama* is the appointed *karma* for Brāhmaṇas, as *tejas* is for Kṣatriyas: an impatient Brāhmaṇa is no good, and a languid warrior is the lowest of men.[22] The usage is not quite settled: whereas *dama* mostly seems interchangeable with *kṣamā*, which it reduplicates in some passages, in his speech on the duties of the castes Bhīṣma distinguishes between the two: *kṣamā* is reckoned as one of the nine virtues common to all castes, whereas *dama* is mentioned in the first place among the characteristically brahmanical virtues.[23] It is true, in any case, that either one or both

---

[21] BhG 18.42-43:
śamo damas tapaḥ śaucaṃ kṣāntir ārjavam eva ca |
jñānaṃ vijñānam āstikyaṃ brahmakarma svabhāvajam || 42 ||
śauryaṃ tejo dhṛtir dākṣyaṃ yuddhe cāpy apalāyanam |
dānam īśvarabhāvaś ca kṣātraṃ karma svabhāvajam || 43 ||

[22] Mbh 10.3.18-20:
prajāpatiḥ prajāḥ sṛṣṭvā karma tāsu vidhāya ca |
varṇe varṇe samādhatta ekaikaṃ guṇavattaram || 18 ||
brāhmaṇe damam avyagraṃ kṣatriye teja uttamam |
dākṣyaṃ vaiśye ca śūdre ca sarvavarṇānukūlatām || 19 ||
adānto brāhmaṇo 'sādhur nistejāḥ kṣatriyo 'dhamaḥ |
adakṣo nindyate vaiśyaḥ śūdraś ca pratikūlavān || 20 ||

[23] Mbh 12.60.7-9:

terms will hardly fail to turn up in contexts enumerating brahmanical virtues.[24]

Now, this dyadic model of *tejas* and *kṣamā* (or *dama*) as the respective ground virtues of Kṣatriyas and Brāhmaṇas is evidently at odds with the monadic model mentioned earlier of *tejas* as the supreme universal energy and the original source of each and every subordinate provincial energy in the different domains of cosmos and society. As has been shown, the roots of such monadic model of *tejas* can be traced back to the upaniṣadic monistic model of the metaphysic absolute *brahman*, as distinct from the dualistic sociological notion of *brahman/kṣatra*. But, in spite of belonging to a different plan, it is equally obvious that the notion of absolute *brahman* is more akin to the *varṇa* concept of *brahman* than to that of *kṣatra*: and hence it happens that, in another set of texts, *tejas*, in its capacity as the energetic counterpart of absolute *brahman*, comes to be conferred on *brāhmavarṇa* as its eminent property. Such texts even appear to be overall more frequent than texts connecting *tejas* with the Kṣatriya. Thus, e.g., in the course of a fervent panegyric of Brāhmaṇas which amounts to a proper love declaration, Bhīṣma compares the supreme *tejas* of the Brāhmaṇa in this world to that of the thousand-rayed sun upon the earth.[25] But a simple comparison is not enough; elsewhere, the sun —usually one

---

akrodhaḥ satyavacanaṃ saṃvibhāgaḥ kṣamā tathā I
prajanaḥ sveṣu dāreṣu śaucam adroha eva ca II 7 II
ārjavaṃ bhṛtyabharaṇaṃ navaite sārvavarṇikāḥ I
brāhmaṇasya tu yo dharmas taṃ te vakṣyāmi kevalam II 8 II
damam eva mahārāja dharmam āhuḥ purātanam I
svādhyāyo 'dhyāpanaṃ caiva tatra karma samāpyate II 9 II

[24] Mbh 1.11.14:
ahiṃsā satyavacanaṃ kṣamā ceti viniścitam I
brāhmaṇasya paro dharmo vedānāṃ dhāraṇād api II 14 II
Mbh 12.182.4:
satyaṃ dānaṃ damo 'droha ānṛśaṃsyaṃ kṣamā ghṛṇā I
tapaś ca dṛśyate yatra sa brāhmaṇa iti smṛtaḥ II 4 II

[25] Mbh 13.9.20:
etad dhi paramaṃ tejo brāhmaṇasyeha dṛśyate I
sahasrakiraṇasyeva savitur dharaṇītale II 20 II

of the foremost *tejas* bearers – is actually subordinated to Brāhmaṇas: such is their supreme *tejas* and *tapas*, that it is thanks to their good offices that the sun shines in the sky.[26] Outstanding Brāhmaṇas are typically described as ablaze with *tejas*: thus Kapila appears to the wretched sons of Sagara as a glowing mass (*tejorāśi*) and burns them up with a fiery glance;[27] after the massacre of the Bhārgavas, a woman escapes bearing in a thigh a flaming embryo, Aurva (later to become the "father" of the fiery submarine mare) who robs the sight of the murderous Kṣatriyas attracted by the glare.[28] Examples could be multiplied.

It must not be overlooked that this *brahmavarṇa* affiliation of *tejas* is by no means novel – nay, it revives the old Brāhmaṇa partition of substance-powers recalled earlier, assigning *tejas* to *brahman* and *ojas* to *kṣatra*, which I had tentatively advanced in my 1992 paper and which has been corroborated in the meantime by Smith's extensive study on Brāhmaṇa classifications.[29] Later on, after and as a consequence of the upaniṣadic rise of *tejas* to all-importance, *ojas* recedes somewhat into the background: *tejas* has now become the mark of pre-eminence that must crown the paramount powers that be.

---

[26] Mbh 3.287.16:
brāhmaṇā hi paraṃ tejo brāhmaṇā hi paraṃ tapaḥ |
brāhmaṇānāṃ namaskāraiḥ sūryo divi virājate || 16 ||

[27] Mbh 3.105.25, 106.3:
[*sagarātmajā apaśyanta*] *kapilaṃ ca mahātmānaṃ tejorāśim anuttamam* |
tapasā dīpyamānaṃ taṃ jvālābhir iva pāvakam || 25 || ...
sa cakṣur vivṛtaṃ kṛtvā tejas teṣu samutsṛjan |
dadāha sumahātejā mandabuddhīn sa sāgarān || 3 ||

[28] Mbh 1.169.20-21:
tāsām anyatamā garbhaṃ bhayād dadhāra taijasam |
ūruṇaikena vāmorūr bhartuḥ kulavivṛddhaye |
dadṛśur brāhmaṇīṃ tāṃ te dīpyamānāṃ svatejasā || 20 ||
atha garbhaḥ sa bhittvoruṃ brāhmaṇyā nirjagāma ha |
muṣṇan dṛṣṭīḥ kṣatriyāṇāṃ madhyāhna iva bhāskaraḥ || 21 ||

[29] Smith 1994: 30 and *passim*. The Mbh quotation (13.104.63) at p. 52, n. 14 and p. 282, n. 55 refers to the vulgate, although the critical edition is mentioned in the bibliography.

It appears, therefore, that in the Mbh we are confronted with basically two sets of texts (which may be multiplied by taking varying degrees of approximation into account). The one set, in a theologico-metaphysical frame of mind, claims supremacy for the Brāhmaṇas as the best mundane representatives and spokespersons of absolute *brahman*, and consequently recognizes them as the best wielders of *tejas* which is the supreme energy of *brahman*. The other set, in a socio-political frame of mind, strives at harmonizing the roles of the two upper castes by a kind of mutual subordination in different respects: to wit, *kṣatra* gets the upper hand, as the foundation of the royal authority – and accordingly takes over *tejas* as the insignia of supremacy from the hands of the Brāhmaṇa; while, on the other hand, the latter is credited with some sort of seniority, conveyed by his peculiar virtue of *kṣamā* now recognized as the source and final resting place of *tejas*.

A telling example of this double attitude concerning the status of the Brāhmaṇa vis-à-vis the Kṣatriya is offered by the different treatment of the well-known story of the archetypal struggle for pre-eminence between the Brāhmaṇa Vasiṣṭha and the Kṣatriya Viśvāmitra in the two epics. Let us take up the *Rāmāyaṇa* first.

The king on campaign with his troops chances upon the *ṛṣi*'s *āśrama*, where he is hospitably entertained with all his retinue thanks to the wondrous powers of the cow of plenty Śabalā. Viśvāmitra covets the cow and demands it from Vasiṣṭha, who refuses to oblige. When the king tries to seize her by force, the distressed Śabalā appeals to her master, who protests his inability to resist the king's might. But Śabalā herself lectures him on the actual power relations between the Brāhmaṇa and the Kṣatriya: there is no true force (*bala*) in Kṣatriyas – the divine force of *brahman* is stronger than *kṣatra*. Viśvāmitra may have great valour (*vīrya*), but Vasiṣṭha's *tejas* is unconquerable.[30] Then, at the *ṛṣi*'s behest, she

[30] Ram 1.53.14-15:

na balaṃ kṣatriyasyāhur brāhmaṇo balavattaraḥ ।
brahman brahmabalaṃ divyaṃ kṣatrāt tu balavattaram ॥ 14 ॥

sends forth hordes of barbarians who crush the king's troops and force him to retreat. A further attempt, after Viśvāmitra has obtained the knowledge of divine weapons from Śiva, is equally fruitless: all *divyāstra*s are baffled by Vasiṣṭha's upraised brahmanical staff (*brahmadaṇḍa*), and even the supreme *brahmāstra* is swallowed up by his *brahmatejas*, while hosts of sages praise his unfailing force and exhort him to restrain his *tejas* by his *tejas*. Finally, Viśvāmitra gives in, sadly confessing his inferiority: fie on *kṣatriyabala*, the *bala* of *brahmatejas* is true *bala*.[31]

In this passage *tejas* is attributed exclusively to *brahman* and its representative Vasiṣṭha; in this connection, it is noteworthy that the author even takes care to avoid the use of such a stereotyped and altogether common epithet as *mahātejas* with reference to Viśvāmitra within the context of the struggle. Instead, Viśvāmitra is said to possess *vīrya* or *bala*: the latter term is also employed of Vasiṣṭha, but in a peculiar way which only serves to underscore its Kṣatriya specificity: whereas at the outset the *ṛṣi* protests its helplessness to oppose *bala* which is the reserve of the warrior, he is reminded that Brāhmaṇas do possess another sort of "*bala*" – i.e., *brahmatejas* – which is indeed the true *bala*. Viśvāmitra says the same in his concluding remark. To sum up, it appears from this text that *tejas*, as the supreme power of *brahman*, is the reserve of the Brāhmaṇa, whereas the Kṣatriya must content himself with some lesser forms of energy such as *bala* and *vīrya*, which are not, however, true power in its fullest sense.

The Mbh version (1.165.2-144), in spite of being shorter, interestingly brings to bear the alternative model of *kṣamā* and

---

aprameyabalaṃ tubhyaṃ na tvayā balavattaraḥ |
viśvāmitro mahāvīryas tejas tava durāsadam || 15 ||

[31] Ram 1.55.16, 20, 23:
tad apy astraṃ mahāghoraṃ brāhmaṃ brāhmeṇa tejasā |
vasiṣṭho grasate sarvaṃ brahmadaṇḍena rāghava || 16 || ...
tato 'stuvan munigaṇā vasiṣṭhaṃ japatāṃ varam |
amoghaṃ te balaṃ brahmaṃs tejo dhāraya tejasā || 20 || ...
dhigbalaṃ kṣatriyabalaṃ brahmatejobalaṃ balam |
ekena brahmadaṇḍena sarvāstrāṇi hatāni me || 23 ||

Brāhmaṇa acquiescence on the notion of *brahmatejas* and Brāhmaṇa dominance which is at home in the Vasiṣṭha-Viśvāmitra legend. When the *ṛṣi* refuses to surrender the cow (here called Nandinī) Viśvāmitra introduces the theme, declaring that *vīrya* is the prerogative of Kṣatriyas as *śama* is of Brāhmaṇas: he will seize the cow by force (*bala*) according to *svadharma*. Vasiṣṭha acquiesces, reiterating the principle that *vīrya* and *bala* belong to the warrior. Moved by the piteous cries of the cow, he explains that he cannot help the forceful abduction, for he is a Brāhmaṇa abiding in *kṣamā*; and a few lines later he explicitly declares that *tejas* and *kṣamā* are the respective *bala*s of Kṣatriyas and Brāhmaṇas: patience being his own lot, the cow may go if she pleases.[32]

While at this point in the Ram version the cow had stirred the *ṛṣi* himself into action, proclaiming the superiority of *brahmatejas* over *kṣatriyabala*, the Mbh lets the *ṛṣi*'s *kṣamā* remain intact. The cow herself takes the initiative in emitting the hosts that will rout the king's army, although the author hastens to point out that no lives were taken, lest the *ṛṣi*'s exemplary forbearance should be in any way diminished by his indirect consent to a slaughter. At this point the story draws to an end without more ado. Witnessing the wondrous feats of *brahmatejas*, Viśvāmitra is disgusted with his *kṣatra* nature, and confesses in exactly the same words as the Ram: *dhig balaṃ kṣatriyabalaṃ brahmatejobalaṃ balam.*[33]

---

[32] Mbh 1.165.28:
kṣatriyāṇāṃ balaṃ tejo brāhmaṇānāṃ kṣamā balam |
kṣamā māṃ bhajate tasmād gamyatāṃ yadi rocate || 28 ||

[33] Mbh 1.165.41-42:
dṛṣṭvā tan mahad āścaryaṃ brahmatejobhavaṃ tadā |
viśvāmitraḥ kṣatrabhāvān nirviṇṇo vākyam abravīt || 41 ||
dhigbalaṃ kṣatriyabalaṃ brahmatejobalaṃ balam |
balābalaṃ viniścitya tapa eva paraṃ balam || 42 ||

A similar acknowledgement of the superiority of *brahmatejas* versus *kṣatriyabala* resonates a few chapters before (Mbh 1.155.27-28ab) in the words spoken by king Drupada to enlist Brāhmaṇa help against his Brāhmaṇa opponent Droṇa:
brāhmam uccārayaṃs tejo hutāhutir ivānalaḥ |
sametya sa [scil. Droṇa] *dahaty ājau kṣatraṃ brahmapuraḥsaraḥ* |

The ending of the story could not have been different without impinging on the rights of tradition; but the author of the Mbh version appears to have made a conscious effort to rework a well-known apologue of Brāhmaṇa supremacy so as to adapt it to a regime of diarchy, where the Kṣatriya, as the wielder of the actual political power, is ready to take over *tejas*, while the Brāhmaṇa retains a sort of honorary primacy as the repository of spiritual authority, expressed by his newly acquired virtue of *kṣamā*.[34]

This shift of prerogatives is most pregnantly illustrated by a peculiar formula that is reiterated identically no less than four times in the *Udyoga-* and *Śantiparvan*, according to which

> fire is born from the waters, *kṣatra* from *brahman* and metal from stone: the all-pervading *tejas* of the three (viz. fire, *kṣatra* and metal) becomes extinguished in their respective wombs.[35]

The formula first occurs in connection with the story of Nahuṣa, when Agni, invited to seek out Indra's hiding place, protests his inability to enter the waters, lest they should quench his *tejas*. Then it is taken up by Vidura in the course of his advice to Dhṛtarāṣṭra, and again by Bhīṣma in his instruction to Yudhiṣṭhira. This latter instance is the more relevant to our subject. To the question as to what should be done in case Kṣatriyas should misbehave towards Brāhmaṇas, Bhīṣma replies that they should be restrained by all means, because *kṣatra* originates in *brahman* – then, after citing our formula, he expands it by specifying that whenever an iron

---

brahmakṣatre ca vihite brahmatejo viśiṣyate ‖ 27 ‖
so 'haṃ kṣatrabalād dhīno brahmatejaḥ prapedivān |
Here too, as in the traditional Viśvāmitra-Vasiṣṭha contest, *tejas* is consistently attributed to *brahman* alone, in contradistinction to *bala* as the lesser power of *kṣatra*.

[34] In this connection, it may be interesting to remark that the proportion of co-occurrences of *kṣamā* and Brāhmaṇa in the Ram and Mbh is of zero to several.

[35] Mbh 5.15.32, 38.13; 12.56.24, 79.22:
adbhyo 'gnir brahmataḥ kṣatram aśmano loham utthitam |
teṣāṃ sarvatragaṃ tejaḥ svāsu yoniṣu śāmyati ‖
Cf. also Mbh 13.34.15, 58.24.

weapon hacks at a stone, fire enters water or a Kṣatriya displays hostility towards a Brāhmaṇa the three of them are subdued: thus it is that the aroused invincible energies and forces (*tejāṃsi ca balāni ca*) of the Kṣatriyas come to nought in *brahman.*[36]

Whereas in the Vasiṣṭha-Viśvāmitra story warrior *bala* was set up against brahmanical *tejas*, according to the present doctrine both *bala* and *tejas* are claimed by the warrior, while the once fiery Brāhmaṇa has become *saumya* to the Kṣatriya as water is to fire: another way of conveying the same sort of complementary opposition elsewhere expressed by the polar couple *tejas/kṣamā*.

TEJAS/KṢAMĀ AND THE KING

It is now time to turn to the previously hinted at anomaly of the king as subsuming and integrating this same polarity into his encompassing nature. I have already mentioned king Bṛhadratha's resembling the sun in *tejas* and the earth in *kṣamā*: the comparison is a stereotyped one. The twin similes here occur juxtaposed in a single half *śloka*: *tejasā sūryasadṛśaḥ kṣamayā pṛthivīsamaḥ*.[37] The half *śloka* recurs with a slight variant in connection with king Avi-

---

[36] Mbh 12.79.23-24:
yadā chinatty ayo 'śmānam agniś cāpo 'bhipadyate |
kṣatraṃ ca brāhmaṇaṃ dveṣti tadā śāmyanti te trayaḥ || 23 ||
tasmād brahmaṇi śāmyanti kṣatriyāṇāṃ yudhiṣṭhira |
samudīrṇāny ajeyāni tejāṃsi ca balāni ca || 24 ||

It is incorrect to summarize all these passages as saying that "the *tejas* of water is more powerful than the *tejas* of fire", as Whitaker (2002: 410) does to support his (mis)interpretation of the Dhundhu myth (see footnote 17) to the effect that Kuvalāśva subdues the *tejas* of Dhundhu's fire by the *tejas* of his own sweat. As I have shown, these passages belong in a dyadic scheme of complementary, hence mutually exclusive terms: in this scheme, *tejas* "becomes extinguished" (*śamyate*) in something else, which by definition is *other than tejas*. This is made quite explicit in the texts by the use of the "feminine" word 'womb' (*yoni*) as opposed to the unmistakably "masculine" overtones of *tejas* (also a word for 'sperm').

[37] Mbh 2.16.14:
tejasā sūryasadṛśaḥ kṣamayā pṛthivīsamaḥ |
yamāntakasamaḥ kope śriyā vaiśravaṇopamaḥ || 14 ||

kṣit.[38] An almost identical expression, yet split to make up the 1st and 4th *pada*[39] of a *śloka*, is employed in connection with Śantanu. Dying Bhīṣma is said to equal Brahmā in *kṣamā* and the sun in *tejas* in two similes occurring in the 2nd and 4th *pada*.[40] The more usual coupling of *kṣamā* with the earth also occurs elsewhere with reference to Bhīṣma, in a comparison spanning two *śloka*s.[41] Arjuna himself is credited with seer-like *dama*, in addition to sun-like *tejas* and earth-like *kṣamā*.[42] The latter couple is found once also in the Ram, with reference to Rāma.[43] The underlying structure in (nearly) all these examples is a fourfold comparison building up *pada*-wise the *śloka*: within this structure, the similes involving the couple *tejas/kṣamā* exhibit the utmost degree of stereotypy with respect to the other similes in the quoted instances.

The joint inherence of both energies in a single subject, which has already been recognized as exceptional, is here grounded in the peculiar status of the king in the epics as has been highlighted by

---

[38] Mbh 14.4.20:
tejasādityasadṛśaḥ kṣamayā pṛthivīsamaḥ |
bṛhaspatisamo buddhyā himavān iva susthiraḥ || 20 ||

[39] Mbh 1.94.12:
tejasā sūryasaṃkāśo vāyuvegasamo jave |
antakapratimaḥ kope kṣamayā pṛthivīsamaḥ || 12 ||

[40] Mbh 13.27.1:
bṛhaspatisamaṃ buddhyā kṣamayā brahmaṇaḥ samam |
parākrame śakrasamam ādityasamatejasam || 1 ||

[41] Mbh 5.154.2-3:
bṛhaspatisamaṃ buddhyā kṣamayā pṛthivīsamam |
samudram iva gāmbhīrye himavantam iva sthiram || 2 ||
prajāpatim ivaudārye tejasā bhāskaropamam |
mahendram iva śatrūṇāṃ dhvaṃsanaṃ śaravṛṣṭibhiḥ || 3 ||

[42] Mbh 5.88.30:
tejasādityasadṛśo maharṣipratimo dame |
kṣamayā pṛthivītulyo mahendrasamavikramaḥ || 30 ||

(Of course, in spite of not being formally a king, Arjuna is in fact the ideal king of the Mbh; cf. Biardeau 1994, part 4).

[43] Ram 5.33.9:
tejasādityasaṃkāśaḥ kṣamayā pṛthivīsamaḥ |
bṛhaspatisamo buddhyā yaśasā vāsavopamaḥ || 9 ||

several scholars. Pollock has laid stress on the "functional" divinity of the king which entailed "regard[ing him] as substantially identical to various divine powers" (Pollock 1984: 525). This multiplicity of divine powers incorporated by the king could be more accurately characterized as a virtual totality, exemplified among others by the self-contained model of the *lokapāla*s; according to a well-known passage of the *Mānavadharmaśāstra,* it is indeed from perennial particles of the *lokapāla*s that the omnipotent made up the king for the purpose of protecting the world from fear.[44] An echo of this is found in the Mbh in Vidura's farewell to Yudhiṣṭhira going into exile after the fatal game of dice: among other words of praise, Vidura urges the royal Pāṇḍava to fix his resolve on victory which is in the nature of Indra, on suppression of wrath which is the appurtenance of Yama, on liberality as befits Kubera and on self-restraint belonging to Varuṇa. In addition to the virtues of the regents of the main quarters, Yudhiṣṭhira is directed to learn further virtues from cosmic entities, among which once again *kṣamā* from the earth and *tejas* from the solar orb.[45]

---

[44] Manu 7.3-5:

arājake hi loke 'smin sarvato vidrute bhayāt |
rakṣārtham asya sarvasya rājānam asṛjat prabhuḥ || 3 ||
indrānilayamārkāṇām agneś ca varuṇasya ca |
candravitteśayoś caiva mātrā nirhṛtya śāśvatīḥ || 4 ||
yasmād eṣāṃ surendrāṇāṃ mātrābhyo nirmito nṛpaḥ |
tasmād abhibhavaty eṣa sarvabhūtāni tejasā || 5 ||

Calling attention to this passage at the very outset of his article, Vogel expressed his wonder at its neglect by so many authors dealing with Indian kingship, remarking that "[i]mmers hier vindt men de eigenlijke kern der Indische opvattingen omtrent den koning. Hij is meer dan een heerscher bij de gratie Gods; hij is samengesteld uit de essentie der goden en is dus zelf een godheid" (Vogel 1930: 84). A quarter of a century later, Gonda (1959: 172) based his account of the "*deva*-ship of the ruler" on this same *locus.*

[45] Mbh 2.69.16-18ab:

aindre jaye dhṛtamanā yāmye kopavidhāraṇe |
visarge caiva kaubere vāruṇe caiva saṃyame || 16 ||
ātmapradānaṃ saumyatvam adbhyaś caivopajīvanam |
bhūmeḥ kṣamā ca tejaś ca samagraṃ sūryamaṇḍalāt || 17 ||
vāyor balaṃ viddhi sa tvaṃ bhūtebhyaś cātmasaṃbhavam |

For his part, Hiltebeitel understands the peculiar status of the king not so much in terms of encompassing divinity as in terms of "wholeness, soundness or perfection" both physical and moral, i.e. as being *sarvaguṇasaṃpanna* or 'endowed with all the virtues' (Hiltebeitel 1990: 198-199). Amidst the vast array of virtues that he draws from supporting texts he however fails to recognize a distinct specificity of the couple of *tejas* and *kṣamā*.[46]

On the other hand, while disclosing "la silhouette du roi" at the very heart of the Mbh,[47] Biardeau has shown how his all-embracing nature as the earthly vicar of the great *bhakti* god must of necessity entail a *coincidentia oppositorum* under the guise of *brahman* and *kṣatra*, *vaiṣṇava* and *raudra* components (Biardeau 1994: 171) – or, we may now add, *kṣamā* and *tejas*.

---

[46] I am less than convinced by Hiltebeitel's attempt to discern a trifunctional patterning of "all the virtues" of the king, in the wake of Dumézil. While avowing that the texts "will not allow one to insist that any single set of individual virtues forms the original 'endowment'", he believes that "if one assumes a basic structure rather than an original combination" one can adduce several passages which "demonstrate a predilection for trifunctional groupings of royal virtues, whether these be in triads, tetrads or pentads" (Hiltebeitel 1990: 202, 215). In fact, the trifunctional table he ends up with requires a fair amount of manoeuvering to constrain what looks like a disparate assemblage into the procrustean scheme. Even Dubuisson (1978: 25), while bent on much the same attempt, warns that "on constate que, dès la période épique, ce lien génétique, nourri de spéculations socio-fonctionnels, s'est transformé, cédant la place à d'autres représentations"; although he still believes, like Hiltebeitel, in the persistence of the "thème du roi 'complet' qui doit sa réputation à la possession d'un éventail de qualités réparties sur les trois niveaux", he quotes Dumézil's own significant opinion that by the epic times the theme of trifunctional completeness has become virtually undistinguishable from the "thème plus général, simplement cumulatif, souvent moral, de l'homme complet". Then, as the French would say, we ought not to be "plus réalistes que le roi"! In the context of the present paper, I must particularly question the 3rd function value of *kṣamā*, which has rather been shown to be a specifically brahmanical prerogative; and even for *tejas*, a first function virtue according to Hiltebeitel, things are not quite so simple, as it is the purpose of the present paper to show.

[47] "L'épopée n'est pas un récit gratuit [...] Elle met en scène de bons et de mauvais rois [...] Il s'agit donc d'un enseignement dispensé aux rois, o – le bon souverain apparait comme indissociable de l'*avatāra* auquel il se substitue [...] les devoirs du roi sont la préoccupation centrale des auteurs, et l'*avatāra* est la forme du divin qui peut en donner la justification ultime" (Biardeau 1994: 61 f.).

The most meaningful illustration of the need for the joint inherence of the complementary energies of *tejas* and *kṣamā* in the ideal king is no doubt to be found in the conversation between Draupadī and Yudhiṣṭhira soon after the Pāṇḍava's withdrawal into exile. Grieving over the hardships they have to endure in the forest, Draupadī blames Yudhiṣṭhira for his submissiveness in terms stressing the need for wrath (*manyu*), equated with *tejas* as the Kṣatriya's own nature:

> There is no such thing as a mild warrior, according to the pronouncement of the world: but today I see in you, a warrior, quite the reverse. A Kṣatriya who does not display *tejas* at the proper time is despicable to all creatures; therefore, you should not indulge *kṣamā* against enemies under any circumstances.[48]

She goes on to relate a conversation between Bali and Prahlāda on the occasions respectively fit for *tejas* and *kṣamā*, showing that even according to her there is no question of absolutely denying *kṣamā* for the king, but only of appropriately timing the exercise of both *tejas* and *kṣamā*: as she conclusively says, "he who knows the right time for each of them is indeed a king".[49] For his part, Yudhiṣṭhira replies distinguishing between wrath (*krodha*) and *tejas*: only the ignorant mistake the former for the latter, while truly warrior-like virtues such as prowess (*śaurya*) and righteous indignation (*amarṣa*), which are varieties of *tejas* (*tejaso guṇāḥ*), cannot be attained by him who is overpowered by wrath.[50] He winds up by

---

[48] Mbh 3.28.34-36:
na nirmanyuḥ kṣatriyo 'sti loke nirvacanaṃ smṛtam ।
tad adya tvayi paśyāmi kṣatriye viparītavat ॥ 34 ॥
yo na darśayate tejaḥ kṣatriyaḥ kāla āgate ।
sarvabhūtāni taṃ pārtha sadā paribhavanty uta ॥ 35 ॥
tat tvayā na kṣamā kāryā śatrūn prati kathaṃ cana ।
tejasaiva hi te śakyā nihantuṃ nātra saṃśayaḥ ॥ 36 ॥

[49] Mbh 3.29.35cd:
kāle prāpte dvayaṃ hy etad yo veda sa mahīpatiḥ ॥ 35 ॥

[50] Mbh 3.30.20:
dākṣyaṃ hy amarṣaḥ śauryaṃ ca śīghratvam iti tejasaḥ ।
guṇāḥ krodhābhibhūtena na śakyāḥ prāptum añjasā ॥ 20 ॥

quoting some "stanzas about the forbearing" (*gāthāḥ kṣamāvatām*) once sung by a great-souled and forbearing descendant of Kaśyapa, in which *kṣamā* is successively equated to notions typically belonging in a brahmanical sphere, like *brahman*, *satya*, *tapas*, *śauca*, etc.[51] Thus even here the respective pertinence of *tejas* to *kṣatra* and *kṣamā* to *brahman* is not denied, but subsumed within the encompassing horizon of the king.

This passage has an interesting parallel in the dialogue of the Brāhmaṇa ascetic Kauśika with a *pativratā*,[52] featuring once again characters of either sex discussing the respective merits of *tejas* and *kṣamā*: this time the male character is a Brāhmaṇa, though, and he will be subjected to the humiliation of being lectured by a woman on *dharma*. After a foreboding incident (in a fit of temper he kills with an angry glance a crane guilty of inadvertently defiling him) Kauśika calls at a house to beg for food but is kept waiting by the mistress, who attends her husband first. When Kauśika, inflamed with wrathful *tejas*, remonstrates boasting his brahmanical might,[53] the devoted wife retorts in appeasing, yet reproachful words: the feats of the *tejas* of brahmans are all too well-known; but however great their wrath, their grace is (read: ought to be) just as great[54] –

---

[51] Mbh 3.30.35-37:
atrāpy udāharantīmā gāthā nityaṃ kṣamāvatām |
gītāḥ kṣamāvatā kṛṣṇe kāśyapena mahātmanā || 35 ||
kṣamā dharmaḥ kṣamā yajñaḥ kṣamā vedāḥ kṣamā śrutam |
yas tām evaṃ vijānāti sa sarvaṃ kṣantum arhati || 36 ||
kṣamā brahma kṣamā satyaṃ kṣamā bhūtaṃ ca bhāvi ca |
kṣamā tapaḥ kṣamā śaucaṃ kṣamayā coddhṛtaṃ jagat || 37 ||

[52] For an interpretation according to a different perspective see Brinkhaus 1994: 275 ff.

[53] Mbh 3.197.19ab:
brāhmaṇaṃ krodhasaṃtaptaṃ jvalantam iva tejasā |
and later on (22ef):
brāhmaṇā hy agnisadṛśā daheyuḥ pṛthivīm api |

[54] Mbh 3.197.24ab, 27cd-28ab:
jānāmi tejo viprāṇāṃ mahābhāgyaṃ ca dhīmatām | ... | ...
krodhaḥ suvipulo brahman prasādaś ca mahātmanām || 27 ||
asmiṃs tv atikrame brahman kṣantum arhasi me 'nagha |

or does he want to burn her up just as he did to the bird? Then she directs him to a virtuous fowler to set right his shaky notions of morals; the choice of the fowler is obviously meaningful: the fowler blamelessly kills birds in accordance with *svadharma* (and so does the king indulge violence when required), whereas the Brāhmaṇa killed the unhappy *balāka* out of mere unbrahmanlike impatience.

So the joint lesson of both episodes is that, whereas *tejas* has now become the property of the Kṣatriya, the king shall do well to exercise both *tejas* and *kṣamā* as the situation requires, and to shun mere rashness (i.e. *tejas* = *krodha*) while displaying rightful energy in wielding the *daṇḍa* at appropriate times; whereas for the Brāhmaṇa no such distinction seems to apply: he is taught to renounce all display of *tejas*, which in his case is squarely equated with unlawful *krodha*, because

> the gods regard him as a true Brāhmaṇa who gives up anger and delusion [...] and although harmed does not harm anybody.[55]

In conclusion, the dialectics of *tejas* and *kṣamā* may be viewed as yet another attempt towards a solution to the thorny problem of the mutual relationship between the two highest powers, both claiming divine status: the king as a 'human god' (*naradeva*) and the Brāhmaṇa as a 'god on earth' (*bhūmideva*)[56], in whose harmonious cooperation and synergy, the epic authors do not tire of repeating, is rooted the welfare of the terrestrial world.

Of course, with these scanty remarks we have but grazed the surface of a question that would require much further *vicāraṇa* to

---

[55] Mbh 3.197.31cd, 32cd:
yaḥ krodhamohau tyajati taṃ devā brāhmaṇaṃ viduḥ || 31 || ...
hiṃsitaś ca na hiṃseta taṃ devā brāhmaṇaṃ viduḥ || 32 ||

[56] See Gonda 1969: 62 ff. and Hopkins 1915: 64. It must be noted that whereas in the Mbh the appellation *naradeva* for the king is extremely common, nay stereotyped, the corresponding Brāhmaṇa appellation is only attested (to my knowledge) by solitary and variable instances – they are styled, e.g., *bhūmidevā-* in Mbh 13.128.30 and *martyeṣu kṣitidevatā-* in Mbh 13.129.2.

be adequately investigated. Our present aim, however, has been merely to shed light on some facets of a notion – that of *tejas* – that proves to be connected in multifarious ways to central nodes of the epic (and puranic) ideology.

REFERENCES

BIARDEAU, Madeleine 1994. *Etudes de mythologie hindoue II. Bhakti et avatāra.* Pondichery: EFEO.

BRINKHAUS, Horst 1994. Weltflüchtige und innerweltliche Askese im Mahābhārata. *ZDGM* Supplementband 10: 273-281.

DUBUISSON, Daniel 1978. Le roi indo-européen et la synthèse des trois fonctions. *Annales. Economies, Civilisations, Sociétés* 33.1: 21-34.

GLASENAPP, H. von 1940. *Entwicklungsstufen des indischen Denkens. Untersuchung über die Philosophie der Brahmanen und Buddhisten.* (Schriften der Königsberger Gelehrten Gesellschaft. Geisteswissenschaftliche Klasse, 15/16 Jahr, Heft 5.) Halle: Max Niemeyer Verlag.

GONDA, Jan 1952. *Ancient-Indian* ojas, *Latin* *augos *and the Indo-European Nouns in* -es/-os. Utrecht: A. Oosthoek's Uitgevers Mij.

—— 1957. *Some Observations on the Relations between 'Gods' and 'Powers' in the Veda apropos of the Phrase* sūnuḥ sahasaḥ. `s-Gravenhage: Mouton & Co.

—— 1959. The sacred character of ancient Indian kingship. In: *La Regalità Sacra. Contributi al tema dell'VIII Congresso Internazionale di Storia delle Religioni* (Roma, Aprile 1955): 172-180. Leiden: E. J. Brill.

—— 1969. *Ancient Indian Kingship from the Religious Point of View.* Leiden: E. J. Brill.

HILTEBEITEL, Alf 1990. *The Ritual of Battle. Krishna in the Mahābhārata.* New York: SUNY.

HOPKINS, E. Washburn 1915. *Epic Mythology.* (Grundriss der Indo-arischen Philologie und Altertumskunde, 3.1.B.) Strassburg: Karl J. Trübner Verlag.

MAGNONE, Paolo 1992. The development of tejas from the Vedas to the Purāṇas. *WZKSA* 36, Supplementband: 137-147.

—— 2002. Paraśurāma's rise to avatāra-hood: A glimpse of early avatāra-theology. *Rendiconti dell'Istituto Lombardo Y Accademia di Scienze e Lettere (Cl. di Lett. Y Sc. Mor. e St.)* 136.2: 195-210.

POLLOCK, Sheldon 1984. The divine king in the Indian epic. *JAOS* 104.3: 505-528.

SMITH, Brian K. 1994. *Classifying the Universe. The Ancient India Varṇa System and the Origins of Caste*. New York: OUP.

VOGEL, J. Ph. 1930. *Het sanskrit woord tejas (= gloed, vuur) in de beteekenis van magische kracht*. Amsterdam.

WHITAKER, Jarrod L. 2000. Divine weapons and tejas in the two Indian epics. *IIJ* 43.2: 87-113.

—— 2002. How the gods kill: the nārāyaṇa astra episode, the death of Rāma and the principle of tejas in the Indian epics. *JIPh* 30: 403-430.

Some Aspects of the Character of Bhīṣma in the *Mahābhārata*

RAM KARAN SHARMA

In his Introduction to *Anuśāsanaparvan* of the Mbh, Dandekar has brought to light some burning problems relating to some aspects of the character of Bhīṣma. One such problem relates to Bhīṣma's celibacy. Was Bhīṣma a celibate from birth? Or was he married before Śantanu's marriage with Satyavatī, and was it only to facilitate his father's marriage that he took the terrific vow of lifelong celibacy?

Let us first understand the problem, as raised by Dandekar, in his own words:

> In 153.11d, it is said that, when Yudhiṣṭhira set out for Kurukṣetra to be present at Bhīṣma's *niryāṇa*, he took with him Bhīṣma's sacred fires ... – in other words, that Bhīṣma was married. The question whether Bhīṣma was married or not has been much debated. Those who believe that Bhīṣma was a *naiṣṭhika* brahmacārin, that he had not married at all, point out that there is no clear mention anywhere in the epic, of Bhīṣma's marriage. On the other hand, Bhīṣma's vow of *brahmacarya* is referred to very prominently (1.94.86-88; 6.15.12, 115.1). But what did this *brahmacarya* actually imply? When Satyavatī's father hesitated to marry his daughter to Śantanu for fear that, since Bhīṣma had already been anointed *yuvarāja*, the son born to Satyavatī would have no chance to succeed to Śantanu's throne, Bhīṣma nobly vowed that he would not only renounce his right to Śantanu's throne but that, in order that there should be no trouble of any kind between his progeny and Satyavatī's progeny, he would also observe complete *brahmacarya*. His exact words are:

adya prabhṛti me dāśa brahmacaryaṃ bhaviṣyati |
aputrasyā 'pi me lokā bhaviṣyanty akṣayā divi || (1.94.88)

The crucial words here are *adya prabhṛti.* Those words would suggest that Bhīṣma was already married but that he vowed to observe *brahmacarya* – that is to say, he vowed not to have sexual relations with his wife – *from that day onwards.* In the *Bhīṣmaparvan,* Bhīṣma is said to have performed thirty Aśvamedhas (6.22.15). And only a married person is entitled to the performance of a Vedic sacrifice. ... It would thus appear that Bhīṣma was duly married, that he had set up the sacred fires for the purpose of Vedic rites, but that he later took the vow of strict sexual abstinence with a view toward facilitating his father's marriage with Satyavatī. The *bhīṣmatva* of Bhīṣma's vow would perhaps be better appreciated if it were remembered that continence in the married state implied greater austerity than not marrying at all. (*Anuśāsanaparvan,* pp lxxviii-lxxx.)

Dandekar also quotes from the *Pāṇḍavacaritra* the following in support of Bhīṣma being a *gṛhamedhin,* i.e. a *gṛhastha* leading a married life (Mbh 1.217):

The gods said:
sarve 'pi jñānino brūta pṛcchāmaḥ khecarā vayam |
yady etad vratam ārabdhaṃ kenā 'pi gṛhamedhinā || 217 ||

Indian tradition in general believes in Bhīṣma as a model of *ūrdhvaretas* – a *naiṣṭhika brahmacārin.* Let us have a look at the traditional point of view on this problem in the words of the eminent traditional commentator on Vācaspatimiśra's *Sāṃkhyatattvakaumudī* on *Sāṃkhyakārikā* – Bālarāmodāsīna:

na ca bhīṣmasyorddhvaretastvoktir yuktā, yato mahābhārate "mahatā rājayogena parivāreṇa saṃvṛtaḥ stūyamāno mahārāja bhīṣmasyāgnīn anuvrajan prāpto 'smi samaye rājann agnīn ādāya te vibho" iti vākye tasmin agnihotṛtvasūcakadakṣiṇāgnigārhapatyāhavaniyākhyāgnitraya – saṁbandhasyā 'gnīn iti bahuvacanena pratītiḥ teṣāṃ cā 'patnīkena sambandhāsambhavāc ca patnyāś ca vivāhasaṃskāreṇa sampadyamānatā sa ca samskaraḥ ... ūrdhvaretastvaviruddha iti vācyam | *vaiyāghrapādyagotrāya sāṃkṛtyapravarāya ca gaṅgāputrāya bhīṣmāya ājanmabrahmacāriṇe aputrāya dadāmy etad udakaṃ bhīṣmavarmaṇe vasūnam avatārāya śāntanor ātmajāya ca arghyaṃ dadāmi bhīṣmāya ābālyabrahmacāriṇe iti pādme tarpaṇārghyadānamantrābhyām "ayam pitaram ājñāya kāmārtaṃ śantanuṃ purā ūrdhvaretasam ātmānam cakāra" iti mahābhāratīyavacanena cāsya naiṣṭhika-*

> *brahmacāritvasya kaṇṭhata evodghuṣyamāṇatvāt* I *na ca "tvām hi rājye sthitam sphīte samagrāṅgam arogiṇaṃ strīsahasraiḥ parivṛtam" iti mahābhārate tasya sapatnīkatvam ucyata iti parasparaviruddhā evaitā yuktaya iti vācyam* I *patnībhinnastrīsambandhoktyā virodhānavatārāt* I *ata eva tasyaiva caturthacaraṇaṃ "paśyāmyaho ūrdhvaretasam" iti paṭhyata iti dik* I (*Sāṃkhyakārikā* 50)

The learned commentator has said all that can be said for and against Bhīṣma being a *naiṣṭhika brahmacārin* from the traditional angle and has concluded in favour of Bhīṣma's *ūrdhvaretastva*, i.e., absolute celibacy from birth, and has also referred to the traditional *tarpaṇa mantra*s and special *arghya* for Bhīṣma during the *pitṛpakṣa.*

Those who do not agree with the traditional point of view on the subject raise the following points to show that Bhīṣma was already married before his father's remarriage with Satyavatī:

1. Bhīṣma's fires – all the three fires – brought by Yudhiṣṭhira at the time of Bhīṣma's *niryāṇa*;
2. Bhīṣma has already been declared a *yuvarāja*;
3. the use of the term *adya prabhṛti* in the relevant passage representing Bhīṣma's terrific vow (1.94.88).
4. Nīlakaṇṭha's interpretation of Satyavatī's advice to Bhīṣma, "*dārāṃśca kuru dharmeṇa*" as "*brahmacaryasaṃkalpāt prabhṛti tyaktān santatyartham aṅgīkuru*" (1.97.11).
5. Bhīṣma's performance of thirty (or three hundred) *aśvamedha* sacrifices.
6. Mbh passages like "*strīsahasraiḥ parivṛtam*".
7. *Pāṇḍavacaritra* passage "*kenā 'pi gṛhamedhinā*".

It is not proposed to pass any decisive judgment over the two conflicting views as stated above. An attempt is made just to give the relevant background material as given in the text depicting Bhīṣma's character in general and his *naiṣṭhika brahmacarya* or otherwise in particular.

The starting point of Bhīṣma's story is his unqualified love for his beloved while he was one of the eight Vasus (Dyaus by name). His beloved is enamoured of Vasiṣṭha's cow Nandinī. She persuades him to bring that cow so that her earthly friend Jitavatī – King Uśīnara's daughter – is rejuvenated and immortalized by drinking Nandinī's milk. Dyaus, along with his seven brothers, unhesitatingly commits the crime of stealing the cow. Vasiṣṭha curses all the eight Vasus to be born on the earth. The curse is later amended and the seven Vasus are destined just to be born on the earth and return to their heavenly abode soon thereafter. But Dyaus has to live long on the earth on account of his direct initiative in the crime. He will be endowed with all the aspects of magnanimity and will observe absolute continence, as per Vasiṣṭha's amended curse, as follows (1.93.37, 39):

ayaṃ tu yatkṛte yūyaṃ mayā śaptāḥ sa vatsyati ।
dyaus tadā mānuṣe loke dīrghakālaṃ svakarmaṇā ॥ 37 ॥

bhaviṣyati ca dharmātmā sarvaśāstraviśāradaḥ ।
pituḥ priyahite yuktaḥ strībhogān varjayiṣyati ॥ 39 ॥

Thus abstinence from sexual enjoyment forms the very origin of Bhīṣma's incarnation on the earth.

Bhīṣma's story brings in another curse from Brahmā for the divine figures of Mahābhiṣa and Gaṅgā. Mahābhiṣa is incarnated as Śantanu – son of Pratīpa. The Vasus do not want to have an earthly mother. So they meet Gaṅgā and request her to be their mother on the earth and throw away the seven of them immediately after their birth. But as stated above, Dyaus was destined to live long. The Vasus' address to Gaṅgā about Dyaus is quite relevant to the problem (1.91.20-21):

turīyārdhaṃ pradāsyāmo vīryasyaikaikaśo vayam ।
tena vīryeṇa putras te bhavitā tasya cepsitaḥ ॥ 20 ॥
na saṃpatsyati martyeṣu punastasya tu saṃtatiḥ ।
tasmād aputraḥ putras te bhaviṣyati sa vīryavān ॥ 21 ॥

So issuelessness (*aputratā*) forms the very basis of Bhīṣma's mundane character.

Any aspect of Bhīṣma's *brahmacarya* or otherwise has to be considered with the two passages "*strībhogān varjayiṣyati*" and "*tasmād aputraḥ putras te bhaviṣyati na saṃśayaḥ*" in the background. As per divine design, Gaṅgā incarnates on earth. She first wants to marry King Pratīpa. But as per divine design, she sits on his right thigh, which is traditionally reserved for the sons, daughters or daughters-in-law. Accordingly, Gaṅgā is married to his son Śantanu (the cursed Mahābhiṣa born on the earth). The condition of the marriage mutually agreed to is that Śantanu would never question any act of omission or commission of the Gaṅgā. So all their seven sons (as already designed) are thrown away by Gaṅgā in her stream without any interference from her husband. But when the eighth son is born and Gaṅgā is about to throw him as well in her stream, the King questions the propriety of this action. As designed earlier, Gaṅgā takes this opportunity to desert the King, saying (1.92.54-55):

> *tat te* [the seven Vasus] *śāpād vinirmuktā āpavasya mahātmanaḥ* ।
> *svasti te 'stu gamiṣyāmi putram pāhi mahāvratam* ॥ 54 ॥
> *eṣa paryāyavāso me vasūnāṃ saṃnidhau kṛtaḥ* ।
> *matprasūtaṃ vijānīhi gaṅgādattam imaṃ sutam* ॥ 55 ॥

Saying so Gaṅgā leaves the palace and departs along with her son (1.93.43-44):

> *etad ākhyāya sā devī tatraivāntaradhīyata* ।
> *ādāya ca kumāraṃ taṃ jagāmātha yathepsitam* ॥ 43॥
> *sa tu devavrato nāma gāṅgeya iti cābhavat* ।
> *dvināmā śaṃtanoḥ putraḥ śantanor adhiko guṇaiḥ* ॥ 44 ॥

Being deserted by Gaṅgā (and also separated from Devavrata/ Gāṅgeya), Śāntanu leads a life of complete abstinence for thirty-six years and Devavrata likewise resembles his father in regimen, character, and conduct (even though living separately) (1.94.18-19):

sa samāḥ ṣodaśāṣṭau ca catasro 'ṣṭau tathāparāḥ |
ratim aprāpnuvan strīṣu babhūva vanagocaraḥ || 18 ||
tathārūpas tathācāras tathāvṛttas tathāśrutaḥ |
gāṅgeyas tasya putro 'bhūn nāmnā devavrato vasuḥ || 19 ||

But the father and the son meet accidentally. Śantanu is surprised to see the river Gaṅgā covered with arrows. He is surprised to see this "transhuman" (*atimānuṣa*) action of someone (unknown to him). The Gaṅgā introduces Devavrata, his eighth son, to him and allows him to take this great archer, conversant with the essence of polity (*rājadharma*) home (1.94.25, 31, 36):

tāṃ śarair āvṛtāṃ dṛṣṭvā nadīṃ gaṅgāṃ tadantike |
abhavad vismito rājā karma dṛṣṭvātimānuṣam || 25 ||

yaṃ putram aṣṭamaṃ rājaṃs tvaṃ purā mayy ajāyithāḥ |
sa te 'yam puruṣavyāghra nayasvainaṃ gṛhāntikam || 31 ||

maheṣvāsam imaṃ rājan rājadharmārthakovidam |
mayā dattaṃ nijaṃ putraṃ vīraṃ vīra gṛhān naya || 36 ||

Śantanu takes Devavrata home and (as he happens to be the only surviving successor) he is coronated as a *yuvarāja* (1.94.38cd):

pauraveṣu tataḥ putraṃ yauvarājye 'bhyaṣecayat || 38 ||

There is no mention whatsoever about Devavrata's marriage either in Gaṅgā's or Śantanu's home. Could Devavrata of "transhuman action" be declared as *yuvarāja* without marriage?

For most of his career as the seniormost living successor of his family, he not only plays a unique role of *bhīṣmatva* as matchmaker for his younger brother Vicitravīrya by forcibly bringing the three princesses of Kāśirāja, one of whom (Ambā) eventually becomes the source of his *niryāṇa*. He also arranges the marriages of Gāndhārī with Dhṛtarāṣṭra, Mādrī (and Kuntī) with Pāṇḍu, as well as Devaka's daughter with Vidura. A matchmaker-in-chief without himself being married! That is Bhīṣma's character.

Had he been married, Paraśurāma would not have persuaded him to marry Ambā and there would have been no need to invoke *svapanāstra* from his Vasu-brothers in order to defeat his Guru. Had he been married, Satyavatī would not have advised him to marry according to *dharma*: "*dārāṃś ca kuru dharmeṇa*" (1.97.11). It may be noted in this connection that Nīlakaṇṭha interprets this clause as "*brahmacaryasaṃkalpāt prabhṛti tyaktān santatyartham aṅgīkuru*". So Nīlakaṇṭha as well is of the view that Bhīṣma was earlier married. But is there any textual support for this supposition? Mirashi (1959) is very much opposed to this viewpoint, including that of Nīlakaṇṭha. He says that if the Mbh text supported the prior marriage of Bhīṣma, then the text would read as follows:

dārāṃś caivābhigaccha tvaṃ mā nimajjīḥ pitāmahān.

Had Bhīṣma been married, his deserted wives must have found a place in the comprehensive list of persons accompanying Yudhiṣṭhira to Kurukṣetra on the eve of Bhīṣma's *niryāṇa* (13.153.9-11):

dhṛtarāṣṭraṃ puraskṛtya gāndhārīṃ ca yaśasvinīm |
mātaram ca pṛthāṃ dhīmān bhratṝṃś ca puruṣarṣbhaḥ || 9 ||
janārdanenānugato vidureṇa ca dhīmatā |
yuyutsunā ca kauravyo yuyudhānena cābhibho || 10 ||
mahatā rājabhogyena paribarheṇa samvṛtaḥ |
stūyamāno mahārāja bhīṣmasyāgnīn anuvrajan || 11 ||

Besides, Bhīṣma's wives do not appear even during the performance of Bhīṣma's last rites (13.154.16cd-17ab):

kṛṣṇena ca bharatastrībhir ye ca paurāḥ samāgatāḥ || 16 ||
udakaṃ cakrire caiva gāṅgeyasya mahātmanaḥ |

In the absence of the depiction of the death of Bhīṣma's wife or wives anywhere in the text, they should have found a prominent place in the list of the party visiting Bhīṣma on the eve of his *niryāṇa* – as they would have been the most senior members of his royal palace!

Thus if we take an overall view of the textual references to Bhīṣma's character, we do not perhaps find any support for Bhīṣma's marriage anywhere.

As regards the use of the clause *adya prabhṛti* in the words of Bhīṣma's terrific vow, the term does not necessarily convey the sense of his non-celibate character prior to the vow. In view of what has been stated above, the clause conveys the sense that such a vow was not taken earlier; the vow would be effective from that very time and date and not from any later date. It may also be noted that even the Nīlakaṇṭha edition of the text uses this poetic formula *adya prabhṛti* in the beginning of the verse twelve times!

As to the performance of thirty or three hundred *aśvamedha* sacrifices by Bhīṣma, this is perhaps a problem of textual criticism. The relevant text must be further examined. Our critical edition reads "*yenāhṛtās triṃśato vājimedhāḥ*" (6.22.15) with a wavy line under *triṃśato*. The Nīlakaṇṭha version reads "*yenāhṛtās triśataṃ vājimedhāḥ*" (Nīlakaṇṭha maintains a dignified silence here). D₁ (the Adyar ms reads "*yenārditās traiśatāḥ śaurisaṅghāḥ*". Unless all the available variants are duly reexamined, it is not possible to arrive at any definite conclusion.

Mirashi, agreeing with the learned editor Belvalkar, rightly points out that Sītārāmaśāstri's view of Bhīṣma being married on the basis of the statement (in the text) of Bhīṣma's performance of 300 or 30 *aśvamedha* sacrifices is not tenable at all. He further says that Bhīṣma perhaps passed away at the age of 186. How was it possible for him to perform 300 or even 30 *aśvamedhas*? Yudhiṣṭhira performed one after the Mahābhārata war. Even historically speaking, Samudragupta performed just one *aśvamedha*, Puṣyamitra two, and Pravarasena four.

As regards Bhīṣma's three fires and such descriptions of Bhīṣma as "*strīsahasraiḥ parivṛtam*", both the points have been well-reconciled by Bālarāmodāsīna as quoted above. Pāṇḍavacaritra's version (*kenā 'pi grahamedhinā*) may also be reconciled on similar lines.

We must not forget the fact that the text does not describe Bhīṣma as a recluse. Bhīṣma is rather depicted as a model of the *Gītā*'s ideal (BhG 6.1):

anāśritaḥ karmaphalaṃ kāryaṃ karma karoti yaḥ I
sa saṃnyāsī ca yogī ca na niragnir na cākriyaḥ II 1 II

Thus Bhīṣma of the Mbh is a model of the *Gītā*'s *karmayoga*. He is not a recluse but he lives mostly as a recluse, even while enjoying the life of a palace. Sometimes, he overacts, as in the context of the elopement of Kāśirāja's three daughters or his encounter with his Guru – Paraśurāma. Sometimes he maintains his position as an impartial observer, as in the case of Draupadī's open insult during *dyūtakrīḍā*. Against his wishes, he fights on behalf of Duryodhana for ten days during the eighteen days of the Mahābhārata war. As the first commander-in-chief of the Kaurava army, he persuades the desperate army to fight by presenting the code of conduct of Kṣatriyas (6.17.11):

adharmaḥ kṣatriyasyaiṣa yad vyādhimaraṇaṃ gṛhe I
yad ājau nidhanaṃ yāti so 'sya dharmaḥ sanātanaḥ II 11 II

There is perhaps nothing in heaven nor on earth that he does not describe to Yudhiṣṭhira in the *Śānti* and *Anuśāsana Parvans*. So "*strībhogān varjayiṣyati*" and "*tasmād aputraḥ putras te bhaviṣyati na vīryavān*" – as corroborated by numerous statements in the text – go to show the transhuman (*atimānuṣa*) nature of Bhīṣma's character and conduct.

Thus as far as I can see, the text does not appear to favour the concept of Bhīṣma's marriage at any stage.

REFERENCES

Anuśāsanaparvan (1966). Ed. by Ramachandra Narayana Dandekar. (The Mahābhārata ... critically edited, 17.1-2.) Poona: BORI.

MIRASHI, V. V. 1959. Bhīṣma Vivāhit hote kay. In: *Yugvāṇī* Dec. 1959.

Sānkhyakārikā (1991-92). By the Great Sage Ishwarakrishna with a commentary called Sankhya – Tattvakaumudi by Shri Vachaspati Mishra and another commentary called Vidvattoshinī by Shri Balaram Udāseen. Varanasi: Bharatiya Vidya Sansthan.

The *Mahābhārata* as a Source of Inspiration for Viśākhadatta's Drama *Mudrārākṣasa*: A Case Study of Intertextuality

GEORG VON SIMSON

1. INTRODUCTORY REMARKS

a. The Mbh as a source of inspiration for other literary works

It is well-known that the *Mahābhārata* has been the source of inspiration for an abundance of literary works in Sanskrit, e.g. for six of the plays attributed to Bhāsa (especially the *Dūtavākyam*, about Kṛṣṇa's vain mission to Hastināpura); Kālidāsa's *Śakuntalā*, Bhāravi's *Kirātārjunīya*, Māgha's *Śiśupālavadha*, Bhaṭṭa Nārāyaṇa's *Veṇīsaṃhāra*, and Śrīharṣa's *Naiṣadhacarita*.[1]

What these works have in common is that they do not borrow the whole plot of Mbh, but take either selected episodes of the main story or independent stories (like the *Nalopākhyāna*) to elaborate on them and make them the main plot of their own work. The borrowing is not hidden, but visible on the surface of the new works as these keep the names of characters (like Arjuna, Śakuntalā, Nala) so that in a way they are the same persons as in the epic.

As I am going to show, the relation between Mbh and the *Mudrārākṣasa* (MR) is of a different nature: Viśākhadatta, the

[1] Brockington 1998: 484-491; van Nooten 1971: 81-92.

author of the play,[2] is apparently inspired by the basic structure of the epic, though he bases his plot on a traditional non-epic story.

b. Sources of *Mudrārākṣasa*

Walter Ruben, the author of the most thorough analysis of MR (Ruben 1956), in his chapter on the sources of the play does not mention the Great Epic at all. Apart from the *Kauṭalīya Arthaśāstra*, whose influence makes MR a political play with exceptional features – exceptional for example insofar as women do not play any major part and any erotic atmosphere is completely absent from it – the obvious sources of MR, extensively discussed by Ruben (1956: 153-171), are the legends about the fall of the Nanda dynasty, which are preserved in the *Bṛhatkathā* tradition.[3]

In addition to these main sources which concern the historical background of the play – that is to say, the fall of the Nanda dynasty and the coming into power of the Maurya dynasty with Candragupta Maurya as one of the main characters and his minister Cāṇakya (who is seen as identical with the political author Kauṭilya) as the main agent – Ruben discusses as possible sources of inspiration Śūdraka's play *Mṛcchakaṭika* and Bhāsa's play *Pratijñāyaugandharāyaṇa* (Ruben 1956: 177-185).

The consequence of Ruben's overlooking the Mbh is that he has to consider the other central character of the play, Rākṣasa, as Viśākhadatta's invention. According to him, the author also invented the aim of the play's plot, the winning over of Rākṣasa, who finally is forced to accept the position as Candragupta's minister (Ruben 1956: 175).

---

[2] On the author and his date see Warder 1977: 257 f.

[3] See also Raghavan 1948: 64-67.

2. *MUDRĀRĀKṢASA* AND *MAHĀBHĀRATA*

a. The verse MR 2.16

In the following I am going to show that neither this motif nor Rākṣasa himself were quite original inventions of the play's author, but that Viśākhadatta was inspired by Mbh. The influence of the Great Epic on our play might not seem obvious to begin with. The identity of the main characters in MR in relation to historical persons on the one hand and the *Bṛhatkathā* tradition with its well-known legendary stories about these characters on the other, may have prevented scholars from considering the Mbh as a possible source. But there is at least one verse where indeed explicit reference is made to the epic; it is verse 16 of the second act (Hillebrandt's edition):

> *karṇeneva viṣāṅganaikapuruṣavyāpādinī rakṣitā*
> *hantuṃ śaktir ivārjunaṃ balavatī yā candraguptaṃ mayā* ।
> *sā viṣṇor iva viṣṇuguptahatakasyātyantikaśreyase*
> *haiḍimbeyam ivaitya parvatanṛpaṃ tadvadhyam evāvadhīt* ॥

In Kale's literal translation:

> The potent poison-maid, destined to kill one man, whom I had reserved for the destruction of Candragupta, came in contact with king Parvataka, and to the great good luck of Viṣṇugupta, killed him whose very death was sought by him (i.e. Viṣṇugupta), just as the powerful missile, the oneman-slayer, which was kept in reserve by Karṇa in order to kill Arjuna, smote, to the great interest of Viṣṇu (Kṛṣṇa), the son of Hiḍimbā, whom he (Kṛṣṇa) wished to make its victim.[4]

This verse refers to an important episode of the main plot of Mbh[5]: Karṇa had received an infallible spear (*śakti*, a word that at the same time means 'power') from Indra in exchange for his golden armour. Since that weapon could be used no more than once, Karṇa intended to use it against Arjuna, the only enemy that was equal

---

[4] Kale 1965: 107 (2.15).

[5] About the probable year-myth background of this story see von Simson 1994: 234 ff.

to him in strength. In order to foil this plan, Kṛṣṇa arranges that Karṇa is forced to apply the lethal weapon against Bhīma's son Ghaṭotkaca, a *rākṣasa* from his mother's side.

Our verse contains a multiple comparison: Rākṣasa compares himself with Karṇa, Cāṇakya with Kṛṣṇa, the Maurya king Candragupta with Arjuna, and Parvataka, king of the barbarians, with Ghaṭotkaca, the son of the *rākṣasī* Hiḍimbā. The action lying at the basis of the comparison is the redirection of a lethal weapon. In the case of Mbh it is Karṇa's *śakti* which kills Ghaṭotkaca instead of Arjuna, and in the case of MR it is the poisonous girl. According to Rākṣasa's plan, she should kill Candragupta, but Cāṇakya uses her instead to kill the barbarian king Parvataka.

The peculiar correlation between these two episodes consists not only in the motif of the redirection of a lethal weapon that could be used against one man only, but also in the rather strange fact that the weapon is used against an ally of one's own party: Bhīma's son Ghaṭotkaca is fighting on the side of the Pāṇḍavas, and Parvataka is Candragupta's ally against the Nandas. The reasons for killing one's own ally are in both cases similar, but not identical: Kṛṣṇa wants Ghaṭotkaca dead because he is a *rākṣasa*, and that means one who hates brahmins and sacrifices.[6] Parvataka, too, stands as a barbarian outside the brahminical order of society, but in his case there is a solid political motive that makes Cāṇakya want to have him removed. The price Candragupta had to pay for his alliance with Parvataka was that he had to let him have half the empire, and this was of course unacceptable for a politician whose king according to *Arthaśāstra* concepts should not share power with anybody.

There is nothing to support the assumption that this Parvataka was a historical king.[7] I would rather agree with Ruben who sug-

---

[6] Mbh 7.156.26 *eṣa hi brāhmaṇadveṣī yajñadveṣī ca rākṣasaḥ*. (All quotations refer to the Critical Edition by V. S. Sukthankar et al., Poona: BORI, 1933-66.)

[7] About the hypothesis of some historians that he might be identical with king Porus of Greek sources see Ruben 1956: 176 with fn. 1.

gests that Viśākhadatta here follows the *Kauṭalīya Arthaśāstra*[8] (7.14.27), which recommends that a weak king "should secure the services ... of heroic men from bands, robber-bands, foresters and *Mleccha* tribes" (*śreṇīpravīrapuruṣāṇāṃ coragaṇāṭavikamleccha-jātīnām*, Kangle's translation). Parvataka means 'Little Mountain' and also his son's name Malayaketu, 'Banner of the Malaya', may be associated with a mountain. This may have been inspired by popular ideas about *rākṣasa*s, which we encounter in Mbh where Ghaṭotkaca when threatened by Karṇa's *śakti* makes himself as huge as the foot of the Vindhya mountain (7.154.55 *kṛtvātmānaṃ vindhyapādapramāṇam*) (or as the Vindhya mountain itself: v.l. *vindhyaśailapramāṇam*) or where he some verses later looks like a cloud-mountain (7.154.59 *babhau ... meghaśailaprakāśaḥ*) and where his huge body in his fall crushes a part of Dhṛtarāṣṭra's army (7.154.61 *hato 'py evaṃ tava sainyekadeśam apothayat*). After being slain, Ghaṭotkaca's body looks like a scattered mountain (7.155.1 *haiḍimbaṃ nihataṃ dṛṣṭvā vikīrṇam iva parvatam*). The word *parvata* used here for 'mountain' is reminiscent of the name of king Parvataka/Parvateśvara in MR.

b. Candragupta compared with *candra* 'the moon'

Leaving the question of the meaning of king Parvataka aside for a moment, let us have a look at other details of the comparison given in MR 2.16. To emphasize the parallelism between his play and the epic, Viśākhadatta calls Cāṇakya here Viṣṇugupta and Kṛṣṇa Viṣṇu, recognizing thus the Mbh hero's divinity and connecting both characters with the god Viṣṇu.

In the same way as the name Viṣṇugupta establishes a connection with Viṣṇu, the author deliberately connects Candragupta with *candra*, the moon, more than once. Already the prologue associates Candragupta with the moon in a playful way: The stage manager's wife announces that she has invited brahmins to perform a worship

[8] Ed. by R. P. Kangle, Bombay, Part I (Critical Edition) 1960, Part II (English Translation) 1963.

of the moon who is threatened by an eclipse. The *sūtradhāra*, who presents himself as an accomplished astrologer, sets her right pointing out that "This cruel grasper Ketu wants to overcome the full orb of the moon by force, but the union with the planet Mercury protects him" (1.6). Cāṇakya, who is just entering the stage, misunderstands this verse believing that somebody is threatening his king, taking *candra* as Candragupta and *ketu* as the name of the barbarian king Malayaketu.

If this was the only instance of connecting the characters of the play with astronomical/astrological entities, one could consider it as just another playful way of starting the main plot of the drama. But Candragupta is also compared or associated with the moon at other places.[9] At the beginning of Act III, when the king is to act independently for once, he orders the Kaumudī festival to be celebrated. The Kaumudī night in the month Kārttikeya at the end of the rainy season in autumn is the holiest full-moon night of the year. Verse 11 of the same act imputes to Rākṣasa the intention to "take away the lustre of the Maurya-moon" (*mauryendoḥ śriyam apaharāmīti*); in verse 9 of Act IV Rākṣasa complains that the Kaumudī festival is going to be celebrated under Candragupta whom he refers to just by *candra*, 'moon', and not under the Nanda king, another 'moon among kings' (*nṛpacandra*). Further examples are 4.19, 21; 4.1 and the interpolated verse 7.16 (Hillebrandt's edition).

That Viśākhadatta's persistent association of Candragupta with *candra*, the moon, is more than a play with a historical king's name seems to be further evidenced by the comparison of the king with the epic hero Arjuna. As I have pointed out at an earlier occasion (von Simson 1994), some aspects of the main plot of Mbh can be better understood if we see in the epic heroes reflections of natural phenomena. The Pāṇḍavas seem to represent powers of moon and wind and the Kauravas powers of sun and clouds or, to be more

---

[9] Also in his other play, *Devīcandragupta*, of which only some passages are preserved, Viśākhadatta seems to play with the name of its hero, the Gupta king Candragupta, and *candra*, 'moon' (cf. Warder 1977: 263).

specific, Arjuna and Kṛṣṇa are representatives of the white and the black moon and Karṇa and Bhīṣma of different aspects of the sun. Thus Candragupta of MR and Arjuna of Mbh correspond perfectly to each other, both representing the bright moon.

c. Cāṇakya compared with the planet Mercury; Malayaketu compared with the *graha* Ketu

But what about Cāṇakya alias Viṣṇugupta: does he, as Kṛṣṇa in Mbh probably does, represent the black moon? The answer is no – the archaic concept of the black moon, the moon during the new moon period, has by now been replaced by Mercury, the planet that in the same way as the black moon is close to the sun. Already the *Jaiminīyagṛhyasūtra* (2.9) associates Mercury with the god Nārāyaṇa, most likely to be understood as just another name of Viṣṇu in this case. Viśākhadatta follows the same tradition. To quote again the ambiguous verse of the prologue (1.6): "This cruel grasper Ketu wants to overcome the full orb of the moon, but the union with the planet Mercury will protect him," meaning in the context of the play's plot: "King Malayaketu wants to overcome king Candragupta, but the union with Cāṇakya-Viṣṇugupta will protect him."

There is one other passage, 4.19, where Cāṇakya is represented by the planet Mercury (*budha*, 'the intelligent one'):

> *astāhimuhe śūle udide śampuṇṇamaṇḍale cande* |
> *gahavadibudhaśśa*[10] *lagge udidastamidammi kedummi* ||

Kale, who follows Ḍhuṇḍhirāja's commentary, translates:

> You should go[11] when the sun is about to set, and the full-orbed Chandra (moon) has risen in conjunction with Budha (the planet mercury; and when Ketu has risen and set (i.e. Rāhu's head is rising and its tail disappearing).

---

[10] Various readings: *gamaṇe vuhassa, gamaṇaṃ buhassa, gayaṇaṃ budhassa,* etc.

[11] Kale reads in *pāda* c *gamaṇaṃ* instead of *gahavadi-*.

The verse is spoken by Cāṇakya's agent Viṣṇuśarman, who under the disguise of the Jaina monk Jīvasiddhi gives astrological advice to Rākṣasa. As *candra*, moon, here again points to king Candragupta, the reference to Budha's *lagna* (*budhaśśa lagge*), the meeting place with the planet Mercury, can only refer to Cāṇakya, confirming the association of Viṣṇu with this planet.[12]

Turning back to the *Jaiminīyagṛhyasūtra* (2.9), we find that the *graha* Ketu is associated there with the region of the mountains (*parvata*): *rāhus tu pūrvadeśikaḥ ketuḥ parvata iti*. It seems that this or a similar text has inspired our author to make prince Malayaketu whom he associates both in the prologue verse (1.6) and in the just quoted verse 4.19 with the *graha* Ketu, the son of a king Parvataka, 'mountain, hill'. There is no need, therefore, to look for a historical king with that name.

d. Rākṣasa compared with the sun

If Cāṇakya gives his support to a king who is consistently associated with the moon, and if Viśākhadatta was inspired by Mbh, one would expect that his antagonist Rākṣasa is associated with the sun. This is indeed the case. The first hint is given in our key verse 2.16, where Rākṣasa compares himself with Karṇa, a hero who according to Mbh is son of Sūrya, the sun-god, and who is provided with clear solar features in the epic.

More explicit is a passage in Act IV where the sun metaphor is used three times in connection with Rākṣasa. In verse 4.19 (see above), the same verse which identifies Cāṇakya with the planet Mercury, the moon – Pkt. *canda* = Skt. *candra*, pointing to king Candragupta – is said to have risen with its full orb (*śaṃpuṇṇa-maṇḍale cande*) while Ketu – and this can only refer to prince Malayaketu – has vanished immediately after having risen.[13] The

---

[12] About the association of the sun with Rākṣasa in this verse see below.

[13] *udidastamidammi kedummi*. About the possible astronomical meaning of this expression see Ḍhuṇḍhirāja's commentary and Kale's translation quoted above.

statement that the sun is facing its setting (*astāhimuhe śūle*) therefore necessarily refers to Rākṣasa, the Prākrit allowing a pun: *śūla* may stand for both Skt. *sūrya*, sun, and *śūra*, hero.[14] The astrologer's preceding remark in prose which states that Rākṣasa is marching from North to South (*tumhāṇaṃ uttalāe diśāe daḥkhiṇaṃ diśaṃ pastidāṇaṃ*) can thus be interpreted as a clear reference to the *dakṣiṇāyana*, the second half of the year, when the sun is moving southward.

It is thus safe to assume that the sunset imagery at the end of Act IV, too, is meant to be applied to Rākṣasa himself.[15] It is introduced by the servant's reply to Rākṣasa's question about the hour of the day: "His reverence the sun desires to set" (*atthāhilāsī bhaavaṃ sūro*), where once again the use of the Prakrit word *sūra* allows the simultaneous understanding *sūrya* and *śūra* with a metaphorical reference to Rākṣasa himself.[16]

e. Rākṣasa and Karṇa (Mbh)

If we compare Rākṣasa with Karṇa, the sun-hero of Mbh, we see some striking similarities. Both are open, straightforward and generous characters[17], loyal towards their kings, Karṇa towards Duryodhana and Rākṣasa towards his Nanda king, and both act as brave and efficient army leaders.[18] In Act II, Rākṣasa generously takes jewels he had received from Malayaketu off from his person to give them as a reward to Siddhārthaka, an agent of Cāṇakya's, just like Karṇa who takes his golden armour and ear-rings from his body to confer them on Indra (Mbh 3.284-294). Generosity as well as association with gold and wealth are characteristic features of

[14] Cf. Ḍhuṇḍhirāja's commentary and Kale, footnote *ad locum*.

[15] Cf. Ruben 1956: 93 f.

[16] Ḍhuṇḍhirāja sees here a double allusion to both Malayaketu, who is facing his downfall, and Rākṣasa, who desires *artha*: *śūro malayaketur astomukhaḥ śūro rākṣasaś cārthābhilāṣī iti copaśrutir dhvanitā*.

[17] "Rākṣasa is inclined to be too generous and too trusting" (Warder 1977: 266).

[18] On Rākṣasa as an army leader see Vogel 1946: 6 ff.

the sun, and Rākṣasa's friendship with the jeweller Candanadāsa might thus emphasize his solar character. Another feature of the sun, its association with snakes and poison, seems to be hinted at by the fact that Rākṣasa's agent Virādhagupta is a snake charmer and by the poison-maid he uses in his attempt to kill Candragupta.

But there is one more specific feature that should be mentioned. In strong contrast to the epic Kṛṣṇa and Cāṇakya of the MR who are described as coolly calculating politicians – though Cāṇakya is also prone to anger (*krodha*) – , both Karṇa and Rākṣasa are much more compassionate, emotional and soft characters. As Karṇa sheds tears over Dhṛtarāṣṭra's son Durjaya when he is slain by Bhīma[19], Rākṣasa too is more than once shown as being about to weep, so in Act II, stage direction before verse 5, and Act IV, stage direction before verse 5 and 15 (*sabāṣpam*), or having tears in his eyes: stage direction Act II, before verse 7, and Act VI, between verse 8 and 9 (*sāsram*).

Van Buitenen speaks of "Rākṣasa's brand of compassion and devotion" (van Buitenen 1968: 45), and in a similar way, Ruben describes Rākṣasa as the compassionate one[20] and considers compassion (Mitleid) as one of the issues of MR (Ruben 1956: 177). Looking for a correspondence among natural phenomena, one would think of the sun during the rainy season, the sun shedding tears as it were in the first part of the *dakṣiṇāyana*.

There is one point that establishes an even closer relation between Rākṣasa and Karṇa, and that concerns the main motif of the play: In the same way as Cāṇakya tries to win Rākṣasa over, so Kṛṣṇa – that is to say the epic counterpart of Cāṇakya – makes an attempt to win over Karṇa to the side of the Pāṇḍavas. This is related in the *Karṇopanivādaparvan* ("The Temptation of Karṇa", as van Buitenen translates this title)[21], the 7th Subparvan of the *Udyogaparvan*.[22] Unlike Cāṇakya, who finally forces Rākṣasa to

---

[19] Mbh 7.108.39: *rudann ārtas tava sutaṃ karṇaś cakre pradakṣiṇam.*

[20] Ruben 1956: 147 "Er ist der ausgesprochen Mitleidige".

[21] Van Buitenen 1978: 442.

yield, Kṛṣṇa does not succeed in persuading Karṇa. The half-brother of the Pāṇḍavas remains loyal to Duryodhana, though he clearly sees the omens and portents that predict Yudhiṣṭhira's victory in the approaching battle (Mbh 5.141.1-40). He is a fatalist like Rākṣasa, who listens to the astrologer in Act IV and who in Act II blames Lakṣmī, the personified fortune.

f. Rākṣasa and Bhīṣma (Mbh)

This failure to win Karṇa over – the hero will fight and die towards the end of the battle on the side of the Kauravas – makes him an imperfect counterpart of Rākṣasa. But as a representative of the sun, Karṇa himself is incomplete. His complement is Bhīṣma, the old hero who dies at the beginning of the *uttarāyaṇa* and thus in my opinion represents another aspect of the sun: the sun towards the end of the year, the sun approaching the winter solstice (von Simson 1984: 195). He supplies those features of Rākṣasa that are missing with Karṇa. Like the latter, he is fighting on the side of the Kauravas to whom his loyalty belongs, but unlike Karṇa, he has a weak point that makes it possible to overcome this otherwise invincible hero: Already towards the end of the *Udyogaparvan*, under the preparations for the war, Bhīṣma declares that he will not fight against a woman or one who was a woman before, and that he therefore will not kill Śikhaṇḍin who in a former existence had been a woman, Śikhaṇḍinī (Mbh 5.169.16-20). He confirms this decision during the battle when the Pāṇḍavas ask him to disclose by which means he can be killed (Mbh 6.103.53-82). The Pāṇḍavas are thus able to overcome Bhīṣma by placing Śikhaṇḍin like a protecting shield before Arjuna. Bhīṣma is not immediately killed in the decisive duel with Arjuna. He survives for several weeks on the battle-field, time enough to confer all his knowledge on Yudhi-

[22] Mbh 5.138-148. Immediately before the battle starts, Kṛṣṇa makes another fruitless attempt to win over Karṇa and make him fight on the side of the Pāṇḍavas as long as Bhīṣma is alive (Karṇa hates Bhīṣma after being humiliated by him) (Mbh 6.41.84-87).

ṣṭhira. Unlike Karṇa, he is thus finally won over and transfers his loyalty to the new ruler.

Like Bhīṣma, who refuses to fight against a woman, Rākṣasa too is overcome by taking advantage of his morality. When fleeing from the capital he had entrusted his wife and his son to his friend, the jeweler Candanadāsa. By putting Candanadāsa under arrest and ordering him to be impaled for sheltering Rākṣasa's family, Cāṇakya forces Rākṣasa to make an attempt to rescue his friend and thereby gets the opportunity to seize him and to put him under pressure so that Rākṣasa finally sees no other way than to yield to Cāṇakya's demands.

As we see, the details are different – what is common is only that in both cases the hero is bound by moral obligations so that he finally has to give up his resistance that could not have been overcome in open battle.

Like Rākṣasa, who no doubt has a terrifying name[23] which would normally denote a demon, Bhīṣma's name, too, means 'terrifying', and – unlike Rākṣasa – he at one occasion indeed acts as a *rākṣasa*: he abducts the daughters of the king of Kāśī with the intention to let them be married with his half-brother Vicitravīrya (Mbh 5.170). Ambā, the eldest of these three sisters, is later reborn as Śikhaṇḍin. Karṇa and Bhīṣma may – as we have seen – be considered a complementary pair. Their names remind us of the *rākṣasa*-brothers of the *Rāmāyaṇa*, Kumbhakarṇa and Vibhīṣaṇa. This Vibhīṣaṇa, in spite of being a *rākṣasa*, is a pious man who, like Bhīṣma of Mbh and Rākṣasa of MR in the end becomes an invaluable supporter of the virtuous heroes of their respective epics.

---

[23] This makes Kale think that Rākṣasa must be a historical person, because Viśākhadatta would never have invented "such a reprehensible name" (Kale 1965: xxx).

3. CONCLUSION

I think we may understand the idea behind the plot of MR – the winning over of Rākṣasa – if we consider the different roles to be played by Cāṇakya and Rākṣasa. These are the roles of *yoga* and *kṣema* according to the *Arthaśāstra* tradition: *yoga* meaning the winning of power, *kṣema* meaning securing it and enjoying it under peaceful circumstances governed by *dharma*. Cāṇakya alias Viṣṇugupta alias Kauṭilya plays the role of Viṣṇu who helps a weakened Indra or a king in distress to regain his power. In astronomical/astrological terms, this is the task of the black moon or of his neighbour, the planet Mercury: to bring the bright moon to power again after the new-moon period. He has to re-establish *dharma* using if necessary *adharmic* methods. And he has to tame the dangerous hostile power, the power of the Rākṣasa, the power of the sun, in order to make it a protective power, and this can happen only in the *dakṣiṇāyana* when the sun's power is declining.

When Cāṇakya in MR retires after accomplishing his task of winning over Rākṣasa, he just follows the example of Kṛṣṇa in Mbh. There it is related how Yudhiṣṭhira after the war expresses his gratefulness to Kṛṣṇa, whose divine *buddhi* l ıs granted victory to the Pāṇḍavas (Mbh 12.45.18 f.). But then Kṛṣṇa reveals his insight which he just has won in deep meditation: Yudhiṣṭhira is advised to present himself to the dying Bhīṣma, the bearer of all knowledge or rather: of all the single sciences (Mbh 12.46.17 *ādhāraṃ sarvavidyānām*) he will need as a king (Mbh 12.46). Bhīṣma is called *pitāmaha*, the grandfather; he is the bearer of the tradition, he knows past, present and future (Mbh 12.46.19), he knows everything about the Vedas, the ritual, the *āśrama*s and the *dharma* of the four *varṇa*s, and when he dies[24], knowledge will be diminished (Mbh 12.46.22 f.).

But, interestingly, even in this late chapter of the *Śāntiparvan* where Kṛṣṇa as the incarnate god Viṣṇu extols Bhīṣma's know-

[24] Mbh 12.46.23. The author uses the sun-metaphor: *tasminn astamite bhīṣme*!

ledge, he does not fail to mention that former rākṣasic deed of Bhīṣma's: the abduction of the three young women (Mbh 12.46.13). It is apparently an integrating part of Bhīṣma's personality characterizing him as somebody who forcibly takes care of the continuation of the dynasty and thereby of life on earth, even though this eventually, through Ambā's curse and her rebirth as Śikhaṇḍinī, will cost him his own life.

As Bhīṣma is the "grandfather", who is in possession of the knowledge of the ancestors, so Rākṣasa is the minister inherited from the former Nanda king, his knowledge is therefore indispensable and cannot be replaced by Cāṇakya's *buddhi*. Intelligence cannot replace traditional knowledge and life-experience. Rākṣasa's name – if not invented by Viśākhadatta – might therefore originally have referred to the demons' protective power (*rākṣasa* < √*rakṣ* 'to protect'), which is well attested (Hopkins 1915: 38).

Summing up: I hope to have made plain that MR, regardless of its novel features as a political drama with a highly sophisticated and artificially designed plot, is in a surprising way indebted to traditional patterns that are discernible in Mbh. On the other hand, its undisguised metaphorical references to astronomical entities (moon, sun, the planet Mercury and the eclipse demon Ketu) confirm my conviction that the Great Epic as well can be interpreted on these lines.

REFERENCES

BROCKINGTON, John 1998. *The Sanskrit Epics.* (Handbuch der Orientalistik. 2.12.) Leiden: Brill.

BUITENEN, J. A. B. van 1968. *Two Plays of Ancient India. The Little Clay Cart; The Minister's Seal. Translated from Sanskrit and Prakrit, with an Introduction.* New York: Columbia University Press.

—— (trans.) 1978. *The Mahābhārata*, III: *4: The Book of Virāṭa; 5: The Book of the Effort.* Chicago: The University of Chicago Press.

HILLEBRANDT, Alfred 1912. *Mudrārākṣasa by Viśākhadatta. Edited from MSS. and provided with an Index of all Prākrit words.* (Indische Forschungen, 4. Heft.) Breslau: M. and H. Marcus.

HOPKINS, E. Washburn 1915. *Epic Mythology.* (Grundriss der Indo-Arischen Philologie und Altertumskunde, 3.1.B.) Strassburg: Karl J. Trübner.

KALE, M. R. 1965. *Mudrārākshasa of Viśākhadatta. With the commentary of Dhuṇḍirāja. Ed. with an English translation, Critical and Explanatory Notes, Introduction and Various Readings.* (Revised and enlarged edition with Hindi translation.) 5th edition. Delhi: MLBD.

NOOTEN, Barend A. van 1971. *The Mahābhārata.* New York: Twayne Publishers.

RAGHAVAN, V. 1948. *The Mudrārākṣasanāṭakakathā of Mahādeva. Ed. with Introduction, Notes etc.* (The Sarasvati Mahal Series 1.) 2nd revised edition. Tanjore: T.M.S.S.M. Library.

RUBEN, Walter 1956. *Der Sinn des Dramas "Das Siegel und Rākshasa".* (Deutsche Akademie der Wissenschaften zu Berlin, Institut für Orientforschung, Veröffentlichung Nr. 31.) Berlin: AkademieVerlag.

SIMSON, Georg von 1984. The mythic background of the Mahābhārata. *Indologica Taurinensia* 12: 191-223.

—— 1994. Die zeitmythische Struktur des Mahābhārata. In: Reinhard Sternemann (ed.), *Bopp-Symposium 1992 der Humboldt-Universität zu Berlin*: 230-247. Heidelberg: Universitätsverlag C. Winter.

TELANG, Kāshināth Trimbak 1884. *Mudrārākshasa by Viśākhadatta. With the commentary of Ḍhunḍhirāj. Ed. with critical and explanatory notes.* Bombay: Government Central Book Depot.

VOGEL, J. Ph. 1946. *De Zegelring van Rāksjasa door Wisjākhadatta. Indisch Tooneelspel uit sanskrit en prākrit in het nederlandsch vertaald.* Leiden: E. J. Brill.

WARDER, A. K. 1977. *Indian Kāvya Literature,* III. (Chapter XXIX: Viśākhadatta, pp. 257-277). Delhi: MLBD.

Indra in the *Harivaṃśa*

RENATE SÖHNEN-THIEME

INTRODUCTION

The *Harivaṃśa* is a text in transition from the epic tradition (parts of which already appear to be transitional) to that of the Purāṇas proper, in which the full development of new systems of theological orientation is completed. Being an appendix to the *Mahābhārata*, the HV shows the same setting and is to a great extent indebted to its lore as well as its worldview. A study of the representation of any god in the HV has thus to draw upon the evidence found in the Mbh as necessary background. For a god like Indra who has already a long and varied history in texts predating the Mbh, one might watch out for even older references. At any rate, the direction of comparison would be rather looking backward into history than forward into later purāṇic developments.

Indra, as Viṣṇu's senior colleague or elder brother, might be expected to be much more closely connected to Viṣṇu/Kṛṣṇa than Vedic Rudra and epic-purāṇic Śiva.[1] Both Indra and Viṣṇu have, of course, quite a different development after their appearance in the *Ṛgveda*: whereas Viṣṇu is accepted by the Brāhmaṇa texts as the deity of the sacrifice or identified with the sacrifice,[2] Indra, to

---

[1] P. Schreiner remarks, in a footnote at the end of his paper on Śiva in the Harivaṃśa (Schreiner 2005), that "Indra's presence in the HV is surprisingly pervasive and dominating"; he adds that he regretted the absence of a paper on that topic.

whom sacrifices were mainly addressed, is made more and more suspect; his great deeds are belittled, his sovereignty is contested.[3] The sacrifice is no longer a means to worship the gods and to obtain their favour, but becomes an end in itself, higher than any god. Gods and Asuras both strive to perform sacrifices.[4] Viṣṇu, permeating the whole universe with his three strides and identified with the sacrifice, becomes the highest god in some of the Brāhmaṇa texts, rising far beyond the ancient gods of the Ṛgvedic period.

There is one trace, however, pointing to Indra's unparalleled supremacy, in spite of all brahmanical attempts to put it into doubt, and this is the name Indra itself, which assumes an appellative meaning independent from the god Indra, being either used in the sense of 'lord, king' and 'leading, preeminent',[5] transferable to any person worthy of it. Apart from this, Indra's individual position, the rank and office of the ruler and protector of all the worlds and beings,[6] becomes in some contexts separated from its original holder; it can be attained by performing sacrifices and obtaining merit and can be lost again, due to misbehaviour or when the merit is even-

---

[2] Cf., e.g., *Śatapathabrāhmaṇa* 1.1.2.13: *yajño vai viṣṇuḥ*, or 14.1.1.6: *sa yaḥ sa viṣṇur yajñaḥ saḥ*, etc.; this identification is also taken up in HV App. 29:779.

[3] Cf. Söhnen-Thieme 1997.

[4] Cf., e.g., *Jaiminīyabrāhmaṇa* 1.153: *devāsurā yajñe 'spardhanta*; 1.321: *prajāpatir yajñam asṛjata, taṃ devebhyaḥ prāyacchat ... tenājayanta*. The idea of the gods performing a sacrifice can actually already be found in the latest book of the ṚV, in the *Puruṣasūkta*: *táṃ yajñáṃ barhíṣi práukṣan púruṣaṃ jātám agratáḥ, téna devā́ ayajanta* ... (ṚV 10.90.7).

[5] This usage does not seem to be attested before Manu or the epics (cf. PW s.v.).

[6] The term *indratva-* n., denoting Indra's rank and power, seems to occur first in Mbh 3.218.14: Being offered the chance to become "Indra" by Indra himself (13), after defeating the gods, Skanda refuses: *śādhi tvam eva trailokyam ... ahaṃ te kiṃkaraḥ śakra, na mamendratvam īpsitam* ('you alone are to rule over the three worlds ... I am your servant; I do not wish for Indra-hood'). How Indra himself became "Indra", is stated in Mbh 14.5.7: *vāsavo 'py asurān sarvān nirjitya ca nihatya ca | indratvaṃ prāpya lokeṣu tato vavre purohitam | ... bṛhaspatim*. ('Having obtained his Indra-hood by defeating and slaying the Asuras, Vāsava chose Bṛhaspati as his family priest'). In both cases the *indratvam* seems to be the reward for being brave and victorious.

tually exhausted. The loss of his Indra-hood happens to Indra himself after killing Triśiraṣ and Vṛtra and thereby incurring the sins of brahmin-murder and of untruthfulness upon himself,[7] and it is only when his substitute, e.g. Nahuṣa in the Mbh, has shown himself unworthy that Indra can resume his old position.

As for *indra* meaning 'lord, king; preeminent', there are innumerable attestations of *rājendra*, *narendra*, *gajendra*, *daityendra*, *viprendra*, *dvijendra*, etc., in the HV as well as in any other post-Vedic text. Probably it is due to this development of the appellative meaning of *indra* that it became necessary to specify Indra the Vedic Lord of the gods as *devendra* or *mahendra*, or to use unambiguous hereditary epithets from the Vedic tradition, like *śakra*, *śatakratu*, *puraṃdara*, *śacīpati*, *maghavān*, etc. (some of which, e.g. *śakra* and *vāsava*, appear as names replacing the name Indra in later tradition), or to denote him by his specific rank as *devarāja*, *surādhipa*, *sureśa*, etc.[8]

1. NAMES AND EPITHETS OF INDRA

a. Distribution in different sections of HV

Before presenting the evidence in the *Harivaṃśa*, some practical issues should be taken into consideration. A difficult problem seems to be the segmentation of the text for comparative statistical purposes, when dealing with the distribution of names and epithets. On the one hand one would like to compare segments of approximately the same length, and on the other one would wish to separate layers corresponding to the textual development. Since both objectives cannot be harmonised, no statistical evaluation is attempted.

---

[7] In the story as it is told in the *Udyogaparvan* of the Mbh, Vṛtra is slain with a *vajra* made of foam (Indra's stratagem to overcome Namuci in Brāhmaṇa legends); for this reason Indra is *anṛtenābhibhūto*, as well as he was *traiśīrṣayābhibhūto ... pūrvaṃ brahmahatyayā*, and has to hide in the water (Mbh 5.10.42-43).

[8] For names and epithets of Indra in the Mbh cf. Brockington 2001.

There is also the problem of the evaluation of the star passages in the critical edition and their relationship to the appendix passages, the appendix passages themselves being of a quite different nature: whereas shorter appendix passages might be treated as lengthy star passages, the larger appendix passages (e.g. App. 29, App. 41, App. 42-42B) have to be treated as separate text segments.

In order to give at least a provisional impression of the distribution of the most important names and epithets of Indra, I have selected three significant sections, representing three parts of the HV: the PPL section of the *Harivaṃśaparvan* (ch. 1-29), ch. 30-92 of the *Kṛṣṇacarita*, and App. 42 and 42B (24 chapters in the Vulgate), to which have been added App. 41 (with 26 chapters) and App. 29 (12 chapters), each of which shows remarkably different frequencies. The names and epithets of Indra are listed in the sequence as given in Brockington's account of the frequencies in the Mbh[9]; to this list is added the Vedic epithet *puruhūta* at the end, since it occurs quite often (also in passages not included in the table, like App. 18). – One might have added more of the epithets combining a synonym for 'gods' with a synonym for 'lord, king, most eminent' (like *devendra*, *surādhipa*, *amaraśreṣṭha*, *tridaśeśvara*, etc.), which are especially frequent in App. 29, but this would have inflated the list without giving much interesting information. Epithets belonging to an individual context (like *kauśika*, *hariśmaśru*, etc.) are also excluded from the table, but they are dealt with in the subsequent analysis.

Even though the number of stanzas in each segment varies considerably, one can easily recognise the differences between them. Thus App. 41 does not provide much more than the name Indra itself: *śakra* (line 260) seems to be used as designating Indra's function[10] and *maghavān* appears only as a highly dubious reading in line 1616 and most probably does not refer to Indra.

---

[9] Brockington 2001: 68 f.

[10] *aham aindre pade śakraḥ* (Nārāyaṇa's statement).

TABLE 1

	PPL ch. 1-29 (1363 stanzas)	*Āścaryaparvan* ch. 30-92 (3251 stanzas)	App. 42, 42B (24 chapters) (ca. 1850 stanzas)	App. 41 (26 chapters) (ca. 990 stanzas)	App. 29 (12 chapters) (ca. 740 stanzas)
Śakra	12 (+ 7*)	58 (+ 13*)	41 (+ 8*)	1	24
Indra	9 (+ 6*)	7 (+ 3*)	11 (+ 2*)	7 (+ 1*)	9
– (as title)	4	2	2	–	–
Vāsava	2 (+ 1*)	14 (+ 1*)	21 (+ 4*)	1	2
Devarāja	–	11 (+ 4*)	6	–	10
Vajrin, Vajrabhṛt, etc.	3 (*vajrapāṇi*)	3	1	–	2
Mahendra	–	7	13	2	26 (+1*)
Puraṃdara	1 (+ 3*)	8 (+ 3*)	21 (+ 4*)	1	4
Śatakratu	5	2 (+ 2*)	2 (+ 2*)	–	2
Maghavān	6 (+ 1*)	1	–	1	–
Sahasrākṣa, Sahasradṛś	1 (+ 1*)	3 (+ 2 *śatadṛś*)	6	–	2
Pākaśāsana	5 (+ 3*)	2 (+ 2*)	1	–	3
Sureśvara, Sureśa	–	1	4 (+ 2*)	–	6
Śacīpati	(1*)	2 (+ 4*)	4	–	–
Vṛtrahan(tṛ)	–	2 (+ 5*)	1	–	2 (*-nāśana*, *-ghna*)
Puruhūta	(1*: Viṣṇu)	6	5	–	–
Balabhid	–	–	–	–	2 (+ 7 other cpds)

The other passages show a clear preference for the name Śakra over any other name (except for App. 29, where Mahendra is slightly more frequent than even Śakra), the name Indra being proportionately rather less represented than in the Mbh. Indra is outnumbered by Vāsava in the *Kṛṣṇacarita* and in the *Prādurbhāva* episodes in App. 42 and 42B of the HV (except if Mahendra is counted together with Indra); in App. 29 this name has lost its importance again. Quite striking is the growing frequency of Puraṃdara, which is undoubtedly due to formulaic expressions like *puruhūtaḥ puraṃdaraḥ* (59.7, 62.3), *puraskṛtya puraṃdaram* (38.65) or *puraṃdaram puraskṛtya* (74.19*829 and App. 42:612), *puraṃdarapurogamāḥ* (6.18; App. 42:505), possibly also *paulomyeva puraṃdaraḥ* (88.35), all with alliteration.

If App. 41 shows little interest in mentioning Indra, quite the opposite is true for App. 29, an elaborate version of the *Pārijātaharaṇa* episode. Since it is a story in which Indra plays an important role, his names and epithets abound. Apart from the popularity of the term Mahendra,[11] there is especially an increase in variation of epithets denoting Indra's supremacy over the gods, like *devarāja* (10),[12] *sureśvara* (6), *devendra* (4), *amarasattama* (4), *deveśa* (3), *surapati* (2), *amareśvara* (2), *amaraśreṣṭha* (2) *suraśreṣṭha*, *amarottama*, *surottama*, *surādhipa*, *vibudhādhipa*, *amaramukhya*, *suramukhyeśa*. Quite a number of these occur as vocatives in Nārada's two speeches and may not be taken too seriously.[13]

A similar variety can be found in epithets referring to Indra's deeds in the remote past, especially his victory over Vala (spelled *bala* throughout), which, however, does not seem to have been

---

[11] In some cases the names Indra and Mahendra are used together with Kṛṣṇa's name Upendra, in a kind of play with words: *mahendrānujaṃ draṣṭuṃ gato 'ham* (App. 29:510); *upendro 'ham, mahendreṇa lālanīyaḥ* (line 620); *upendrasya mahendra.ayam ... niścayaḥ* (line 634); *indropendrau* (line 1018); *mahendropendratanayau* (line 1083); *upendraṃ na mahendro'tha...* (line 1384).

[12] In four instances the stem *devarājan-* is used (ll. 712, 1224, 1252, 1572), the stem *devarāja-* appears thrice in declined forms and thrice in compounds.

[13] Vocatives like *bhuvaneśvara* (App. 29:856) or *bhāvana* (line 529), otherwise addressed to the Supreme God, do indeed seem overexaggerated.

understood properly any longer; beside older *balabhid* (i.e. *vala-bhid*) in ll. 391 and 1391, new formations are used which suggest a demonic person (*baladehabhid, balanāśana, balāntaka, balaripu, balaniṣūdana*), even if *adrighātin* (line 339), possibly parallel to *balaghātin* (line 440), appears to reflect the notion of a rock.[14]

b. Some epithets in detail

As stated before (p. 337), some of Indra's epithets are already used in the *Ṛgveda*, such as *śakra* 'the potent one', *puraṃdara* 'the destroyer of strongholds', *śatakratu* 'possessing a hundred powers of will', *maghavan* 'bountiful/powerful', *vṛtrahan* 'destroyer of Vṛtra', *śacīpati* 'lord of might or help' (later understood as Śacī's husband). Epithets like *sahasrākṣa* or *puruhūta* occur in the ṚV as well, but are not exclusively used for Indra.

Of the epithets referring to Indra's specific weapon, the *vajra*, *vajrin* and *vajrabhṛt* can be found in the ṚV, whereas *vajrapāṇi* (PPL section 3.106, 209; 21.12)[15] and *vajradhara* (*Kṛṣṇacarita*, HV 89.40) are not attested before the epics, *vajrāyudha* not before the HV. Likewise compounds referring to Indra's splitting open the *vala* (the rock or mountain in which the cows were hidden)[16] do not appear before the epics (*balabhid, balanāśana*) or even before the HV (*balaniṣūdana* etc.).

Although the name Vāsava does not occur in the ṚV, it can be found in the *Atharvaveda* (AV 6.82.1). Presumably it is an innova-

[14] The compound *adrighātin-* itself does not appear in the Skt. dictionaries; it may be synonymous with *adribhíd-* (ṚV 6.73.1), said of Bṛhaspati (who is closely associated with Indra in the Vala myth; cf. Schmidt 1968). But one has also to consider the feat of Indra striking down the mountains, a popular concept which is reflected in a considerable number of similes (cf. below p. 349).

[15] Its Ṛgvedic equivalent is *vajrahasta*. – In the PPL section it occurs in the context of Indra cutting the embryo in Aditi's womb to pieces, a myth invented for the (pseudo-)etymological explanation of the Maruts' name from *mā rodīḥ* 'don't cry'.

[16] Cf. e.g. ṚV 2.11.20: *bhinád valám índra* ... 'Indra split the mountain cave'; 2.24.3: *úd gā́ ājad ábhinad bráhmaṇā valám* 'he drove the cows out, he split the mountain cave with a poem', etc.

tion derived from *vásu* 'good', which is not infrequently used in the vocative sg. to address Indra, and in the plural to denote the Ādityas; the formation *vāsavá* from *vásu* may be compared to that of *brāhmaṇa*, *rākṣasa* from *bráhman*, *rákṣas*.

Another name which does not actually occur in the *Ṛgveda*, but can be traced back to it, is Pākaśāsana, which might originally have meant 'instructor of the ignorant' (cf. *prá pākaṃ śāssi* ṚV 1.31.14), but was later interpreted as 'punisher of (the demon) Pāka', although no story seems to have emerged to support this interpretation. Here it might rather be intended to mean 'the ruler over the ripening (of fruit)',[17] in agreement with Indra's function as god of fertility, who has to provide the necessary rain, and in keeping with the other occurrence of *pra* + *śās* in the ṚV. This seems to be reflected in the formula *nāvarṣat pākaśāsanaḥ* (HV 9.95, 10.10, 24.5, 29.31).[18] Indra's connection with rain is further expressed in *pravavarṣa sahasrākṣaḥ* (29.33), in *vavarṣa harivāhanaḥ* (24.6), which refers to Indra's bay horses known from the ṚV, in *śivaṃ varṣati vāsavaḥ* (41.13), and in the loc. abs. *mandaṃ varṣati vāsave* (77.29).

In *kāle devaś ca varṣati* (44.58) the reference may be either to Parjanya (cf. *kālavarṣī ca parjanyaḥ* in 28.13) or to Indra.[19] The relationship between Indra and Parjanya is not very clear. In 59.17, in the speech of the shepherd explaining the Indra festival to Kṛṣṇa, the name Parjanya seems to refer to Indra, similarly in 61.19, in the description of the thunderstorm descending on the Govardhana mountain. But Indra and Parjanya, who share the function of providing rain, seem to retain their original status as two separate deities in the list of Ādityas in the Mbh as well as in the HV, except

[17] Cf. Hopkins 1915: 122: "[Pākaśāsana] means 'ruler of crops' (vegetables) but is understood as ruler or slayer of Pāka (demon)".

[18] Cf. also (non-formulaic) Mbh 1.218.45: *bhūyaḥ saṃvardhayām āsa tad varṣaṃ pākaśāsanaḥ* (with K2 Ñ2 B D). – The other occurrences of *pākaśāsana* in the HV (3.105 and star passages) do not seem to have any connection with this concept.

[19] Cf. also Ram 1.10.29: *vavarṣa sahasā devaḥ*.

in the list of the twelve Ādityas in the era of Manu Cākṣuṣa in the PPL section (3.50-51), where Parjanya does not occur:

> *tatra* (1)*viṣṇuś ca* (2)*śakraś ca jajñāte punar eva hi* |
> (3)*aryamā caiva* (4)*dhātā ca* (5)*tvaṣṭā* (6)*pūṣā tathaiva ca* || 50 ||
> (7)*vivasvān* (8)*savitā caiva* (9)*mitro* (10)*varuṇa eva ca* |
> (11)*aṃśo* (12)*bhagaś cātitejā ādityā dvādaśa smṛtāḥ* || 51 ||

In the list found in 8:35*158 and in App. 42B:23 ff. both deities are named separately:

> (1)*dhātāryamā*(2) *ca* (3)*mitraś ca* (4)*varuṇo* (5) *'ṃśo* (6)*bhagas tathā* ||
> (7)*indro* (8)*vivasvān* (9)*pūṣā ca* (10)*parjanyo daśamas tathā* |
> *tatas* (11)*tvaṣṭā tato* (12)*viṣṇur ajaghanyo jaghanyajaḥ* ||

It is noteworthy that the sequence in these two lists[20] is quite different, especially concerning Viṣṇu, who heads the list in 3.50, but appears as the last-born in the lists found in the star passage and in App. 42B which agree with one of the lists found in the Mbh.[21] Not only in this list, but also in all the other lists of Ādityas found in the Mbh Viṣṇu appears as the last-born, whatever the sequence of the other eleven: so we have to assume that the list in HV 3.50 f.,

---

[20] There are two more lists of Ādityas in the Appendices, one in App. 41: 551 ff.:

> (1)*indro* (2)*viṣṇur* (3)*bhagas* (4)*tvaṣṭā* (5)*varuṇo* (6) *'ṃśo* (7) *'ryamā* (8)*raviḥ*
> (9)*pūṣā* (10)*mitraś ca varado* (11)*manuḥ* (12)*parjanya eva ca*

and another one in App. 42:357 f.:

> (1)*aryamā* (2)*varuṇo* (3)*mitraḥ* (4)*pūṣā* (5)*dhātā* (6)*puraṃdaraḥ* (7)*tvaṣṭā*
> (8)*bhago* (9) *'ṃśaḥ* (10)*savitā* (11)*parjanya ceti viśrutaḥ*

the first of them listing Indra and Viṣṇu at the beginning, i.e. they share the same place but the order is reversed, whereas in the latter list Viṣṇu is missing (but the list seems to be incomplete, counting only eleven Ādityas, except in ms D6, which reads *parjanyo viṣṇur eva ca* in the last *pāda*). In all these lists Parjanya is listed as separate from Indra.

[21] Mbh 1.114.55-56ab, in the version of the Southern Recension; the critical edition reads for the last two lines:

> (7)*indro* (8)*vivasvān* (9)*pūṣā ca* (10)*tvaṣṭā ca* (11)*savitā tathā* |
> (12)*parjanyaś caiva* (13)*viṣṇuś ca ādityāḥ pāvakārciṣaḥ* ||

arriving at thirteen Ādityas.

headed by Viṣṇu and omitting Parjanya, must be an innovation, furthest from the ṚV, where Viṣṇu is not included (see below).

Another name which goes back to the Vedas is Kauśika, used as patronym in HV 23.84, App. 6B:33, App. 42B:2174, 2404, 2420). It appears first, as a vocative addressed to Indra, in ṚV 1.10.11 (*ā́ tū́ na indra kauśika ...*), in a hymn ascribed to Madhucchandas, son of the Kauśika Viśvāmitra, and probably has the original meaning 'friendly to the Kauśika family'. Sāyaṇa in his commentary, however, understands Kauśika as a patronym (*kuśikasya putra*) and quotes the following story from the *Anukramaṇikā*:

> *kuśikas tv auṣīrathir indratulyaṃ putram icchan brahmacaryam cacāra. tasyendra eva gāthī putro jajñe.*

In the Mbh, this Gāthin is twice mentioned as Gādhi, son of Kuśika and father-in-law of Ṛcīka, in 3.115 and 5.117, and appears again in 12.49 where the story of the *Anukramaṇikā* is reformulated in verse. A similar, but slightly shorter version is found in the PPL section of the HV (and in App. 6B:26-33):

Mbh	**HV**
*... **kuśiko** nāma dharmajñas*	*babhūva mṛgayāśīlas*
***tasya** putro mahīpatiḥ* ‖ 12.49.3 ‖	***kuśikas tasya** cātmajaḥ* ... ‖ 23.82 ‖
*ugraṃ **tapaḥ** samatiṣṭhat*	*kuśikas tu **tapas** tepe*
*sahasrākṣa**samo bhuvi*** |	***putram** indrasamaṃ **vibhuḥ*** |
***putraṃ labheyam** ajitaṃ*	***labheyam** iti;*
trilokeśvaram ity uta ‖ 4 ‖	
***tam** ugratapasaṃ dṛṣṭvā*	***taṃ** śakras*
sahasrākṣaḥ puraṃdaraḥ |	
samarthaḥ putrajanane	
*svayam ev**aiti**, bhārata* ‖ 5 ‖	*trāsād abhyetya jajñivān* ‖ 83 ‖
putratvam agamad, rājaṃs,	
tasya lokeśvareśvaraḥ |	
***gādhir** nām**ābhavat** putraḥ*	*sa **gādhir abhavad** rājā*
***kauśikaḥ** pākaśāsanaḥ* ‖ 6 ‖	*maghavān **kauśikaḥ** svayam* ... ‖ 84 ‖

App. 6B repeats 23.82-84ab, but inserts after 23.83:

> *pūrṇe varṣasahasre vai* ***taṃ*** *tu śakro hy* ***apaśyata*** ।
> ***atyugratapasaṃ dṛṣṭvā sahasrākṣaḥ puraṃdaraḥ*** ॥

The second line is a slightly changed version of one line from the Mbh passage (12.49.4ab) and must have been added into the PPL passage, which may have existed independently. Interestingly, the PPL account provides a motive for Indra becoming Kuśika's son: *trāsāt* 'out of fear'; no doubt Indra is afraid of a potential rival.

Apart from the Ṛ̣V, the epithet *kauśika* occurs also in the *Subrahmaṇya* formula, attested in some Brāhmaṇas and Śrauta-sūtras, for which different explanations are given in the Brāhmaṇas themselves. One of them refers to Indra's love affair with Ahalyā, faintly echoed in Mbh 12.329.14, amongst curses by brahmins.

The three occurrences of Kauśika in App. 42B have no connection with any of these stories, but simply show *kauśika* as a well-known epithet: *kauśiko vāsavaḥ prabhuḥ*, and *kauśika- harivāhana-* (in nom. and loc.), the second epithet, also found in HV 24.6, referring to Indra's bay horses in the Ṛ̣V. A totally new explanation of *kauśika* is given in App. 42:424-425:

> *jātamātro 'tha bhagavān adityā sa kuśair vṛtaḥ* ॥
> *tadāprabhṛti deveśaḥ kauśikatvam upāgataḥ* ।

> Then, as soon as he was born, Aditi covered him with Kuśa-grass; from this time onward the lord of the gods assumed the state of being Kauśika.

Hariśmaśru (referred to in Mbh 12.329.14.1) appears as an epithet in App. 42B:505 and 2381, but it reflects rather the Ṛgvedic epithet *hariśmaśāru* than the context of the Mbh occurrence, where Indra becomes 'gold-bearded' because of Gautama's curse. Likewise the epithet *sahasrākṣa* (which is not restricted to Indra in the HV) is not yet understood in the naturalistic way and does therefore not need a story explaining the origin of these eyes, as told in various Purāṇas.[22]

[22] Cf. Söhnen-Thieme 1996: 49 f.

Thus one can see that, apart from individual explanations that are not found in other texts, the epithets in the HV are in some respect more traditional than those in the Mbh.

2. INDRA IN SIMILES

Like some of the epithets, similes drawing on Indra, his exploits, his qualities and attributes, etc., as an *upamāna* belong to a stock of formulae that must have developed long before the epics took their present shape. They refer to a conception of Indra that predates the specific brahmanic lore developed in the Brāhmaṇa texts to which many stories in the Mbh can be traced. In the HV these similes naturally rather occur in contexts without Indra as acting figure, but there are also exceptions, for instance in App. 42B: even although Indra is one of the main protagonists in the Vāmana episode, there are many comparisons referring to him, to his weapons, or to former deeds, especially his cutting off the wings of the mountains, in order to stabilise the earth.

Comparisons with reference to Indra can be grouped as follows:

(a) compounds with the meaning 'Indra-like': *śakratulya-*, *indrasama-*, *vāsavopama-*, etc. (to which may be added compounds meaning 'of the same valour as Indra', e.g., *pākaśāsanavikramaḥ*).

(b) comparisons referring to a constellation, e.g. 'like Indra' with respect to the gods or vice versa; 'like Indra' together with Śacī, 'like Indra' in his abode, etc.

(c) comparisons referring to certain deeds of Indra, especially his battles with demons;

(d) comparisons with Indra's weapons, most frequently his *vajra*, to which any other weapon, including bows (*cāpa*), lances (*śakti*), and clubs (*gadā*), may be compared;

(e) comparisons with the *vajra* as the 'thunderbolt' (*aśani*), with which the wings of the mountains were cut; this topic is by far more frequent than the slaying of Vṛtra.

In the PPL section similes referring to Indra are comparatively infrequent and seem to be restricted to formulaic expressions. Thus *yathā śacyā śatakratuḥ* appears in 19.5 (King Brahmadatta enjoying life in the forest with his wife) and *yathā śacyā śacīpatiḥ* in 174* (Balarāma enjoying life with Revatī). A similar idea is expressed in the simile in 18.2 (*nandanaṃ maghavān iva*): the king of Benares enters the forest, together with his harem, like Maghavan resorting to his pleasure-grove Nandana. The third simile (15.52) appears in dubious advice given to Ugrāyudha when he is about to enter into a battle with Bhīṣma (the first-person narrator of the passage): he should not fight, but use conciliation, gifts, and disunion (*sāma*, *dāna*, and *bheda*), like Maghavan when he defeated Śambara (*śambaraṃ maghavān iva*). The Śambara myth is quite obscure; there is no clear account either in the ṚV (where it is only alluded to) or in later literature; the means alleged are not mentioned anywhere with respect to Śambara.

All three similes occur in the *Pitṛkalpa* section, whereas the PPL proper confines itself to formulaic compounds like *śakratulya-parākramaḥ*, (said of Bhagīratha in 221*, of Dharmaratha 23.24, and of Arjuna 24.23, whose father is said to be Indra, anyway), and *indropamatejasaḥ* (said of the sons of Purūravas 21.10 and Nahuṣa 22.1), the common quality being valour in battle. It is perhaps noteworthy that the names and epithets used in similes so far (Indra, Śakra, Maghavan, Śatakratu, and Śacīpati) belong to the oldest stock found already in the ṚV.

The *Kṛṣṇacarita* section presents a more varied picture. As for compounds, beside *śakrasamaḥ putraḥ* (69.15), we find *vajra-dharopamaḥ* (89.40) and *vāsavopamavikramaḥ* (said of Viṣṇu, the *vāsavāvarajaḥ* 'younger brother of Vāsava' in 92.1); in star passages moreover *pākaśāsanavikramaḥ* (893*) and even *mahendra-samavikramaḥ* (870*), apart from the older formula *śakratulya-parākramaḥ* (said of Jarāsaṃdha in 910*).

As for similes with *iva* and *yathā*, there is one instance with a notion akin to *yathā śacyā śacīpatiḥ*, viz. *paulomyeva puraṃdaraḥ* in 88.35, used as a standard for Kṛṣṇa's enjoyment with his newly wedded wife Rukmiṇī.[23]

The remaining similes concentrate mainly on the relationship between Indra and the gods: *te 'pi govṛttayaḥ ... kṛṣṇaṃ* I *upāsaṃ cakrire, svarge śakram ivāmaraḥ* 64.24; *taṃ ... yādavāḥ ... rājānam* (Ugrasena) I *anujagmuḥ ... devā iva śatakratum* 78.4; ... *tam upendram* ... I *anujagmuḥ yaduganāḥ śakraṃ devagaṇā iva* 79.29, all of them characterising the gods as obedient followers of Indra. This ties in very well with the frequent use of formulaic compounds like (*devāḥ*) *śakrapurogamāḥ* in 22.1, 36.60, acc. 21.10, *indrapurogamān* 35.7, *puraṃdarapurogamaiḥ* 6.18, and expressions combining *puraskṛtya* with *puraṃdaram* (38.65, 829*).

There are couple of other similes with Indra: in 44.9 Nārada (characterised as *śakrasakha-* 'Indra's friend' in 46.6) is compared with Indra *sākṣāc chakra ivāparaḥ* (but the reading is not quite certain),[24] and one simile refers to Indra's fight with Vṛtra: *jarāsaṃdhasya ... rāmeṇāsīt samāgamaḥ* I *mahendrasyeva vṛtreṇa* ... (82.5); interestingly Balarāma is compared to Vṛtra, "bad" king Jarāsaṃdha to Indra (as also in 910*, cf. above):[25] is this the result of Vṛtra's reputation being raised in some Mbh passages?

More frequent in similes than Indra himself is his main weapon, the *vajra*, no longer consistently 'club', but sometimes combined with *aśani* as a 'thunderbolt',[26] as in 31.120 *surendra-vajrāśanitulyasāraiḥ* (qualifying Rāma's arrows), in 61.5 *vajrāśanisama-*

---

[23] In a star passage in the same chapter a similar idea is expressed in a Vaṃśasthavila stanza: *evaṃ vivāhaṃ ... kṛtvā ... pure tu tasmin nyavasat sukhaṃ hariḥ* I *yathaiva śakraḥ svapure jagadguruḥ* (1021*), but without reference to Indra's wife.

[24] 5 Southern mss read *chakrasakho/chakrasakhā muniḥ* for *chakra ivāparaḥ*.

[25] In 942* Jarāsaṃdha is placed even above Indra in a rhetorical question: *ko nāma hi jarāsaṃdhaṃ raṇe jetuṃ mahīpatiḥ* I *śaknuyāl lokavikhyātaḥ sākṣād api śatakratuḥ*?

[26] In 1049* ll. 14 f. (*punas tu ... murur gṛhya mahāgadām* I *indrāśanir ivendreṇa visṛṣṭa iva nisvanaḥ*) the sound of Muru's mace seems to be compared to that of Indra's *aśani*, but the syntax is garbled, and the variant readings do not yield a simple solution.

prabham (qualifying the rain and storm with which Indra wants to punish the herdsmen who have given up the Indra festival), and in 59.14 where *vajrāśanisama-* qualifies the sounds of the monsoon clouds.

On the whole, it does not look as if the *vajra* was actually used as a weapon to kill demons (especially Vṛtra); the most frequent reference is to mountains that were struck down. Thus in 37.43 the demon Kālanemi strikes down the gods with rocks and sharp-topped (?) trees (*śailaśṛṅgāgrapādapaiḥ*), like the mountains with the bolt/club (*vajreṇeva mahāgirīn*); the same phrase turns up in 76.6, when Saṃkarśana strikes Andhramalla on the head (*muṣṭi-naikena ... sāśani-stanayitnunā* I *śirasy abhyahanat... vajreṇeva mahāgirim*): in both cases one has presumably to supplement Indra as agent in the simile.[27] Other instances are 54.18, where in the description of heavy rains the downpour of water is compared to the *vajra* (*vajreṇevāvarugṇānāṃ nagānām* ... I *srotobhiḥ parikṛttāni patanti śikharāṇi*); in 77.48 the simile *vajrāhatam ivācalam* qualifies Ugrasena's son Kaṃsa, who has been killed by Kṛṣṇa; a similar expression (*vajrabhinna ivācalaḥ*) is used in 74.38, with reference to Kaṃsa's elephant, who falls to the ground, struck down by Kṛṣṇa with its own *vajra*-like tusk (*vajrakalpena svena dantena*). In 58.49 and 51 (as well as in 76.6 mentioned above), it is Baladeva's fist which is likened to the *vajra*, which might suggest the old Ṛgvedic meaning 'club'. In one instance (637*, only ms D2) it is Vṛtra struck down by Indra's *vajra*, to whom the demoness Pūtanā is compared: this seems to be more in line with the older concept of Vṛtra being a demon. – A more metaphorical use of the *vajra* is found at 56.17 *vajrapātopamaṃ vacaḥ*,[28] referring to the alarming news of Kṛṣṇa being in the power of Kāliya.

---

[27] It is not quite clear which myth or legend is alluded to with these similes. It seems rather unlikely that the idea of the mountains being split in order to give way to the rivers, as described in ṚV 4.19, is still alive in the minds of the narrators (although similes may preserve earlier concepts), but the Brāhmaṇa legend of how Indra cut off the mountains' wings (not yet found in the ṚV) does actually not fit very well either.

The other weapon that appears in similes is Indra's bow (called *mahendrāyudha* in 58.5, *indracāpa* in 699*, and *śakracāpa* in 1059*); but the reference is presumably rather to the rainbow than to a bow used as a weapon.

Let us now look at the appendix passages. The highest number of similes occurs in App. 18 (consisting of 1105 lines), in which Indra does not appear at all, its main topic being the conflict between Kṛṣṇa and Jarāsaṃdha. Both opponents seem to be compared to Indra, cf. *jarāsaṃdho ... pākaśāsanavikramaḥ* (line 12) vs. *sahasrākṣasamadyutiḥ ... kṛṣṇaḥ* (ll. 775 f.), *keśavaḥ prasthito 'dhvānaṃ yathendras tridivam* (line 1072), and *anujagmur yadu-gaṇāḥ śakraṃ devagaṇā iva* (line 1098). Apart from them, there are kings like Yadu, the founder of the Yādava clan, who is twice compared to Indra (line 97 *indrapratikāśaḥ* and line 126 *tasmai ... indrasamāya*), the king of the Cedis (*uvāca rājā cedīnāṃ devānāṃ maghavā iva* line 700), and King Mucukunda (*nṛpaśreṣṭhaḥ ... devaśreṣṭhaparākramaḥ* line 177).[29] This is presumably in agreement with the normal epic use of similes drawing upon Indra for the illustration of heroic and royal qualities. Interestingly even Garuḍa is reported to have assumed a divine shape as impressive as that of Indra (*śakrasya sadṛśaṃ rūpaṃ divyam* line 598), in order to fetch a diadem (*mauli*) for Viṣṇu from the ocean.

As in the *Kṛṣṇacarita* section to which this appendix belongs, there are quite a number of comparisons referring to Indra's *vajra*: in his martial address to his army Jarāsaṃdha refers to his royal allies (*ete nṛpāḥ*) as *vajrapratimagauravāḥ* (line 684); the mountain which they are ordered to besiege shall experience a danger similar to that of the *vajra* (*vajraprapātapratimaṃ bhayam* line 695). Set on fire, the mountain emits stones, as though it was split by Indra's *vajra* (*vajreṇa puruhūtasya yathā syād dāritas tathā* line

---

[28] Cf. also Ram (Vulgate) 2.12.53 (= critical edition App. I no. 9:82) *tāṃ hi vajrasamāṃ vācam ākarṇya ...* (referring to Kaikeyī's speech).

[29] His city is compared to that of Indra already in line 174 (*tāṃ purīṃ dhanavatīm puruhūtapurīprabhām*).

748). Kṛṣṇa's act of reprisal with his discus has an effect on Jarāsaṃdha's army similar to that of the *vajra*: *cakrānalajvalahetoḥ ... petuḥ yathā vajrahatās tathā* (line 852). The last simile refers to King Sṛgāla who is struck down with the discus like a mountain (... *taṃ nipatitaṃ vajrapātād ivācalam* line 1026).

Hardly any comparison drawing upon Indra is found in App. 29, the elaborate story of Kṛṣṇa's theft of the Pārijāta tree from Indra's heaven (comprising 1685 lines). This is not surprising since Indra is one of the main actors who cannot very well be compared to himself. There is only one simile, describing the gods, who are like Indra (*devā deveśvaropamāḥ* in line 475), as paying homage to sages and ascetics devoted to Śiva.

One might expect the same infrequency of Indra similes in App. 42B (3070 lines), since Indra, as the leader of the gods in the battle against Bali and his army, is again involved in the story. This is, however, not a mere family quarrel, more or less restricted to two brothers, but a great battle involving many combatants on both sides; thus it is perhaps not surprising that there is not only a considerable number of similes referring to the *vajra/aśani*, but also to Indra himself. They illustrate the valour of both gods and Dānavas in turn; cf. *sarve divaukasaḥ ... śakrasya samavikramāḥ* (line 500) vs. *sahasrāṇi ... dānavānām ... śakrapratimatejasām* (line 1866). Bali's father Virocana is the best of Asuras as Indra the best of gods (*surāṇām iva vāsavaḥ* line 253); the Asuras follow Hayagrīva into battle as the gods follow Indra (*tridaśagaṇā iva vāsavaṃ prayāntam* line 197).

Indra's function of giving rain is drawn upon metaphorically, when "showers" of arrows are "poured down" on the enemy: on Niṣkumbha by the Daitya Vṛṣaparvan (*niṣkumbham ... mahendra iva dhārābhir śaravarṣair avākirat* line 1805), on the god Bhaga by Śambara (line 1237 *abhyavarṣac charair enaṃ parjanya iva vṛṣṭimān*). Taking a huge shape, Śambara fills the atmosphere with noise and the earth (presumably with water) like Indra (*varṣate vāsavo yathā* line 1254); here Śambara seems to be imagined as a kind of cloud demon.

Of Indra's great deeds in the past it is, as in the *Kṛṣṇacarita* section, only Indra's smashing the mountains that is taken up in comparisons. In the same way as Indra with his weapon (*vajra* or *aśani*) acted against the mountains, Māruta throws his spear against Bāṇa (*śaktiṃ... cikṣepa baliputrāya śakro 'sanim ivādraye* line 915); similarly Tvaṣṭṛ at Maya (*śaktim... daityendre saṃnyayātanat ... puraṃdara ivāśanim* line 1043), whereas the Dānava Maya strikes Tvaṣṭṛ with his club (*gadayā ... vajreṇendra ivācalān* line 1059);[30] the gods have to watch how their elephants are struck down like the mountains by Kujambha's club (ll. 1425-1430): *vajrahatā ivendreṇa viśīrṇā iva parvatāḥ* (line 1430).

Indra's *vajra* or *aśani*, with which he split or struck down the mountains, is also several times referred to in compounds. The Daityas themselves are *mahendravajratulyavegāḥ* line 103; Bali's bows (*dhanūṃṣi*) are *vajrāyudha-saprabhāṇi* line 433; the heroes on both sides fight each other with *vajra*-like arms and fists (*bāhubhir muṣṭibhiś caiva vajrakalpaiḥ ... praharanti vīrāḥ parasparam* line 1500 f.). From these similes one cannot get a clear idea what the *vajra* is actually like, and the same is true for the *aśani*: *indrāśani-samaspṛśa-* qualifies arrows in line 1614 (*indrāśani-samaspṛśair vegavadbhir ajihmagaiḥ*), and in line 1974 (*vajrāśani-samasparśair bāṇaiḥ*), whereas in line 1182 it is Pūṣan's bow that is compared to the bolt (*śakrāśanim ivāparam*). In one instance, they are even compared with each other: *vajrair aśanikalpaiḥ* line 907. Thus, as in the other similes, there seems to be no real distinction between the *vajra* (originally a club, presumably made of wood, with spikes) and the stone-like thunderbolt called *aśani*. Both are used in similes involving a club (of the demons Maya, Kujambha, and Bāṇa), swift or pointed arrows, and a bow (Pūṣan,

---

[30] The great club of the Dānava Bala is compared to Indra's bolt (*mahāgadā ... indrāśanir ivendreṇa* ll. 954 f.). His fight with Dhruva is compared to that between the *vajra* and the mountain in line 977 (*vajraparvatayor iva*).

Bali);[31] apart from that, the *aśani* appears twice in connection with spears (Vāyu, Tvaṣṭṛ), and the *vajra* (once) in connection with arms (*bāhu*).[32]

3. VIṢṆU/KṚṢṆA AS INDRA'S YOUNGER BROTHER

In the Vedic period Viṣṇu actually appears, not as Indra's younger brother, but as his friend and ally (*sákhi-*, e.g. ṚV 1.22.19, 4.18.11, etc.), who assists him in the fight with Vṛtra (cf. also ŚB. 5.5.5.1 ff., JB 2.242 f., and PB 20.15.6); in the ṚV the two names are not infrequently joined together in the *dvandva* compound *indrāviṣṇū* (ṚV 4.2.4 etc.). This *dvandva* compound can also be found in the epics,[33] where it may be considered as formulaic; similar ones are modelled after it, like *śakraviṣṇū* (three times), *vāsavācyutau* (once), and *indropendrau* (twice). Nearly all of these *dvandvas* are found in similes.[34]

The name Upendra for Viṣṇu is not attested before the epics; it occurs on its own in the Mbh, *Āraṇyakaparvan* App. 1, no.1:13, where the gods are qualified as *sopendrāḥ samahendrāś ca* (in Yudhiṣṭhira's hymn to the sun-god) and in 8.51.31, where the residence of the Yādavas, protected by Upendra (here clearly Kṛṣṇa), is compared to the three heavens protected by Indra. Most of the other occurrences of Upendra, however, are found in similes: thus the twin brothers Nakula and Sahadeva are compared to Indra and Upendra in 6.79.55, likewise Kṛṣṇa and Sātyaki, who are just friends, in 9.33.14; Arjuna's son (and thus Indra's grandson, so to speak) Abhimanyu is compared to Upendra twice (6.108.38 and 7.50.23). Rudra, Upendra, and Indra (in this sequence) together

[31] The common quality may be the sound, cf. line 1235: *śrūyate dhanuṣaḥ śabdo visphūrjitam ivāśaneḥ*.

[32] Whether this is like a resonance of the old Vedic epithet *vajrabāhu*, qualifying Indra, is open to speculation.

[33] Cf. Brockington 2001: 71.

[34] Exceptions: *indrāviṣṇū* 9.44.4, in a list of gods participating in Agni's consecration, and *śakraviṣṇū* 2.22.16: Kṛṣṇa uses the same chariot as Indra and Viṣṇu in the battle with Tāraka.

serve as standard of comparison for Aśvatthāman (7.31.46), Karṇa (7.150.46), and (without Indra) for Bhīṣma (8.51.31). In these similes Upendra certainly refers to (Vedic) Viṣṇu, not to Kṛṣṇa, one of the actors in the story. In the Ram Upendra is found only twice: Ram 1.49* (*upendrasamaś ca kaḥ*) and in 6.105.15 (in Brahmā's eulogy of Rāma, identifying Rāma with Viṣṇu/Kṛṣṇa as highest deity): ... *tvam upendro madhusūdanaḥ*[35]. In the second instance *upendra*, followed by *madhusūdana*, refers most likely to Kṛṣṇa,[36] not to Viṣṇu (if the two can be separated at all at later stages).

The meaning 'Indra's younger brother' of *upendra* is suggested mainly by synonyms like *indrāvaraja* (Mbh), *vāsavānuja* (HV), *indrānuja* (HV, Ram), etc.; in the Ram the relationship between Rāma and Lakṣmaṇa is often compared to that between Indra and Viṣṇu. The concept of Indra and Viṣṇu as brothers presumably goes back to the development of the list of Ādityas, in which Viṣṇu was not included before the epics. Indra, also originally not belonging to this group,[37] is identified as seventh son of Aditi[38] in Brāhmaṇa texts, e.g. MS 1.6.12[39] as well as in a list in TĀ 1.13.3 (quoted by Sāyaṇa on ṚV 2.27.1).

In the HV the specific family relationship between Indra and Viṣṇu/Kṛṣṇa seems to be expressed more frequently than in the epics: in epithets like *vāsavānuja* (HV 79.21, 91.32, 92.35, 92.70; App. 29:1500; App.42 B:14), *puruhūtānuja* (App. 18, 51*), *indrānuja* (App. 29:25, 510, 804, 841), *puraṃdarānuja* (App. 29:1573), and *indrād avaraja-* (32.5), beside *upendra-*, which seems to be especially frequent in App. 29 (HV 62.56 f., 64.23, 67.3, 79.37;

[35] The whole *śloka* (Ram 6.105.15cd-16ab) runs as follows:
prabhavaś ca apyayaś ca tvam upendro madhusūdanaḥ |
indrakarmā mahendras tvaṃ padmanābho raṇāntakṛt |

[36] In the previous *śloka*, Viṣṇu and Kṛṣṇa are listed separately (*ajitaḥ khaḍgadhṛg viṣṇuḥ kṛṣṇaś caiva bṛhad-balaḥ*). The name Kṛṣṇa does not seem to appear anywhere else in the Ram (critical edition).

[37] He is addressed as Āditya once in the ṚV, in a Vālakhilya hymn (8.52[4].7)

[38] Aditi is said to have given birth to eight sons in ṚV 10.72.8-9; their names are, however, not listed (except for Mārtāṇḍa, the last of them).

[39] Cf. Hoffmann 1957.

App. 18, 61*; App. 29:620, 634, 767, 797, 1018, 1083, 1383, 1448). It is provided with a new explanation in 62.44 (see below). Except for 32.5 and App. I no. 42B, these epithets refer now to Kṛṣṇa, who is, strictly speaking, a brother of Baladeva, not of Indra. In large sections of the HV, however, Kṛṣṇa is now conceived as Viṣṇu's earthly form, usurping all of Viṣṇu's names and epithets, including *upendra*, etc.

Viṣṇu being the later born, younger brother of Indra seems, however, to have presented a problem for at least one of the composers of the HV. This is clearly expressed in Janamejaya's question at the beginning of App. 42B (line 14): *sraṣṭā yo vāsavasyāpi sa kathaṃ vāsavānujah?*[40] which is preceded by another question (line 13): *adityā devamātuś ca kathaṃ garbhe 'bhavat prabhuḥ?* In his reply, Vaiśaṃpāyana first gives a list of Ādityas (discussed above), confirming Viṣṇu's birth as the youngest of the Ādityas, he then tells the elaborate story of Viṣṇu's dwarf incarnation, which provides an answer to both questions (see below).

An especially cunning way to correct Viṣṇu's inferior status as younger brother of Indra, his *upendratva*, would be to interpret the compound *upendra* in a different way, not as a *tatpuruṣa* compound (like 'subcommentary', 'subsection', etc.),[41] but as a *bahuvrīhi* with a preverb as first member,[42] meaning 'above Indra'.[43]

---

[40] This question may be associated with a statement about Nārāyaṇa (identified with Hari) in HV 32.5: *aditer api putratvaṃ etya yādavanandanaḥ* | *eṣa viṣṇur iti khyāta indrād avarajo 'bhavat.*

[41] Cf. *upa* in Wackernagel & Debrunner 1957, § 102 ("Präverbiales Vorderglied in Tatpuruṣas"), e.g. *upākhyāna* (*upendra* is not mentioned). One may add *upapurāṇa* beside *purāṇa*, the metre *upendravajra* beside *indravajra*, etc.

[42] Similar *bahuvrīhis*, with a preposition governing the second member, are e.g., *údanta-* ('den oberen Rand erreichend'), *ánuśiśu-*, *víloman-*, etc. (cf. Wackernagel & Debrunner 1957, § 110); they belong rather to the older language (but note *atyāditya-* 'beyond the sun' in *Meghadūta* 1.46). Even as a *bahuvrīhi* it might in the first place be understood to mean 'below Indra', cf. P. 1.4.86: *hīne*.

[43] Paraphrase according to P. 1.4.87: *upo 'dhike ca* '*upa* (with loc., see P. 2.3.9) also in the meaning of "above, supra".' In HV 62.44, *upa* is glossed as *upari* (with gen.).

One can indeed find a similar interpretation in the HV, put into the mouth of Indra himself, in his eulogy of Kṛṣṇa in ch. 62, after Kṛṣṇa had propped up the Govardhana mountain in order to protect the cows from Indra's torrents and thunderstorms. In his speech, Indra outlines the different layers of the worlds, the highest being Goloka with Kṛṣṇa as its overlord, gives an explanation of *govinda* (*tvaṃ gavām indratāṃ gataḥ* 62.43) and then explains in stanza 44:

> *mamopari yathendras tvam sthāpito gobhir īśvaraḥ* |
> *upendra iti kṛṣṇa tvāṃ gāsyanti divi devatāḥ* || 44 ||
>
> Since you have been established by the cows as their sovereign, the Indra above myself, the gods in heaven will sing your praises, Kṛṣṇa, calling you "Upendra" ("above Indra"). (HV 62.44)

This interpretation does not seem to have been successful in the later Indian tradition (it is not even listed in Sanskrit dictionaries, but constitutes a real basis for Pāṇini's *sūtra* 1.4.87, as opposed to the examples invented by the *Kāśikā*).[44] The idea of Viṣṇu as Indra's younger brother must have become so strongly rooted that it ruled out the alternative explanation of the compound.

To sum up: In the Mbh *upendra* appears as epithet of Viṣṇu, used mainly in similes, often grouped with other Vedic deities like Indra or Rudra; there is one instance where it refers to Kṛṣṇa, who is then compared with Indra. In the Ram the relationship between Indra and Viṣṇu serves to illustrate the relationship between Rāma and Lakṣmaṇa, but *upendra* is not used in this context. In the HV *upendra* occurs most frequently in the *Kṛṣṇacarita*, where it refers always to Kṛṣṇa. It is usually taken to mean 'Indra's younger brother', 'little Indra', and this relationship is especially drawn upon and discussed in App. I no. 29. At the end of the Govardhana myth Indra himself provides it with a new explanation ('above Indra'). It does not appear at all in the PPL section, and in the

---

[44] It can actually be found as an alternative in Ganguli's translation of Mbh 13.135.30, following Śaṅkara's commentary on the *Viṣṇusahasranāmastotra* (referred to by Nīlakaṇṭha): "He that is the younger brother of Indra (or He that transcends Indra in accomplishments and attributes)."

Prādurbhāva section (App. I no. 42B) it qualifies Viṣṇu, born (later than the other gods) from Aditi as a dwarf,[45] in order to help the gods against Bali.

4. INDRA AS PROTAGONIST IN NARRATIVES

Looking at stories with Indra as an active figure, one can find a characteristic difference between the narratives within the Kṛṣṇa cycle or the sections on Viṣṇu's *prādurbhāva*s and narratives that are outside these cycles, such as the PPL section and the frame story.

a. PPL (ch. 1-29) and *Bhaviṣyaparvan* (ch. 114-118)

The PPL section contains three comparatively short accounts in which Indra plays a role. One is the story of how Indra (as Vajrapāṇi) enters Diti's womb, in order to cut the Maruts to pieces, invented to explain the name of the Maruts.[46] Another is the story of Indra's birth as Kuśika's son Gādhi, explaining Indra's epithet Kauśika as Kuśika's son, which has been discussed above. The motif of Indra taking his birth as son of a valiant king appears again in the third Indra story in the PPL section, the story of King Raji (HV 21.11-27), a grandson of Purūravas:[47]

In one of the battles between gods and Asuras Brahmā announces that the party on whose side King Raji fights will win. Both groups try to win Raji for themselves,[48] but since the Asuras

[45] This connection is also found in Mbh 13.135.30, where Upendra is followed immediately by Vāmana and contrasted with Atīndra in the next line.

[46] This myth, which is told in greater detail in Ram 1.44.14–46.9, but is not found in the Mbh (cf. Sørensen 1904-25), seems to belong to the purāṇic tradition.

[47] He appears also in the Mbh (1.70.23), but no story is told about him.

[48] Similar stories can be found in the Brāhmaṇas: in *Aitareyabrāhmaṇa* 3.39.1 the gods try to secure Agni's help in the battle against the Asuras, and Agni agrees under the condition that he is praised (*stuta*). The gods comply, and Agni helps them with three battle lines in the form of the three Vedic metres (*gāyatrī, triṣṭubh, jagatī*). – In *Śatapathabrāhmaṇa* 1.4.1.34 each of the two parties want to secure the *gāyatrī* (identified with the earth: *iyaṃ vai sā pṛthivī*) as guarantee

refuse to let Raji become their "Indra", whereas the gods offer this position to him, he decides to fight on the gods' side and wins Śrī from the Asuras. By means of a trick Indra becomes Raji's son and eventually regains his position as "Indra".

There is one more appearance of Indra in a story without any connection with Viṣṇu/Kṛṣṇa, viz. in the frame story told by the Sūta to Śaunaka at the end of the HV (critical edition ch. 118), after Vaiśampāyana has completed his story of Mbh + HV. When Janamejaya performed a horse sacrifice, Indra, desiring Janamejaya's queen, defiled it by entering the body of the horse, with whom she has to lie together according to the rules of the sacrifice. The *adhvaryu* at the sacrifice, becoming aware of this, tells Janamejaya about it. Thereupon Janamejaya curses Indra never again to be worshipped with a horse sacrifice, and banishes his wife as well as the sacrificial priests involved in the procedure. But then the Gandharva Viśvāvasu points out to him that Indra, being afraid of him, did not want the horse sacrifice to be completed, and that it was unjust of Janamejaya to banish his innocent wife and the officiating priests, since it was not their fault. The king then acts according to Viśvāvasu's advice and lives with his wife happily ever after.

In this story we actually get the only one explicit reference to Indra as a womaniser in the HV, a motif found in allusions to the Ahalyā story[49] and in the story of Cirakārin in the *Śāntiparvan* of the Mbh.[50] The motif of Indra preventing the completion of a horse sacrifice, out of the fear that the sacrificer might surpass him in the number of sacrifices (*śatakratu* in the later meaning of 'having performed 100 sacrifices'), has parallels in the *Rāmāyaṇa* (*Bāla-*

---

of victory for themselves. They both send a secret messenger to invite her, but she follows Agni, the messenger of the gods, and the gods are victorious.

[49] Cf. Söhnen-Thieme 1996.

[50] There is an allusion to Indra's attachment to another brahmin's wife in App. 29:872 f., but his intentions seem to have not been successful and only incurred a 'mental curse' (*apadhyāna*), which Kaśyapa feels obliged to appease (see below p. 362).

kāṇḍa) version of the Śunaḥśepa story, in several versions of the Gaṅgāvataraṇa myth, and in Kālidāsa's *Raghuvaṃśa* (ch. 3), where Raghu fights with Indra about the horse needed for the completion of his father Dilīpa's sacrifice. Obviously both motifs have been amalgamated in the final ḤV story.

To sum up: in the sections that are not connected with Kṛṣṇa, Indra is seen in a quite negative light. He can maintain his supremacy only by tricky devices; his actions are dubious (in PPL) or even sinful (in the frame story). Thus the development that can already be traced in stories indebted to brahmanic lore in later parts of the Mbh is further continued.

b. *Kṛṣṇacarita* (including App. I no. 29)

Turning to the *Kṛṣṇacarita* section, which forms the greatest part of the HV, we find two longer stories, telling of the confrontation of the older god Indra with the new supreme god Kṛṣṇa. In the first story[51] the Indra festival is replaced by a festival in honour of the Govardhana mountain, and Indra's revenge in the form of torrents of rain cannot achieve anything, because Kṛṣṇa uses the mountain as an umbrella for cows and herdsmen (this is mentioned already in the Mbh 5.128.45: *govardhano dhāritaś ca gavārthe*). Indra has to submit and to accept that Kṛṣṇa is 'above Indra' (see p. 356 above).

The other story is that of the Pārijāta tree stolen from Indra's heaven by Kṛṣṇa, in order to please his wife Satyabhāmā, and the ensuing battle between Indra, who wants to retrieve his property, and Kṛṣṇa, who predictably proves to be superior to Indra.[52]

[51] Different versions of this story are analysed in Gangoly 1949.

[52] This conflict is also mentioned in a list of Kṛṣṇa's victories over various enemies in ch. 105 of the HV (starting with two Dānavas):

vāsavaṃ ca raṇo jitvā pārijāto hṛto balāt |
nirjitaś caiva bhagavān varuṇo lohitahrade || 10 ||

The Vedic gods are then followed by Śiśupāla (11), Bali's son Bāṇa (12), Pāvaka, Sālva, Saubha (13), Hayagrīva (14), Jarāsaṃdha (15), and the Khāṇḍava forest (16). This sequence seems odd, since in the Mbh the killing of Śiśupāla occurs later than the burning of the Khāṇḍava forest, and Jarāsaṃdha is killed by Bhīma.

This story, which has also become very famous and has been retold in various Purāṇas, is actually not included in the text of the critical edition, but relegated to App. 29. In the critical edition, the chapter preceding App. 29 tells of Kṛṣṇa killing the demon Naraka, from whose treasury Aditi's earrings are obtained, and Kṛṣṇa's visit to Indra's heaven to restore them to Aditi. At the end of his visit Kṛṣṇa accidentally sees the Pārijāta tree in Indra's abode; he uproots it and places it on Garuḍa, before returning home to Dvāravatī (HV 92.65; accidentally or perhaps deliberately not translated by Bose):

saṃrakṣyamāṇaṃ devais taṃ prasahyāmitavikramaḥ |
utpāṭyāropayām āsa viṣṇus taṃ vai mahādrumam || 65 ||
(v.l. *taṃ garuḍopari*)
... *tataḥ prāyād dvāravatīm* ... || 66 ||

Indra seems to agree:

śrutvā tad devarājas tu karma kṛṣṇasya vai tadā |
anumene mahābāhuḥ kṛtaṃ karmeti cābravīt || 67 ||

There is no conflict; chapter 93 describes Kṛṣṇa at Dvāravatī, the tree is not mentioned any more. Like the Govardhana episode, Kṛṣṇa's theft of the Pārijāta tree is already known in the Mbh, it is alluded to in 7.10.22 f.:

vainateyaṃ samāruhya trāsayitvāmarāvatīm |
mahendrabhavanād vīraḥ pārijātam upānayat || 22 ||
tac ca marṣitavāñ chakro jānaṃs tasya parākramam |

which seems to be roughly in agreement with the account quoted from the HV (critical edition), and in 5.128.48: *pārijātaṃ ca haratā jitaḥ sākṣāc chacīpatiḥ*, which somehow suggests a conflict in which Indra is actually defeated. This conflict is perhaps first fully narrated in part 5 of the *Viṣṇupurāṇa*,[53] but must at some point have

[53] ViP 5.30.30–31.13 [= BrP (ASS) 203.26–204.13]. When Kṛṣṇa and Satyabhāmā see the Pārijāta tree in Indra's pleasure grove, Satyabhāmā asks for it,

been felt to be lacking in the HV by the transmitters. Thus App. I no. 29,[54] which supplies the missing conflict, was added after ch. 92, ignoring stanza 92.65 in which the theft had already been told. The story, which here in the HV starts with an elaborate prehistory of the theft and includes long speeches by the go-between Nārada and the two brothers Indra and Kṛṣṇa, runs as follows:

> After Kṛṣṇa's return to Dvārakā, Nārada pays him a visit, during which he gives him a flower from the Pārijāta tree, which Kṛṣṇa passes on to Rukmiṇī. Hearing about it, Satyabhāmā is extremely offended and announces that, neglected by Kṛṣṇa like this, she will commit suicide. Kṛṣṇa promises her to fetch the whole tree from Heaven. He sends Nārada to Indra with the message that he should allow the Pārijāta tree to be taken to Dvārakā. Indra refuses, giving several good reasons. Nārada replies that he had already pointed out these arguments to Kṛṣṇa, but Kṛṣṇa had insisted on his wish as Indra's younger brother who has to be indulged (*upendro 'ham mahendreṇa lālanīyaḥ sadā* line 622) and had threatened to hurl his club on Indra's chest, if Indra did not comply with his wish. Now Indra recollects how often he has tolerated Kṛṣṇa's acting unfavourably towards him, whereas he has treated his younger brother affectionately. He sends Nārada back with the message that being challenged he will not withdraw (*āhūto na nivarteyam* line 699); he will not strike first, but he will not give the tree to Kṛṣṇa, unless he is defeated. Nārada warns Indra that his younger brother is in reality the Lord of the world and must not be contradicted, but Indra remains firm and insists that Kṛṣṇa should respect the decision of his elder brother, even more so if he is the highest Lord. Nārada returns to Kṛṣṇa and reports Indra's refusal. Kṛṣṇa is not surprised and sends Nārada back with a declaration of war. Now Indra asks Bṛhaspati's advice, Bṛhaspati seems to disapprove of any vio-

---

reminding Kṛṣṇa of his declarations of love for her. Kṛṣṇa places it on Garuḍa. The guards warn Kṛṣṇa that this tree belongs to Śacī, Indra's wife, but Satyabhāmā rebukes them. They inform Śacī, who incites Indra to fight against Kṛṣṇa; in the ensuing battle Indra and the gods are disarmed. Satyabhāmā teases him, but Indra replies that it is not dishonourable to be defeated by Kṛṣṇa. When Kṛṣṇa apologises and offers to restore the tree to its proper place, Indra grants him to have it in Dvārakā as long as he stays on earth.

[54] It is not found in the oldest and most reliable mss Ś1 and M1-3 (cf. HV, critical edition, p. xxxi) and appears at the end, after App. I 42 B, in two Newari mss (only one of which was used by the critical edition; cf. Brinkhaus 2002: 171 and 173), which shows that it was added later to these mss; in the Vulgate it is found after ch. 92, similarly in the younger mss used by the critical edition (cf. also Schmid 1997: 247, fn. 2).

lence, but nevertheless tells Indra to fight; he then withdraws to the ocean and tells Kaśyapa (husband of Aditi and father of the gods, including Indra and Viṣṇu) about it. Kaśyapa becomes angry and tells Bṛhaspati that he is staying in the ocean in order to appease the mental curse (*apadhyāna*) of the brahmin Devaśarman, whose wife Indra had once desired. Then Kaśyapa sets out to worship Śiva. Pleased with Kaśyapa's long hymn, Śiva shows himself and tells him that Kṛṣṇa will take the tree to Dvārakā. Meanwhile Kṛṣṇa sets out for Indra's pleasure grove, together with his son Pradyumna and his friend Sātyaki. He extracts the tree and places it on Garuḍa; Indra, informed by the guards, arrives on his elephant Airāvata, accompanied by his son Jayanta with a chariot, in order to retrieve the tree. In the ensuing battle Pradyumna fights with Jayanta, Sātyaki fights with Indra's friend Pravara, Airāvata fights with Garuḍa; when Indra and Kṛṣṇa fight with each other, Indra's elephant is seriously wounded and sinks down on the Pāriyātra mountain. They settle for a break, during which Kṛṣṇa worships Śiva with a hymn; Śiva endorses Kṛṣṇa's victory. Then the battle is taken up again, with the gods and celestial sages as spectators. In the end Indra's and Kṛṣṇa's parents intervene, and the two brothers agree to their mother Aditi's wish that the tree should be given to Kṛṣṇa for one year, after which it should return to Heaven.

There are several changes in the story, as compared with the ViP/BrP version: Nārada is introduced as a protagonist (he also gives some detailed information about the Pārijāta tree which link it with Śiva); Satyabhāmā's wish for the Pārijāta tree is motivated by jealousy; the fight is preceded by long discussions between Kṛṣṇa's messenger Nārada and Indra, in which the relationship between Indra and Kṛṣṇa is a prominent topic; the conflict appears to by a family feud between the two brothers (the gods are not involved, except as spectators);[55] the argument is eventually settled by a de-

---

[55] The only reference to them as Indra's troops is in line 1376 (Kṛṣṇa challenging Indra): *mahendram āhvayām āsa* ... | *satkṛtaṃ puṣkarābhyāśe sarvair devagaṇaiḥ saha* (where *satkṛtaṃ* is presumably an inferior reading for *saṃsthitaṃ* V2.3 B1.3 D5.6, supported by Ñ1 *saṃskṛtaṃ* and Ñ2 *saṃsthitaḥ*). In 1382 f. the troops are defeated without having attacked Kṛṣṇa: *tato 'hanad raṇe viṣṇur bāṇaiḥ* ... | *sainyāni devarājasya* ... (evidently they play only a passive or decorative role); likewise Indra showers arrows on (Kṛṣṇa's) troops in ll. 1388 f. *sainyāny api ca devendraḥ śarair* ... *chādayām āsa* ...; thus C. Schmid's statement (1997: 250) "Il s'agit ... également des troupes de dieu qui, honorant Indra, combattent à ses côtés face à un Kṛṣṇa qui est évidemment sans armée", with which she wants to support the opposition between Indra's emphasis on authority

cision of the brothers' parents, who bring about a reconciliation.[56] The outcome of the conflict between Indra and Kṛṣṇa is predicted and confirmed by Śiva, who is addressed with hymns by Kaśyapa as well as Kṛṣṇa: this is clearly an innovation influenced by Śaiva tendencies.[57]

Quite striking in this episode is the multi-faceted relationship between Indra and his "younger brother", especially since the new deity appears on three layers:[58] as Viṣṇu the origin and creator of the universe including the gods and their king Indra;[59] as a son of Aditi and Kaśyapa and thus Indra's younger brother;[60] and as the son of Devakī and Vasudeva, where no special relationship with Indra can be implied.[61] Thus

Nārāyaṇa, the highest god and origin of the cosmos
is reborn as

Viṣṇu, son of Kaśyapa and Aditi, the youngest of the Ādityas,[62]	Kṛṣṇa Vāsudeva, son of Devakī, a human Superman.

(embodied in his army) vs. Kṛṣṇa's relying only on the friendship of his helpers, does not agree with the evidence of the text. Both sides of combatants are rather strikingly symmetrical.

[56] There is no dialogue between Satyabhāmā and Indra, and Kṛṣṇa does not apologise; the stay of the tree in Dvārakā is however limited for one year only.

[57] Cf. Schreiner 2005: 333 f., 343 f.

[58] I am, of course, aware of the fact that there is no strict distinction between these three layers; Kṛṣṇa and Viṣṇu are much more conceived as one identical person than, e.g., the previous human *avatāra* Rāma and Viṣṇu.

[59] Thus in Nārada's speech instructing Indra about Kṛṣṇa's true identity: *nārāyaṇo mahātejāḥ sarvakṛl lokabhāvanaḥ ... brahmā devagaṇāś cānye paścāt sṛṣṭā mahātmanā* ... (ll. 754, 756).

[60] *sa jātaḥ sarvakṛd devo bhrātā tava sureśvara | nārāyaṇo mahātejā yam upendraṃ pracakṣate | icchann eva harir devaḥ kāśyapatvam upāgataḥ* (Nārada's speech ll. 766 ff.)

[61] *hitāya jagato 'dyāpi loke vasati mānuṣe | upendro jagato nāthaḥ* ... (Nārada's speech ll. 796 f., after a survey of Viṣṇu's other *avatāra*s).

[62] Apart from the continuous reference to Kṛṣṇa as Indra's younger brother, this layer is manifest in the description of how Indra and Kṛṣṇa pay their respect to their mother Aditi.

As a human, Kṛṣṇa may of course worship any deity as his *iṣṭa-devatā*; in App. 29 it happens to be Śiva. In this way Śiva may appear to be superior to Kṛṣṇa, but not necessarily to Viṣṇu (with whom he is identified in Nārada's speech anyway); so there is no problem of superiority in this layer. Kṛṣṇa even promises to help Śiva against the demons in Ṣaṭpura (this story will be told in App. I no. 29B). The problem of Indra's relationship with Kṛṣṇa, however, is that Indra has to respond to all three layers at once – at least this is what Nārada conveys to him. Indra has only the choice to submit totally to this three-layered Viṣṇu/Kṛṣṇa and worship him or to try to keep his own ground against all odds. Indra chooses to fight for what he thinks is his right; and he does not fail totally, although he has to give up the tree temporarily. Evidently even the narrator of this passage, who depicts the relationship between the combatants in a much less favourable light than the narrator in the ViP (BrP), does not take the risk of having Indra completely defeated.

c. *Prādurbhāva* section (App. I no. 42B)

Quite different from the *Kṛṣṇacarita* episodes concerned with Indra are those connected with the *Prādurbhāva* section,[63] as for instance Viṣṇu's Vāmana-*avatāra* in App. 42B.[64] Here there is no antagonism between Indra and Kṛṣṇa, the conflict is between the gods and the Asuras, who have become strong under their ruler Bali and need to be defeated. Not surprisingly it turns out that only Viṣṇu can control Bali in the end. Battle scenes abound, mostly one god against one demon, who then turns out to be victorious; the god has to retreat and seek shelter with Indra. When Indra eventually enters the battle himself, he is not really defeated; a heavenly voice ad-

[63] App. 42-42B are missing only in Ś1; this section must have belonged to the HV already in a comparatively early period (cf. Brinkhaus 2002, who is doubtful about Vaidya's decision to exclude these appendixes from the text of the critical edition).

[64] The development of this myth in the Vedic texts and in the Mbh is presented in Tripathi 1968, who also investigates this HV version, but from a different aspect. (His hypotheses require revision in the light of the critical edition.)

vises him to withdraw, since his enemy Bali is invincible due to a boon granted to him by Brahmā.

The only way to defeat Bali is that Viṣṇu should take his birth as a Dwarf in Aditi's womb and win over Bali by means of a trick. Since in that way Viṣṇu is born from Aditi later than Indra and the other Ādityas,[65] the name Vāsavānuja is justified.

App. 42B shows some interesting features in the description of Indra. As opposed to the *Kṛṣṇacarita* and the appendix passages related to it, where Indra mounts his elephant Airāvata, he is equipped in App. 42B with his chariot (*śakraratha* appears in ll. 935, 1201*65, 1529*96), drawn by bay horses (as in the ṚV): *ratham harihayair yuktvā sa prāyāt samaraṃ prati* (line 505);[66] his horses are referred to in line 559: *te devarājasya puraṃdarasya hayāḥ*, and in the comparison in line 625: *hayair varaiḥ śakrahayapratikāśaiḥ ... yuktān rathān āruruhuḥ surāḥ*. The epithet *harivāhana-* (ll. 2404 and 2420) has been already mentioned before, likewise the epithet *hariśmaśru* (in line 505, where he is also called *harinetra*, and in line 2381, where he is also called *harikeśa*).

Whether these features can be taken as an indication that these passages are comparatively early is, however, difficult to establish; one has to take into consideration that episodes referring to battles between gods and Asuras in the pre-epic, prehistoric Vedic times may have suggested the use of Vedic (or pseudo-Vedic) allusions, without being very early.

To sum up: there are actually not many stories about Indra in the HV; Indra's fight with Vṛtra, which appears in three versions in the Mbh, is only referred to in a simile (drawing on the Vedic myth, not on the Mbh stories). Apart from the PPL section, the new

---

65 This would suggest that Viṣṇu had not been born from Aditi, before the gods were confronted with Bali, and that the myth presupposes an older list of Ādityas, which did not yet include Viṣṇu.

66 In App. 18 Indra's chariot, drawn by bay horses and equated to a rock, appears in a simile illustrating the marvellous chariot of King Sṛgāla (*khe gateneva śakrasya haryaśvena rathādriṇā* line 975), who belongs to the hostile camp and is killed by Kṛṣṇa at the end of App. 18.

stories in the HV are more interested in the relationship between the Vedic main god in confrontation with the newly celebrated hero and god Kṛṣṇa. Their antagonism is first expressed in the Govardhana myth, which clearly settles the question of supremacy: the traditionally worshipped agricultural deity is defeated by the new pastoral deity Kṛṣṇa, whose identity with Viṣṇu is not yet emphasised. The equally popular story of Kṛṣṇa's theft of the Pārijāta tree, told in App. I no. 29, teaches Indra that Kṛṣṇa is licensed to do anything he likes, being now fully identified with the highest deity. The story of Indra's fight with Bali (App. I no. 42B), which is not found in the Mbh, celebrates Viṣṇu in his dwarf incarnation; there is no confrontation between Indra and Viṣṇu, which reflects the relationship as found in Vedic texts.

The only story of Indra (apart from an faint allusion in App. I no. 29) as an adulterer is found at the end of the HV, in the *Bhaviṣyaparvan* section, which deals with events beyond the account as given by Vaiśampāyana; it may indicate the tendency which Indra stories will take in future.

CONCLUSION

Although many details have still to be investigated more thoroughly, some observations may be formulated as preliminary results. Looking at the traditional Vedic main god, one has, of course, to distinguish between short references (allusions, formulaic expressions, or similes referring to Indra), which generally represent the ideas of an earlier stage than that of the composition of the text, and the evidence of more detailed narratives, which are most likely to reflect new developments (even if they are elaborating on allusions found already in the epic). Names and epithets occurring in these narratives abound in variations upon the older inherited ones, as is evident especially in the similes used in the *Kṛṣṇacarita* section, whereas App. I no. 29 elaborates on epithets glorifying Indra's greatness as king of the gods, quite out of keeping with the story it has to tell.

REFERENCES

Texts and Translations

Das Aitareya Brāhmaṇa (1879). Ed. by Th. Aufrecht. Bonn: Adolph Marcus.

The Aitareya Brahmanam of the Rigveda (1922). Ed., trans. and explained by M. Haug. Allahabad: S. N. Vasu, Panini Office.

Atharva Veda Sanhita (1924). Ed. by R. Roth & W. D. Whitney. 2nd edition by M. Lindenau. Berlin: F. Dümmler.

Atharva-veda Saṃhitā (1903-05). 2 vols. Trans. with a critical and exegetical commentary by W. D. Whitney, rev. ed. by C. R. Lanman. Cambridge, Mass.: Harvard University Press.

Sanskrit Indices and Text of the Brahmapurāṇa (1987). By P. Schreiner & R. Söhnen. Wiesbaden: Harrassowitz.

Brahmapurāṇa. Summary of Contents, with Index of Names and Motifs (1989). By R. Söhnen & P. Schreiner. Wiesbaden: Harrassowitz.

The Harivaṃśa, being the khila or supplement to the Mahābhārata (1969-71). 2 vols. Critically ed. by P. L. Vaidya. Poona: BORI.

Harivamsha (1940) [1944?]. Trans. into Engl. prose by D. H. Bose. DumDum (Bengal).

Das Jaiminīya-Brāhmaṇa in Auswahl (1919). Text, Übersetzung, Indices. By W. Caland. Amsterdam: J. Müller. (Reprint: Wiesbaden: M. Sändig, 1970.)

The Mahābhārata (1927-66). For the first time critically edited by V. S. Sukthankar, F. D. Edgerton etc. 22 vols. Poona: BORI.

The Mahabharata of Krishna-Dwaipayana Vyasa (1981). Trans. by Kisari Mohan Ganguli. [First publ. 1883-96.] 4th edition. New Delhi: Munshiram Manoharlal.

Pāṇini's Grammatik (1887). Ed. by O. Böhtlingk. Leipzig: Verlag von H. Haessel. (Reprint: Hildesheim: G. Olms, 1970.)

The Vālmīki-Rāmāyaṇa (1960-68). Critically ed. by G. H. Bhatt [etc.]. 7 vols. Baroda: Oriental Institute.

Die Hymnen des Rigveda (1861-63). 2 vols. Ed. by Th. Aufrecht. Berlin: Dümmler. (Reprint: Hildesheim: G. Olms, 1973.)

[*Śatapatha-Brāhmaṇa*:] *The çatapatha-brāhmaṇa in the Mādhyandina-çākhā with extracts from the commentaries of Sāyaṇa, Harisvāmin and Dvivedagaṅga* (1855). Ed. by A. Weber. Berlin: Dümmler. (Reprint: Varanasi: Chowkhamba Sanskrit Series Office, 1964.)

The Śatapathabrāhmaṇa, according to the text of the Mādhyandina School (1882-1900). 5 vols. Trans. by J. Eggeling. Oxford: Clarendon Press. (Reprint: Delhi: MLBD, 1972.)

Taittirīyasaṃhitā (1871-72). 2 vols. Ed. by A. Weber. Leipzig (Indische Studien, 11-12). (Reprint: Hildesheim: G. Olms, 1973.)

Śrī Viṣṇupurāṇa (1933). With Hindi trans. by Śrī Munilāl Gupta. Gorakhpur: Gītāpress, V.S. 1990.

Secondary Literature

BRINKHAUS, H. 2002. The division into Parvans and the Bhaviṣyaparvan of the Harivaṃśa. In: M. Brockington (ed.), *Stages and Transitions: Temporal and Historical Frameworks in Epic and Purāṇic Literature. Proceedings of the Second DICSEP August 1999*: 157-175. Zagreb: Croatian Academy of Sciences and Art.

BROCKINGTON, J. 2001. Indra in the Epics. In: K. Karttunen & P. Koskikallio (eds.), *Vidyārṇavavandanam: Essays in Honour of Asko Parpola* (Studia Orientalia, 94): 67-82. Helsinki: Finnish Oriental Society.

GANGOLY, O. C. 1949. Indra-cult versus Kṛṣṇa-cult. *Journal of the Ganganath Jha Research Institute*, 7.1: 1-27.

HARA, M. 1975. Indra and tapas. *Adyar Library Bulletin* 39: 129-160.

HOFFMANN, K. 1957. Mārtāṇḍa und Gayōmart. *Münchener Studien zur Sprachwissenschaft* 11: 85-103.

HOLTZMANN, A. 1878. Indra nach den Vorstellungen des Mahābhārata. *ZDMG* 32: 290-340.

HOPKINS, E. W. 1915. *Epic Mythology*. (Encyclopedia of Indo-Aryan Research, 3.1.B.) Strassburg: Karl J. Trübner. (Reprint: Delhi: MLBD, 1974.)

KIRFEL, Willibald 1947. Rāmāyaṇa Bālakāṇḍa und Purāṇa: ein Beitrag zur chronologischen Fixierung des ersten Buches. In: *Die Welt des Orients* 1: 113-128. (Reprinted in: Robert Birwé (ed.), *Kleine Schriften*: 76-91. Wiesbaden: Steiner, 1976.)

SCHMID, C. 1997. La rivalité de Kṛṣṇa et d'Indra: l'enlèvement de l'arbre Pārijāta dans le Harivaṃśa. *Bulletin d'Études Indiennes* 15: 247-297.

SCHMIDT, Hanns-Peter 1968. *Indra und Bṛhaspati: Untersuchungen zur vedischen Mythologie und Kulturgeschichte*. Wiesbaden: Harrassowitz.

SCHREINER, P. 2005. Śiva in the Harivaṃśa. In: P. Koskikallio (ed.), *Epics, Khilas and Purāṇas: Continuities and Ruptures. Proceedings of the Third DICSEP September 2002*: 325-345. Zagreb: Croatian Academy of Sciences and Arts.

SÖHNEN-THIEME, R. 1996. The Ahalyā story through the ages. In: J. Leslie (ed.), *Myth and Mythmaking*: 41-62. Richmond: Curzon.

—— 1997. Rise and decline of the Indra religion in the Veda. In: M. Witzel (ed.), *Inside the Texts – Beyond the Texts. New Approaches to the Study of the Vedas*: 235-244. Harvard, Mass.: Harvard University, Dept. of Sanskrit and Indian Studies.

SØRENSEN, S. 1904-25. *An Index to the Names in the Mahābhārata*. London. (Reprint: Delhi: MLBD, 1963).

TRIPATHI, C. G. 1968. *Der Ursprung und die Entwicklung der Vāmana-Legende in der indischen Literatur*. Wiesbaden: Harrassowitz.

WACKERNAGEL, J. & A. DEBRUNNER 1957. *Altindische Grammatik*, II.1. Göttingen: Vandenhoeck und Ruprecht, 1957. (Reprint: 1985.)

Bhīṣma's Discourse as a *śokāpanodana*

Muneo Tokunaga

1. METAMORPHOSIS OF THE *MAHĀBHĀRATA*

It is a common understanding among epic scholars that the *Mahābhārata* attributed to Kṛṣṇa Dvaipāyana Vyāsa developed from a heroic poetry of a relatively small size[1] into the present form of ca. 75,000 verses (Critical Edition), or into the "Dharmaśāstra" of 100,000 verses, which has traditionally been called *Śatasāhasrī Saṃhitā*.[2] There is no doubt that this enormous enlargement is a result of incorporating huge amounts of didactic material as a discourse of Bhīṣma on the *dharma*s into the *Śānti*- and the *Anuśāsanaparvan*.[3] It is therefore of special importance, in understanding the textual development of the Mbh, to investigate *why* and *how* didactic material was introduced into our text.

---

[1] The Mbh goes back to the text of 24,000 verses, called "Bhārata" (besides *upākhyāna*s) and ascribed to Vyāsa (1.1.61). Further, some manuscripts refer to the text of 8,800 verses, again ascribed to Vyāsa. However, this passage is omitted from the text of the Critical Edition (cf. *Ādiparvan*, Vol. 1.2, p. 884, App. 1, No. 1, line 15). See Brockington 1998: 21.

[2] As to the "Collection of a hundred thousand verses", cf. 1.56.13; 12.322.36. 331.2; Winternitz 1972: 464; Brockington 1998: 131.

[3] Outside the *Śānti* (26,325 lines) and the *Anuśāsana* (13,402 lines), we find didactic texts in Mbh 3.29-23 (conversation between Yudhiṣṭhira and Draupadī, 634 lines), 3.196-206 (story of Satī and the teaching of Dharmavyādha, 927 lines), 5.33-41 (teaching of Vidura, 1,086 lines), 5.42-45 (*Sanatsujātīya*, 268 lines), 6.23-40 (*Gītā*, 1,400 lines), 11.2-7 (*śokāpanodana* by Vidura, 226 lines), 14.16-50 (*Anugītā*, 2,062 lines). *Śānti*, *Anuśāsana*, and these passages amount to 46,330 lines, i.e., 30.6 % of the whole text (151,166 metrical lines).

2. ORIGINAL SIZE OF THE *MAHĀBHĀRATA*

In my paper "*Udakakriyā* and the Śāntiparvan", I pointed out that the first forty-five or so chapters in the *Śāntiparvan*, which I call "Śānti opening", belongs in essence to the original Mbh attributed to Kṛṣṇa Dvaipāyana Vyāsa as the *dénouement* of the life-long, fierce struggle between the princes of the Bharata lineage (Tokunaga 2005). Further, I suggested that the original Mbh actually ended with Yudhiṣṭhira's consecration in Hāstinapura (chapter 40), just as the story of the *Rāmāyaṇa* actually ends with Rāma's triumphant entry into Ayodhyā. In this respect, it deserves attention that John Brockington (2002: 128) reports there is never any depiction of any episode occurring after the end of the battle among the many Mbh relief narratives in existence.

3. ABSENCE OF BHĪṢMA'S DISCOURSE IN THE ORIGINAL *MAHĀBHĀRATA*

From the viewpoint of textual development, no one would deny that originally Bhīṣma's discourse was not a part of the Mbh. After a long battle in the first ten days described in Book 6, Bhīṣma was shot by Arjuna with innumerable arrows and finally fell down, making the earth resound (6.114.84). Saṃjaya reports this scene to Dhṛtarāṣṭra:

> When Bhīṣma, the son of Śantanu and the doyen of the Bharatas, was killed (or struck down), your sons, O Bhārata, did not know what to do.[4]

In 1898 E. W. Hopkins discussed this topic and argued that Bhīṣma was killed right on the tenth day of the war in the earlier version of the epic, based on the words *hata*, *nihata*, *vinihata*, which, in his interpretation, mean "slain" (Hopkins 1898: 9). I do not totally op-

---

[4] Mbh 6.115.15:
hate śāṃtanave bhīṣme bharatānāṃ pitāmahe ।
na kiṃcit pratyapadyanta putrās tava ca bhārata ॥ 15 ॥

pose his theory but the root √*han* and its derivatives are, at any rate, ambiguous in meaning. My view is that, in spite of the fatal shot on the tenth day, Bhīṣma somehow kept his life for some time on the battlefield. However, he did not survive for such a long time as to deliver an enormous discourse after the war. This assumption is supported by the following passages.

When Bhīṣma fell down on the earth, Karṇa, who will later succeed Droṇa as commander-in-chief of the Kaurava army, swears,

> I shall carry out this noble duty of a righteous person. I will follow [the path of] Bhīṣma when I give up my life.[5]

Bhīṣma is still alive at this moment.[6] However, it is indicated in his words that Bhīṣma's death is imminent. Similarly, he says,

> Even if the all-destroying Death, who is always vigilant, protects Arjuna in the fight, I will encounter and kill him in the battle. If not, I will follow in the footsteps of Bhīṣma to Yama.[7]

Let me quote another passage from Book 11. After the end of the great war and the succeeding night-attack on the camp of the Pāṇḍavas by the survivors of the Kaurava army, Vyāsa grants Gāndhārī spiritual eyes to see the site of the fierce battle. At the sight of Bhīṣma's dead body, Gāndhārī surmises that Bhīṣma, although a mortal, maintained (*adhārayat*) his life like an immortal[8] and wails in sorrow,

> Devavrata, the best of men who is similar to a god, having gone to heaven, whom shall the Kurus, O Mādhava, now consult about the *dharmas*?[9]

---

[5] Mbh 7.2.20ab:
kartāsmy etat satpuruṣāryakarma tyaktvā prāṇān anuyāsyāmi bhīṣmam ।

[6] He converses with Bhīṣma in the next chapter.

[7] Mbh 7.2.32:
taṃ cen mṛtyuḥ sarvaharo 'bhirakṣet sadāpramattaḥ samare kirīṭinam ।
tathāpi hantāsmi sametya saṃkhye yāsyāmi vā bhīṣmapathā yamāya ॥ 32 ॥

[8] Mbh 11.23.21:
dharmātmā tāta dharmajñaḥ pāraṃparyeṇa nirṇaye ।
amartya iva martyaḥ sann eṣa prāṇān adhārayat ॥ 21 ॥

It is clear from these passages that Bhīṣma survived for a while on the field and died before the war ended.

We can describe the structure of the original Mbh without Bhīṣma's discourse ending actually with Yudhiṣṭhira's enthronement in Figure 1.

FIGURE 1
Outline of the Development of the *Śāntiparvan*

I: Arguments between Yudhiṣṭhira and his companions over the meaning of the war

II: Yudhiṣṭhira's attainment of mental peace, entry into Hāstinapura and consecration

B: Bhīṣma's discourse

(Stage 1) Śānti opening (the original *Śānti* without Bhīṣma's discourse)

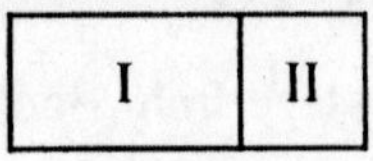

(Stage 2) Bhīṣma's discourse inserted before Yudhiṣṭhira's consecration

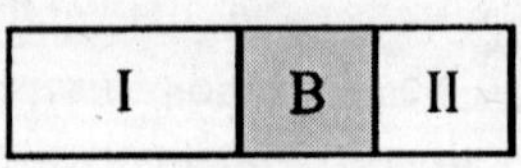

(Stage 3) Bhīṣma's discourse enlarged and moved to the place after Yudhiṣṭhira's consecration

(Stage 4) Insertion of the *Nārāyaṇīya* into the *Śāntiparvan* and addition of Book 14 as continuation of Bhīṣma's discourse

---

[9] Mbh 11.23.25:
dharmeṣu kuravaḥ kaṃ nu paripraksyanti mādhava I
gate devavrate svargaṃ devakalpe nararṣabhe II 25 II

4. ORIGINALLY BHĪṢMA GAVE A RELATIVELY SHORT INTRODUCTION TO YUDHIṢṬHIRA

In the present circumstances it seems almost impossible to provide an accurate chronology of all the events described in the Mbh. The present form of the Mbh consists of diverse elements or layers belonging to different stages of textual development. This is especially the case with the part of the Mbh which deals with the "revived" Bhīṣma and his discourse (Book 12 to the beginning of Book 14). We have seen above that Bhīṣma was defeated on the tenth day of the battle and died before the end of the war. But, to the surprise of the reader, he reappears after the war as an instructor in the *dharma*s. Even if we admit round numbers, this part of the Epic contains the following conflicting expressions of the dates or periods of events, presumably due to the "revival" of Bhīṣma and other factors.

(A) Having performed a water-libation to Karṇa in the Ganges, Yudhiṣṭhira stays on the bank of the river with his companions for one month (*māsam ekam*) in order to get rid of impurity (*āśauca*) (12.1.2).

(B) Just before the commencement of Bhīṣma's discourse, Kṛṣṇa predicts that Bhīṣma has fifty-six days (*pañcāśataṃ ṣaṭ ca*) until he dies on the winter solstice (12.51.14).

(C) After the end of Bhīṣma's discourse, Yudhiṣṭhira once returns to Hāstinapura and stays there for fifty nights (*śarvarīḥ ... pañcāśat*),[10] waiting for the winter solstice (13.153.5).

(D) Yudhiṣṭhira comes back to the battlefield to see Bhīṣma again just before the latter's *niryāṇa*. Then Bhīṣma tells him that he has been on the arrow-bed for fifty-eight nights (*aṣṭapañcāśataṃ rātryaḥ*) since he fell down on the tenth day of the war (13.153.27)

---

[10] As a solution for the unconformity, Dandekar cites the variant reading: *śarvarīṃ ... pañcāham* (Critical Edition, Vol. 17, Introduction, p. lxxxii).

Concerning the above expressions, it must be noted first that (C) and (D), occurring in the same chapter, cannot be treated independently. If they thus form a set, there is little time for Bhīṣma's discourse, taking into account the last eight days of the war. As a consequence, we cannot but conclude that the "revived" Bhīṣma, if ever, had only a short time to talk to Yudhiṣṭhira after the war.[11]

Now, as to the expressions (A) and (B), neither one agrees with the chronology produced from (C) *plus* (D). If Bhīṣma had been alive for fifty-six days from the beginning of his speech to his death on the winter solstice (B), we would need at least sixty-four days as the period of his survival (8 days before and 56 days after the war), ignoring the one-month *āśauca* (A) and all other events between the end of the war and the commencement of his discourse.[12]

It is not difficult to understand the intention behind the expression (B). Disregarding descriptions in the earlier version, a later compiler felt the necessity of securing a long period of Bhīṣma's survival for the sake of including a vast amount of Bhīṣma's discourse in the Mbh. It should be noted that (B) occurs not before but after Yudhiṣṭhira's attainment of mental peace and consecration ceremony. We will come back to this point later.

The expression (A) is hard to adjust to the other dates. The one-month residence on the bank of the river Ganges seems to upset the whole chronology of the events during the period in question. Even if we subtract eighteen days of the war from the month,[13] it does not solve the question. Did the one-month *āśauca* enter the text due to a new theory of the period of *āśauca* or was it due to a new calculation of the period from the beginning of the war to the winter solstice? This passage requires further investigation.

---

[11] Cf. also editor's critical note on 13.153.5 (Vol. 17, p. 1120).

[12] Cf. again critical note on 12.51.14 (Vol. 13, pp. 656-657) for the editor's desperate attempt to find a consistency in the expressions of the present Mbh.

[13] Cf. Nīlakaṇṭha on 12.1.2; editor's endnote on p. 635 of Vol. 13.

5. ORIGINALLY BHĪṢMA INSTRUCTED YUDHIṢṬHIRA IN THE *RĀJADHARMA BEFORE* THE LATTER'S CONSECRATION

As mentioned above, the Śānti opening, i.e., the first forty-five or so chapters of Book 12, comprises the main features of the original *Śāntiparvan.* Arguments between Yudhiṣṭhira and his wife and brothers about the legitimacy of the war in this opening later incited epic compilers to develop full expositions of the *dharma*s in the succeeding part of this opening. At the same time, the *parvan* name *Śānti*, which originally meant the Śānti opening, was expanded to these expositions and finally became the title of the whole text covering the *Rājadharma*- (with the Śānti opening as the beginning part of it), the *Āpaddharma*-, and the *Mokṣadharma-parvan.*[14] This assumption is supported by the names of one hundred sub-*parvan*s listed in the *Parvasaṃgraha*, which registers the *parvan*s that constituted the Mbh before they were grouped into eighteen major *parvan*s (leaving aside the *khila*, i.e., 99 *Harivaṃśa* and 100 *Bhaviṣyat*) on the final stage of compilation. Interestingly, the three sub-*parvan*s (the eighty-sixth to the eighty-eighth) of the present *Śānti* are, in the *Parvasaṃgraha* 1.2.64, called *Śānti* (instead of *Rājadharma*!), *Āpaddharma* and *Mokṣadharma.*[15]

Since the Mbh seems to have ended originally in Yudhiṣṭhira's attainment of mental peace and his *abhiṣeka* described in the Śānti opening, it appears reasonable to assume that Bhīṣma's discourse, at first, entered the text, in a short form, not *after* but *before* Yudhiṣṭhira's consecration ceremony. There are two reasons for this assumption.

[14] For the detail, see Tokunaga 2005. Cf. also Sukthankar 1928: 177, fn. 8.

[15] Mbh 1.2.64:

śāntiparva tato yatra rājadharmānukīrtanam |
āpaddharmaś ca parvoktaṃ mokṣadharmas tataḥ param || 64 ||

(1) Bhīṣma's discourse as a *śokāpanodana*

After his inauguration in Hāstinapura, Yudhiṣṭhira the king, being accompanied by Kṛṣṇa, visits Bhīṣma in Kurukṣetra. Meeting him on the field, Kṛṣṇa requests Bhīṣma to give instructions in the *Rājadharma* and to tell Yudhiṣṭhira about the righteous way of life as a king without sorrow for the slaughter of his kinsmen:

> So dispel, O Bhīṣma, the sorrow of this eldest son of Pāṇḍu who is tormented by the loss of his relatives. (12.50.30)
>
> So pull out with your wisdom the sorrow, O best of men, which has risen in the mind of the son of Pāṇḍu. (12.50.36ab)
>
> Tell him meaningful words concerning *dharma*, *artha* and concentration [of mind]. Dispel his sorrow. (12.51.18cd)[16]

Soon after the conversation, Bhīṣma begins his instruction to Yudhiṣṭhira in the royal duties and other *dharma*s in the present Mbh.

After his long discourse on the *dharma*s, which covers the greater part of Books 12 and 13, Yudhiṣṭhira regains his normal state of mind (13.152.2 *prakṛtim āpannaḥ*). Then Bhīṣma says to him, "Enter the town, O king. Let your mental agony go away" (13.152.5cd).[17] And when Bhīṣma has gone to heaven on the winter solstice, Kṛṣṇa consoles Yudhiṣṭhira with the words,

> You have heard royal duties from Bhīṣma, the son of the Ganges. Abandon your sorrow, O great king, for it (i.e., slaughter of kinsmen) was doomed that way.[18]

---

[16] Mbh 12.50.30:
tad asya tapyamānasya jñātīnāṃ saṃkṣayeṇa vai |
jyeṣṭhasya pāṇḍuputrasya śokaṃ bhīṣma vyapānuda || 30 ||
Mbh 12.50.36ab:
sa pāṇḍaveyasya manaḥsamutthitaṃ narendra śokaṃ vyapakarṣa medhayā |
Mbh 12.51.18cd:
prabrūhi dharmārthasamādhiyuktam arthyaṃ vaco 'syāpanudāsya śokam ||

[17] Mbh 13.152.5cd:
praviśasva puraṃ rājan vyetu te mānaso jvaraḥ || (Cf. also verse 7.)

From these passages we may be justified in assuming that Bhīṣma originally delivered his instruction *before* Yudhiṣṭhira's inauguration in Hāstinapura, because his instruction was intended to remove sorrow from Yudhiṣṭhira (*śokāpanodana*) who would not enter the town due to his remorse over the slaughter of kinsmen.

I concentrated on the *śokāpanodana* of the *Śāntiparvan* in the third DICSEP (2002). In the ritual texts of ancient India, *śokāpanodana* is prescribed in obsequial rites for a bereaved family who performed a water-libation to the dead in the sacred river. It is so prescribed because a bereaved family are not allowed to bring their sorrow back into their ordinary life. This is why they must perform the rite of *śokāpanodana* before they enter the town or village. It is clear that Bhīṣma's instruction to Yudhiṣṭhira in the present Mbh violates the position of *śokāpanodana* prescribed in the ritual texts. Bhīṣma's instruction as *śokāpanodana* is required prior to Yudhiṣṭhira's entry into the capital.

(2) Yudhiṣṭhira ascends the throne twice in the present Mbh

Near the end of Book 13 there is an interesting passage, which deserves special attention in understanding the textual development of the *Śāntiparvan*. This passage is found *after* Bhīṣma's long discourse.

> *tataḥ kuntīsuto rājā paurajānapadaṃ janam* |
> *pūjayitvā yathānyāyam anujajñe gṛhān prati* || 1 ||
> *sāntvayāmāsa nārīś ca hatavīrā hateśvarāḥ* |
> *vipulair arthadānaiś ca tadā pāṇḍusuto nṛpaḥ* || 2 ||
> *so 'bhiṣikto mahāprājñaḥ prāpya rājyaṃ yudhiṣṭhiraḥ* |
> *avasthāpya naraśreṣṭhaḥ sarvāḥ svaprakṛtīs tadā* || 5 ||
> *dvijebhyo balamukhyebhyo naigamebhyaś ca sarvaśaḥ* |
> *pratigṛhyāśiṣo mukhyās tadā dharmabhṛtāṃ varaḥ* || 4 ||
> *uṣitvā śarvarīḥ śrīmān pañcāśan nagarottame* |
> *samayaṃ kauravāgryasya sasmāra puruṣarṣabhaḥ* || 5 ||

---

[18] Mbh 14.2.5-8:
śrutāś ca rājadharmās te bhīṣmād bhāgīrathīsutāt | ...
tyaja śokaṃ mahārāja bhavitavyaṃ hi tat tathā |

> Then the king, son of Kuntī, duly honored and allowed townsmen and villagers to leave for their home. And the king, son of Pāṇḍu, with a lot of gifts, consoled women who had their brave sons and husbands killed. A man of great wisdom having been consecrated, Yudhiṣṭhira having obtained his kingdom, the best of men then having placed all his subjects [in their respective offices], the best of righteous men having received inestimable blessings from twice-borns, best warriors and merchants on all sides, a man of prosperity having lived fifty nights in the best town, the bull of men remembered his promise to the foremost of the Kauravas. (Mbh 13.153.1-5)

This passage overlaps in essence with a (much longer) passage occurring *before* Bhīṣma's discourse. The correspondence between the two passages is remarkable. We find the people's expression of their enthusiastic welcome for Yudhiṣṭhira and Yudhiṣṭhira's donation to the Brahmins, who recite blessings for him, in the first half of chapter 39, the consecration ceremony of Yudhiṣṭhira in chapter 40, Yudhiṣṭhira's appointment of his brothers and subjects to their respective offices in chapter 41, and the *śrāddha* ceremony and Yudhiṣṭhira's bringing consolation to women who lost their husbands and children in the war in chapter 42 of the *Śāntiparvan*. It must be emphasized that the description in the above passage is not a recapitulation of the events that occurred in the earlier part of the text. It is palpable to the reader that it runs as a part of the basic story. We must admit therefore that Yudhiṣṭhira ascends the throne *twice* in our Mbh.

It is not uncommon to find remnants of the earlier version in the Mbh, which suffered repeated revision and enlargement. This passage is one of the good examples. It is evident in this passage that Bhīṣma originally delivered his discourse *before* Yudhiṣṭhira entered the capital and ascended the throne as king of the Bharatas.

6. THE ORIGINAL LOCATION OF BHĪṢMA'S TEACHING

If Bhīṣma delivered his instruction before Yudhiṣṭhira's *abhiṣeka*, we might be able to find the original location of Bhīṣma's instruction in the text preceding Yudhiṣṭhira's *abhiṣeka*. Our attempt, in fact, is not in vain. When we read the text carefully from the beginning of the *Śāntiparvan*, we come across a strange passage in chapter 38. A clear change in Yudhiṣṭhira's mind is recognized in this chapter. Although he persistently refused to become a king in the preceding part of the text, Yudhiṣṭhira, in this chapter, asks Vyāsa about the righteous way of life as a king. Vyāsa himself does not answer the question. Instead, Vyāsa abruptly recommends Yudhiṣṭhira to go and see Bhīṣma on the battlefield for the instruction (12.38.6).[19] This is the first place in which Bhīṣma reappears after his fall on the tenth day of the war. Vyāsa emphasizes Bhīṣma's excellent knowledge of *Rājadharma* and other topics:

> He who knows the *dharmas* and who knows the mysterious truth about *dharma* and *artha* will tell you. Go to him before the person who knows the *dharmas* leaves his life.[20]

Kṛṣṇa endorses Vyāsa's proposal (21) but, for no clear reason, Yudhiṣṭhira does not follow their advice. Then the topic of Bhīṣma is discontinued and the story turns quickly to the climax in the Mbh.

> Appeased by these and many other people, noble-minded Yudhiṣṭhira cast off his mental suffering and agony. The son of Pāṇḍu, who had heard the words [of the elders] and the source [of the truth], with a thorough knowledge of what had been heard and what was to be heard, resolutely achieved peace of mind (*śānti*).[21]

---

[19] Mbh 12.38.6:
śrotum icchasi ced dharmān akhilena yudhiṣṭhira |
praihi bhīṣmaṃ mahābāho vṛddhaṃ kurupitāmaham || 6 ||

[20] Mbh 12.38.16:
sa te vakṣyati dharmajñaḥ sūkṣmadharmārthatattvavit |
tam abhyehi purā prāṇān sa vimuñcati dharmavit || 16 ||

[21] Mbh 12.38.28-29:
etaiś cānyaiś ca bahubhir anunīto yudhiṣṭhiraḥ |
vyajahān mānasaṃ duḥkhaṃ saṃtāpaṃ ca mahāmanāḥ || 28 ||
śrutavākyaḥ śrutanidhiḥ śrutaśravyaviśāradaḥ |
vyavasya manasaḥ śāntim agacchat pāṇḍunandanaḥ || 29 ||

Released from his mental agony at last, Yudhiṣṭhira sets out for Hāstinapura (verses 30-31), settles in the palace and ascends the throne as king of the Bharatas (chapter 40). It appears strange that Vyāsa refers to Bhīṣma as the instructor and the topic is not continued in this chapter. What is the need of referring to his name in this passage? If Bhīṣma had actually removed sorrow from Yudhiṣṭhira with his (presumably short) instruction in this place, the story would have taken a natural course to Yudhiṣṭhira's freedom from agony, attainment of mental peace, procession to Hāstinapura and consecration ceremony, that is, to the finale of the life-long struggle for supremacy between the rival princes of the ancient Kuru kingdom.[22]

REFERENCES

BROCKINGTON, John 1998. *The Sanskrit Epics*. (Handbuch der Orientalistik, 2.12.) Leiden: E.J. Brill.

—— 2002. Visual Epics. In: Danuta Stasik & John Brockington (eds.), *Indian Epic Traditions – Past and Present. Papers presented at the 16th European Conference on Modern South Asian Studies, Edinburgh 5-9 September 2000* (RO, 54.1): 111-131. Warsaw: Polska Akademia Nauk, Komitet Nauk Orientalistycznych.

HOPKINS, E. W. 1898. The Bhārata and the Great Bhārata. *American Journal of Philology* 19.1 (No. 73): 1-24.

SUKTHANKAR, V. S. 1928. Epic studies. *Journal of the Bombay Branch of the Royal Asiatic Society*, N.S. 4

TOKUNAGA, Muneo 2005. *Udakakriyā* and the Śāntiparvan. In: Petteri Koskikallio (ed.), *Epics, Khilas and Purāṇas: Continuities and Ruptures. Proceedings of the Third DICSEP September 2002*: 169-181. Zagreb: Croatian Academy of Sciences and Arts.

WINTERNITZ, Moriz 1972. *History of Indian Literature*, I. 2nd English edition. Delhi: MLBD.

---

[22] I advanced in this paper my assumptions as to the passage of the *Śāntiparvan*, in which Bhīṣma appears on the scene anew in the guise of the instructor of Hindu *dharma*s. I hope at least this paper will attract readers' attention to this strange passage, which, in my view, is essential to the understanding of the transformation of the Mbh from an heroic poetry to the Dharmaśāstra. I am thankful to Dr. W. Knobl's help in improving my expressions in this paper.

INDEX

1. Wake early (at the same time every day).
2. Clean your face, teeth, and mouth. Brush your teeth, scrape your tongue, and gargle with some warm water. The tongue accumulates bacteria overnight. This helps diminish their numbers. While your local drugstore may carry plastic or rubber tongue scrapers, I prefer the Indian-style stainless-steel ones. You can find sources for these in Appendix A.
3. Drink a glass of warm water. This stimulates a bowel movement and cleanses the gastrointestinal tract.
4. Eliminate.
5. Apply cooling salve or cool water to the eyes. This refreshes the eyes.
6. Gargle with salt water and use a neti pot to irrigate the nasal cavities with salt water. These steps should only take about 3 minutes total. Put ¼ teaspoon of noniodized sea salt in the bottom of your neti pot, fill with warm water, and follow the clear directions that come with the pot. You can find where to get this in Appendix A. We are all exposed to a multitude of pathogens every day, especially if we work or live with a lot of other people. Being exposed to pathogens is not the problem. The problem is proliferation of the pathogens, which often occurs in the nasal passages or throat. Rinsing the nasal passages and gargling with salt water helps us avoid proliferation of bacteria and viruses that we are exposed to and prepares us nicely for doing some breathing exercises, which we will discuss later.
7. Meditate, engage in quiet contemplation or read inspirational material for 15 to 60 minutes. If you don't have a meditation practice, this could be a time of prayer or gentle breathing exercises that you can learn from a yoga practitioner. In any case, the goal is to quiet the mind. This is useful for calming the spirit.
8. Apply warm oil to your body. It is ideal to massage it in for about 15 minutes, but even a simple application of oil, which only takes a few minutes, is beneficial. This encourages the nervous system to be calm for the rest of the day. It can be a powerful medicine for calming a threadbare nervous system and gradually restoring hormonal balance. (See page 291 to learn how to do this.)
9. Follow your self-massage by bathing and dressing.
10. Take a brisk half-hour walk, followed by 5 to 10 minutes of gentle yoga. This is useful for calming the spirit. In general, if you are very thin or weak, a slow, stretchy restorative yoga, tai chi, or qi gong routine will be good. If you are heavy, a more vigorous form of exercise, such as a strenuous, vigorous form of yoga or jogging could be appropriate. If you are unsure which is best for you, consult an Ayurvedic lifestyle counselor. Appropriate exercise encourages a calm spirit and smooth flow of qi and nourishing fluids. Remember: Blood follows qi and qi follows the spirit. If the spirit is calm, and qi and blood flow smoothly, and hormones will be more balanced. It is not a problem to exercise later in the day, if that works better in your life or in certain seasons, weather, or climates, but it is important to include exercise in your life and doing it first thing in the day ensures it won't be missed.